AF469133

SETON GORDON

SETON GORDON

The Life and Times of a Highland Gentleman

RAYMOND EAGLE

Published by Lochar Publishing Ltd
MOFFAT DG10 9ED

British Library Cataloguing in Publication Data

Eagle, Raymond
Seton Gordon : the life and times of a
Highland gentleman.
I. Title
508.092

ISBN 0-948403-83-7

Typeset in Linotype Walbaum by Inforum Typesetting, Portsmouth

Printed by Scotprint.

Designed by John Leath MSTD

To

Lorna Davidson, Violet Strachan, Dennis Burnett.

Good hiking companions
who shared the excitement
of my first meeting
with Seton Gordon

CONTENTS

ACKNOWLEDGEMENTS

THERE ARE MANY PEOPLE to whom I would like to offer my deep thanks for information and guidance in preparing this biography. Several are named in the text and their contribution is evident as the reader progresses through Seton Gordon's life. My special thanks goes to these people. The Gordon family, Caitriona Macdonald-Lochart, Bridie Prettejohn and Alasdair Gordon were wonderfully patient despite the many times I asked each one for information or clarification.

I made many friends and received wonderful hospitality while engaged in research, especially from Mrs 'Puchi' Cameron-Head of Inverailort; Captain and Mrs Alwyne Farquharson of Invercauld; Simon and Caitriona Macdonald-Lochart, Dunsyre; Mrs Violet Humphrey, Aboyne; Major Ruaraidh Hilleary, Greshornish, Skye and Mr. Jonathan MacDonald, Duntulm, Skye.

There are others I would be remiss in not thanking for so readily responding to requests for information or offering other forms of assistance:

Sir William Heseltine, KCVO, CB, former Private Secretary to Her Majesty The Queen; Colonel Sir Donald Cameron of Lochiel, KT, CVO, 26th Chief of Clan Cameron; Iain Thornber, FRSA, FSA, JP, Deputy Lieutenant of Inverness-shire; Lady Anne, Countess of Dunmore; Dr. J Morton Boyd; S. M. Simpson, National Library of Scotland; William Sinclair, broadcaster, Inverness; Dr John Maddicott, Exeter College, Oxford; Susan Reynolds, MA, Lady Margaret Hall, Oxford; Frank Hamilton and Michael Everett, Royal Society for the Protection of Birds; Mr. John Cook, ChM., FRCS(Ed), Clehonger, Hereford; Mrs Sheila Lochhead, Swansea; Professor Toby Jackman, Victoria, Canada; Lieutenant-Colonel A. A. Fairrie, (Retd), Queen's Own Cameron Highlanders; Alex and Norma MacLean, Linicro, Skye; Anthony Ottway, London; Jack Edwards, Waltham Cross, Herts; Mrs Mairi Bremner, South Uist; George Ridley, the Grosvenor Estates; Squadron-Leader Douglas Salter, RAF (Retd); Miss Jean M. Whyte, Ditchling, Sussex; Donnie MacKenzie, Barnet, Herts; Miss Mary L. T. Brown, New York; John Swindell, London; Jack and Beryl Hulbert, Aylesbury, Bucks; David Saunders of the Dyfed Wildlife Trust; Peter Grant, Aberdeen Public Library; Miss Mary Williamson, Aberdeen University Library; the proprieters of the *Oban Times*; British Airways and British Rail for assistance with travel; Mr Norman Miller Miller who gave permission for his portrait of Seton Gordon to be reproduced on the jacket.

I would also like to give special thanks to my wife, Maureen, for her patient help with proofing and general encouragement, and to Natasha Betancor-Leon for her help with word-processing.

My thanks are due to the following publishers and authors for permission to quote passages from their publications:

From Seton Gordon's books:

Macmillan & Co: *Highways and Byways of the West Highlands*, *Highways and Byways of the Central Highlands*, and all of Seton Gordon's books originally published by Cassell; Robert Hale Ltd: *The Highlands of Scotland*; Methuen Publishers: *In Search of Northern Birds* and *A Highland Year*; Paul Hamlyn Publishing: *Afoot in the Hebrides*; B. T. Batsford Ltd: *Wild Birds in Britain*; Canongate Press: Alistair Campsie's *The MacCrimmon Legend*; Jonathan Cape Ltd: Prince Felix Youssoupoff's *Lost Splendour*; Chambers Publishers: Alasdair MacGregor's *Over the Sea to Skye;* Methuen Publishers: H. V. Morton's *In Search of Scotland* and Michael Powell's *A Life in Movies*; Walker and Co: Elizabeth Montgomery-Campbell's *The Search for Mhorag*; *National Geographic Magazine*: Robert J. Reynold's 1952 article on Skye; *The Scottish Field*: A 1955 article by Seton Gordon; *The Scots Magazine*: Tom Weirs last interview with Seton Gordon.

A special thanks to *British Birds* magazine for permission to reprint a collection of Seton Gordon's bird photographs.

FOREWORD

MY EARLIEST RECOLLECTIONS of Seton Gordon are from boyhood. He used to come to give lectures at my school, illustrating his talks from a magic lantern with wonderfully exciting photographic plates. Many years were to intervene before I saw him again. By then much water had flowed under the bridge when, in the aftermath of war, I came to make my home at the Castle of Invercauld, along the headwaters of the Dee amid the surrounding grandeur of the Cairngorms. This was Seton's heartland and into its fabric his roots were inextricably woven. Its people he knew intimately, a friend in every bothy and cottage along the way. Its hills and glens he had traversed from end to end, familiar with their ever-changing moods as with those of a friend, from the relentless arctic severity of midwinter, to the gentle peace of a midsummer's day.

Nothing escaped his quick eye. He was alive and sympathetic to nature's ways and responded to them as the wild creatures with whom he shared its kingdom. Though his sense of hearing was impaired he carried still ringing in his ear, all the diverse cadences of birdsong heard in the days of his youth. As for plants, whether of the seashore, of forest, of meadow and moor, or of cliff and scree, these were his fellow travellers. With advancing years he looked forward with growing eagerness to annual pilgrimages to the high tops to review with renewed delight the re-emergence of those alpine gems from the recedence of the melting snows.

What a wonderful companion he was, full of reminiscences and steeped in the stories and traditions of the Highlands. He had a delighful sense of humour, perceptive and entertaining, kindly, never cynical or derogatory, and all the more telling for that. As a raconteur his style was inimitable. Often did I listen to a familiar story, yet always somehow he contrived to extract in the retelling some nuance of difference which gave it a fresh and subtly distinct flavour. His memory was remarkably retentive and he could draw upon it at will, instantly recalling the smallest detail of incidents that had happened long ago.

Seton Gordon had a lifelong devotion to the pipes and an abiding reverence for 'Ceol Mor', the great music composed for them in distant, bygone times. Though never ranking among the foremost players, his knowledge of the music was none the less profound, and he was in demand as a judge at well known competitions and kept in touch with the leading players of the day as well as oncoming talent.

As to his undoubted contribution to the study of nature, others more competent than I will pass judgement. His long life spanned an era of rapid and unprecedented development in science and technology, yet he remained singularly untouched by a changing world, inviolate as the hills around him. Through his writing he reached out across oceans and continents, evoking for his countless readers and admirers the spirit of his homeland. He was generous to youth, offering encouragement and for some he was the inspiration which set their steps along a chosen path.

He was indeed a Highland gentleman, and the author has rendered service to future generations through his painstaking research into the life and times of one of Scotland's most distinguished sons, who is rightfully acclaimed as both naturalist and author. Those who would follow in his steps have but to search the high tops and they will find his bright eye gazing toward heaven above in the star of the cushion pink, hear his voice in the song of the snowbunting, his humour in the laughter of the mountain stream; they have but to release their spirit and it will soar with his, free as the wind on the wings of the golden eagle, king of birds.

Captain Alwyne Compton Farquharson of Invercauld, MC

Chief of Clan Farquharson

PREFACE

THE ISLE OF SKYE, over which the Cuillin Hills form an impressive backdrop when viewed from the mainland, is the largest island of the Inner Hebrides. Almost every island in the Hebrides has been the subject of song. Skye holds a special significance and has been immortalised by more songs than any other, *The Skye Boat Song*, *The Road to the Isles*, *The Skyline of Skye*, *Island for Dreamers* and the *Bonnie Isle of Skye*, to name a few.

Many books have also been written about 'Eilean a' Cheo', the Isle of Mist, and countless others have included large sections devoted to Skye: Martin Martin's *Description of the Western Isles* written in 1695, through Samuel Johnson's *A Journey to the Western Isles* in 1775, Alexander Smith's *A Summer in Skye* in 1865 to J.A. MacCulloch's *The Misty Isle of Skye* in 1905. Contemporaries of Seton Gordon who also wrote about the island include Alasdair MacGregor, Thomas Nicol, T. Ratcliffe Barnett and H.V. Morton.

In the summer of 1925 Seton Gordon and his wife of ten years, Audrey, rented Tayinloan Lodge, just north of Portree and near the junction of the Dunvegan road. Seton's diaries show clearly how quickly he fell under the spell of Skye. With his gift for description he was able in the next few years to convey this strongly in his books and articles.

In the autumn of that year they rented Duntulm Lodge, located at the north end of Skye, from the Department of the Secretary of State for Scotland. Close by are the ruins of Duntulm Castle, the ancient fortress home of the MacDonalds of the Isles. Facing the Minch, with a view across to the Outer Isles, it is a magnificent place. They would have liked to make it their permanent home but could not persuade the Department to sell it. In 1931 a final move was made to the Manse at Upper Duntuilm, just a few miles south. Once known as the Lodge of Osmigarry, it is an imposing stone house exposed to the westerly gales that race across the Minch. In addition the Gordons purchased the glebe of about seventy acres. This provided a challenge for their agricultural talents.

The fact that Skye was chosen as a permanent home is significant to the story of Seton Gordon's life. It was a merging of man and place. Though expressing a love for the Cairngorms on whose slopes much of his early nature lore was learned, some of his finest prose is found in the descriptions of the Hebrides and the west, where the light and the distances have an ethereal quality found in few places on earth.

Skye offers an infinite variety of landscape and mood, from the serrated skyline of the Cuillin Hills to the large expanses of moorland and the ever changing seascapes around its hundreds of miles of shoreline. Because of its history and the movements of races throughout the last thousand years, there are numerous forts and castles that have been the homes of principal families, both Norse and Scots.

The history of Skye is a microcosm of the history of the Highlands, with all its romance, bravery, treachery, cruelty and pride. Here then was a place that he never tired of writing about when he returned from other parts of the country. A land where a wealth of legend and folklore waited to be examined and explained. Where the golden eagle nested only a walk from his back door. Where the weather was ever changing and could swing from shrieking gale to dream-like calm, sometimes producing effects of light and cloud that belong to some other dimension.

Upper Duntuilm became home to Seton Gordon for the next forty-seven years. A short walk across the moors, past Loch Sneosdale are the cliffs and crags of this hauntingly beautiful northern tip of Skye. The colour and mood change throughout the year and are perhaps at their best on a winter afternoon when the westering sun slants across the landscape shining palely on the lochans and delicately tinting the cliffs of Beinn a' Sga.

Whatever the time of day or time of year, Seton Gordon retained an impression and made it come alive in one of his narratives. Every sunrise, every sunset, every cloud formation and nuance of light was important and would be minutely observed.

Thus we have a seventy-year record of summer calm, still autumn days, winter storm, the renewal of spring, natural aberrations and man-influenced environmental changes. There are some who say that his bird-watching records are of limited practical use to other ornithologists because they lack precise data. Yet reading his long observation of the eaglets he named Cain and Abel and the delightful way in which he gives them personality, the strength of Seton Gordon's writing is seen. He addressed these critics specifically in one of his last radio interviews, when he said, Although I took a science honours degree, I do not consider myself a scientist, and my approach is more a love of birds, and while studying them to treat them as fellow beings - fellow creatures. I think nowadays, too much importance is being paid to the scientific side. I think there is a tremendous lot still to be learned from, you might say, the unscientific side of bird watching.

In his approach, Seton Gordon was like one of his heroes in nature writing, W.H. Hudson, whose book *Birds and Man* has that same wonderful quality of simplicity in his descriptions of the south and west of England which he roamed in pursuit of birdlife.

Nowadays it is possible to stay in the comfort of one's sitting room and watch on television the habits of the golden eagle while in the space of an hour or less, a commentator describes the life of the bird. It took Seton and Audrey weeks of cold and discomfort in cramped hides, using primitive heavy equipment. Seton once watched at an eyrie site where the ledge was not wide enough for a proper hide. It was a day of bitter north wind with driving snow showers and he remained motionless for nearly five hours covered in a piece of sacking. At the end, his legs had lost all feeling and he was unable to descend the cliff. Audrey, who was just recovering from a sprained ankle, climbed up and guided Seton's feet into the footholds as he made a painful descent.

His descriptions give a sense of 'being there' as much as the TV screen, because his writing forces us to use the inner mind. He helps us to see things that are given a mere passing reference by the television commentator.

The west is not the same as when he first journeyed there; when bothies, blackhouses and thatched roofed cottages merged with the landscape. His record though, deserves to be kept as much as those of earlier chroniclers, because he witnessed more changes.

The uniqueness of Seton Gordon's writing is that it constantly demonstrates his sense of wonder. It has been drawn upon often in these pages to show the vision with which he was blessed. He has been accused of repetitiveness, and if the number of times that he describes seeing St Kilda from all points of the Hebrides and the western mainland are counted, this could be true, but it was always as though he was seeing that distant island group for the first time. Occasionally it would seem that an editor gave too much license and could have been heavier with his pencil. At its best his writing was outstanding, as when he was in the heart of the Cuillin Hills at night and experienced a severe thunderstorm, or when he first climbed the Red Cuillin hill, Beinn na Caillich.

From his childhood on Deeside, Seton Gordon's life was to be a long and interesting one. He later had to overcome the affliction of deafness, but achieved fulfilment as few can claim to have done: A writer, living on Skye – his choice of location – with total freedom to roam, yet countered with the discipline to learn, to record and to write prolifically on all aspects of the Highlands and Islands. He earned the affection and respect of countless numbers of people from all walks of life, and kept his curiosity alive right up to the time of his death, two weeks short of his ninety-first birthday.

John O'Groats
Cape Wrath
Thurso
Wick
CAITHNESS
SUTHERLAND
Lewis
Stornoway
Harris
The Highlands
North Uist
ROSS-SHIRE
Fraserburgh
Elgin
Buckie
Banff
Nairn
Peterhead
Skye
Inverness
MORAYSHIRE
Grantown-on-Spey
INVERNESS-SHIRE
South Uist
Loch Ness
Monadhliath Mts.
Speyside
ABERDEENSHIRE
The Cairngorms
Aberdeen
Deeside
Glen More
Rum
Banchory
Ballater
Braemar
Eigg
Grampian Mts.
Fort William
The Angus Glens
Loch Rannoch
Coll
Kirriemuir
Montrose
Tay
Forfar
Strathmore
Aberfeldy
Tiree
Loch Tay
Arbroath
Dundee
PERTHSHIRE
Mull
Firth of Tay
Oban
Perth
St. Andrews
Crieff
FIFE
ARGYLL
STIRLINGS.
Loch Lomond
Firth of Forth
Jura
DUNBARTONSHIRE
EAST LOTHIAN
Edinburgh
Glasgow
Berwick-upon-Tweed
The Lammermuirs
Islay
RENFREWS.
KINTYRE
Peebles
Tweedale
Arran
Ayr
AYRSHIRE
The Borders
Cheviot Hills
Mull of Kintyre
DUMFRIESSHIRE
0 25 miles
0 40 km.
Dumfries
Annan
GALLOWAY
WIGTOWNSHIRE
Carlisle
Stranraer
Wigtown

CHAPTER

1

A DEESIDE CHILDHOOD

SETON PAUL GORDON was born on 11 April, 1886. His father, William, came from an old Aberdeenshire family. He was town clerk of the City of Aberdeen, a position to which he was appointed in 1875. Forty-seven years old at the time of his son's birth, he completed nearly sixty years of service to the city, dying in office in March 1924 at the age of eighty-five.

In April 1881 William Gordon married Ella Mary, daughter of horticulturalist William Paul of Waltham Cross, Hertfordshire. Ella Mary was eighteen years younger than her husband and of a totally different nature. William, described as quiet, almost withdrawn, was an austere man totally concerned with intellectual pursuits. Ella Mary, a romantic, wrote poetry and sacred songs. From glimpses that are recorded of her she was outgoing and kind. She became known as the 'Queen's Poetess' and was described by the press as a 'sweet singer' and a favourite of Queen Victoria.

William had been born in Aberdeen in 1839, the eldest son of William Gordon, stock and share broker. Educated at the West End Academy and Marischal College (1854-57), he became a law apprentice with the firm Adam and Anderson and was admitted to the Society of Advocates in 1864. In 1866 William was appointed to the combined offices of city chamberlain and deputy town clerk. In 1874 the city council chose him unanimously to fill the town and harbour commission clerkships, and he became the first town clerk to receive a salary. Previously called principal common clerks, they held office under commissions of appointment, their incomes derived from fees. In 1903 William received an Honorary Doctorate of Law from Aberdeen University.

The eulogies following his death in 1924 provide a description of Seton Gordon's father. In a speech to council on 13 March, the Lord Provost, William Meff, said:

> We have lost an extremely capable official, whose services cover a period of almost sixty years. During his long career he saw many Town Councils come and go. He was jealous in guarding everything pertaining to the honour and importance of the City, which he maintained with a dignity all his own. Though silent, he was the power behind the scenes.
>
> Closely associated as we have been for over thirty two years, I had opportunities for knowing him better than many, and I will cherish the memory of one from whose sound advice, general information, and personal friendship, I have derived so much benefit.

A comment in the *Aberdeen Press and Journal* said of him:

> First impressions might suggest a personality that was not really approachable, but longer experience removed any such feeling, and revealed an official ready and anxious to put his wide experience to service.
>
> Occasionally there might have been – and was – excuse for a little austerity towards those whose methods were not altogether his own.

In addition to his professional duties William Gordon was a Justice of the Peace and a member of the General Council of the University of Aberdeen. He was also proficient in six languages. Thus, there was no question about intellectual stimulus in the Gordon home, with a father of great intellect and a mother who was a poet, composer and singer. Though educated at home apart from a brief period at a private school in Rugby, there is no doubt from his later achievements at Oxford that Seton was a willing student and eager to expand his knowledge.

The Gordons lived at 26 Rubislaw Terrace, and owned a chalet-style house at Aboyne on the south side of the Dee close by the bridge, to which they moved after giving up Rubislaw Terrace in 1902. It stands on a bluff overlooking the river and the town beyond to the north. In the distance is the hill, Morven, rising 2700 feet above the Dee valley. This hill played an increasingly significant part in Seton's early life.

The name 'Auchintoul' was chosen for the chalet, after the branch of the Gordons from which William believed he was descended, 'rightly or wrongly'. John Cook, a retired surgeon and grandson of William's sister Evelyn, has done some research into the family's origins and thinks it more probable that they are descended from the Ardmeallie branch, a small estate in the parish of Marnoch, Banffshire. The crest of this branch, a boar's head over a scrolled motto 'Byde be' is the one William refers to in some later correspondence with his son. One member of the family who adopted the Ardmeallie crest was Sir Gordon Gordon-Taylor, an eminent surgeon who was John Cook's guardian and a first cousin to Seton Gordon.

Seton Gordon's grandfather, also William, came from Rothes, Morayshire and moved to Aberdeen as a young man working for the London Shipping Company before going into business for himself as a sharebroker.

Twice a member of Aberdeen City Council, he held the post of treasurer until his retirement in 1866, the year that his son became employed by the city. He and his wife, Margaret, had seven children. Seton's father was the eldest. Alice Miller Gordon, born in 1842, married a London wine merchant, John Smeaton Taylor. It was their son Gordon Gordon-Taylor who became a surgeon and was later knighted.

James Miller Gordon, born in 1845, had a distinguished career in the Royal Scots Fusiliers, rising to the rank of Lieutenant Colonel. Hodgson Campbell Gordon, born in 1848 became a partner in his father's firm. Evelyn Margaret, born in 1850, married John Cook, a director of the Union Bank of Scotland. They had two sons, John and George. The latter was father of the present John Cook.

William Gordon, Hon. LLB *Seton Gordon's father*

Ella Mary Gordon, FRS*Lit, Seton Gordon's mother*

Ella Mary's family was descended from the Pauls of Newseat in Aberdeenshire, an estate near Peterhead. Originally called St Pol, they fled from France at the time of the Hugenot persecution. The family came from Chateau d'Amoy near Orleans.

On April 21st 1881, at Cheshunt, Hertfordshire, William, the eldest of a family of seven, married Ella Mary, the second eldest of a family of ten.

William Paul, father of Ella Mary, was a successful nurseryman and writer on horticulture. His father, Adam, founded a nursery at Churchgate in Cheshunt, after walking south from Aberdeenshire in 1806, where his father was Laird of Newseat. The youngest child, he was not included in his father's will. In the words of descendent Douglas Breeze, who until his death in March 1988, lived in 'Holly Lodge', a house built for William Paul: 'Adam's eldest brother had some compassion, and giving five golden sovereigns, told him to go and make a fortune, which he did'. His first house still stands in the lane opposite Cheshunt Church where Ella Mary married William, and several generations of Pauls are buried. The original nursery is now a park.

Adam had two sons, William and George. William quickly showed his total dedication to horticulture, helped by an enquiring mind. He stayed within his father's business for many years during which he published several books and papers. The assurance displayed by the Paul family is demonstrated by an act of impudence when in about 1850 they fenced off 70 acres of Crown land in Epping Forest. Close to High Beech, a woodland nursery was created which flourished for many years. It would have continued but for a decision by the Crown, under whose jurisdiction Epping Forest came, to transfer the land to the City of London Corporation. The City, concerned over this anomaly, took steps to have the acreage returned. The Pauls were instructed to give the land back to the City, but in actual fact had the use of it for several years. The woodland nursery still appears on old maps and is seen as an arc shape on the road from Epping to Loughton.

William was not only a brilliant horticulturalist but also a prolific writer. In his early twenties he wrote *Observations on the Cultivation of Roses in Pots*, a book which went into eight editions, with translations into French, German, and Spanish.

William's best known work *The Rose Garden* was written in 1848. It went into ten editions, later ones illustrated by his daughter Florence. *The Rose Garden* was reprinted in 1978 by Earl M. Coleman Inc. of New York. William Paul also published the *The Rose Annual* from 1860 to 1881. William Paul broke away from the family business. His development of the now famous 'Scarlet Climber' rose caused a rift with his brother George, whose premise was that the original work was done while William was still in the partnership of Adam Paul and Sons, and therefore he could not take full credit. The dispute was arbitrated by the Rose Society. This body found in favour of William because he worked as an individual, and in his own time.

In 1871 William bought Waltham House from Anthony Trollope and established his nursery in the extensive grounds, which were ideal for the purpose. Under William's management the business flourished, and because of the patronage of Queen Victoria, it became known as the Royal Nurseries and remained in the Paul family for another generation, then continued for a few years under a new owner, until Waltham House was taken over as a convent school. In 1936 the house was torn down to make way for a road improvement project.

William and Amelia-Jane Paul had ten children, five boys and five girls. The boys all went into law or the church. Of the girls, Ella Mary became a poet and Florence an accomplished artist and illustrator. Ella Mary wrote several books of poetry: *Golden Rain*, *Flashes and Reveries*, *Firelight Fancies*, *White Heather*, *Purple Heather*, and *Quiet Thoughts*. Also published was a thirty-two verse poem to George Gordon, Lord Byron.

Ella Mary claimed her poems were written simply to sell at Bazaars to raise money for charities. *Golden Rain* was published to help build a new parish hall at Aboyne. Yet they were read avidly in all parts of the United Kingdom, and long reviews appeared in many newspapers throughout the British Isles.

She became a Fellow of the Royal Society of Literature, with an impressive list of nominees, and also came to the attention of Queen Victoria. Dr Ramsay Colles, JP, LLD, FRHS, FRSAI, of Dublin, writing in the *Irish Masonry Illustrated* stated: 'Queen Victoria . . . was no mean judge of poetic workmanship. No wonder that considerable interest should be excited in the poems and the personality of a writer whom the Queen has been delighted to honour, for her praise was never carelessly bestowed'.

From the descriptions that survive, Ella Mary had a kind nature which she used to help people in practical ways. As an only child Seton was doted on, and it is to his credit that he later displayed none of the behaviour – vain, self-centred, and spoilt – which so often develops with an over-loving, over-protective mother. Each book of Ella Mary's poetry was awaited by the middle and upper class ladies of her day with eager anticipation. To the old Queen, in her years of mourning, they helped assuage her grief.

In a small book written by Helen Jerome, *Ella Mary Gordon at Home*, published in 1901, she was described as 'having a charming personality, magnetic and attractive. Endowed with a sweet sympathetic nature, she is filled with a tender pity for the unfortunate ones in life'.

A letter received by Seton Gordon in 1934 shows a practical streak worth more than all the flowery descriptions of her. It provides a glimpse of the Gordon family life before the turn of the century and of a very young Seton preoccupied with his nature interests before the family left Aberdeen. It was written from Johannesburg, South Africa by Nan Yorke-Mitchell:

> Dear Seton Gordon,
>
> Your article in *John o' Gordon's* [a magazine] is my excuse for writing to you. Many years ago in Aberdeen, I had the pleasure of knowing your gifted mother, Ella Mary Gordon, 'The Queen's Poetess'.
>
> You would not remember me. You were a young lad with a penchant for wandering in hills and dales and hobnobbing with birds and beasts.
>
> You flashed in and out of your mother's drawing room like a Will o' the Wisp. She used to ask me to lunch. Your father turned up now and again, quiet, reserved, saying little or nothing. Your mother did all the talking.
>
> Came a time when I needed advice – your mother was wonderful to me and gave me expert advice. Eventually came an offer to trek to S. Africa. She gave me a dressing case on my departure.
>
> In 1909 I came back on a visit. I called at the chalet in Aboyne. I saw your father and mother. She had changed very much and was ill; eventually I heard that she had died.
>
> You were flashing around in a tweed kilt. I think you had tea with us. This is the last time I ever heard of you, but seeing your article and knowing your whereabouts I decided to write to you. Your mother was a sort of guardian angel to me in my extreme youth.

At the time of Nan Yorke-Mitchell's visit to the chalet, Seton Gordon was twenty-three, and in his second year at Oxford. His first book had been published and he was well established as a freelance writer.

Even today it does not take long to leave Aberdeen and be in attractive countryside. Then it would have taken an even shorter time. There was an abundance of woods, fields and streams to lure a small boy away from the town. Although some of his earlier trips were taken in the company of a governess, it was not long before he was going on his own. Several summers were also spent at the Aboyne chalet before the permanent move was made.

In her 1901 book Helen Jerome also said: 'The poetic temperament so beautifully illustrated in the verses of Ella Mary Gordon, is inherited by her only son, Seton, a tall, handsome boy who is being educated at Mr Wise's school, Oakfield, near Rugby'. Just how long Seton Gordon remained at Oakfield is impossible to discover, but it played a very minor part in his overall education. By 1901 he was at the upper age range for attendance at a prep school, and it is unusual for a boy to be sent away to school for the first time at fifteen. He never spoke about the time spent at Oakfield and it was not possible to have remained there for more than a year at the most. At that age, contemporaries would leave for their next school. Seton left to return home and continue with private tuition.

It is generally accepted that he published his first article at the age of about fifteen. Many of his articles are preserved in scrap-books and it is odd that the first one was not kept. Early photographs show the reason why Seton Gordon was able to take his mother's idolisation in his stride and not be affected by it. As well as being an attractive child with an open expression, there is a self-assuredness which is remarkable in that there is no hint of precosity. He admitted that being an only child made him serious minded early in life and he felt comfortable in the company of much older people.

In most of these pictures Seton is wearing Highland dress, a not unusual feature of posed photographs of the period. In one he is wearing a tweed kilt similar to that referred to in Nan Yorke-Mitchell's letter. The main difference between these and thousands of other Victorian portraits, including those of the Royal Family, is that he continued to wear the kilt at all times and in all weathers for the rest of his very long life.

Seton Gordon's reminiscences of those early years indicate a freedom bestowed on few boys to follow his interests, roving the countryside around Aberdeen and Aboyne for hours at a time. Some of his earlier recollections told at various times show a clear independence of spirit. The earliest one he puts at about the age of five. It was an accident that might have been fatal. On a summer visit to Aboyne he was playing on the village green with a friend, Gordon Stewart Duncan, a year older than himself. During a practice at golf Seton 'paid the penalty for standing too close' and was was hit by Gordon Duncan's cleek in a back-swing. The blow hit him above the right eye and the local doctor said that he had literally escaped within an inch of his life.

Another memory concerned a fish and also took place before the turn of the century. Close by the old Dee Bridge, a more ornate structure than the present one, a large pike lived in a backwater. Seton Gordon was determined to catch it. With a small fish for bait he hooked it while his governess held him around the middle as he drew it in. Lord Huntly, Chief of Clan Gordon, happened to pass by and expressed surprise that so small a boy had caught a 7lb fish.

To someone with a strong childhood memory of 'cheery' oyster catchers playing their game of 'follow the leader' along the river, there could be only one avocation, and it was followed unwaveringly. The gift of a bicycle was a landmark, and allowed further freedom to roam and observe.

After the move to Aboyne in 1902, when Seton Gordon was sixteen, the chalet became their permanent home for several years. Seton was by this time a proficient photographer and for some years had used the Aboyne garden to observe and record the behaviour of some of the more common birds. A pair of bullfinches nested in the garden and one summer Seton visited the nest frequently while the hen was brooding on her eggs. When the young hatched, the mother allowed him to stroke her on the nest, and she would alight on his hand

and take hemp seed from it, shelling each seed carefully. She would then feed her family on the seed. The bird became so tame that she would take hemp seed held between his lips. He later wrote: 'The delight of having a truly wild bird fly off the nest and settle in one's hand is worth the hours spent in establishing contact.'

On one occasion the bullfinches had their nest blown down, and Seton found the young birds scattered, already cold and stiff. Set before the kitchen fire, they revived and he put them back in the nest which he moved to a small table on the balcony of the house. He was relieved when the mother flew to the new location and fed her young.

This intense interest could not long be contained in a garden. North of Aboyne, the hill Morven, rising beyond the town, beckoned Seton Gordon irresistibly. On its slopes are found ptarmigan, red grouse, curlew, lapwing, lark and golden plover. It was on this hill that he began bird photography seriously, experimenting with his camera. Nature photographers up to that time were mainly content to obtain pictures of eggs in the nest, but some, R.B. Lodge and Richard Kearton among them, began to photograph nesting birds. Seton Gordon's inspiration came from the latter.

Soon he was venturing into the Cairngorms. They are higher than the West Highlands, many summits above 4000 feet, whereas in the west only Ben Nevis exceeds this. Lochnagar, at 3786 feet, is closer to Aboyne. One day, at the end of May 1903, he was on its western slopes where large snow patches still lay, when at about 3000 feet he watched a ptarmigan in flight. He noticed it hesitate for a few seconds then continue on its way. Keeping an eye on the spot where the ptarmigan had dropped, he crossed a snow patch and there found a hen on the nest. A decision was made that led to another step in his career as a naturalist. He knew that Richard Kearton did not possess a picture of a nesting ptarmigan. Seton Gordon quickly set off down to Ballater, where for the cost of sixpence, 'a fortune then to a boy' he sent a telegram to Kearton, who replied that he was coming north on the next train.

He met Kearton at Ballater railway station the next day. It was late when he arrived, and they walked all night. It was sunrise when they arrived at the corrie where the bird was nesting. Kearton's excitement was so great that Seton thought he was going to drop the camera, not realising that the bird was comparatively tame. The picture was a success, and in telling the story more than seventy years later Seton Gordon ended with a modest chuckle about his first brush with fame as a naturalist.

In 1901 Queen Victoria died. The significance of her reign on Seton Gordon's life went far beyond her liking for his mother's poetry or grandfather Paul's plants. From the time of her first visit to the Highlands in 1842 she had encouraged an interest in Highland music, dress and customs.

The presence of the court at Balmoral and the outdoor activities associated with the monarch's visits, fishing, stalking, and the Highland Gatherings along the Dee valley, fostered skilled fishermen and fine shots. Equally the men that served them, the stalkers and ghillies, were of high calibre and knew their mountains and their craft well. Many of these men were first class players of the Highland bagpipe. Seton Gordon acquired his lifelong passion for this music from early association with them.

The best found themselves in royal service, and from these would be chosen men to be honoured with the title 'Queen's Piper'. There are always two, and when not acting in an official capacity at formal or informal events, they are employed as ghillies or stalkers on the Balmoral estate. The tradition survives under our present Queen, and Seton Gordon maintained his association with each generation of pipers to the reigning monarch during his lifetime. Piping is an essential part of Balmoral activities, especially when the Royal Family is in residence. There were occasions before the Second World War when as many as seven or eight estate workers played the pipes around the table after dinner.

Although Seton Gordon was not afraid to criticise keepers, as he sometimes did when he felt they were killing protected species unnecessarily, he remained on good terms with the majority of them. Many were counted among his personal friends.

With one family in particular, the McDonalds, who produced at least three generations of keepers, he maintained an unbroken association. Donald, Sandy and their unmarried sister Nell still live in Braemar, and Donald, who has retired as head stalker on the Invercauld estate, has many memories of Seton. He was a toddler when Seton first appeared at their home early in the century.

Sandy McDonald senior was for fifteen years a keeper at the Bynack Lodge in the Mar Forest, south-west of Braemar. In the Scottish tradition the family is still known as 'Bynack'. Miss Nell 'Bynack', now in her eighties, recalls Seton as a young man walking through the glen to visit them. In 1914 the family moved to the Lui Beg Cottage after the death of keeper Donald Fraser, a favourite of Edward, Prince of Wales and his aunt, the Princess Royal.

John MacIntosh was another upper Deeside stalker with whom Seton spent many hours. For many years he stayed each summer at Corrour bothy. He was a good piper in his day and Seton would take his pipes there for a shared session.

Before John MacIntosh was at Corrour it was in the care of Charles Robertson, who was of great age when Seton Gordon first met him. In describing the old man, he creates a wonderful picture:

> Charles Robertson, even as an old man, was agile and active. This was especially so during his many crossings of the River Dee. When the river was in spate extreme care and precision were needed to leap from boulder to boulder, and although I had youth on my side I was never able to emulate his skill. He was a character and greatly impressed me on my first meeting, which was to be one of many. He used to tame the mice in the bothy, and they would come fearlessly to him, sit on his boot and take crumbs.

Another stalker of Seton's acquaintance, Finlay MacPherson of the now ruined Loch Builg Lodge, had a Cairn terrier called Toddles. The dog and MacPherson were inseparable, though Toddles was not the most obedient dog. Seton Gordon carried fond memories of his master shouting 'Come back Toddles!' as the dog wilfully disappeared, followed by a stream of forceful remarks, usually ending 'Got TAMM you, Toddles!' the dog knowing that no physical force would be forthcoming to bring him into line.

One man who played an important part in Seton Gordon's early years was Charles MacIntosh, second keeper on the Balmoral estate. Among other outdoor skills, he was an expert fly-fisherman, preferring to be on the river before sunrise or at dusk, to savour the quiet gloom of these special times of the day. Writing in the mid-1940s Seton Gordon looked back on these hillmen of his youth, and rejoiced that he had been privileged to live among them and associate with them daily.

Even after her death, Queen Victoria's influence on Deeside and its close ties with her family were too strong to be broken. Edward VII continued the annual visits and used Balmoral very much as his mother had done. He enjoyed Highland customs and the wearing of Highland dress. The popularity of Deeside never faltered.

For his seventeenth birthday in 1903, Seton Gordon received from his parents a half-plate Thornton Pickard Ruby camera with a Dallmeyer lens. This opened up new opportunities for bird photography which he was quick to seize. It is easy to forget, when one looks at the myriad of wildlife and bird photographs contained in 'coffee table' books today, that he was a pioneer in bird photography, working alone and developing his own skills and techniques. When he began, he stalked his birds. To obtain a picture of a bird as wary and unapproachable as the curlew on the nest was a considerable feat.

With the variety of cameras available today it is a temptation to always want the latest and most up-to-date equipment available. Seton's Thornton Pickard was still in use thirty years later. His only other cameras were a Kodak and an Ica, both hand-held cameras using 3¼ × 5½ format. From 1920, He also used a Una Sinclair with a Ross telecentric lens. This camera gave some very fine results and was not affected by being partially submerged in water when left below the high tide mark during the 1921 expedition to Spitsbergen! The Kodak was new in 1908 and with a special lens the cost was just over £5. It was used chiefly for seabirds. As there was no independent focus it was necessary to judge accurately the distance between the bird and the camera.

Seton Gordon once observed that despite the considerable increase over the years in wildlife photographers, most lacked the patience of the early school. Strangers would write, usually in the spring, and say that they had planned during the season to photograph all the rare birds in the Highlands – would he therefore tell them how to set about it and where exactly to find their nests!

The year after receiving the Thornton Pickard, he took his first picture of a golden eagle eyrie. The nest was in a Scots fir, and built far out on a strong lateral branch, slightly more than halfway up the tree. The location was in a deer forest, on the beat of Charles MacIntosh. The bird had an alternative nest which it used some years, on a rock not far from the tree.

Seton Gordon had by this time acquired a motorcycle and trailer to carry his photographic equipment. The trailer was actually a wicker bath-chair, which, having a small wheel and handle at the front was easily adapted for this use.

He and Gordon Duncan, who several years before had almost been responsible for Seton's early demise, were out with MacIntosh when they spotted the eyrie. The first branch was at least 12 feet off the ground, and to get the heavy camera into place they brought a ladder and a length of rope from MacIntosh's cottage. The keeper gave the tree a smart whack with his stick and the head of the eagle appeared over the side glaring fiercely. She then rose, 'slowly and flew heavily until she cleared the neighbouring treetops before spiralling upwards until out of sight'.

The ladder did not reach the first branch and to overcome the problem, MacIntosh lifted it and Seton Gordon, steadying it against his chest until Seton was able to grasp the branch. From there he hauled up the equipment. There was a large branch on which to steady the camera. Seton looked into a huge nest 8 feet wide, with two eggs, blotched and spotted rusty red, one slightly bigger than the other. He took several photographs of the nest and its eggs. Returning a few weeks later he found two eaglets, already feeding well, with the remains of a stoat and a red grouse in the eyrie.

The motorcycle and trailer provided some adventures and amusement. On one occasion Seton took a girlfriend for a ride. As they drove out of Aboyne he was thrilled to find the bike performing exceptionally well and actually accelerating uphill. He turned and called over his shoulder 'I have never seen her climb this hill so fast before'. To his great consternation there was no passenger – and no trailer either. About a hundred yards to the rear he saw the trailer in a cloud of dust, and the girl sitting in a 'very undignified posture' on the road beside it, fortunately unhurt but with an extremely angry expression on her face.

It was not long after this that he bought his first car, a 1906 12 h.p. Humber, which was as much an adventure to ride in – but more difficult to fall out of. There was no self-starter, the lamp burned paraffin and the sidelights carbide. There was no spare wheel and a flat tyre had to be mended by the roadside. The motorcycle remained in use for carrying the photography equipment, though never beyond the end of a forest service road, or to the base of a moor. From these points the equipment was carried, however far.

Time spent in the Cairngorms increased so that summer or winter, hardly a week went by that he was not in them, sleeping in the bothies, which were in much better shape then. They were built of stone, sometimes with a tin roof and always a fireplace. Used by deer watchers through the summmer months, they were primitive but could be made comfortable. The Corrour bothy was Seton Gordon's favourite.

It was in 1906 that Seton Gordon first climbed to the summit of Braeriach. In a deep corrie known as the Garbh Choire Mor, at 3800 feet, he saw a large snowfield. There are many in the Highlands that last from year to year, though most disappear in exceptionally warm summers. It was 1960 before he was able to write that the corrie was free from snow and no moisture could be found in the scree that it usually covered.

Aboyne was the home of a noted amateur ornithologist, Arthur Murray Farquhar, a career naval officer who was promoted to Rear Admiral in 1906. He was a frequent contributor to *Ibis* and also shared with Seton Gordon a love of fly-fishing and golf. During periods of leave he returned to his estate, Granville Lodge, and was a companion on bird watching expeditions. A favourite location was Mount Keen, a high conical hill to the south of Glen Tanner. Rich in birdlife, it is now a nature reserve. Farquhar came from a long line of distinguished sailors: both his father and grandfather reached the rank of Admiral. A knighthood was conferred upon his grandfather in 1815, and Arthur Murray assumed it on his father's death in 1908.

He played an important part in shaping Seton Gordon's life, perhaps even more vital than William Gordon. Seton described the Admiral as lovable, and pictures suggest that he would be as much at home on his country estate as on the deck of a battleship. At home the Admiral divided his time beween birds, golf and fishing. He was in his day one of the finest fishermen on the Dee. His sons, Malcolm and John, both retired naval captains, had many memories of those far off times in Aboyne. They recalled outings with Seton Gordon before they were ten years old. He took them in his wicker trailer to see an eyrie in Glen Tanner. They remembered being assisted up an old Scots pine tree to peer into the nest. Another time he took them to a plover's nest and for their benefit turned one of the eggs around while the mother was away. They waited for her to return, whereupon she turned it so that the thinner end pointed in. Seton was a frequent visitor to their home, especially when their father was on leave. They joined in many golf games and fishing expeditions as they grew older.

Another boy who enjoyed frequent outings with Seton was closer in age than the Farquhar brothers. A few miles west of Aboyne is the estate, Dinnet, and in 1896 it was purchased by the Barclay-Harvey family. Their son Malcolm, also an only child, was six years old at the time, four years younger than Seton. They became firm friends and as he grew older Malcolm joined in many of the birdwatching expeditions.

With so many outdoor-loving friends of all ages and walks of life Seton had ample opportunity to pursue both golf and fly-fishing. They were recreations that he continued to enjoy, with opportunities to fish lochs, rivers and pools across the breadth of Scotland from the Dee to the Outer Hebrides. He learned to play golf well enough to continue at university and to represent Oxford at inter-varsity matches, earning his 'Blue'.

In 1907 at the age of twenty-one Seton Gordon published his first book, *Birds of the Loch and Mountain* illustrated with ninety of his own photographs. Timing was excellent. Although the camera had been in use for perhaps thirty years, not too many had used the instrument as a means of fostering an interest in nature. Few people were better equipped to follow the Kearton brothers. The book contained information on twenty-one birds, eagle, ptarmigan, capercailzie, grouse, woodcock, goosander, golden plover, curlew, sandpiper, redshank, oyster catcher, common tern, common gull, black-headed gull, grey crow, water ouzel (dipper), ring ouzel, bullfinch, meadow pipit, willow warbler, and peregrine falcon.

The book received very good reviews and showed Seton Gordon's dedication to ornithology and his unusual grasp of detail. His study of upland birds in all weathers, especially in blizzard conditions, helped to point out the hardiness of many species. It also showed the hardiness of the author, who descibed many days of great discomfort, yet the rewards, in viewing natural phenomena and moments of exquisite beauty, were to him well worth it.

Seton Gordon thought that the Wild Birds Protection Act was ineffective. Among birds lacking protection were the black-headed gull and the peregrine falcon. In 1908, the black-headed gull was removed from the Act with disastrous results. He personally saw keepers breaking eggs and destroying nests. In one instance a keeper was busily filling a bucket with eggs, while a gull with both wings broken by shot lay helpless in the water. Many keepers thought of the black headed gull as a deadly enemy of grouse and pheasants, but Seton did not think it was a common occurrence, provided other food was plentiful. On the other hand the gulls helped farmers immensely by feeding on the deadly grubs of the daddy-long-legs or crane fly, so injurious to young oat.

Seton's concern for the peregrine was supported by an event which happened in late April 1908. He discovered one brooding on Clach-na-Ben and planned a series of photographs right up to the hatching of the young. It was in connection with the peregrine that he was most critical of keepers:

> It is regrettable that this bird is fast decreasing as a nesting species, to a great extent through the constant warfare waged by nearly all gamekeepers. Many are under orders from their masters, who are ready to sacrifice the peregrine for a few extra grouse on the 12th. A keeper boasted to me of killing a falcon on the wing with his rifle, though he had absolutely no excuse for this contravention of the Wild Birds Protection Act.

The site which he found was on a ledge half way down a rock face, near the summit of the mountain. There was no nest, just a slight depression scraped in the earth, but there were five eggs. On the way up he was surprised by the number of grouse, some of them flushed within a few feet of the nesting rock. It seemed that they were not unduly worried by the presence of the peregrine.

Nine days later he returned with his half-plate camera. Although it was now early May, there had been a heavy snow storm the previous day. Despite this, Seton, now accompanied by Malcolm Barclay-Harvey, reached the rock by 8 a.m. They were rewarded by a view of the hen poised ready for flight at the edge of the nesting ledge. She flew off at speed and did not return while they were in the vicinity.

At the base of the rock a freshly discharged cartridge was found, evidence that a keeper knew of the nest and had already attempted to shoot the bird, no doubt why she was more wary on this visit than on the previous one. The camera posed some difficulty because of the nest's location. Seton hauled it up by rope, and after a good deal of manoeuvering, found a precarious vantage point. He exposed four plates, and all turned out well.

On the 18 May, they returned to the rock to begin a series of photographs of

Braemar Gathering in 1908 (By kind permission of Dr. Euan Dawson). Seton Gordon was correspondent for The Times *and* Morning Post

the young birds as they developed. Setting out before 5 a.m. on a day of cold north wind, when he and Barclay-Harvey reached the top it was enveloped in thick mist. They expected any moment to see the peregrine leave her nest but found only two eggs that had been moved along the ledge a distance of nearly 2 feet. There was the mark of a pellet in the rock, with a corresponding groove in the nest.

It was plain that the keeper had crept up and shot the unsuspecting bird while she brooded. Seton could see the marks made by her claws as she writhed in her death agony and several feathers were lying around, some of them of extraordinary beauty, tinged with greenish yellow. To show how the eggs were found Seton had the rope thrown up to haul the camera into place. The cock peregrine was flying in the far distance, and did not come near.

As well as writing nature articles, Seton Gordon was now covering the Braemar Gathering for both *The Times* and *Morning Post*, which he did until 1913, the last year of Highland Games until after the Armistice of 1918. In a dispatch to the *Morning Post*, Seton Gordon wrote:

> The Braemar Gathering is noteworthy in that here one sees three distinct clans muster in full kilt dress, and march to the gathering ground with their pipes in full cry and their banners waving in the wind. The custom of the Gathering of the Clans is in danger of lapsing. Many of the old land owners are in straitened financial conditions and the expense incurred to upkeep a clan is a very considerable item. Few of the clansmen are willing to bear the cost of their Highland dress. Braemar is one of the few districts where Highland matters flourish. The clansmen of the Duke of Fife number 100, reinforced by the Invercauld Highlanders and the Royal clansmen of Balmoral; close to 300 men in all. Their burnished claymores and formidable Lochaber axes glint in the sun, making a picture, which once seen, remains long in memory.
>
> In front march the Royal Highlanders, dressed in Royal Stuart tartan, in each bonnet a thistle and oak leaf. The pipers were led by the King's piper, Pipe-Major Forsyth. At the head of the clan Mr Charles MacIntosh bore the Royal Standard. At three o' clock, great cheering announced the approach of the King and Queen, riding in a carriage with postillions. The King and Prince Albert wore the kilt, the King having three eagle plumes on his bonnet, the badge of chieftainship. The crowd cheered again and again as they proceeded to the pavilion to the stirring strains of 'Hielan Laddie'. The clansmen again marched around the enclosure as the King took the salute.

The clansmen were provided with a meal between the proceedings, fortified by several 'drams'. It was towards the end of one such Braemar Gathering that a marcher, spotting Seton Gordon, came up to him in a very happy frame of mind and pointing unsteadily at the sky said, 'Eagles, Mr Gordon – hundreds of them!!'

The tradition of providing Highland dress must have carried on for a while beyond 1918 because Donald McDonald, who would have been too young to march before the war, was a clansmen with the Duke of Fife's Mar contingent. He said that everything was provided except the shoes.

Another interest, in total contrast to nature and piping was shared with Malcolm Barclay-Harvey. They were railway enthusiasts and frequently travelled on the footplate of the Deeside trains which ran from Aberdeen to Ballater, becoming proficient enough to sometimes drive the engine. Seton used his photographic skills to take scenes along the track from the engine cab. The collection is among his papers in the National Library of Scotland and show considerable inventiveness, as many of the pictures are taken at speed. Despite all the swaying and vibration, they are clear and in focus.

Two favourite drivers were James Hay and James Wilcox. On one journey while Seton Gordon was with Wilcox an incident occurred at his home station. Arriving from Aberdeen on the evening train, Seton was driving and though he applied the brakes in good time, they were not working well that day. There was a slight down gradient into the station from the east and in consequence Seton overran the platform. His anxiety was great as he watched the businessmen jump down from their carriages onto the line, hoping that he would not be seen, and associated with such indifferent driving.

In the summer of 1908 Seton Gordon registered at Aberdeen University for a fifty lecture course in zoology. The lecturer was Sir Arthur Thompson, a professor with an international reputation. The course material was designed for those intending to read for a degree in natural science. The tuition covered dissection, 'illustrative of the various classes of animals, supplemented by demonstration, practice in microscopy, and identification of representatives of the local fauna'. A number of field trips would be included.

Although Seton had immense experience in the field, his private education allowed little opportunity for laboratory work. This was required to satisfy the entrance requirements for Exeter College, Oxford, where he had applied to read natural sciences. This included botany, zoology and chemistry. In having Sir Arthur Thompson as his first tutor in these subjects he was fortunate. Thompson had held senior teaching posts in zoology for ten years and was known in Canada and the United States, where he was a visiting professor at both MacGill and California. His showmanship was an attraction, aided by a 'clear-cut face, and a pleasing though slightly high-pitched voice, used to good effect to deliver lectures with great lucidity, imagination and flashes of humour'.

During the summer Seton learned that he had been accepted at Exeter College, and went up for his first term in October, 1908.

CHAPTER

2

FROM THE COUROUR BOTHY TO OXFORD HONOURS

In choosing Exeter College, Seton Gordon was in good company. A list of past members picked at random includes J. R. R. Tolkien, who was a contemporary. In more recent years the actor Richard Burton was up in 1944 and Sir Roger Bannister in 1946. A few years ahead of Seton Gordon were Lord Fisher, Archbishop of Canterbury from 1945 to 1961, and 'Tubby' Clayton, founder of Toc H. Sir Frederick Soddy, who received a Nobel Prize for his pioneering work in chemistry, attended in 1919. William Morris and Edward Burne-Jones were undergraduates in the early 1850s. Their art is represented by a Morris tapestry of the Adoration of the Magi, designed by Burne-Jones. In the college library is the Morris 'Kelmscott Chaucer', an oustanding piece of book decoration.

In describing Exeter as the twentieth century approached, Dr J. R. Maddicott, tutor in medieval history and college archivist wrote:

> The tone of the college is more difficult to describe than its constitution. Mark Pattison spoke of it as 'genteel but unintellectual'. Another memoir writer of the 1850s says 'it was an axiom that no scholarly distinction was to be expected from Exeter'. Ascribing its failings to the recruitment of tutors from a narrow circle. Neither observation is entirely accurate . . . Exeter [later] contained some remarkable men among its senior members: Ray Lancaster, the pioneer biologist; J. A. Froude, the historian and one of the last great Devonians to be associated with the college; W. A. Sewell, the founder of Radley, who was said to be one of the best tutors in Oxford; F. T. Palgrave, the poet and compiler of the *Golden Treasury*; and C. W. Boase, a Fellow for over fifty years and the college's historian. These five very different figures suggest the variety and talents which found a home at Exeter.

Seton Gordon was twenty-two when he went up to Oxford, a little older than the average student, most of whom came up from the more traditional route of the public schools. The enrolment record for 1908 has fifty-seven entries, all

Seton Gordon in 1906, at age 20

handwritten in 'copperplate' writing in a large ledger. The entries include seven Rhodes scholars from: Rhodesia, Natal, Transvaal, Bermuda, and the United States. Other students came from an equally varied range of places: Germany, Constantinople, Punjab, Paris, Lahore, and Russia. One quaint feature of the ledger was that the column for the father's name included, not his occupation but his 'quality'. Many called themselves simply, gentlemen or landowners. There were doctors, lawyers, accountants, engineers and clergy-men. The appearance of Rhodes scholars only five years before had introduced a new dimension to college life, perhaps not always appreciated by the established elite, which at the time still dominated life at England's two ancient universities. With the start of the First World War, changes were set in motion, greater than the impact of Rhodes scholars, which opened up the ancient seats of learning to a diversity of people. To some, the changes made Oxford an alien place.

The distractions for a new arrival at Oxford were many. For Seton Gordon to be suddenly thrust into university life with some 4000 undergraduates, even for someone as outgoing as he, would be overwhelming – societies to join, interests to engage in, new friends to make, old friends to spend time with, including Malcolm Barclay-Harvey who had entered Christchurch to read law. Seton Gordon enjoyed college life to the fullest, but admitted to spending too many hours playing golf, which is probably why in June of his first year he failed a zoology exam and in December failed a botany test. These, his only failures, may have been enough to make him give sober thought to the future.

There was little indication that Seton Gordon suffered the financial stress that plagues so many students. Still sought after as a freelance writer, as his knowledge increased through university tuition, more articles were sold on resource related subjects. A second book was also being prepared. Students were always dipping their hands into their pockets to buy a variety of items, but food especially. Even later when he developed friendships with Prince Felix Youssoupoff and Edward, Prince of Wales, he seemed to have little difficulty in keeping up with them.

Two outstanding scientists provided tutelage in botany and natural sciences during Seton's years at Oxford. The first was Professor Sydney Vines who in 1888 was elected to the Sherardian Professorship. When Seton returned to obtain a Diploma in Rural Economy and Forestry it was under Professor, later Sir William, Somerville. Vines' published works included *Lectures on the Physiology of Plants* and a translation of Sachs' *Textbook of Botany*.

Whenever an opportunity presented itself, Seton returned to Deeside where he continued his interest in birds and plants. The frequent diary references to birdsong suggests that at this point his hearing was not too impaired. There is no doubt that from the 1920s onwards his hearing deteriorated rapidly.

Despite early academic failures, he was enrolled in the honours schools. Some students, through laziness, too much time spent on extra-curricular activities, or inability, were 'sent down' because of repeated failures. Many went on to fame or achievement in their chosen career, but university life was not for them. Of all the people with wealth attending Oxford at that time, Seton Gordon established a friendship with one whose wealth exceeded all others: one of the most unusual men of our century, who felt called upon to do something completely foreign to his nature – assassination. The man was Prince Felix Youssoupoff of Russia.

This association began when they met at Braemar Castle, as guests of the English-born Princess Dalgorouky, and was surprising in that they were so different in outlook and background. Seton came from an Aberdeen middle-class family with a father who would today be described as a 'workaholic'. Youssoupoff came from the wealthiest family in Russia, later married Irina, a niece of Tsar Nicolas II, and until well into adult life thought only of the pleasures his wealth could bring.

There were Youssoupoff palaces in St. Petersburg, Petrograd, and Moscow as well as thiry-seven estates across Russia. Included in these were coal and iron mines, oilfields, mills and factories. One estate stretched 120 miles along the shore of the Caspian Sea. Crude oil here was so abundant that it soaked the ground and the peasants used it to grease their cart wheels. The Youssoupoff wealth was accumulated through generations of imperial service. There was hardly a Tsar or Empress who did not have a Youssoupoff as a close personal adviser.

A brief summary of Felix's life will reveal why his personality was so out of the ordinary. Born on 24 March, 1887, he was so puny that he was not expected to live beyond 48 hours. His mother, Princess Zenaide had longed for a daughter and because of her disappointment, Felix was dressed as a girl until he was five years old. The ugly baby was now attractive, and was later described as the most beautiful young man in Europe. He admitted to being such a detestable child that he went through a succession of nannies, governesses and tutors. He once bit the finger of a music teacher so badly that she could not play the piano for a year. Not until the death of his brother in a duel when Felix was twenty-six, did he decide to give up a life entirely devoted to pleasure; 'to think only of my own desires and ways to satisfy them . . . I loved beauty, luxury, comfort, the colour and the scent of flowers'.

Now the sole heir to the family's vast fortune, Felix came to Oxford in 1909 and enrolled at University College. He developed an immediate liking for Oxford and the British, finding them 'attractive, hospitable, self-possessed, and imbued with a sense of their own superiority'.

Felix returned to Russia before commencing the autumn term at Oxford and it was then that he first met Rasputin, the so called mystic who had such a profound influence on the Tsarina. He had come to the attention of Tsar Nicolas II and Tsarina Alexandra when it was discovered that their only son, Alexis, was a haemophiliac. From that moment, the Tsarina was convinced that Rasputin could help alleviate the boy's suffering. By the time of his assassination, Rasputin had more influence than either the Court or government ministers. His powers appeared to be such that during the worst periods of the disease when Alexis was in great pain and the bleeding could not be stopped medically, he alone seemed to be able to arrest it and calm the boy. There have since been medical theories put forward to suggest how this came about, ruling out the use of mysticism.

Rasputin had a strange hold over most women. He had gained the affection of a mother and daughter who were close friends of Youssoupoff and Rasputin had expressed a wish to meet him.

The killing of Rasputin has been well documented elswhere, but the utter revulsion felt by Youssoupoff for him is less well known. When the Prince became aware of his influence on the Tsarina, and its effects on Russia, he felt compelled to act. In his book *Lost Splendour* Youssoupoff describes Rasputin and their first meeting:

> From the very first his self assurance irritated me and there was something wicked, crafty and sensual in his unctuous countenance which disgusted me. He was of middle height, muscular and thin, with arms disproportionately long. Just where his untidy crop of hair began to grow there was a great scar. His face was framed by a shaggy beard and his small shifty eyes had a revolting expression. They were close together and so deep sunk that at a distance they were invisible. His sweet and insipid smile was almost as revolting as the

> expression in his eyes. He was not in the least like a holy man. On the contrary he looked like a lascivious, malicious satyr.

Youssoupoff returned to Oxford shortly after his first meeting and it was several years before he met Rasputin again. While making no claim to being a scholar, he enjoyed meeting and talking to people from many different parts of the world, and examining their ideas, morals and customs. He was not cast in the ordinary mould, yet his zest for life made him popular. Although Felix was known to the college servants and porters as 'Mr Elkins' there was little doubt as to his true identity. Travelling by train he was in the habit of booking a first class compartment for himself, though it is certain that he would have shared it with his university friends.

In his second year Felix rented a small house on King Edward Street where for several months Seton Gordon shared rooms with him. Among the luxuries were a Russian chef, a French chauffeur, an English valet, and a housekeeper whose husband cared for Youssoupoff's three horses, a hunter and two polo ponies.

sw0 The diversity of students ensured a wide range of opinions – the essence of a university education, though many of the wealthier students had little incentive to take academic life seriously. Their future was assured in the estates and London houses to which they confidently knew they would succeed, each with its army of servants and retainers. In Seton Gordon's time there, few had any premonition that they were living in the last of a golden age, and that the First World War and its aftermath would change the social order so drastically and permanently. These are the people so readily associated with Oxford. As Jan Morris wrote, ' the picture of a nostalgic idyll, of privileged persons enjoying outmoded delights, attended by servants, to the sound of bells'.

Seton Gordon took full advantage of what Oxford had to offer, though he preferred to spend his vacations on Deeside. Here his social life was widened by visits to Braemar Castle, leased over many years by an intriguing couple, Prince and Princess Alexis Dalgorouky. Like Youssoupoff, Dalgorouky had estates in Russia, but much of his time was spent in Britain where he was drawn to the way of life of the British aristocracy. His father had held high office as Secretary of State and Privy Seal to Tsar Alexander II, and Alexis himself served with distinction in the Russian army during the Russo–Turkish war. He was for a time a chamberlain to the Emperor. In 1898 he had married Frances Pellew-Wilson, heiress of Fleetwood Pellew-Wilson of Wappenham Manor, Northamptonshire. Braemar Castle, leased from the Farquharsons of Invercauld, became their Scottish seat. The Princess was more prominent in local affairs than her husband, and gained a reputation for her hospitality. During her summer visits she held numerous house parties, balls and dinners.

The Princess had her own piper and even followed the tradition of her Royal neighbours by having pipe music played at breakfast, and around the table after dinner. Seton would sometimes play with him and they were occasionally joined by John MacIntosh from the Corrour bothy.

To Nell McDonald, Princess Dalgorouky was a familiar figure as she passed the school while setting out to visit the homes of her humbler neighbours, taking tea with them. Nell remembered her as a magnificent figure in furs and fashionable hats.

It was Seton Gordon who first persuaded the Princess to take a ride in a motor car, when she wished to visit Mrs Charles MacIntosh at the Ballochbuie. A promise was made that he would not go over 10 miles an hour. The Deeside roads were in good condition even in those days and Seton realised this would be impossible on a downhill gradient. Keeping the car at a steady 15 miles per hour, he gradually increased to 20. The Princess appeared very comfortable but could hardly fail to notice the speedometer. Seton reassured her by saying 'That dial shows the engine revolutions'. Despite this deception, she took frequent drives with him and finally bought her own motor car, a magnificent vehicle driven by a liveried chauffeur.

As well as a house in London, the Dalgoroukys had an estate, Nashdom, near Taplow in Buckinghamshire. This later became a monastery. The Prince died in June 1915 and so did not live to see the upheavals in his native land. The Princess, who was active during the First World War organising for the welfare of the troops, died in August 1919. Both were buried near their Buckinghamshire home.

The Dalgoroukys' butler was a Mr Connor, who had great dignity and bearing though already elderly. In January 1910 Seton and a friend, Dick Crewe, while staying at Braemar Castle, set out early to climb Ben MacDhui. It was 5:50 a.m. as they descended the stairs to find Connor in white tie and tail coat, 'presiding over a breakfast of porridge, eggs, bacon, toast and coffee. He was as cheerful as though the hour were 9 a.m.' The pair were going to spend several days at the Corrour bothy, and the trip might have ended in disaster had Seton not known the mountains so well. He was carrying his pipes in their wooden case, an extra weight that he later almost regretted. It was bitterly cold, and soon after reaching the bothy a fire of peat and bog fir was burning strongly.

The next day, Seton and Crewe were some miles from the bothy when snow started to fall thickly. They returned quickly. It was not until darkness fell that the storm reached its height and when in late evening the blizzard passed the Lairig was as bright as day under a full moon. Across the ground, the snow had been drifted by the gale. They piled the fire high with fuel, yet in that small room a basin of water, placed on the table by the window, froze solid.

The weather gradually improved and they set out for the Derry Lodge. There was less weight to carry, but the pipes in their case were difficult to transport on steep icy slopes. The snow surface was so frozen that it bore their weight as they fought the bitter frost-laden wind. Despite the intense cold, Seton was compelled to play his pipes that day. He admitted: 'My fingers, in a temperature of 15 degrees of frost and a bitter wind of perhaps 30 miles an hour, were stiff, and not in the best form for excecuting the grace notes of a pibroch. Except for my friend there was no living thing within earshot – ptarmigan were in the shelter of the corrie below, and even the eagle, king of birds, was in a more sheltered and less airy site'.

They were without ice axes and the snow had been swept off many slopes by the force of the wind. This left large areas of old snow, thawed and fozen several times until its surface was like glass. Extreme care was necessary to avoid slipping over a precipice and into a rock-filled corrie. When Seton and Crewe finally reached Donald Fraser's door, it was opened by his wife who after an astonished glance, broke into peals of laughter. This was very disconcerting until they saw themselves in a mirror – two unshaven faces, black from a week of peat smoke in the confines of the bothy!

In 1911 Seton Gordon was preparing to take his degree, and in the summer he sat the final botany examination. He regretted the many hours spent on the golf courses around Oxford, and did not feel over-confident about his prospects. Despite this, with Malcolm Barclay-Harvey, he took off for the north on the weekend before the examination and took the overnight train to Aviemore. The destination was again the Corrourbothy where he worked on alpine flora notes. Seton Gordon recalled: 'Most of my friends thought I was mad to obtain a week-end leave of absence so near to my finals, but it turned out to be most fortunate for me that I did so'.

Back at Oxford he entered the examination hall with some trepidation and studied the question papers in front of him. One asked 'Write as fully as possible what you know about the Alpine Flora of Britain'. Years of observation in the Cairngorms and Deeside, and that final weekend honing, paid off. Seton wrote 2500 words. When he met the distinguished examiners for his *viva voce* test a few days later, he realised they were treating him with an undeserved deference:

> I soon discovered from the questions that they considered me an authority on alpine plants, and my difficulty was to cloak my ignorance when they asked me, among other questions, the name of the saxifrage which grows only on Ben Lawers among British hills. I did not know it was the last stronghold of *Saxifraga cernua*. In the end I gained second-class honours, and, as up to that time no first class honours had ever been awarded in the Honours School of Botany, I realised my extreme fortune. I do not suppose that either before or since, the Corrour bothy has been the means of obtaining an honours degree for a student'.

The following year Seton Gordon returned to Oxford for postgraduate studies under Professor Somerville. The Professor was aware of Seton Gordon's knowledge of the Cairngorms and asked if he would assist in a search for the rare white flowered variety of *Silene acaulis*, the cushion pink. In early July 1912 he took the Professor to the Corrour bothy from where they set out in search. They were walking along a ridge, some distance from each other, when Seton found a clump right in his path. Several days might have been taken up without success and he often wondered if Somerville realised how fortunate they were to have found it so soon. They also found some *Linnae borealis* in bloom and visited a golden eagle eyrie before returning to Oxford.

William Somerville's knowledge was gained from practical as well as academic experience. After his father's death in 1879 he ran the family's Lanarkshire farm for six years before attending Edinburgh University, where he was one of the earliest graduate students in agriculture to obtain a degree. He obtained an appointment to the Chair of Agriculture and Forestry at Durham College of

Science. Eight years later Somerville moved to Cambridge where he remained for twelve years, until offered the position of Assistant Secretary at the Board of Agriculture and Fisheries. After four years he was drawn back to academic life when offered the Sibthorpian Chair of Rural Economy at Oxford and a Fellowship of St John's College. Somerville found time to buy two derelict farms, in Sussex and Gloucestershire, and bring them to full production. His interests were remarkably close to Seton Gordon's, with a love of field botany which was pursued as actively as possible. Other interests in common were ornithology and fly-fishing.

Although Seton was aware of his good fortune to receive tutelage from two such eminent men as Vines and Somerville, the temptation to play golf sometimes became too strong. In 1911 he won his 'Blue' in a match against Cambridge. He played under a number of captains, Jim Robertson-Durham, 'Chubby' Hooman, and Denys Finch Hatton. 'Chubby' was still corresponding with Seton into the early 1960s, from his home near Wimbledon Common. He was a magnificent golfer who inspired Seton to play above his average performance. Denys Finch Hatton was the son of the Earl of Winchelsea and Nottingham and had gone up to Brasenose to study Modern History. His fame was recently revived as the hero in the film *Out of Africa*. The portrayal by Robert Redford failed to capture the uniqueness of Finch Hatton, which Seton Gordon said he never encountered in anyone else during his long and varied life. He recalled Finch Hatton as charming, quite fearless, and with a reputation for saying exactly what he thought, regardless of the consequences. Even this description is barely adequate. In Errol Trebinski's biography of Finch Hatton, *Silence will Speak* she said of him: 'Any commitment which enforced his running with the herd would have been intolerable'. Karen Blixen, in her book *Out of Africa* wrote after his death in a flying accident: 'What they [the colonists] remembered about him was his absolute lack of self-consciousness, self-interest, and unconditional truthfulness which outside of him, I have only met in idiots'.

At Oxford, Seton Gordon recalled a match which they played with a distinguished don who later became a university vice-chancellor. Finch Hatton insisted on addressing him as Watkin. After a time the professor said 'Look here Finch Hatton my name is not Watkin but –'. He calmly replied, 'I prefer to call you Watkin'. He also had a quick repartee, and one of Seton Gordon's favourite and oft repeated anecdotes relates to a particular inter-varsity match. Finch Hatton, always very generous on the green, gave away putts to his opponent, the Cambridge captain. Eventually a spectator could stand it no longer and getting close to him said, 'Finch Hatton, do remember you are playing for your side and not for yourself'. The immediate reply was, 'And do remember that you are playing for neither!'

Added to Seton Gordon's hours on the fairway were those spent writing articles. A selection of those published in 1912 included 'Grouse Prospects' for *Country Life*; 'A Motor Tour' for the *Graphic*. On 6 August he covered the funeral of the Duke of Fife for the *Morning Post*; then wrote another article for the *Graphic* 'On Highland Gatherings'; two more for *Country Life*, 'Wild Country Life' and 'After Gannnets on Suilsgear'. For the *Morning Post* he also wrote

The Hon Denys Finch Hatton golfing partner to Seton Gordon at Oxford

'Stalking Prospects' and 'A Day in the Forest'. He was also paid for pictures by the *Onlooker* and the *Illustrated London News*. The fees ranged from three guineas to a high of seven guineas. Before the First World War, when weekly wages were measured in shillings for the vast majority of people, this represented a good income for a student. Gathering the material meant frequent trips to Scotland. Here the information was readily found, in activities that he enjoyed. The motor tour item retraced an itinerary which he did with Felix Youssoupoff in the Highlands by Loch Awe, Connel, Ballachullish and Fort William, one of many such journeys that they made together.

In 1912 he also published his second book with Cassell *The Charm of the Hills* compiled from various articles written for *Country Life* and the *Scotsman*, and was exclusively about the Cairngorms and the Dee. It was illustrated with forty-two of his own photographs. Many expeditions on to the hightops are described. The last quarter of the book is divided into the four seasons and he takes the reader through them, in a 'nature note' format. There are no diaries available before 1912, but the contents of this section of *The Charm of the Hills* suggests that they were used, but have been lost, because many of the notes have specific dates.

The first diary entry for 1912 is 25 February when he was visiting Chateau d' Amoy at Vouzon, near Orleans. This was the home of the St Pol family from which the Pauls of Newseat were descended before crossing to Scotland and settling on the Aberdeenshire coast. The entry is not auspicious, and notes only that the daffodils are in bloom and an adder was killed. In a one page summary of family history written for his granddaughter Susan, he says: 'The tradition in the family is that the Pauls, at the time of the persecution of the Hugenots, fled from France and settled near Peterhead, where they landed. The French family of St Pol are a very old, (though nowadays very poor) family, and an ancestor took part in the first crusade, and have a cross as their crest. A later St Pol did great deeds at the battle of Cressy and was made a Viscount. I stayed with the St Pols in 1912 at Chateau d' Amoy, and one of them later came to stay with us on Skye'.

The first nature notes appear towards the end of March:

> Saturday 23rd – Visited first the Glen —— eyrie on the W. slopes 1600 ft. Found it repaired to a certain extent with cowberry, ling, and fresh fir branches. two eggs – are almost white. Should say bird has been brooding a week. No sign of hen, but eggs warm. Many blackcock about. Glorious sunny day.
>
> 25th – Watched oyster-catcher at Braemar Castle. Seemingly jerk their heads in similar manner to sandpiper or redshank. Visited Beinn —— eyrie and watched the eagle sitting from a distance of less than 100 yards without putting her off. Seemed young bird very tame. Was sitting down wind. Glorious fine day – fine and mild.
>
> 6 April – Went to Clach na Beinn with Arthur Murray Farquhar. A fine sight of the peregrine as she sped off the rock and over the hillside across the wind, which was blowing at approx. 70 miles per hour. Got over the rocks with

some difficulty, but no sign of nesting yet. A.M.F. says he has never been here in such a wind. Many trees blown over.

22nd – The sandmartins have arrived at the sand bank near Bletsoe. Went up Loch —— and after considerable difficulty found the eyrie of the peregrine. Three eggs. The hen showed conspicuous bravery, alighting from her eggs while we watched from a distance of some 60 yards.

23rd – The Glen —— eyrie has been robbed! Visited other eyrie but no sign of birds. Excellent view of peregrine crossing corrie. Motored to Corrie ——, then on by foot. A very interesting view of a pair of merlins pursuing g. eagle. Merlin's flight to my mind like that of a swift.

These entries indicate a tremendous freedom of movement and enthusiasm for recording all he saw. Most of May was taken up with making forestry notes at the Oxford University Experimental Area at Bagley Wood just outside the city. Most of his notes were on natural regeneration. In June he was back in Scotland spending several days camped on the Braeriach, where he was joined by Somerville. As well as stocking Lochan Uain with fingerling trout, they visited several golden eagle eyries.

Seton motored over to the Inverary Forest nursery, another experimental area where he spent several days. Here he saw the first croft worked under a new afforestation scheme. On 8 July he attended the Duke of Fife's funeral as a special representative for the *Morning Post* – 'Very picturesque and impressive sight. Pipers led by Colin Cameron playing "The MacIntosh Lament".'

The following day he gave a lecture at Aboyne – 'very well attended, excellent reviews', then travelled on to Dinnet to hear a pibroch competition, where he had a long talk with Colin Cameron. He told Seton of the occasion in 1861 when at the age of eighteen he won first prize for pibroch at the Inverness Northern Meeting. Cameron, whose brother Sandy was piper to Cameron of Lochiel, was at this time sixty-eight years old and still an outstanding piper.

On an outing with Malcolm Barclay-Harvey to climb Beinn MacDhui, Seton noted: 'Weather changed at 1:30 p.m. and later almost constant rain. M.B.H. and self went on to Loch Etchachan. Excellent sighting of a hill fox asleep at burnside. Heather magnificent. Returned to Dinnet at 8 p.m. – CATASTROPHE !!'

This note may be the first mention of a facet of Seton Gordon's life which became a legend, and made him the despair of hostesses – his total disregard for time, which made him frequently late for dinner. So immersed was he in thought or conversation that he would sometimes walk into the dining room and find the assembled guests already seated in formal splendour!

In 1912, Edward, Prince of Wales, went up to Oxford, and became a member of Magdalen College. A common interest in piping brought him in touch with Seton Gordon. They received tuition from Pipe-Major 'Wullie' Ross, who later directed the military piping college at Edinburgh Castle. From these sessions in Ross's class a close friendship developed despite an age difference of several years, the Prince being eight years younger.

The piping class met once a week and Seton Gordon remembers the Prince working hard on 'Invercauld's March', which he was determined to master. Edward was a competent and enthusiastic piper and a very apt pupil. He later took on the Presidency of the Scottish Pipers' Society. When official duties would allow, he was a frequent attender at the Oxford University Caledonian Society Dinners. On one occasion Pipe-Major Ross and Seton Gordon piped the Prince down the 'High' to his college at midnight. In doing so they were breaking university rules, but were delighted to observe that although the proctors accompanied them on the opposite side of the street, they did not dare interfere because of the presence of the Prince of Wales.

The Prince continued his enthusiasm for the pipes and in 1935 composed a slow march, which he called 'Mallorca'. His original, handwritten manuscript was presented to the Scots Guards. It was so enthusiastically received that it was put into the regular music programme, and included in Changing of the Guards ceremonies at Buckingham Palace.

Another regular attender at the dinners was Gerald 'Long' Hay, a fellow student who stood 6 feet 11 inches. Hay joined the Argyll and Sutherland Highlanders in 1914 and had the distinction of being the tallest officer in the British army. Gerald, or Fitzgerald Hay, to give him his full Christian name, was a rare character with a nice touch of madness for good measure. He was a frequent patron of the New Theatre, and in a letter to Seton Gordon many years later, an amusing incident was recalled by the late S. C. Dorrill, MBE, whose family were long time proprietors of the theatre. There were frequently obstreperous students in the audience and Hay, because of his size, could always be counted on to help eject any who went too far in their behaviour. Dorrill thanked him on one occasion, and asked why he was so helpful, whereupon Hay replied, 'You wait, one evening I will come back disguised – you won't recognise me and I will just kick up hell!' A few nights later he arrived with three friends, all wearing false moustaches and beards. Dorrill immediately told him that they would not be admitted and Hay, feigning disappointment, said 'Oh dear, I was afraid you might recognize me!' The students disappeared and returned a few days later with a photograph of themselves in their 'get-up', which they then signed and gave to Mr Dorill. He treasured it for many years.

The Prince was frequently absent from Oxford, performing official duties both at home and on the continent. Compared to other undergraduates, more self-discipline was required in Edward's life, and as heir-apparent his upbringing was a shade more spartan than Youssoupoff's. His one luxury was clothes, and he wore the latest styles. The letters to Seton Gordon show an enthusiasm and zest for life, with many dashes and exclamation marks. He did not obtain a degree, unlike the present Prince of Wales and Prince Edward, but he enjoyed the social contact with the wide variety of people with whom he came into contact, and was popular with fellow students at Magdalen.

One of the luxuries the Prince was allowed at Oxford was his Daimler, and he was very generous in sharing it with his friends. Seton Gordon accompanied him on a number of fishing expeditions along the backwaters of the Isis and Cherwell Rivers. There were also golf games at Frilford and other local clubs. On at least one occasion they travelled together in the Highlands, where a photograph shows the Prince's car perched precariously across the old small and primitive Ballachulish ferry.

George V endured much agonising before deciding that his son should be allowed to enjoy the life of a normal undergraduate. There is every reason to believe that Edward revelled in the innocent camaraderie and there was a large circle of commoners whose company he enjoyed. Their names came up frequently in letters. For Edward to take the trouble to write to Seton Gordon from Sandringham on Christmas Day, would indicate a reciprocity of friendship.

The Prince was eighteen when he went up to Oxford. Seton was now twenty-six, but still visited Oxford in his postgraduate work. Photos of this period show him to be very mature, thoroughly dependable and, though serious looking, he was known for his sense of humour as well as a gift of mimicry. This dependability may have been why the Prince was attracted to him. Edward looked, if anything, younger than his eighteen years, was never a serious student, and knew that maintaining friendships would be difficult because of the duties and obligations that faced him.

There were other interests Seton and Edward shared, aside from piping. Both were competent golfers, and both had a fetish for physical fitness. Seton Gordon had built up his powers of endurance through years of hill-walking, and was a very keen swimmer, often taking a dip in the ice-cold waters of Highland pools and lochans. The correspondence between them began in January 1913, when Seton wrote to the Prince and told him of his activities during the Christmas vacation at Alnwick on the Northumbrian coast, and his visit to Holy Island. He also mentioned a planned visit to France to study forestry methods there.

On 13 January Edward replied from York Cottage, Sandringham, in Norfolk: . . . 'I should say it was a good idea to go to France for a study of your subject for it is a great agriculture country, & you would, no doubt be able to pick up a lot there. All you tell me about Holy Island is of great interest; both the wild geese and the wigeon haunt our coastline on The Wash, & their habits are curious. We have been shooting almost every day here, & have killed a lot of woodcock and seen a large number. Today I got 25!! In fact the last fortnight, the snow and cold have made these birds take refuge in most parts of Norfolk. Hoping you are very fit, I remain, yrs ever, Eddie.'

The Duke of Windsor's letters are included by kind permission of Michael Bloch, counsel for the estate of the late Duchess of Windsor

In two short notes in the middle of February there is an apology for missing an evening with Pipe-Major Ross, and the hope of being there the following week. The other was a request to bring forward a golf game. The Prince spent a lot of time apologising for postponing or cancelling arrangements, because of demands on his time, or family commitments, which he found frustrating. A reserve, and a natural modesty are evident in his letters especially when mentioning his family.

In 1913 Edward visited Germany twice, and kept up a regular correspondence with Seton Gordon. These letters reveal little of the tension that was building between the two countries. The first letter came from the Principality of Wurttemburg, where he stayed with King Wilhelm and Queen Charlotte. He found 'Oncle Willie' easy going and apt to doze off during carriage rides that they would sometimes take – the Queen would jab him to make him acknowledge the salute of one of his subjects.

On 12 April Edward wrote from the Wilhelmspalast:

> My Dear Seton,
>
> Many thanks for your letter. I am staying here with the King and Queen of Wurttemburg, and had a very nice motor trip from Cologne; by Coblenz, Wiesbaden, Darmsdadt, Heidelberg and Karlsruhe. On Sunday afternoon I had a fine run in the car to the Lake of Constance, to Friedrichshapen where I spent a couple of nights and and on Monday saw over the Zeppelin airship garage and works, and saw the ship make an ascent . . .*
>
> I hope you will have a good trip to Russia; the scheme sounds a very good one. I hope to get a chance of shooting a capercaillie before I leave. I fancy one has to do a lot of stalking. Well, good luck Seton, Hoping to see you next term, I remain yrs. ever, Eddie.

*The Prince was shown over the airship plant by Count Zeppelin himself, then a vigorous seventy-four years old.

The Prince began to confide to his friends how Oxford was changing his outlook. His letters and notes to Seton Gordon tell of his impatience with official duties, which he now saw as a waste of time. He was frequently summoned by his father to attend formal occasions such as welcoming a foreign dignitary. One such occasion was to meet the President of the French Republic, Raymond Poincaré, when the Prince deputised for his father. His own account of the event was in a letter to Seton Gordon dated 25 June 1913:

> It is most awfully good of you to give me such a ripping and useful present & I thank you most sincerely for it. It was nice seeing you again in camp for a few minutes. I got home alright & am having a busy time here. I went down to Portsmouth yesterday to meet the French President & it was heavy work. I shall be going to Germany again in about a weeks time I expect. I hope you get through your schools alright & that we shall meet again on Deeside. With renewed thanks & wishing you the best of luck, I remain yrs ever, Eddie.

In the spring of 1913, Seton Gordon was invited to Russia by Prince Felix Youssoupoff, who had returned there to continue the improvements to his estates. He had asked Seton to become a forestry adviser and though this never came about, it provided a first-hand opportunity to see Russia as a guest of the wealthiest family, and to meet the Russian aristocracy. He also had a close look at Russian forestry practices at that time. Seton often wondered what his fate might have been had he taken up the offer from Youssoupoff, and whether he would have survived the events of 1917.

It is worth reflecting that Seton Gordon saw a way of life and opulence that a mere four years later was wiped out. In this he shared a coincidence with the Prince of Wales who was unknowingly at the same time witnessing the last years of the German aristocracy, many of whom were related to the very people that Seton met. Despite the tragedy that overtook the Imperial Family, several of their close relatives escaped, including Felix and his wife, Irina. Her mother, the Grand Duchess Xenia and her sons, were also among those who got away, as were several Dukes together with senior military and naval officers. They were all eventually taken to England on the H.M.S. *Marlborough*. During the Second World War when the Grand Duchess Xenia stayed at Balmoral, she nursed Seton Gordon's Aunt Florence during her last illness.

When he arrived in Russia, Seton was taken to the Moika Palace in St Petersburg, and he was immediately struck by the leisurely tempo of life there compared to British cities: 'People strolled through the streets as though they were inhabitants of a country village. They were kindly and cheerful'. When he entered the door of the palace, he saw his first Cossack guards, 'Men of distinguished presence – and fully armed!' He met Youssoupoff's mother, Princess Zenaide, who had a well-deserved international reputation for her grace and charm.

Entertainment was lavish. Each evening there was a dinner party for forty to fifty guests, the ladies wearing expensive jewelery, and the men in various uniforms. Conversation never flagged, and was conducted in French, Italian, German, and English, but little Russian. The servants were impressive, with their epauletted coatees and wigs. Moika had an art gallery filled with paintings by Rubens, Rembrandt, Vandyke and Tiepolo. The city was still in the grip of winter weather, and one thing that Seton Gordon recalled were the sleigh-rides. He wrote:

> There were long sledge journeys amid interminable forests, the bells ringing cheerily as it was drawn over the frost encrusted snow. In the evenings we would listen to the tuneful singing of sad Russian folk songs. The Russian peasant and the Hebridean crofter would find much in common with their folk music. Another link would be their love of hospitality and the friendly evening gatherings which are a feature of both countries.

With so many estates to choose from in a matter of weeks, it was not possible to see them all, and Cocoze, in the Crimea, was decided upon. It was April, and the trees were in bud, compared to the snow in St Petersburg and Moscow. He was taken around the countryside and took many photographs of peasants and Tartars. There were some of the interior of the palaces visited, and one of Felix standing in front of the house at Cocoze.

Seton chose not to remain in Russia because the pattern of his life showed more strongly each year his attachment to the traditions and music of his native country. It was also likely that he was disturbed by the great contrasts in life-style, especially those between peasants and the land-owning class in Russia. This applied more in the remote areas, such as the Crimea, than in the vicinity of Moscow and St Petersburg, where Seton has already made reference to the warmth of the ordinary people. The peasants, although obviously hardy, lacked the independence of the folk among whom he had grown up. On Deeside the Royal Family were treated with respect, and even a sense that they were a part of the community of Deeside; never with awe bordering on superstition.

E. K. C. Hamilton, who became Dean of Windsor and a Bishop of Salisbury, was also a contemporary of Seton Gordon and Felix Youssoupoff at Oxford. He also went to Russia, as a guest of Felix, in 1910. At Archangelskoe he witnessed an incredible scene. After church, a line of several hundred peasants filed past Princess Zenaide:

> For over one and a half hours the Princess stood and heard their welcomes and complaints, receiving from the men the large brown, salted loaves, a token of prosperity, and from the women a plate of eggs. The women were very frightened, some beginning to cry. Many of them knelt to kiss the ground on which the Princess stood. It was an extraordinary sight.'

Seton Gordon would not have been happy spending several years in a land where there was such a disparity between the classes. For this reason he returned happily to Britain. The only reference that he ever made to birdlife in Russia was the profusion of the grey crow, which he saw everywhere he went.

Another event which took place in 1913 was the meeting at the Vincent's Club ball with undergraduate Audrey Pease. They were introduced by her brother Cuthbert, who also moved in the Prince of Wales' circle and was already an acquaintance of Seton's. It was discovered that they had many interests in common. Audrey was a keen ornithologist and accomplished photographer, who from her home, Otterburn Towers in Northumberland, had observed and photographed many species of moorland and seabirds.

She was small in stature, with a wistful look and an enchanting profile, set off by short fair hair and a fresh complexion. She was not afraid to endure hardship in the pursuit of ornithology; her size and appearance belied her toughness. She had celebrated her nineteenth birthday in August of that year, and had gone up to Lady Margaret Hall in 1912 to study natural sciences, the same courses that Seton had taken for his degree. The Hall was one of only three women's colleges at that time in the university.

Howard Pease, father of Audrey and Cuthbert, was a merchant banker, a business in which the family had been engaged for generations, and had helped to finance the building of the London-North Eastern Railway. A forbear, Edward Pease, a devout Quaker, was known as the 'father of the English railway'. A forward-thinking man, he had long been interested in the idea of a public railway, and in 1821 met George Stephenson, who at the time was an enginewright at the Hillingworth Colliery. Pease took an immediate liking to him, and they were soon working together to build the Stockton-Darlington Railway. Edward Pease became a wealthy man in the latter half of his life, because of the success of a venture which interested him more as a benefit for the public good.

The Pease family were well known in the north of England, more especially in Darlington where there are several reminders of their industry. The woollen mill owned by Edward Pease survived until 1983. His most fitting memorial is Locomotion No. 1, now at Bank Top station. This primitive locomotive was the first train to cover the Stockton-Darlington line on 27 September 1825, and was in service for twenty-five years.

Women's education was only just beginning to be taken seriously by the time of Audrey's enrolment at Lady Margaret Hall in 1912. Their colleges were administered by women who not only had strong ties to the Church of England, but were, in the main, daughters of clergymen who held high office. The first Principal of Lady Margaret Hall, Elizabeth Woodsworth, was the daughter of the Bishop of Lincoln, who had been Headmaster of Harrow. When she retired in 1908, her place was taken by Miss Henrietta Jex-Blake, a daughter of the Dean of Wells Cathedral and former Headmaster of Rugby. Both women saw Lady Margaret Hall as the extension of their own youthful privileges extended to a wider family circle, with little sympathy for the aspirations of modern women scholars. Woodsworth stated that goodness was more important than cleverness. Despite these assertions, most students saw it in a different light. One graduate described her austere college life as characterised by 'a diet of stew, rice pudding, and Sunday observance.'

Audrey Pease was already an independent spirit, and like her future husband was educated privately. In that wild border country surrounding Otterburn she had become an expert horsewoman, riding astride rather than sidesaddle, as was the custom for women then. Audrey's knowledge of the birds of Northumberland was equal to Seton's knowledge of those on Deeside. One difference, which later influenced his methods, was that she used a hide.

Her notebooks show a precise and detached study. They record each spring the species observed, the number of nests found, and their location. A description of the eggs and the number in the nest is noted, and later, the date of hatching, and an account of the progress of the birds. On record also is the date on which the various migratory birds were first seen. On a July 1913 visit to the Farne Islands there are notes on bird markings in a coded form which shows great attention to detail. Although these are quite the opposite to Seton's notes, which he kept in a pocket diary, and were not written up regularly, his more emotional approach was better suited to the production of articles. Combining the different approaches was later the key to their success as a partnership.

Most women enrolling at Oxford in 1912 had no thought of a career, and to most of them a degree would be of little value. It was only the year before Audrey's arrival that any recognition was given to examinaton results, when the Delegacy for Women Students was established. This gave accreditation to 'registered women students' but the act of receiving a degree did not come until a few years later. Although she graduated with honours in zoology, Audrey received only a certificate to show she had been a registered women student for twelve terms, with a statement of examination results. Some women students received their degrees retroactively, after the First World War, when women were included in the ceremonies.

Segregation of the sexes was still officially very strict other than formal invitations at prearranged events, such as debates. The Ball where Audrey and Seton met was at a university club, Vincent's, whose members were made up of undergraduates who had won their 'Blue' in the particular sport at which they excelled. Membership was kept to one hundred students. Seton's was won in golf, and Cuthbert won his in hockey, though he was also a keen football player.

One of the peculiar 'perks' of the club was that each member could mail up to six letters per day, with the club paying the postage.

Audrey and Cuthbert were very close, and he had known Seton for some time. He doubtless arranged the introduction with their common interests in mind, and their friendship opened up new horizons for Seton. Audrey introduced him to the Northumbrian coast, where her Aunt Ella Pease had a house at Alnmouth, a few miles down the coast from Holy Island and the Farne Islands. Otterburn is close to Carter Bar and the Cheviot Hills.

Almost from their first meeting, every opportunity was taken to share knowledge and continue developing their skills. A difference in the method of photography was that Seton stalked his subject, while Audrey had for some time used a hide. Though more time is required for hide photography, to allow the occupants of the nest to get used to its proximity, the results are infinitely better. In stalking, Seton Gordon acknowledged that the bird can become uncomfortable in the presence of the 'cyclops eye of the camera'.

The summer vacation allowed them to spend time in each other's company, exploring Northumberland, with a few days on Deeside. In September Seton returned to Scotland, where he and the Prince of Wales met and exchanged notes. Although Seton was enjoying his old haunts, as autumn lengthened other things were on his mind. Audrey returned to university for her second year. In that last year of peace, and the old order, the university carried on the traditions that had developed over centuries, seemingly insulated from all time.

At the end of September, Seton proposed to Audrey and was accepted. One of the first people to whom he broke the news was Edward, who wrote again on 5 October:

> My Dear Seton,
>
> Very many thanks for your letter. My most hearty congratulations on your engagement. I had no idea this was coming off & I am delighted for your sake. I hope you will both be very happy. When will the wedding take place? I am sorry I will not be at the Derry when you walk over. I only hope you can come up to Oxford soon. If Archie [Ritchie] cannot put you up I will see what I can do; something must be arranged.
>
> Are you going to try our first wine? I am afraid I shall miss it as we have a family wedding on the 15th* & we have a lot to do in town. However there will be more during term so you must come to one of those. We all go south next Friday which is very sad as I have had such a grand time up here. Well goodbye old Seton & please excuse this awful scrawl. I cannot tell you how pleased I am to hear your news, but I shall say nothing about it. All the best of good luck to you!! Yrs ever, Eddie.

*Prince Arthur of Connaught to Princess Alexander, daughter of Princess Loiuse, the Princess Royal, and the Duke of Fife.

This letter suggests that the time was not ripe for a general announcement of the engagement. Seton now spent more time between Braemar Castle, Dinnet, and Oxford than at Auchintoul, so it is possible that his parents had not yet been informed. Another letter on 20 October provides an insight into life at Balmoral and the bond that existed beween the Royal family and their staff:

> . . . How I do envy you being still up in Scotland. I am glad to hear you were at the Derry the other day and saw Donald Fraser and Sandy McDonald. They are both such nice men & I am glad they liked the presents. I always try to give them things that are and will be useful to them through the winter, & I know their tastes and requirements pretty well now!!
>
> I had an awful five days in town with never a moment to myself; a lot of shopping and then the wedding on top of it all. I got back to Magdalen on Thursday evening & have seen many friends; Archie, Hugo Pitman, Gerald Hay, etc.
>
> My Dear Seton I must again tell you how pleased I am to hear about your engagement; I think it is splendid. Of course Cuthbert Pease is a great friend of Archie's. You simply must come up for the Caledonian Ball or something. Well, so long Seton & good luck. Yrs ever, Eddie.

The Prince clearly shows his desire to be accepted by his fellow undergraduates, and as much as his position would allow, to be a part of them. In his 1947 autobiography, *A King's Story*, he wrote: 'But, while my father was showing me how he entertained foreign Royalty, and I was doing my best to play my part at these court functions, I was beginning to form my own ideas about all this lavish hospitality. Although all this State ceremony had previously seemed exciting and colourful and I had accepted it all without question, my association at Oxford with men so far removed from the trappings of Royal life had begun to give me a more sceptical view . . .'

One of the more significant visits took place in November 1913 at Windsor. The guests were the Archduke Franz Ferdinand, heir to the Austro–Hungarian Empire, and his wife, the Furstin Hohenberg. In the Prince's words, 'No suggestion of tragedy then touched this elegant couple who only seven months later would fall before the assassin's fateful bullets at Sarajevo'.

In early December, Seton gave a lecture at Oxford, on the natural history of the Cairngorms, which was attended by the Prince. In November 1986, one of the posters came to light. The tickets were three shillings and two shillings, with unreserved seats at the back one shilling! Archie Ritchie, a Fellow of the Zoological Society, was in the chair. The Prince of Wales did some lobbying for Seton to ensure its success. He had been prodded by Audrey Pease, who received a note from him on 24 November:

> Dear Miss Pease,
>
> Very many thanks for your note and for sending me the notice of Seton's lecture. I shall certainly come, & get as many people to go as possible. I have heard Seton lecture & he is very good at it, & has a wonderful knowledge of natural history. I saw him this morning and he told me about the lecture and how expensive it is to get up, so I can only hope he gets a good audience. I can assure you I will do all I can to make it a success. I remain, yours sincerely, Edward.

After the lecture, in thanking Audrey for an invitation to tea, the Prince wrote:

The wedding of Seton and Audrey at Otterburn, Aug 19, 1915

> The lecture last night was really a great success wasn't it? The hall was very full & Seton showed the slides very well indeed. It was of course particularly interesting to me knowing that part of Scotland so well. Again thankyou very much for your kind invitation, & remain, Yours very sincerely, Edward.

In December Seton Gordon wrote to the Prince from Deeside to report on the condition of Donald Fraser of the Derry Lodge, who was recovering from an operation. With the Christmas holiday at Sandringham in full swing, Edward found time to reply to Seton on Christmas Day, 1913:

> Very many thanks for your letter and that ripping picture of Deeside which I am delighted with, and have already hung it in my room. It is really awfully good of you to send it to me.
>
> Thanks for telling me how old Fraser is doing. I am so glad he pulled through the serious operation. I read the extract from your letter to both my father and the Princess Royal who were very anxious to know how he was.
>
> I shall have plenty of shooting all January. We got 13 woodcock on Tuesday which was good. I hope you are having a good time. Please thank Audrey for her kind message. Again very many thanks for the capital picture. With all good wishes for Xmas & New Year, Yrs. ever, Eddie.'

By the end of December, Fraser had died, and on the 29th the Prince replied from Sandringham to Seton's news of his passing:

> Thanks so much for your letter and telegram. I was awfully sorry to hear of poor old Fraser's death; I was very surprised, as the accounts were so good. However he was very old. He will indeed be a great loss at Mar & we shall miss him at the Derry. My aunt, the Princess Royal is staying here now & I gave her the sad news last night at dinner, & she felt it very much. It was very nice of you letting me know by wire. I return Miss Fraser's nice letter; I feel for her & the poor old mother very much. I think Sandy McDonald is going to move to the Derry now.
>
> I am glad you spent a happy Xmas at Newcastle, and that you and Audrey have tested my glass* again & find it a good one. With all my best wishes for good luck and prosperity in the New Year, I remain, Yrs ever, Eddie.'

*An inscribed stalking telescope, still in the possession of the Gordon family.

A few days into the new year Seton visited Novar, an estate of 4000 acres on the Cromarty Firth, where considerable research was being carried out with several types of conifer that were native to the west coast of North America. As a result of this visit, a two-part article was published later in the *Scotsman*.

The estate has belonged to the Munro Ferguson family for more than 300 years. The present owner, Mr Arthur Munro Ferguson has continued to purchase land and now has 20,000 acres.

The purpose of the article was to describe the forestry practices on Highland estates then, and how they were incorporating these new species whose natural habitats range up to 10,000 feet above sea level. One that has become common in Scotland is the Menzies spruce (Sitka spruce) which in its native setting is a magnificant tree. Many 'old growth' Sitkas on Vancouver Island have attained heights in excess of 300 feet and environmentalists have won protection for a large grove near Pacific Rim National Park. The monotonous lines seen in the Highlands, and the dire visual results, bear no resemblance to a mature western Canadian natural growth Sitka forest.

Douglas fir was also introduced at Novar. In America some attain gigantic proportions. Seton Gordon noted in his article that a tree in Washington State reached 340 feet in height, with a circumference of 42 feet. Its age was estimated at 300 years, and it contained 8000 cubic feet of wood. (The tallest tree ever discovered was found in North Vancouver in 1902. It was a Douglas Fir measuring 415 feet. Unfortunately it was immediately felled.) His article ended:

> If ever the State should enquire into, and find satisfactory for afforestation purposes, the land offered by the Duke of Sutherland to the nation, the forestry methods at Novar would prove of the utmost service to pioneers of sylviculture on the Sutherland lands, for nowhere in this country, or even in Europe, can be found such interesting forestry as can be seen on the Novar estate.

On 10 January 1914 a letter of Seton Gordon's, also on the subject of forestry, appeared in *The Spectator*. There had been considerable correspondence on the subject as a result of an editorial criticising a Liberal Government policy paper on afforestation schemes throughout the British Isles. Correspondents included several leading landowners of the period, Sir John Stirling Maxwell, Chairman of the Royal Scottish Arboricultural Society, H.J. Elwes of Cheltenham, who had appeared before a committee of the House of Lords, and Lord Northumberland, whose seat was Alnwick Castle. Some felt the proposals had merit, though much more so for the Highlands than the rest of Britain. Seton Gordon wrote strongly in favour of state supported private forestry as a means of stopping further Highland depopulation. He defended the initiative by saying:

> It is being recognised more fully every year that the most satisfactory method of retaining the rural population of the Highlands of Scotland, is by the formation of extensive State forests in certain Scottish glens where the soil is too poor for the successful cultivation of crops, but where the tree growth is vigorous.
>
> One of the most significant features of the present time is the steady emigration of the poorer classes of agriculturalists from Scotland to the colonies. The living made by Highland small-holders is a precarious one, and there is only one way to improve the lot of the small-holder in the Highlands. That is by giving him some means to supplement the necessities of life, which he obtains from his holding. This is no idle theory, but what is being actually put into practice by some of the leading Scottish landowners at the present day. As regards the repopulation of the Highland glens, it has been proved beyond doubt that forestry is the only way of achieving this end . . .

> It was calculated by the Coast Erosion Committee of 1909 that we were sending out of the country some £30,000,000 every year for timber and forest products which might be grown on these islands on the nine million acres suitable for forest planting in Great Britain and Ireland. It is obvious that as the price of wood rises, the amount of capital leaving this country will rise greatly, a fact which admittedly is not to the public advantage.
>
> I am, Sir &c., Seton Gordon.'

From the contents of both letter and articles, it is obvious that he was putting the knowledge gained from the rural economy study to good use. He had visited the Inverlever Forest nursery the previous July, where saw what he described as 'the first croft worked under the new afforestation scheme.'

Much of what Seton Gordon saw at Novar spread throughout the Highlands, and after the Second World War, the use of the North American Sitka grew rapidly. Fortunately there are still areas where the old Caledonian forests of Scots pine survive, particularly on the Rothiemurchus estate by Aviemore, which has been in the hands of the Grants of Rothiemurchus for generations.

Mr Arthur Munro Ferguson, in some 1987 correspondence, has outlined the results of the forestry practised on the estate since Seton Gordon's article. There are many similarities to those at the time of the 1914 visit:

> Considerable areas of European larch were suffering from canker towards the end of the last century and it was decided to thin them out to 200 trees to the acre and underplant with various species. Underplanting is still practised here and elsewhere.
>
> The Sitka spruce is a popular tree here, particularly on the west coast where there is a higher rainfall. There are many critics of afforestation with conifers even where the site conditions and soil are quite unsuitable for hardwoods, and the main demand for wood in this country is softwood. We still import about 90 per cent of the timber and timber products used in this country.

Still continuing with his forestry studies, in late February Seton spent some time at the Oxford School of Forestry's Experimental Station in Bagley Wood. It had been acquired by the university in 1907, and had many different types of deciduous trees, including American oaks. From this visit Seton Gordon wrote a two-part article for *Country Life*, 'Forestry at Oxford'.

In early March he paid a second visit to France, this time to study Mediterranean forestry practices along the Cote d'Azur. He visited Toulon, Cannes and Nice, where he arranged with the Inspectur Adjoint to see plantations in the Alpes Maritimes, particularly the Forest of Estrell.

There are some very intensive diary notes, especially on the Cimbra pine, a tree he was anxious to see. Because of deep, soft snow at the higher elevations, 6000 feet plus, it took several attempts. He noticed that clear-cutting was hardly ever carried out, only certain of the older trees being marked. There were visits to several locations ravaged by forest fire, including one of 4600 acres. In the company of a French forester, Seton Gordon visited the mountain village of Molieres, at 5300 feet. On the way up, they had a good view of a golden eagle and the forester said he had seen a white-tailed eagle a few days before. The section of Italian forest adjoining the border was more accessible from the French side, and an arrangement had been made between the two governments for the French forester to supervise it.

Seton Gordon had with him the telescope which the Prince of Wales had given him just a few months before. As they crossed the frontier into Italy he saw no reason to hide it. Accommodation was found in a small village on the Italian side. Before they retired for the night, the Frenchman came into Seton's room very worried. He had heard that the villagers suspected his companion of being a French officer sent to spy on the area, and he was to be apprehended the next morning and taken to the nearest town, some miles away over snowy hill passes. The forester suggested abandoning the tour and returning to the French side as soon as there was sufficient light. Next morning, leaving before the village was astir, they walked briskly down the valley, anxiety causing them to walk with increasing speed towards the frontier, at this point not even marked. The Frenchman looked anxiously around as they hurried, but suddenly relaxed and smiled, 'We are now back in France'. Seton Gordon observed that no spy would carry a telescope in full view, but the forester pointed out that the villagers were primitive peasants, and their suspicion had been aroused. A cryptic diary note on 24 March says, 'A forced descent made by Garde and myself, with fears of arrest – we were glad to be across the burn and into France!'

Enough material was assembled by the middle of April to complete an article on Mediterranean forestry, and he now moved on to Gavarnie, near the border with Spain. From here, on 1 April he set out with a *Garde Foretier* to walk in the Pyrennees.

Seton Gordon remained in France for a few more days, visiting Vouzon and Orleans before returning to Oxford. The trip had provided an opportunity to compare the reaction of familiar trees to differing environments, especially at high elevations.

In the middle March Seton Gordon joined Audrey at Otterburn. They had several outings in Audrey's trap, and serious observation was done on a family of ravens. A hide was set up and some good pictures obtained. As well as these they spent time looking at curlew, lapwing, woodcock and golden plover.

Over the next few weeks Seton was constantly on the move, to Speyside to search for greenshank, then south to London where he had talks with Cassells, his publishers. He was told that only twnty-nine copies of *The Charm of the Hills* were left on their shelves. During this time several cheques were received for articles written, which with the royalties on his book appeared to provide a comfortable lifestyle, though he still sought employment in any field allied to his studies. There are several diary notes referring to job interviews, including one with the Secretary of the Board of Agriculture.

CHAPTER

3

WARTIME ADVENTURES ON THE WEST COAST

THE INTERNATIONAL SCENE was tense during the first half of 1914. The British government had several committees at work on contingency plans for home defence. In his book *Supreme Command* Lord Hankey comments: 'The early months of 1914 gave little indication of the immensity of the coming catastrophe'. Despite his close association with the events, Hankey recalled how short the crisis was and how rapidly it burst into war.

The Prince of Wales was enjoying his last few months at Oxford (he left in June), while Seton was moving between Scotland and the south. Before he left Oxford, Edward held a dinner party for his friends to show them photographs of Norway, where tried cross-county skiing and had written enthusiastically about it to Seton.

By early June Europe was enjoying gloriously warm, sunny weather, which lasted most of the summer. In a note to Seton on 7 June from Oxford, Edward commiserated with him on the poor weather in Scotland, and was envious at not being there. The Prince instead played tennis and polo. He had walked 25 miles on the downs the day before, saying it was 'a 'grand sweat' as the stalkers would say!!'

In a note on 14 July from Buckingham Palace, the Prince complained how awful his OCTU camp was because of the heat. He was at the time on a month's attachment to the 1st Life Guards: '. . . that is a sweat too & I envy you up in Scotland. Glad the book is nearly finished; you must send me a copy. Hope Audrey is quite well; it was good of you both to send that ripping present for my birthday. Well, so long, no time for more. Shant get north till Sept 20th if at all!! Good luck!! Yrs ever, Eddie.' (Seton Gordon's third book, *Hill Birds of Scotland*, to which the Prince referred, was finally published in 1915)

The assassination of Archduke Ferdinand on 28 June, was not at first seen as politically significant. On 10 July the Foreign Secretary, Sir Edward Grey, referred only briefly to it in some introductory remarks to a speech on foreign policy, nevertheless expressing horror at the crime. It was not mentioned in the House again until 27 July when Grey described the crisis which had developed as a result of the Austrian ultimatum of 21 July.

No wonder Hankey referred to the suddenness of the catastrophe. The final, inevitable events happened in quick succession. On 31 July, Austria, Russia,

Belgium and Turkey ordered general mobilisation. Hostilities began on the Polish frontier. The French government ordered general mobilisation. The British had not yet ordered general mobilisation of the army. On 2 August, the Germans sent an ultimatum to Belgium demanding passage through Belgian territory.

Grey guaranteed the protection of the French coasts against German aggression, one more action in an overall policy which earned the disdain of Ramsay MacDonald. Curiously, from the 1920s on, both men were to earn the affection of Seton Gordon, which he carried until their deaths and beyond.

Sir Edward Grey, later Earl Grey of Fallodon, was British Foreign Secretary from 1908 to 1916. He was a neighbour and close friend of Audrey Gordon's aunt, Miss Ella Pease of Alnmouth, where the Gordons were frequent guests after the war. Seton was attracted by Grey's qualities as a countryman and bird-lover. It was this which he later wrote about in a small volume on the Fallodon bird sanctuary. It would be difficult to find a better example of Grey the statesman than the prescient letter he wrote to Ella Pease in 1908, which showed his intuitive grasp of European politics:

> The German Emperor is aging me (*sic*); he is like a battleship with steam up and screws going, but with no rudder and he will run into something one day and cause a catastrophe. He has made a fool of Germany and all the world is laughing at him and the Germans do not like being laughed at . . .
>
> Germany is very strong and very restless, like a person whose boots are too small for him. I dont think there will be a war at present, but it will be difficult to keep the peace for another five years.

At a Cabinet meeting on 30 July, of eighteen ministers present, twelve were on record as opposing any support for France. Most vociferous was Lloyd George. He was not even sure about fighting over Belgium. On the same afternoon, Liberal backbenchers met in caucus during which they voted four to one for neutrality – 'whatever happens in Belgium or elsewhere'.

However, by the 2nd, when Cabinet reconvened they knew the choice was either to ratify the actions taken by Churchill and Grey or face the House and have the government fall. Approval was reluctantly given, though Grey was instructed to tell the French that no British troops could be sent across the Channel. The following day Germany declared war on Belgium and immediately attacked Liège. The British sent an ultimatum which was to expire at midnight 4 August. No reply was received. Despite the earlier protestations of a majority of the Cabinet, and of the Liberal caucus, the 'war to end all wars' had begun.

The declaration of war had a devastating effect on Grey. Behind the calm exterior was a man of great emotion; a man whose heart had been broken a few years earlier, when his wife had died so tragically. She was thrown from her trap when the pony pulling it shied and she died a few days later without recovering consciousness.

When, on 3 August, Grey gave a summation speech to the House of Commons he was close to tears. He saw in one sweep his personal sorrow now mixed with despair at man's folly, and the the knowledge that 'universal darkness' was about to descend. Grey felt it as a personal failure that he could not preserve peace. 'I hate war! I hate war!' he said despairingly to a Cabinet colleague after his speech. He could not face the crowds on the London streets cheering each company of recruits marching to their barracks, oblivious of the horror that awaited them once the fighting started. Following Grey's speech Ramsay MacDonald stated the position of the Labour party, but war fever was by this time so entrenched that his appeal for a saner appraisal of the long term implications was regarded by some as pro-German.

MacDonald never forgave Grey for what he saw as a disasterous foreign policy, which entangled Britain in the entente between France and Russia. Grey was, in the opinion of MacDonald, so committed to France and Russia that he refused every overture by the German Ambassador to gain Britain's neutrality even when asked to propose his own conditions. Yet, after the war, in his letters to Ramsay MacDonald, Seton Gordon referred to Edward Grey as though the two were friends.

Edward Grey stayed in his post for two more years, ignoring medical advice to resign in order to save his failing eyesight. When he finally retired to Fallodon and his bird sanctuary, his sight was almost gone, and Seton Gordon later wrote movingly about this period of his life.

Seton Gordon was twenty-eight when war was declared. Although he was very fit, his deafness was becoming a little worse each year and may have ruled out his becoming a frontline soldier. His life, like Sir Edward Grey's, was one of reverence for living things. He never owned a firearm or took part in stag hunting and bird shoots in which the Prince of Wales and other friends indulged. He never criticised them either. Anti-blood sport enthusiasts may see this as a sign of weakness, but it is still possible to hold divergent views and enjoy a friendship. He followed the political and international scene with detached interest and noted in his diary when Germany declared war on Russia, and when Britain took the irrevocable step of declaring war on Germany. At Otterburn he and Audrey were excited by the activities of redshanks, kestrels and merlins which they had found in the vicinity. The merlin was of particular interest and the nesting sight was visited regularly.

While the politicians and military leaders plotted strategy, Seton added his own touch of sanity in a visit to the merlins in late June; one which without doubt Edward Grey would have given anything to share:

> A strong breeze of west wind swept the uplands, driving white clouds before it. In the alternating sun and shade the moors were at their best, and many miles of hill-country extended as far as the eye could reach. Curlew and golden plover were here in plenty, the trembling cry of the whaup mingling with the pipe of the plover. There was now a great change in the young merlins, and already their tail feathers were beginning to sprout. The parent bird could be seen high above the moors, in the strong breeze flying light and easily and little affected by the wind.

The first few weeks of the war centred mainly around recruiting and kitting out the new soldiers. The younger students and dons at both Oxford and Cambridge were caught up in the excitement and the number of students declined as they left in great numbers to sign up for the armed forces. On 6 August the Prince asked the King for a commission, which was readily given, and he joined the 1st Battalion, Grenadier Guards. On the same day he sent a hurried note to Seton:

My Dear Seton,
Many thanks for yr. letter. This is all too ghastly and colossal to comprehend. But I feel Germany is doomed!! I fear I cannot possibly meet for lunch as I am so busy these terrible days. Thanks so much for asking me. The die is cast thank goodness for the tension of the last week was awful. Best of luck!! Yrs. ever, Eddie.

On 13 August the Prince again wrote to Seton Gordon, this time from Worley Barracks, Brentford, Essex.

My Dear Seton,
Many thanks for your letter. I joined the 1st Battalion Grenadier Guards here on Monday and have been out drilling and marching twice a day. It is hot and the reservists sweat some which does them a world of good and makes them fit! The officers are a very good lot and I know I shall be happy in this fine regiment. But Worley Barracks is a Godless spot and these barracks are vile and at present overcrowded.

The officers' quarters are a mere pigsty and we have garrets in the most filthy state – with no bedrooms! However we are living here under war conditions and only waiting for orders to move out at any moment, so one does not expect to think about comfort. I can only hope we get out to France. The 2nd Batt. went yesterday. I only hope we see all our friends again. Poor old Archie [Ritchie] left for Paris on Sunday to join the Foreign Legion. He is bound to do well and is just the man for the job as they carry 80 lbs! May all go well with him. So long Seton, we are just going on parade so I must stop. Best of luck, yours ever, Eddie.

P.S. Pathetic to think that grouse shooting started yesterday; no Scotland for me this year!

When this letter was written Edward was in high spirits because he knew it was only a matter of time before the 1st Battalion went to France and he assumed he would go with it as a regular frontline officer. However, his frustration began to show in his next letter, written on 5 Sept:

. . . My Battalion left Worley a fortnight ago, & we are now at Welliegton Barracks. Life is very strenuous though monotonous, as one may imagine. How we long to get out!! [to France] I don't see the names of any of our

> Oxford friends on the casualty lists, so let us hope they will come through alright.
>
> The news is a bit better now & how well the navy is doing. Again thanks so much for yr. letter. Best of Luck!!! Yrs. ever, Eddie.

His battalion was given a short leave in mid-September, a sure sign that it was about to go overseas, but the Prince was instead transferred to the 3rd Battalion, also at Wellington Barracks, confirming that he was to be left behind. The Prince resigned himself to staff duties, and reported to the 3rd Battalion. Twice a week he did duty as Orderly Officer, either at Buckingham Palace or at St James's Palace. His feelings of disappointment were summed up in a letter to Seton on 14 October from Wellington Barracks:

> My Dear Seton,
>
> Thanks for your letter. Yes I was just mad at not being allowed out; it was pretty bad luck wasn't it? I may get some staff later on!!
>
> I am leading a most bloody existence here in London, & you make my mouth water by writing from Braemar!! Now I have missed my stalking this year but we have other and more important things to think about!!
>
> I hope you will get out with yr. friend in his car; you must try for something. Why didn't you apply for a commish [commission] in the Deeside Battalion of the Gordon Highlanders as Alec Stuart did? I had a long letter from Archie, just off from Toulouse!! Best of luck, Yrs. ever, Eddie.

Seton Gordon had his mind set on driving an ambulance. He had made contact with Dr Hector Munro's civilian Field Ambulance Unit, attached to the Belgian army at Furnes. Volunteers were sent out by a committee screening people in London, and he was readily accepted. He had conceived the idea of procuring a large car to take out to France to be used as an ambulance. The Prince of Wales was about to get a later model Daimler and Seton thought his old one would be ideal with some modification. Edward would not agree to this:

> King's Guard, St. James's Palace, S.W. 19 October 1914.
>
> Dear Seton,
>
> Thanks for your letter. I am NOT disposing of my old car. I was at Oxford yesterday, such a changed and depressing spot!! Yrs. ever, Eddie.

> Wellington Barracks, S.W. 20 October 1914.
>
> Dear Seton,
>
> I only got your letter last night & so must apologise for that very curt note written on guard. I was in a gt. hurry & thought you wanted an answer at once.
>
> Your idea is quite a good one, but I didn't think of getting rid of my old car yet. I haven't got the new one though I hope to have it soon, & so shall keep the old Daimler until I have fully tested the new one. There are sure to be a

few things to alter, which will necessitate it going back to the works, & I must have a car. If however I do anything in the way of a field ambulance later I will let you know. Please forgive my note of last night; you must have thought me very rude; but I was very rattled. So long!! Yrs. ever, Eddie.

Seton Gordon's failure to take the Prince's advice to join a Highland regiment should not be seen as a desire not to get involved in the war. The lot of ambulance drivers and stretcher bearers was no better than that of a frontline soldier. The dangers were as great. While this exchange of letters took place, arrangements were completed and by the third week of October he was all set to go to France. The Prince offered his congratulations and expressed his own hope of getting to France in a staff capacity.

Before Seton Gordon had even reported for duty he was taken completely by surprise with a request from the Admiralty to take on a very different task. He described it as coming 'out of the blue' especially as he expected to land in France within days. The Admiralty directive was to organise and command a coast-watching service on the west coast of Scotland, principally for U-boat surveillance. It was to be put in place discreetly, so as not to arouse suspicion, and Seton was instructed to pose as an itinerent birdwatcher. The suddenness of the offer is revealed in a letter from Edward only three days after congratulating him on the ambulance posting:

York Cottage, Sandringham. 31 October 1914.

So now you have another job; how they do chop and change about. But it sounds an interesting one though you must be mighty sick not to get employment on the continent. However some of us must remain & look after the old country I suppose!!

I am here for three nights, my first out of London for 6 weeks!!

I had a capital partridge shoot today which has revived me!! Do write and let me know if you have any adventures!! So long and good luck, Yrs. ever, Eddie.

It was Sir Arthur Murray Farquhar who had recommended that Seton Gordon be recruited for the coast-watching job. Farquhar was promoted to Rear Admiral in 1906, and in 1913 given command of Coast Guards and Reservists. He would be aware, more than anyone, of Seton's qualities for this task, which in the early stages at least, would require a cover.

Farquhar, having known Seton Gordon for so many years, could also vouch for his dependability and happy knack of gaining the friendship and respect of so many people. This would be vital in the job of recruiting the fishermen, crofters, and keepers with whom he would be working. Simple people, yet with an independence nurtured in the tough environment in which they lived. Seton was blessed with an air of quiet authority which drew immediate respect and brought out the best in people.

His instructions were to recruit men throughout the islands of Mull, Coll, Tiree and to include the mainland from Danna, on the Sound of Jura, to

Kilchoan on the Ardamurchan peninsula. Later, a fishing boat, the *Lustre Gem* was put at his disposal, but in the first few months he travelled by regular MacBraynes steamer.

Instead of driving an ambulance in Flanders, on 2 November Seton Gordon found himself ready to report to Mull to begin recruiting coast-watchers. It is not known if he received any training, but an important factor would be ship recognition, to be passed on to his recruits. His starting date was 22 October, and he was to be paid £1 per day.

Sending a man with no previous knowledge of ships or shipping, or technical information about submarines, to set up a chain of crofters and fishermen to look out for enemy submarines sounds rather presposterous. The truth was that the navy was in the dark as to what developments might take place in the early part of the war. The idea might well have paid off. At any time the alertness of one well-placed coast-watcher could have resulted in the capture or destruction of a U-boat. The fact that they spent long, lonely hours and weeks without action or sightings, does not take away from their potential usefulness. The Admiralty did not comprehend how the Germans intended using the U-boat. Winston Churchill actually rejected any thought of using submarines against merchant shipping, stating: 'I do not think this would ever be done by a civilised power.'

An indication of the way that some senior naval officers and politicians viewed them is found in a statement by Rear Admiral A. K. Wilson, VC, Controller of the Royal Navy: 'Underwater weapons they call 'em. I call them underhand, unfair, and damned un-English!'

The Admiralty saw the need for surveillance around the coast. Some senior naval officers regarded the submarine as a vessel well-adapted to monitoring shore installations and ports while submerged. A preoccupation with spies led others to believe that it was also ideally suited to dropping these off in remote areas. In Scotland there were naval bases at Cromarty, Scapa Flow, Loch Ewe, Rosyth and the Clyde. All of them were within easy reach of a spy dropped at some remote sea loch. On 1 September and 17 September, there were reports of U-boats off Scapa Flow. The fleet was ordered to Loch-nan-Cille, Mull. It did not return to Scapa until early 1915, by which time the defences had been strengthened.

Although Seton Gordon's diary note for 2 November said: 'Commenced duties as Admiralty Patrol', it was at least two weeks before he settled at Ardura on Mull and began recruiting, as he was responsible for acquiring all necessary supplies for the job. Friday 13 November: 'get chart showing flags of various nationalities. Telegrams ten shillings; Notebook nine pence'.

Two days later, having arranged accommodation at Ardura on Mull, Seton Gordon began recruiting. The first coast-watchers to be signed on were on the mainland coast, opposite Jura. These were John MacTaggart of Kilmory, Dugal MacFarlane, the ferry master at Craignish, and Archie Graham of Tayvallich. Further notes on this day were: 'All lights within sight of coast to be extinguished'.

On the 25th and 26th he recruited nine watchers, all on Mull. In early

December Seton Gordon visited Coll and Tiree where he recruited a total of thirteen between the two islands. On the 7th he signed on the oldest watcher, John Johnston of Coll who, because of his knowledge of pipe music, would make a lasting impression on Seton.

By 3 January, 1915 he had recruited 104 men. These were strategically placed around the coast of Mull, including Ulva and Iona, with the balance on Coll, Tiree, Lismore and the Ardnamurchan and Morvern coasts.

The pay range was one shilling for day watching and two shillings for a night watch. A four-hour night shift warranted one shilling and threepence. The pay scale could not be entirely at Seton Gordon's discretion, so it must be assumed that any differences reflected the degree of responsibility. Out on Tiree, Alexander MacCallum of Scarnish was signed on as a day and night watcher for three shillings per day, but this was disallowed as there is an immediate large ink note which says, REDUCE PAY! Seton Gordon also had powers to appoint special constables and there were three created, two on Mull and one on Ulva.

His diary has some quaint notations in this period: 'Caragean – a seaweed which boiled with sweet milk and strained, makes a cornflower-like liquid. Excellent for the stomach.' – 'A Feadag when cooked with hare, hind, rabbit etc., imparts its own flavour to the whole.' – 'If a raven croaks, the stalker says "we will have blood today".'

There was a problem with equipping the men. By the end of the year only eight pairs of binoculars had been issued. With the army growing on the western front, and new ships commissioned daily, the question of supplies for coast-watchers would not be seen as a high priority. Seton Gordon was left to use his own initiative in obtaining many of the items required for day-to-day administration of the operation. There were reminders to himself to buy pens, long envelopes, foolscap paper, a dispatch case and a barograph. He also had to order coast-watcher's badges and buttons for general distribution.

There were two categories of watchers. Those receiving pay, drawn from men with irregular incomes, the fishermen and crofters, and a group known as honorary coast-watchers made up of land-owners, businessmen, land agents and pier or harbour-masters. In 1915, several retired officers joined the ranks. Reports coming in during the month of December show the keenness with which the coast-watchers were taking to their task.

Dugal MacFarlane, the second watcher to be recruited, sent the following verbatim reports:

7/12/14: All windows well covered. Books well attended to after work. Keeping a good look-out and nothing strange to be seen.

10/12/14: Sir, was out yesterday in small islands round about here and nothing to be seen and I am keeping a watch on.

14/12/14: To let you know that I am watching for anything in the air and sea and nothing strange to be seen. Windows are well covered about here.

17/12/14: Sir, Keeping a eye all round & nothing strange to be seen. [this later became a favourite line of the Gordon family!]

> 21/12/14: There is kno enemy ships to be seen. Yrs truly . . .

His near namesake, Duncan MacFarlane of Gometra, a small island on the west side of Mull, who was on constant day watch, wrote on the 17th of December:

> Sir, I hope you will excuse i dated the last report wrong i was in a hurry the post was waiting on me we are not sure when the post comes or will he come at all. Yrs truly.

A little later he sent a report:

> Sir a very suspicious block of wood shaped like a fender i had it secured this morning its not mine [a mine] But it seems to be chamber inside and a small connection wire runs inside its in Lochtua ulva side near Gometra when you are round you must see it whether its explosive or not I Dont know its rather suspicious I am your humble servant, D. MacFarlane

Coast watcher A. Graham of Tayvallich sent a report on the 8th ot January 1915:

> Mr Gordon Sir, The wither is that Stormy I cannot geat out with a boat to see onything that is worth reported. Yrs truly.

On the 17th the storm was still raging: 'Sir, I havent seen onything that is worth reported the weather is that stormy I cannot see verry fare I am expecting you over soon I am yours trouly A Graham'.

Before the *Sea Fay* or *Lustre Gem* were made available it was necessary to use the MacBrayne's steamers to visit the islands, and storms were frequent in the first winter of the war. The steamer *Dirk*, then commanded by Captain Black, was the main link from Oban to Coll, Tiree and Kilchoan via Tobermory. On one occasion the storm was so severe that it was impossible to offload passengers at Kilchoan, where there was no pier. A heavy rowing boat was used to ferry passengers and goods to the dock. The rowboat crew were seen struggling valiantly in the heavy seas, but they could not reach the steamer. Two elderly Gaelic speaking ladies had paid their ninepence for passage from Tobermory to Kilchoan, but now had to remain on board for a trip across open water to Coll and Tiree. The gale had veered from south-west to west and the tops of the waves were blown into spindrift. Sheets of water were frequently lifted above the *Dirks*' open bridge, where a canvas 'dodger' afforded meagre protection. Seton Gordon, poor sailor though he was, found the power of the sea a tremendous thrill, and revelled in the excitement of ducking in time to avoid the not infrequent wave that broke over the bridge. When they reached Coll it was impossible to put in, so Black made for Tiree. The pier at Gott Bay was new at this time, and as the steamer edged in they could see huddled figures in the shelter at its end, but no one ventured out to throw a rope.

They again returned to Coll, and in Seton's words, 'For this we had a fair wind and sea, so that in spite of some heavy rolling, I think we must have covered the distance in record time. Loch an Eatharna in Coll gives rather more shelter than the landing place on Tiree. With a slight easing of the gale it was now possible to put ashore the mail and a few half-fainting passengers.'

The final leg back to the mainland was accomplished in good time, with a following sea, and soon they were once again at Kilchoan. The skill of the ferry boat crew brought them alongside, several hours after the first unsuccessful attempt. Seton Gordon, recalling the moment as he stood next to Captain Black on the bridge, felt that on this occasion the unfortunate passengers for Kilchoan were deserving of more than a little sympathy. They had joined the boat at Tobermory, expecting to be set down after a half-hour's sail through comparatively landlocked waters. As it was they endured at least eight hours of wildest Atlantic storm, and ultimately were set ashore at Kilchoan late in the afternoon. Prostrate with sea-sickness, the two ladies were lifted into the ferry boat. The captain, though very sympathetic, could not hold back his sense of humour. As they were rowed the hundred or so yards to the slipway, he remarked to Seton Gordon, 'Well, do you see, they have had their ninepence worth!'

Now that the coast-watching service was established and working, its ranks were swelled by several honorary watchers. Among them were Sir Fitzroy MacLean of Duart, and at least two retired colonels. In all, nineteen were classified as 'gentry'.

Coast-watchers usually worked in groups of three, their stations having been sited at strategic points on the islands or mainland coast. The *Sea Fay*, and later the *Lustre Gem* patrolled between each station, and to keep the men on their toes, visited them at unexpected hours. On a signal from the ship, the duty watcher had to hoist the station flag.

Submarines and mines were now beginning to take their toll. The Wilson liner *Hydro* left Liverpool for Trondheim, on 29 January, 1915 and was torpedoed south-west of Tiree. Wreckage was washed up on the island, and six of the nineteen crewmen landed safely there. Two days later the *Viknor*, an armed merchant cruiser, was torpedoed and lost with all hands in the same area. The ship belonged to the 10th Cruiser Squadron, to which Seton Gordon was posted in 1916.

Captain Stuart Farquhar, a brother of the Admiral, was District Captain, stationed in Edinburgh and in command of Coastguards in Scotland. On 17 February Seton Gordon received the following letter from him:

Dear Seton,

The bit of mine you sent me turned up alright, luckily for you, as it contained one of the most powerful explosives known, and a blow with a hammer might set it off at any time. It is a detonator and evidently when it is pulled, as happened in this case the mine becomes safe. I imagine when the mines are laid it is expected that they can only break away from their moorings by the plug you sent being withdrawn, in which case, of course, the detonator comes with it and the mine is harmless.

Glad you are comfortable at Ardura. If you find any more mines, remember the litle copper tube is the business end of it.

The *Sea Fay* will be laid up the first two or three days in March, but after that you shall have her.

Yours sincerely, J. Farquhar.'

Reports now came in regularly from the coast-watchers, with official forms to write them on. Any urgent messages were wired. The speed at which submarines travelled would negate even the effectiveness of this method of reporting, because of the number of hands the information had to pass through before the navy could take appropriate action. A later directive said:

> If a coast-watcher sees what he undoubtedly knows to be an enemy submarine he should, besides informing Stornoway and myself, telegraph the information to the coast-watching station in the direction taken by the submarine.
>
> Thus the coast-watcher on Iona, on seeing a submarine going north should telegraph the information to Treshnish Point and Coll. And he should add in his telegraph the words – 'Stornaway, Treshnish and Coll informed'. From Rear Admiral R.F. Boyle.

Stories of spies and signalling by enemy agents were frequent, and flickering lights were indeed seen at various locations on the islands and the mainland. Even one of the honorary coast-watchers, Sir Stephen Gatty of Lochbuie House on Mull, described by Seton Gordon as an eccentric, was in the habit of suddenly switching on all the lights in his house around midnight. This raised suspicion as his house faced south-west down the loch to the open sea. It was never established as anything more than an odd quirk. One set of flickering lights on Ulva, observed over several nights, turned out to be a heather fire, thought to have been naturally extinguished. The embers, fanned by wind, momentarily burst into flame, looking exactly like a flashlight signal.

On 5 Februry 1915, Germany warned that after 18 February, the waters around Great Britain would be considered a war zone, in which 'every enemy merchant vessel found in this war region will be destroyed without its always being possible to warn the crew or the passengers of the dangers threatening'.

There were some light-hearted moments, though not many. Unintentional humour was, as we have seen, provided by some of the coast-watcher reports, though it must be remembered that most of these men were Gaelic speakers and their English did not come naturally to them. On 14 March, Dugal MacFarlane asked:

> Mr. Gordon, Dear Sir, Is there anything against a white cloth being left out at night to dry on the ground or hanging up if so let me know & oblige, yrs truly.

The land war in Europe was already showing the pattern that became synonymous with the First World War. Millions of men were bogged down in the most appalling conditions, while the generals, who mostly stayed away from the front, were responsible for a seesaw of battles that went on month after month. Large concentrations of support troops were ready to take over when those in the trenches were exhausted, or, as was frequently the case, had been annihilated in some senseless and bloody advance.

Years later, Seton Gordon expressed the concern that he felt at the time for his friends who had left so willingly to join the army:

> It seemed all wrong that I had this marvellous chance to go where I pleased, landing on uninhabited islands and enjoying wildlife, while friends were being killed in France.

Of the approximately 4000 students attending Oxford when the war began, by October 1914 only about one-quarter remained. Each year saw a decline until by 1918 the number was reduced to under 500, most of them unfit or too young for service. By the end of the war, 2700 Oxonians had died. Part of the early keenness came from a belief that the war would last for only six months, and would provide a brief adventure.

An article on conditions at Oxford during this time, written by Seton Gordon, appeared in the *Scotsman* in February 1915. In it he wrote:

> The greatness of the change wrought in Oxford cannot be exaggerated. The normal undergraduate population of the city numbers, in round figures, 4000. At the beginning of the present term the number has been reduced to 1071 . . . Almost the entire remaining University population is now drilling with the Oxford University Officers' Training Corps, no less than 300 members have taken commissions during the vacation.
>
> A few students have even taken advantage of short leave from the trenches to hurry to their colleges, in uniform, to have degrees conferred on them, which they had earned during, so it seems, days of peace long since gone. In this connecton a certain well known member of Magdalen attracted considerable attention. At 6 feet 11 inches, he naturally was a prominent figure during his recent university career. Convalescing from a wound received while leading his men to recapture a trench, he visited Oxford in the striking uniform of a distinguished Scottish regiment. [an obvious reference to Gerald 'Long' Hay, who had joined the Argyll and Sutherland Highlanders] There are other qualities imparted by Oxford to her sons, which will carry them far – the unselfish spirit, the self reliance, the broad outlook, the great sense of fair play, the good fellowship – all these things are the University's gift of priceless value to those who lived within her walls.

Seton Gordon wrote in the obligatory style of the early war years, boosting the necessity of conflict. At this point there was yet no idea that the war would drag on for another three years. Of his immediate friends, Alasdair Graham-Menzies would soon die and Cuthbert Pease was to die later in the war; Archie Ritchie and Gerald Hay, though wounded, survived, as did Malcolm Barclay-Harvey who was commissioned into the Gordon Highlanders. He attained the rank of captain by 1915, but was invalided out of the army because of a chronic asthmatic condition. He then served on the Home Staff and the Ministry of Munitions. It amused the Prince of Wales that 'Long' Hay, the tallest officer in the British army, should be shot in the foot.

By the end of the war, feelings were somewhat different and there was a greater cynicism. It was said that Oxford was haunted by absent friends. Much literature and poetry was produced in the years following 1918, reflecting the sadness and bitterness of those who survived.

Those who were left behind described the state of bereavement as the casualty lists came in. James Morris wrote: 'Even now it is their standards that this city, half regretfully, half mockingly, still fitfully aspires to. Their fair, frank forms we instinctively look for, and fail to find . . . until soon there will be only memories and legends, of thirty feet of names on a college memorial to remind us what it was'.

While universities felt the impact of the war, towns and villages throughout the British Isles were also losing their men by the hundreds. This was particularly evident in the Highlands and the Hebrides. The Outer Isles had the distinction of sending more men to the front per capita than any other area of the British Isles.

The *Oban Times* provides a powerful record of the Highlands and Islands during the first war. There was an added poignancy with the lengthening In Memoriam column as news came to castle and croft of men who would either return no more, or whose bodies were brought back to be buried with full honours while the pipes played the Flowers of the Forest or other appropriate laments and pibrochs. Among the young men who gave their lives were Captain Campbell, Laird of Jura, and Lieutenant Charles Macleod-Brereton, a cousin and godson of Mrs Cameron-Head of Inverailort. The heir to MacLeod of MacLeod, Lieutenant Iain Breac MacLeod, died in April 1915 at the first battle of Ypres. In September the death was reported of Lieutenant Hugh Munro, Argyll and Sutherland Highlanders, son of Neil Munro the Scottish poet and novelist. One of the most tragic In Memoriam columns appeared on 14 August 1915, with the joint, bordered photographs of Lieutenant Colonel MacDougall, Laird of Lunga, and Captain Iain MacDougall the Younger, of Lunga. They were killed within days of each other.

Recruiting drives were constant. On 17 April there was an appeal from the commanding officer of the 10th Battalion, Seaforth Highlanders. In July, below a bordered picture of Lochiel, Lieutenant Colonel Donald Walter Cameron of Lochiel, twenty-fifth Chief of Clan Cameron, was a lengthy column on his success at raising enough battallions to form a brigade in France, ending with:

> Lochiel is now with his men in the frontline trenches. There we follow him and his warriors with our best wishes and prayers, and soon, doubtless we shall hear the echo of the stirring command, recently given at Neuve Chapelle, 'Camerons advance; advance Lochaber!'

The second battle of Ypres resulted in the loss of another 58,000 men, and with

In the Cairngorms – 1912 – Robert Hargreaves, Graham Menzies of Haliburton and Gerald 'Long' Hay (at 6′ 10″ the tallest officer in the British Army in WWI)

the popularity of the *Oban Times* throughout the west, Seton Gordon could hardly fail to be aware of the casualty lists, adding to his belief that his lot was 'all wrong'. Other correspondence was so far removed from the reality of the war, it almost seemed the writers were unaware of the fact that thousands of men were perishing while their protracted exchanges went on. While Seton Gordon was increasing his knowledge of pibroch through his visits to John Johnston of Coll, two men, thousands of miles apart, engaged in a series of letters on the MacCrimmon notation for the bagpipe.

The letters were often acrimonious, each side accusing the other of knowing nothing about the intricacies of piping. The feud centred upon the interpretation of the MacCrimmon notation as expounded by MacLeod of Gesto, and whether he was, in fact, a piper. The MacCrimmoms were, over several hundred years, hereditary pipers to a succession of Clan MacLeod chiefs. Neil MacLeod of Gesto, who lived on a small estate of that name, not far from Dunvegan Castle, was taught by one of the last MacCrimmons, the chanting sung by the old masters to teach their pupils the tunes they were to learn. He published a manuscript in 1828 allegedly based on this chanting, or in Gaelic, *canntaireachd*.

The protagonists were Simon Fraser of South Geelong, Melbourne, Australia, and John Grant of Edinburgh. Both men claimed to be first class pipers, and in September 1915, Grant published a book on *piobaireachd* (pibroch). The argument went on regularly for more than two years, which said much for the dependability of the mail, despite the war. Sides were taken in the issue and each one had his staunch supporters, some using *nom-de-plumes*. John Grant took on all comers in whatever aspect of piping they cared to express an opinion. Although Seton Gordon was surely aware of this correspondence, such airy dialogue would not have been of much concern to him. He became totally fascinated with the MacCrimmon legend and the tunes attributed to their composition.

The letters demonstrated the controversy which raged around the bagpipe then, and indeed still continues, with recently raised doubts about the authenticity of the MacCrimmons and their significance on piping. A 1980 book by Alistair Campsie, *The MacCrimmon Legend* attributes their tunes to Angus MacKay, at one time Queen Victoria's piper, who was committed to an asylum and drowned in 1859, while trying to escape. Despite a claim to documented evidence that the whole MacCrimmon story was a hoax, it has not gone down well in the piping fraternity. Campsie has felt the wrath of pipers everywhere. In the book he refers to a 1932 letter written by James MacKillop to Seton Gordon concerning the Speckled Pipes at Dunvegan Castle, which will be dealt with in a later chapter.

Seton Gordon was still alive when Alistair Campsie began his research for the MacCrimmon book, but died before it was published. He never tired of their legends, and how he might have handled Campsie's claim can only be speculated, but it is quite certain that it would not have shaken his faith in the MacCrimmon story. He knew their pibrochs so well that when judging, he would follow the pipers playing without a score in front of him, and was always as concerned with the 'soul' of the music, as he was with the dexterity of the piper.

Seton Gordon's life was made easier by the arrival of the *Lustre Gem* to get him around the islands on his regular inspections of the watching posts. The skipper was Gilbert Longstaff, the youngest son of Llewellyn Wood Longstaff, who helped finance Captain Scott's Antarctic expedition with a donation of £25,000. Gilbert's older brother Dr. Thomas G. Longstaff, was a mountaineer who made several climbs in the Himalayas. A Vice President of the Royal Geographic Society, he was a member, with Seton Gordon, on the 1921 Oxford University Spitsbergen expedition. Gilbert Longstaff became an ardent fan of Seton Gordon's later books on the west coast.

The coast-watchers' reports continued to come in, generally showing little or no action, but once in a while giving evidence of a submarine sighting or mines exploding. Their reports included weather conditions as well. Once in a while reports on other topics were received, such as suspected spies. The coast-watchers on Coll reported one incident which was reported in great detail by John Johnston, but no one was caught.

Seton Gordon was fascinated by Johnston and wrote about him in several books and articles. In *Hebridean Memories* Johnston had a whole chapter to himself, 'The Island Piper'. In *Afoot in the Hebrides* there is a good account of their relationship:

> It was on Coll that I first met John Johnston, who played the old pipe tunes

and was versed in their history. His croft was on the western shore. Near his door the waves broke on a bay of golden sand. His thoughts were always on Ceol Mor,* or Great Music of the Highland bagpipe. He was taught by an uncle who learned his skill from a Coll piper who, in turn, had received instruction from Donald Ruadh, the last hereditary piper of the great MacCrimmon family. Thus John Johnston's piping deserved to be treated with respect, and I count my hours spent with him as profitable. I sometimes persuaded him to play his practice chanter, and after fanning the peat fire to a glow, he would begin, haltingly at first, as if his stiff fingers fought to express the music that was in him.

*Ceol Mor is Gaelic for 'big music' or *piobaireachd*, as opposed to Ceol Beag, little music – reels and marches.

He would close his eyes tightly, and play old tuning fragments and pieces from the Great Music. When I had mastered the playing of one of these ancient tunes he was delighted. Jumping excitedly from his chair, he would exclaim, 'That's it; that's it. You have it'. Then he would again play, lovingly, the old piece.

A date had now been fixed for the marriage of Seton and Audrey. This was to be 19 August, in St John's Episcopal Church, Otterburn. The Peases were a large, close family and Audrey was a favourite child, so despite wartime conditions and the grim news from the western front, preparations were underway in the three months remaining before the wedding for a great family day.

On 23 April, Ella Mary Gordon died, and her passing was widely reported in the newspapers throughout Britain. With so much room required for war news, the space allotted to Ella Mary shows the esteem in which she was held.

The Prince of Wales wrote in July from the 1st Corps Headquarters in France:

My Dear Seton,

Many thanks for your letter announcing to me the date of your marriage. Hearty congratulations & I only wish I could be present; its very good of you to suggest it. But I hope you get a hold of old Archie who is now a grenadier; he crocked himself a few weeks ago but I hope he is fit again now!!

Your work at Mull must be very interesting when there are subs about but I suppose they have been more cautious of late. All v. quiet out here; I see Gerald Hay fairly often who is v. fit and in good form. My v. best of luck to you both & I remain, Yrs. ever E.

The Prince was obviously pleased that he could keep in touch with, and occasionally see, his Oxford friends. Both Gerald Hay and Archie Ritchie finished the war with distinguished records. Hay saw service in Salonika as well as France, was twice mentioned in despatches, and finished the war as a staff officer in the Army of the Black Sea. He stayed in the army after the war and in 1927 attended the Royal Military Staff College. He was later attached to the War Office. In the 1920s and 1930s he was a frequent visitor to the Gordons' home and is remembered by the Gordon children for his tremendous consumption of Scotch. Ritchie left the Foreign Legion and joined the Grenadier Guards. He was awarded the MC in 1915, and in the same year was mentioned in despatches and was made a Chevalier of the Legion of Honour. After the war he went out to British East Africa to became a Native Commissioner and Administrator of a big game reserve.

In mid-August, Seton left Mull and headed to Otterburn for his marriage to Audrey. The wedding was a quiet one, as were most weddings in Britain at that time. Seton wore formal Highland dress, and one of the distinguishing features of the wedding was that the hymns were written by the late Ella Mary, and set to music by Sir John Stainer, organist at St Paul's Cathedral. (Dr C. H. Lloyd of Eton College, and Walter Alcock of the Chapel Royal also wrote music for Ella Mary.) There were three officiating clergy, one of them Seton's uncle, The Rev Frederick Paul. There was a small reception, which may have been a matter of personal choice, rather than an economy measure. The bride and groom left soon after for a brief honeymoon before returning to Mull and Seton's coast-watching duties.

At Lady Margaret Hall, Audrey had gained an honours degree in Natural Sciences and a Class III BA She had attended Oxford at a most unfortunate time, with the drastically reduced student population and the mounting toll of casualties in France. Audrey enjoyed her months on Mull immensely and often accompanied Seton on his rounds to coast-watchers on the island. Between whiles he found time to edit, and in October, publish *Hill Birds of Scotland*, his third book. There were 292 pages describing twenty-four birds. Some had not been previously covered: the sea-eagle (erne, or white-tailed eagle), osprey, kestrel, raven, black grouse, snipe, greenshank, snowbunting, crested titmouse and dunlin.

The early months of 1916 saw more activity in the Minch than previously. In March, the steamer *Englishman*, a Dominion liner, was torpedoed off Islay. Thirty-six crew members were saved, but several bodies later washed up on the island. Reports were still coming in regularly, often with quaint spelling. On 2 April, a report was received from Bunessan, Mull: "Sir, Gigha MacLean, Ardchiavaig, reported to me that a submarine was seen halfway beween Colonsay and Torran Rocks S.W. of Ardalanish Point. I went across this afternoon with Strong Oppra Glasses and Kept a lookout but could see nothing I would not miss Dought this Report as the place mentioned is the track of vessels sailing outside the Western Isles. Any other Information Received will be sent by wire. Yrs Respectfully Angus MacGillvray'.

Occasionally the desire for action showed in the reports: 'I have seen no Submarines yet, but if I do I will wire with all speed. Dan McKechnie, Coast-watcher, Hynish, Tiree'.

Seton Gordon received notice from the Admiralty in July that he was to be commissioned to the rank of Lieutenant, RNVR and would be transferred to Aultbea on Loch Ewe, Wester Ross, as Base Intelligence Officer, effective 16 October. The Gordons would leave Mull as a family, for Audrey gave birth to a daughter at Oban on 14 July. She was christened Ella Caitriona.

While Seton and Audrey were preparing to leave Mull for Aultbea, news came of the death of Cuthbert Pease while commanding the Machine Gun Company, 1st Guards Brigade. He died on 18 September, of wounds received while crossing no-man's land in an advance. His letters in the preceding weeks showed his excitement at becoming an uncle. In July he had written:

> Being an uncle in reality is a very different thing from being a fictitious one – as I shall now be responsible for the little animal when it arrives & have to give it a present which will probably only make it cry . . .
>
> As uncle I'm not quite sure whether it's my duty merely to name the child or give it some useful & suitable present such as a teaspoon or desert knife as well – anyway I've got two good names to suggest, Portizje and Mortildje – good sounding names & with a certain Biblical flavour about them, both representing aspects of the war, will be reminiscent in after years. I dont mind which you choose. You might also add the name of your abode – Ardura. Portizje Ardura Seton Gordon & thus it would be well equipped for life's handicaps. I shall call it that whatever you and Seton do about it . . . With love, Cuthbert.

He wrote again on 18 August:

> I'm sorry you didn't choose any of the names I suggested. We've been moving about the country lately & spent some time living in the open air which was rather pleasant as the weather was extremely fine – though rather too hot for moving or anything that requires effort . . .
>
> With love, Cuthbert
>
> Please remember me to Ella Caitriona!

Cuthbert's death was a devastating blow after the joy of Ella Caitriona's birth and it deeply affected Audrey. Fortunately, before taking up the posting at Aultbea she and Seton spent two weeks at Otterburn, giving Audrey time to grieve with her family.

When news of the move to Aultbea reached them, disappointment was expressed by the coast-watchers under Seton's command. John Johnston was especially disappointed, and wrote on 6 September:

> Sir,
>
> I am writing this note to express my sincere sorrow at the prospect of your leaving the district for another one, presumably a promotion, which will be a well merited one. I am confident there is not one coast-watcher in the whole district, and it is an extensive, but what will be exceedingly sorry to lose your superintendence, most worthily and amiably combined with strict adherance to duty, and myself in particular, as I counted it a great pleasure to serve under you. With best well-wishes, I am sir, Yr. ob't serv't, John Johnston.

Seton Gordon acknowledged the two years spent at Ardura as being some of the happiest in his life. The impressions that he stored up were drawn upon when he wrote *Land of the Hills and the Glenns* and *Wanderings of a Naturalist* in the early 1920s. His place was taken by Colonel Ellis, one of the honorary coast-watchers, who, from all accounts was not as popular with the men. Coast-watching continued in much the same fashion to the end of the war.

Seton Gordon was now a serving RNVR officer, commissioned to full lieutenant. This meant that by naval tradition his moustache had to go, though with permission he could have grown a full beard had he so desired. He chose to remain clean shaven. From the time that he grew a moustache in his late youth, this was the only period in his life that he was without it.

At Aultbea he joined the 10th Cruiser Squadron as base intelligence officer, under the command of Admiral Reginald Tupper, who until the previous February had been in command of Patrol Area One, headquartered in Stornoway. Patrol Area One covered operations from Scapa Flow to the Clyde, and included the coast-watchers. In addition there were over seventy small vessels, each armed with a gun, all part of the anti-submarine network. Some were commanded by retired admirals, who had elected to return to service in a reduced rank.

At Aultbea there was less freedom, though Seton Gordon, in the short time that he was stationed there, managed several visits to Osgoode MacKenzie of Inverewe, a fascinating Highland character. As base intelligence officer, Lieutenant Seton Gordon sifted all reports coming in from the ships of the squadron, debriefed the officers as they returned to base from patrol and, on at least one occasion, went to sea for the duration of a patrol into the North Atlantic.

The squadron was formed to blockade the 800-mile stretch from the Hebrides to Iceland and to intercept merchant shipping en route to Scandinavian ports carrying supplies bound for Germany. Careful examination was essential because of the deceit employed to hide their true cargo. These included double bottoms, false decks and bulkheads. Sailing ships were given hollow steel masts which were filled with rubber and copper, while barrels of flour contained gun cotton.

Most of the squadron's ships were commandeered liners, fitted with guns and put into service as auxiliary cruisers. Drastic refitting was necessary, and only their shape revealed what they had once been. Ballrooms and lounges became storerooms and in many cases extra bulkheads were put in place to facilitate gun batteries placed on deck. Many of the original crews volunteered to stay with their ship as RNVR members, including Captain Outram of the liner *Alsatian*, flagship of the squadron. Auxiliary cruisers varied in size, from well in excess of 20,000 tons all the way down to the 6000 ton banana boat, *Patia*. Out of a total of about twenty-five ships, in three years of operation six ships were lost by U-boats, and two more in circumstances that were never fully explained, including the *Viknor*. A total of 103 officers and 1062 men were lost.

Aultbea is in a remote part of the Highlands, and was in those days a strict Presbyterian stronghold. For sailors at the base who came from less restrictive places and were billeted locally, it was not easy to become acquainted with local customs. On the Sabbath, beyond attending church, only reading the Bible and eating were permitted. No one went for a walk, even on a warm sunny day – unless it was to and from church.

One man who resisted the influence of the church was Osgood MacKenzie, Laird of Inverewe. He inherited Inverewe House from his mother, and set about reclaiming land that had not been productive for several years. He established a garden which to this day is world-famous for its beauty, and the unusual plants that were successfully cultivated by him; eucalyptus, mimosa and semi-tropical plants that flourished despite the dire warnings of his friends. Seton Gordon recalls seeing a mimosa in full bloom at Christmas time. During his stay at Aultbea, he was a frequent guest at Inverewe. MacKenzie was an impressive figure, with a full, white beard and like Seton Gordon, he always wore Highland dress. He was also fully fluent in Gaelic.

He had in his possession ten manuscript volumes of Highland memoirs written by his uncle, Dr John MacKenzie, covering the period from 1803 to 1860. With encouragement from Seton Gordon, Osgood MacKenzie began writing his own memoirs to add to those of his uncle. He was by this time in his late seventies and the resulting book, *One Hundred Years in the Highlands* was published in 1921. Seton Gordon assisted with editing and revision. MacKenzie's personal memory went back to the potato famine of the late 1840s, when his mother provided funds to put local men to work in road construction so that the country could be opened up to transportation, and at the same time give them a means of income to buy other foods to offset the loss of potatoes.

MacKenzie's most interesting assertion was a dramatic climatic change, which he claimed had taken place in the preceding forty or more years and was responsible for, among other things, the disappearance of the wild bee. He also claimed that filbert and hazel nuts no longer grew in abundance, and birdlife was diminishing in the northern Highlands. On one west coast property for which MacKenzie had the records covering 1866 to 1916, the highs for red grouse in the early years were 1939 for 1872, diminishing to a mere thirty-one in 1914. He lamented the disappearance of the lesser black-backed gull, then said 'their eggs were a source of food supply in the hungry months of May and June, and collecting gull's eggs on the islands of Loch Maree was a favourite pastime. We used to get from 150 to 200 eggs in an afternoon. Now, alas, they are all but gone.' He recorded drastic reductions in some non-game birds: greylag goose, golden plover, green plover, greenshank, dunlin, and whimbrel. The storm petrel, common guillemot, ring ouzel and nightjar had, he said, disappeared from the area.

A comment on MacKenzie's observations came from a most respected Highland ornithologist, the late Desmond Nethersole-Thompson, who died in March 1989, in his eightieth year. On a two-part BBC biographical programme on Seton Gordon, *What a Life*, produced in the mid-1970s, he talked with warm memories of his first meeting with Seton Gordon high in the Cairngorms. He also wrote the Foreword for the 1980 reprint of *The Golden Eagle – King of Birds*.

In answer to a request for his opinion on MacKenzie's notes he replied:

> MacKenzie's comments on bird numbers are largely anecdotal. I don't think that the ebbs and flows of any bird numbers can be attributed to a single

> factor. Climatic oscillations, however, are important to many fringe species. For example snow buntings almost disappeared from Scotland in warmer climatic changes. There are always seasonal fluctuations which are hard to explain. In my greenshank study area in Sutherland, for example, covering from 1964 to 1982, there were 6–7 breeding pairs in 1966 and 20–23 pairs in 1976. Lapwings suffer severely from hard winters and can take years to fully recover.
>
> All grouse species suffer peaks and crashes. I do not think excessive shooting was the main factor. Without facts and figures and without studying each species it is interesting but rather futile to speculate.

Excesses in shooting were, of course, going on throughout the Highlands during the nineteenth century. In Seton Gordon's notes, figures for birds killed on the Glengarry estate for 1839–40 included: fifteen golden eagles, eighteen ospreys, 614 buzzards, six gyro falcons, 275 kites, 462 kestrels, twenty-seven sea eagles, 63 goshawks, 78 merlins, 93 hen harriers, five marsh harriers and eleven hobby hawks, as well as 109 owls of different varieties.

In January 1917, Seton Gordon was transferred to the Naval Centre at Tynemouth, commanded by Commodore Reginald Tyrwhit, who also commanded the Naval Light Force, comprised of both cruisers and destroyers. It was a busy time for intelligence officers. Reports of enemy sightings, incidents at sea, shipping movements, were coming in hourly. All information had to be verified and documented in logs. This was the first major war where wireless made information instantaneous. Seton Gordon's role now had greater importance, with direct access to the various admirals or senior officers under whose command he came.

Allied intelligence reports late in 1916 indicated a new U-boat offensive, to come into effect early in 1917. It was estimated that by the end of 1916, the British had no fewer than 3000 vessels, from small armed yachts, drifters and sloops to torpedo boats and destroyers, all engaged solely in anti-submarine work.

Seton Gordon stayed at Tynemouth for eight months, and in August 1917 he was transferred to the Naval Centre at Kingstown, now Dun Laoghaire, near Dublin. He remained at Kingstown until May 1919 and was in charge of the Naval Centre (HMS *Boadicea II*) for several months prior to demobilisation. His service records indicate a high level of satisfaction with job performance by the various senior officers under whom he served.

Service in Ireland gave him a new dimension for bird-watching and learning about the lives of another group of Celts. From notes during this period he was able to draw on memories for his second post-war book, *Wanderings of a Naturalist* published in 1921. There are four chapters on Ireland. While he was stationed there, he continued to play the pipes, but does not mention in his notes or diaries, which were resumed in 1919, whether he investigated Irish pipes and music. Irish pipes are sweeter in sound and without the wildnesss of the Highland pipe. Exchanges on piping continued with Johnston, and a letter from Coll in April 1917 mentioned conditions on the island:

Lieutenant Seton Gordon, RNVR – 1917 (with Audrey, baby Caitrion and Calum MacFadyen their Dandy Dinmont)

. . . As to pibrochs, I think I told you before that I was completely out of any knowledge of notation, as such was totally ignored by the old pipers from whom I learned. They simply would have nothing to do with it. But the late Mr Glen of Edinburgh published the MacLean pibrochs before he died and these were put down correctly, as they were originally, and can be had from his firm yet. Several of these are taken down from me, at the insistance of the MacLean Association in Glasgow, particularly those of the MacLean chiefs of Duart.

I did not play any since you were here, only a few beside the fire on New Year's Eve, for my own amusement. I am 'watching' still, but this Spring is a terrible cold one, far more so than the last two preceeding ones. The young man with me helps me considerably – I managed to get him exempted as my only support and the only person able to work the holding. I only hope I shall be able to keep him all along.

Johnston's discourse on pibroch, though hard to follow at times, compliments the arguments in the *Oban Times* correspondence and the disagreements on pibroch technique and interpretation. His next letter tells of an interesting turn of events with the coast-watching:

> Dear Sir,
>
> . . . perhaps you will be sorry to hear that I am no longer coast-watching. The very first time [Colonel] Ellis came to Coll after you left he warned me that I would not be long kept on, but did not say so to any one else in his district. This of course was at the insistance of Ralston [the Laird], as they chummed greatly, but kept me on however until him and Ralston came to my house and began all sorts of accusations and fault findings with everything I did. So much so that after listening patiently for a time I told him at last that that was enough, I would not put up with more & ordered him to CLEAR OUT with his coast-watching – OUT OF MY SIGHT. That stopped him. Ralston was left to put in any one he pleased. I am an old man now but I got along with my work splendidly until I met this 'sprig' of a Laird.
>
> It was a black day when you left the district and even outside the coast-watching work it was a source of immense gratification and strength to me when I was favoured with a visit from you, as you were rather encouraging to me and not attempting to destroy me.
>
> Please accept my best thanks for minding me, and let me assure you sir, from my heart, an old man of eighty years that I shall keep you green in my memory for as long as life lasts.
>
> I am, yours sincerely, J. Johnston.

The correspondence on pibroch continued, and occasionally touched on the war, or conditions on the island. He complained of very wet weather and feared the loss of his crops. Johnston also complained that tea was hard to obtain and as the Gordons found food conditions better in Ireland, they sent butter, sugar, and tea to him and other older coast-watchers.

One of the last hostile acts committed by a U-boat was played out almost in view of Kingstown on 10 October 1918, when the cross-channel mail steamer *Leinster* sailed from Kingston for Holyhead at 9 a.m. and within thirty minutes was struck by two torpedoes. The sea was rough, making it difficult to launch the lifeboats. From the time that the second torpedo hit, the steamer stayed afloat for only three to four minutes. Audrey Gordon wrote an account of the sinking to send to family members. She mentioned that Seton's immediate superior, Commander Bagot was on board, but was rescued by a destroyer. Seton was on duty at the Naval Centre when the news was received. Audrey's account was graphic:

> Every available craft in the harbour steamed out – armed yachts, trawlers, drifters, and one motor launch carrying the Senior Naval Officer, Admiral Denison. It was wonderful to see all the gallant little ships hastening with all speed to the rescue. By the time they arrived, the *Leinster* had sunk and three

boats and many rafts were all that was left of the ship. Many people struggled in the water.

Fifty motor ambulances arrived at Admiralty Wharf and at about 1:30 p.m. the first destroyer came in with survivors. Seton and I went down to the wharf and soon found plenty to do in serving hot drinks to survivors. A large number were stretcher cases, and most could only walk with assistance. One was struck by their terrible blue look and the fact that they trembled so much as to be almost unable to hold a cup in their hands. Practically all had been in the water for upwards of an hour, as only three boats were able to get away, and one capsized before being rescued. Cheers were raised for the rescued, but a band of hooligans and Sinn Feiners marched about singing and laughing and joking, heedless of the grief stricken and anxious people, and the landing of the dead.

Commander Bagot was on board the last destroyer. By 4 p.m. about 187 survivors had been landed, about half of them soldiers. *Leinster* carried about 500 soldiers and 150 civilians, yet she had no escort. The commander, Captain Birch, lost his life. He once told Seton he felt convinced that his ship would be attacked, as he often had no escort. He said, 'My only hope is that she will go down decently, so as to give my passengers a chance.'

Only twelve days later, Prince Maximillian of Baden, the new German Chancellor, ordered the U-boat campaign against merchant shipping suspended in anticipation of the forthcoming Armistice talks, but a mutiny in the German navy hastened the end. The Kaiser signed his abdication papers late on 9 November, and fled to Holland. At 5:40 a.m. on the 11th, Germany signed the Armisice and at 11 a.m. the sounds of battle ceased over Europe.

Seton Gordon was patrolling in the naval drifter *Harry and Leonard* off the small island of Lambay, north of Dublin. His dairy note reads:

> We received the historic signal from the Admiralty saying that an Armistice had been arranged for eleven o'clock that morning, and that enemy submarines were not to be attacked unless they showed hostile intent. The 11th hour of the 11th day of the 11th month! There were those who saw a mystic significance in this. Here, out in the Irish Sea, the light was grey and autumnal and there was not another ship in sight. I saw a wheatear on Lambay; a late date for a summer migrant.

He remained at Kingstown in naval service until May 1919, and was formally demobilised on 1 July. The final report on his conduct from the Senior Naval Officer, Admiral John Denison, reads: 'Lieutenant Seton Gordon has conducted himself to my entire satisfaction and is an able and efficient officer. He has been in charge of the Naval Centre for some months and has done excellent work.'

The additional time at Kingstown following the Armistice allowed Seton to explore parts of Ireland which he had not seen during active service. One such location was the Aran Islands, although he went as one of an official naval group. It was in January 1919, and at that time conditions were more primitive than those in the Hebrides. The names have a fascination of their own, Innishmore, Innishmaan, and Innishear. Being a poor sailor, Seton Gordon would have good cause to remember this voyage to the islands, because weather conditions were even worse than at the time of his sail to Coll and Tiree with Captain Black at the beginning of the war.

Once clear of Black Head, the sea increased to such an alarming extent that after being struck by three heavy waves in quick succession, the boat began to settle by the bows. The skipper gave orders to return to Galway. A ventilator had been washed away and 8 feet of water flooded the men's quarters. She was so low by the head, it was impossible to bring her round, and only by all hands standing over the propellor to give extra weight to the stern, was the screw able to grip the water. Precariously, the boat went astern, the sea rushing across the half submerged bow. The pumps were choked, making it impossible to get rid of the great mass of water on board, and Seton Gordon thought that any minute the ship might founder. The bulkhead held, and with great relief, the shelter of a bay was reached, where the pumps were repaired.

The second trip was made in a trawler, the *Lord Hemmage*, as the motor launch would not start. Their first port of call was Innishmore. As the launch hove to, men came towards them across the bay in their primitive curraghs, made of cowhide or canvas, and peculiar to that stretch of coast. The curraghs were rowed alongside by men who, to quote Seton Gordon, 'Were wild looking in appearance and talking to each other excitedly in Gaelic. Some of the islanders wore a curious shoe, known as a 'pampooty'. It consists of a piece of raw cowhide, with the hair on the outside, laced over the toe and round the heel with two ends of fishing line tied above the instep. Wearing such light and pliable footgear, the islanders have preserved the primitive and graceful walk which has been lost elsewhere with the coming of the unromantic boot.'

Seton Gordon was struck by the absence of any rich pasture land. Walls were few and far between, and he was told that the grass becomes so parched in summer that the ponies were taken across to the Connemara Hills to graze and not brought back until the latter part of September, when the autumn rains had commenced. Owing to this lack of moisture and the limestone nature of the soil there is no peat on any of the islands, and as the islanders burned little else, it was transported from Connemara in smacks. If by any chance the supply became exhausted the islanders used cowdung, a good substitute.

Such excursions were very useful in providing opportunities to examine the ways of another race of Gael, so similar, and yet in many ways so different from those on Scotland's west coast. There were bird-watching excursions to various islands and loughs in other parts of Ireland. One of these was to the Isle of Lambay, an ornithologist's paradise which he visited in both April and May of 1919. In between these he went to London on Admiralty business, and while there met Dick Crewe and Archie Ritchie, who had a flat on Wilton Street.

In early May Seton and Audrey began packing their household goods in preparation for the return to Scotland. Their immediate destination was Otterburn, where they remained for several weeks.

CHAPTER
4
BIRDS, ISLANDS AND BAGPIPES

ON 23 MAY, Seton Gordon reported to the Admiralty in London. This was officially the end of his naval career, though with accrued leave, his actual demobilisation was not until 1 July.

In his early post-demobilisation days, Seton Gordon gave considerable thought to the future. Although he and Audrey took advantage of their new found freedom to travel and explore, he was nevertheless concerned about a career and job prospects. Writing in the *Scottish Field* in August 1955 he admitted that had it not been for the First World War it was unlikely that he would have taken up writing and photography as a profession. Despite his Honours Science degree and a Diploma in Rural Economy and Forestry, he found in 1919 that there were many more applicants among recently demobilised officers than appointments to go round. He said:

> I had always wanted to write, and since I found a wife with the same tastes and same love of nature as myself, we fought through the difficult times of the early 1920s. Between 1915 and 1925 we were on the move, and in that time lived in no fewer than twenty-one houses. After the war we visited much of the Highlands and the Hebrides, staying with crofters, camping on islands, some of them uninhabited, and living the hard way, thus getting to know the crofters' way of life and outlook on the world.

Seton was thirty-three years old, and though he had supported himself ably before the war by writing, he now had more responsibilities. He and Audrey had an advantage that many other job seekers did not possess. Their common interests could, with determination, be used to produce an income. Their combined talents would need to be exploited to the fullest, but there was a market, with a steadily growing interest in all areas of the countryside, especially Scotland. Greater leisure time had encouraged the formation of hiking and rambling groups, and the competition in descriptive writing grew with it in the next decade, and writers on the Highlands found an avid audience: F. Fraser Darling, Alasdair Alpin MacGregor, T. Ratcliffe-Barnett, and Thomas Nicol, to name a few. The Gordons had an advantage with their in-depth knowledge of nature lore.

In the meantime, a brief respite at Otterburn before renting a house in Oban, allowed Audrey's parents to enjoy their granddaughter Caitriona. Seton, restless to be out on the moor, discovered a plover's nest and with Audrey's help built a hide. Ten minutes into his first watch on 26 May, the bird unsuspectingly came back to the nest. The day was hot and windless and she was panting constantly and looking most uncomfortable. When a plate was exposed, the bird was startled. As Seton described it in his diary: 'Upon releasing the shutter – the effect was electric! she sprang up into the air and settled down again almost 10 yards off, and her fright was so great she could scarcely draw breath.'

A sheep-track led past the nest, which she used, running along it rapidly until she got near the nest, when she became extremely wary, and moved stealthily towards her eggs. However, she soon became used to the presence of the hide and nineteen days later, on 12 June, three out of the four eggs were commencing to chip, and Seton could hear the chicks cheeping inside them. He found that after hatching, the young plovers run actively almost from their first hour. The cock bird never came near the nest, though he was frequently seen on the hillside 500 or 600 yards away, but once the chicks were hatched he returned and they were tended carefully by both parent birds.

Still officially on active service until 1 July, Seton made several visits to the Admiralty from Otterburn in connection with the closing down of the Kingstown Naval Centre. On one occasion he was forced to plead that a directive sent asking him to attend a meeting arrived while he was in fact in London visiting another department, and requested a new date. In the same letter he also said, 'I do not know whether under the following circumstances an interview with you is still necessary. At present my position is as follows – I have made application for appointment under the Forestry Authority which is expected to be started on the passing of the new Forestry Act. I should prefer if possible that my demobilisation be postponed until news of the passing of the Bill, and whether there is any likelihood of employment under the Forestry Department.'

On 12 June he reluctantly left the moor and took the night train to London for the postponed Admiralty meeting. The next evening he met Felix Youssoupoff, who told Seton of his various experiences in Russia following the Revolution. Youssoupoff's part in the killing of Rasputin was fully described when in 1952 he published *Lost Splendour*. It tells of the incredible effort that it took, the large quantity of poison Rasputin unknowingly consumed, and the gunshot wounds he suffered, before his body was finally thrown into the river. At least two films have been made on the subject, and after the release of one of them, *Rasputin the Mad Monk* in 1934, Princess Irina sued Metro-Goldwyn-Mayer for libel, and won $375,000. In 1956 Felix sued the American television network, CBS, for $1.6 million over a film on Rasputin's murder, but he lost the case.

Following the killing of Rasputin, Youssoupoff was banished to one of his Crimean estates. It is possible that this helped him to escape the purges, and in 1919 he left his homeland forever. From his vast fortune it is said that he took with him $1 million in jewelery and two Rembrandts. The Youssoupoffs settled in Paris where Felix became known for his generosity to other Russian *émigrés*. He died there at the age of eighty in 1967.

After taking up residence in Oban, Seton Gordon worked on his fourth book, *Land of the Hills and the Glens*, which was published in 1920. During June, Seton traded in his 1906 Humber through Macrae and Dick Motors of Inverness. Unaccountably he exchanged it for a 1909 Wolsely rather than a post-war model. It may have been more economical, but gave little improvement in comfort. There was a noticeable increase in train and bicycle use. During this period every penny was watched, and the diary account columns list each expenditure in great detail, from large items such as train and ferry fares to shoe repairs, down to two pence for scones in one list. Yet where they took taxis or used porters for their camping gear they were generous with tipping. One touching entry was for two shillings to a 'penniless marine'.

On 3 July Seton and Audrey commenced a camping trip on the Treshnish Isles, uninhabited and rocky, but with grass swards where cattle were put to graze. The purpose of the trip was to study puffins and storm petrels, both of them nesting in great numbers here. On the largest island there were also greater black backed gulls which they intended to photograph. The gales continued and they were marooned for a few days, making it necessary to stretch out the rations. Having bought three shillings worth of kippers it was a blow to find they had only half the amount that were paid for. Arriving on the largest Island, called Lunga, though several miles west of the one which so tragically lost its Laird and his heir, they found bullocks (stirks) grazing there. It was necesssary to find a spot where they might discourage these 'destructive' animals from approaching their tents. The location gave them an unsurpassed view in all directions; the hills of Rhum with the Cuillins behind, Mull and Ardnamurchan point. To the west were Coll and Tiree and beyond them the Outer Isles, all of which Seton was quick to record in at least three articles eventually published on this camp.

Both the puffin and the storm petrel were in abundance here, and the puffins Seton estimated in their thousands. They were active at all hours of the day and night. One or two who had young concealed among the rocks, arrived from their fishing grounds in the early hours of the morning, their bills packed with numbers of small fry.

The Gordons noticed that as the birds were about to enter their holes, at the last moment panic would seize them and they circled out to sea again, only to go through the same performance a minute later. Yet they displayed aggression when taking over a rabbit burrow, after evicting the rightful owner. Peering into the mouth of a burrow they could see a puffin pecking angrily at the rabbit with her powerful parrot-like bill, until the animal, thoroughly scared, had to bolt to safer quarters.

Attention was also given to the greater black-backed gulls. It was necessary to locate a nest suitably sited for photographing from amongst the colony at the western end of the island. The hide was carried there on the evening of 3 July. The next morning they retraced their steps, and finding that the gull had become indifferent to the hide, it was moved closer, setting it up about 6 feet from the eggs. Several photographs were taken, but it was thought inadvisable to disturb the bird too much on the first day, so Audrey left the hide. Unfortunately by next morning a catastrophe had occurred. In the night, the bullocks had destroyed the hide; even more distressing, a bullock had lain on the nest and the eggs, very nearly hatched, were hopelessly crushed.

A greater black-back was brooding on her nest halfway up the hill near the middle of the island. They repaired and carried off the hide to this nest which contained two eggs, one of them just chipping. The following morning, soon after Audrey entered the hide, the gull returned and several plates were exposed. By 10 July, one chick was hatched out, while the other was tapping at the egg with its bill and cheeping feebly. Seton described the sitting gull:

> In the hot sun she panted and drops of saliva formed at the end of her bill and dripped to the ground. Close-up, the greater black-backed gull presents a shock. The low forehead, the lack of intelligence or expression, the evil countenance and cold murderous eye – there is nothing to admire here.

The second chick was slow to hatch, and was found crushed and cold one morning, half-hatched, dead and stiff. There were no marks of cattle around this time. Its mother had simply lost patience with it.

During the whole period from mid-May to the end of August Seton Gordon's diary was packed with tightly written notes. Few people could equal his ability to get so much on one page. From the one visit to the Treshnish group, he wrote articles for *Chambers Journal* and *Cornhill Magazine* and it provided information for at least two chapters in *Wanderings of a Naturalist*. Yet he did not confine notes to diaries alone. In his papers at the National Library of Scotland is a file filled with notes and ideas. It is as if an idea would start to form, and whatever was at hand was used to get it down. There are envelopes, bits of ragged edged brown paper, an invitation to a Royal Garden Party on which there are notes about Viking galleys. On the back of a letter from the Gordons' solicitors, Gray and Kellas of Aberdeen, which refers to a surtax assessment notice, is written with only a few minor alterations the text of an article, 'Wildlife in the Highlands' – an indication of Seton's ability to lock out the everyday world, to which many of his friends and a few of his detractors have also made reference.

At the end of August Seton and Audrey left the west coast and returned to Deeside for the Highland Gatherings. On 3 September they attended the Aboyne Games, and the following day were at the Braemar Gathering, the first held since 1913. Seton was again special correspondent for the *Morning Post*. Although as before the war the local clans marched, they were fewer in number and too many men who had marched in 1913 were now in foreign graves, particularly those who had served in the Gordon and Seaforth Highlanders. These regiments recruited heavily in the counties of Aberdeenshire and Kincardine. Familiar names, though, appeared in Seton Gordon's dispatch. Charles MacIntosh was the Royal Standard Bearer, and Sandy McDonald was Standard Bearer for the MacDuffs. The return of the Royal Family was a moving moment, and they were received particularly warmly by the crowd. More uniforms were visible at this first post-war gathering, and few of the men were without decorations.

From Deeside, Seton and Audrey went south to Alnmouth in Northumberland where Audrey's Aunt Ella Pease lived. They remained there until spring, playing golf when they were not out on expeditions along the coast or into the Cheviots. Seton's diary gives little idea of how busy he was, yet he produced several articles on the area. He sailed out to the Longstone lighthouse on the relief boat, saw the tame 'St Cuthberts ducks' at Seahouses, and with Audrey went to Lindisfarne, or Holy Island, crossing through the spring tide-race in a pony and trap.

Piping lessons were resumed with Wullie Ross, Seton travelling to Edinburgh for them. On one occasion he heard John MacDonald of Inverness play. It was the start of a reverence for MacDonald's style and calibre which bordered on hero-worship. He heard MacDonald play 'The King's Taxes'. Seton noted: 'Excellent!'

Not until mid-April 1920 did they return to Oban. A number of stops were made at forestry plantations in the Highlands. At Courrour, the plantation was managed by a forester named Hewlett. In a diary note on 7 April, Seton wrote a quotation attributed to him. It is the only indication in the diary of the stress and frustration that he suffered through lack of success with job applications to the Forestry and Agricultural Departments. The note says: '1. Do as well as you can today, and perhaps tomorrow you may be able to do better. 2. The inner half of every cloud is bright and shining – therefore turn my cloud about, and always wear the inside out.' By Seton Gordon's own admission, despite the qualifications earned at Oxford, his extra-curricula studies both abroad and in the British Isles, and his ability to write on the subject, his interviews had not produced the desired results.

The quotation may have acted as a spur, because soon afterwards more articles were produced, more notes on article ideas were jotted down and there were several urgent reminders to himself to write to the Lecture Society. Articles were written on 'Birds of Deeside' for the *Scotsman*, and 'The Agyllshire Coast' for *Country Life*. By mid-May, three cheques netted £27. From this point also began a long period of bird-watching and travel, which lasted throughout the summer, leading to more articles, and his 1921 book, *Wanderings of a Naturalist*. It was as though Seton finally set aside any thought of a forestry career and made up his mind that he and Audrey would have to rely upon writing and lecturing as their main means of livelihood.

A further boost came with the publishing of his fourth book, *Land of the Hills and the Glens*. For this he drew extensively on his coast-watching years and placed a greater emphasis on the west coast of Scotland. Birds given a whole chapter to themselves include the buzzard, Arctic skua, heron, blackcock, ringed plover, white-fronted goose, and tern. There are chapters on Tiree, the Skerryvore Rocks, the islet of Ernisgeir, and Ardnamurchan Point. The book had a profound influence on many people and started them on a lifelong interest in natural history. The late Desmond Nethersole-Thompson was given the book as a school prize, though it was *Hill Birds of Scotland* and the later *Days with the Golden Eagle* which fired his imagination.

During the first week of May, Seton and Audrey returned to the Cairngorms for a study of both the greenshank and the dotterel, and they stayed well into June. On 10 May they arrived at the nesting site, surrounded by hills on which the snow still lay unbroken. Erecting a tent, they made themselves as comfortable as possible, and began to look for greenshank nests. The search took four days, and on the last, while watching a number of solitary males feeding by a small loch, one of the birds rose and flew a few hundred yards before dropping to the ground and disappearing. They reached the spot, and after a search found a female on the nest under a large dead pine branch. Four eggs were in the nest.

Next day they built a hide some distance from the nest, which was as well because returning the following morning Seton and Audrey were confronted by two egg collectors, with whom, in Seton's words, they had 'a slight brush'. Without revealing the location they informed the collectors that a nest had been found with a sitting greenshank which was to be observed and photographed. Fortunately a 'friendly' arrangement was made, and the collectors took off to try to locate another nest.

However, on the 17th, it looked as though the nest was deserted after all, as the eggs were cold. Two days later they found, with great relief, that the hen was again on the nest. They began to move the hide up closer, until by the 23rd it was within 15 feet. They had with them a new camera and hopes were high for good quality pictures. On 26 May, the hide was moved to within 8 feet of the nest. The day, one of 'brilliant sunshine and tropical heat', was not the most comfortable to be cooped up in the hide. The hen returned, but did not sit on the eggs. Seton was not too concerned about the length of time that she had left her eggs unbrooded, as the intense heat of the day would ensure their continued warmth. When finally the hen did return to the nest for some minutes, she panted continuously in the hot sun. The weather broke next day and remained cool and overcast for the following week.

Chipping noises began and on the 30th three young hatched. The fourth did not succeed: 'The mother greenshank seemed very proud of her young family, brooding them contentedly, though one of the chicks was restless and would not remain under her. She pushed it gently under her breast with her bill.'

On 3 June, Seton noted 'This is the eighth consecutive cool and misty day. This is getting serious! No photography can be done and every day precious at this season.' The next day he exposed six plates. Despite his concern the photographs selected for *Wanderings of a Naturalist* are of a very high quality.

With barely a break from the high tops, on the 9th the tent was struck and taken to the summit of Sgoran where a search began for dotterel. They set out for the summit of Braeriach at 3 a.m. and there watched for an hour and a half a pair of dotterel who fed quite unconcernedly. The sky was again cloudless and the sun warm, but a mist was creeping up through the corries and by 11 a.m. the thin tentacles had almost reached them. Returning to the tent, now enveloped in the mist, they slept until 2. p.m., then decided to descend to the Glen Einich bothy at least temporarily.

Reaching the summit of Braeriach again on 14 June, this time accompanied by Malcolm Barclay-Harvey, a south-east gale was blowing, the wind driving over a snow-filled corrie. A pair of ptarmigan with their young anxiously fluttered their wings and feigned injury to decoy them away. No dotterel nest was found until late in the evening of the 16th when one was spotted on a small grassy island surrounded by smooth gravel. In the nest, a shallow depression scraped out of the grass and lined with dried alpine willow leaves, were three attractively marked eggs.

Despite the wind and cold on the summit, the temperature in the glens was hot and, helped by lighting strikes, several forest fires erupted. Smoke could be seen clearly in several directions. Determined to stay until photographs could be taken, the three went down to Aviemore to get provisions. On the way they encountered a dangerous situation when passing through the Rothiemurchus Forest on Major J. P. Grant's estate. Walking along the shore of Loch Morlich, they were suddenly caught between two fires. Fortunately a squad of forest workers arrived at that moment and took over the fire-fighting efforts of the Gordons and Malcolm Barclay-Harvey. The fire swept right up to Drumintoul Lodge on the estate, but stopped short of destroying it. Finally Aviemore was reached, and Seton recalled, 'I well remember the horrified and shocked faces of the elderly tourists as we entered the hotel. This was before the days of oddly dressed hikers and so our smoke-grimed hands and faces, and our general disreputable appearance were the more obvious'.

The hide went up for the first time on the 24th, by which time the male, who did most of the sitting, had become so used to them that they were able to talk at normal pitch while the bird continued to sit. They were amused by his bored expression. On the 26th the diary reads: 'Could hear eggs chipping. Audrey approached to within a foot and the bird ran away, holding up one wing. He uttered a shriek of alarm as though feigning injury, but soon forgot his uneasiness and began to feed on insects. He went back to the nest after I entered the hide, and almost at once fell asleep. From 9.45 a.m. to 1.15 p.m. he twice left the eggs to feed, the first time for only five minutes, the second time for thirty-two minutes'.

Next day, returning to the hide at 11 a.m. they found two of the three eggs hatched. One chick had already walked a foot from the nest. Seton noted: 'An interesting discovery made about the young dotterel. Noticing they were unskilled in avoiding obstacles, we picked them up and saw that their eyes were still closed. During this time the hen never put in an appearance. Our last sight of her mate was a charming one as he brooded his young, with a plant of cushion pink with rich red flowers blooming profusely nearby. As we left him we wished him well.'

On 10 July Seton and Audrey sailed for the Outer Hebrides, from Kyle of Lochalsh to Lochmaddy. Although he had spent the first three years of the war on the west coast, and had revisited the inner islands since demobilisation, there was no record of Seton Gordon having crossed to the outer isles. For him this was a voyage of discovery, and the wet weather encountered in the coming weeks, the wettest July and August for several years, did not deter him from returning again and again. Neither did it diminish his belief that the outer islands were an extension of his spiritual realm.

In the Outer Hebrides there are over fifty islands of varying size. Because of the hundreds of sea lochs and the interspersing of blue tinged hills throughout, fringed in summer by the green machair and white sandy beaches, it is an inspiring seascape which can be captured particularly well in watercolour. The people, toughened by their environment, have a disarming and unaffected simplicity. The music, in danger of being lost until Marjorie Kennedy-Fraser set about recording it, was in keeping with the atmosphere of the islands.

One who appreciates Seton Gordon's feelings for the isles is Dr J. Morton Boyd, until 1984 Director of the Nature Conservancy Council, Scotland. Although he felt that Seton Gordon's books had a greater appeal to the layman, he wrote: 'Seton lived in wonderment of nature, and responded to the lives of animals and people with a remarkable sympathy and sensitivity. He wrote with a mysticism which was part real, and part imagination, in a simple way which endeared him to both laird and crofter.'

To understand the feelings that Seton Gordon developed for the Hebrides, it is necessary to examine them and the spell they have cast over so many people. To everyone in touch with the earth, there are locations which they descibe as 'magic'. It comes from an intuitive sense of being one with the landscape, the light, and the nuances of dimension, and goes far beyond a passing interest in a pretty view. It transcends ethnic origin, personal background, or any other trappings of culture. Those that possess this sense of oneness are blessed, whether it is for a specific place or many diverse ones. If they can convey it to others, either in words or music, so much the better. It is what Dr Morton Boyd meant when he described Seton Gordon's writing as 'mysticism which was part real, part imagination.'

The titles of the many books that have been written about the Western Isles are indicative of the spell placed upon the writers. Seton Gordon chose among others, *The Immortal Isles*, *Islands of the West*, and the *Charm of Skye*. The Rev. T. Ratcliffe Barnett used some of the most descriptive titles, *The Land of Lorne and the Isles of Rest*, *The Road to Rannoch and the Summer Isles*, *The Land of Lochiel and the Magic West* and *Scottish Pilgrimage to the Land of Lost Content*. Alasdair Alpin MacGregor's book on the 'Misty Island' was called *Over the Sea to Skye*. For another he took a line from a well known poem on Scottish exiles, attributed to Sir Walter Scott, for his title *Behold the Hebrides*:

From the lone shieling on the misty island,
Mountains divide us, and the waste of seas;
Yet still the blood is strong, the heart is Highland,
And we in dreams behold the Hebrides . . .

Each of these authors have, by their prose, communicated an idea, a place set apart from the rest of the world, almost as though another dimension has been manifested. Golden sunlight, distant blue hills, infinity.

The weather on Seton and Audrey's first visit to the Outer Isles could not have been worse, but at times it cleared to reveal many of the visual effects so familiar to readers of Seton Gordon's books. Landing at Lochmaddy on North Uist they visited the cottage of an old man named Lachlan MacDonald to inspect a chanter in his possession. He claimed that it belonged to the celebrated Patrick Mhor MacCrimmon. As they began their travels in the rain, Seton complained that the weather was almost useless for photography. Heading north to Harris, one of the first stops was at Rodel, to see St Clement's Church. He proclaimed it 'the most noble edifice in the Outer Hebrides'.

At Tarbert they found a comfortable hotel and the next day set out to climb Clisham, at 2622 feet the highest hill in the Outer Hebrides. On the summit wild thyme and violets bloomed, and the rocks held saxifrage. For the first time Seton could look eastward across the Minch or to St Kilda in the far Atlantic:

> A mist curtain extended all round except to the north, and while giving some fine effects it greatly restricted the view. Southward beyond Taransay, the Atlantic swell broke on the wild headland known as Toe Head, and on the broad stretch of sands known as Traigh Scarasta and Traigh an Taobh Tuatha, the sun shone. Beyond these were the hills of the Sound of Harris. In the distance could be seen, stretching out into the Atlantic, the north-west point of North Uist. Immediately below us the great Loch Langabhat lay blue in the sunshine. South-east lay Loch Seaforth, the crotal-dyed sails of two fishing boats showing up as dark specks against the water.
>
> Out in the Minch lay the Shiant Isles, soft sunshine lighting up their grassy slopes. Beyond rose the high ground of the north of Skye, and the flat topped hills known as MacLeod's Tables. The Cuillins were indistinct, their topmost slopes hidden in mist.

Seton and Audrey retraced their steps and continued on through Benbecula and South Uist until they reached Barra where two days were spent exploring before heading back to South Uist, climbing Easaval on one of the clearest days of their visit. South of Barra is the island of Mingulay, where at one time there was a population of more than fifty people. Because of its inaccessability, sometime before the First World War they were moved to the larger island of Vatersay – the cliffs which ring the island make a landing difficult. For the Gordons the problem was aggravated by a week of constant storm and a continuing swell. When, on 4 August, they were finally able to attempt a landing, a further aggravation was met: 'The spark plug conked out half a mile off Mingulay and had to finish off with our sails – bad landing place.'

Fortunately there was only light wind, though the sky was heavy with watery looking clouds. With the help of the calm sea a successful landing was made. Next morning was wild and stormy, a gale blowing from the north-east, causing heavy sea around the island. So great was the force of the wind, and so insecure and waterlogged the cliff top, it was impossible to venture near the thousands of nesting guillemots and razorbills. Throughout the day the gale continued, but by the next morning, 6 August, the wind had moderated and the sun shone brightly.

Mingulay is a nesting ground for enormous numbers of sea fowl, but there are only one or two places where it is possible to climb down to nesting birds. At one point – immediately below Biulacraig – the rock drops sheer 700 feet, and almost the whole way up the cliff guillemots and razorbills nest. The young of both species leave their nesting ledges for the water at the age of about ten days, many weeks before they are able to fly. Seton surmised that many fall from the ledges to the sea, perhaps being killed by some projecting point of rock. They saw, floating at the base of the cliffs, the small bodies of several unfortunate chicks which had come to an untimely end.

By 8 August, a freshening breeze and falling glass suggested more unsettled weather to come and they left the island. Next day a north-westerly wind brought more rough seas.

The Hebrides in the early 1920s was a different place than it is today. Living conditions for most of the people were primitive compared to the standards of even the most rural areas throughout the rest of the British Isles. The black-house was still a common dwelling, with a hole in the roof for the peat smoke to escape, and a dirt floor on which fresh sand was sprinkled periodically, yet the inhabitants had a dignity and outlook found in few other places. They were in touch with the elements, which circumscribed their lives. Although to Seton Gordon and other previously mentioned writers, a fine day in the outer isles is like a day in heaven, many wet ones have to be endured. This is hard on the crops, already difficult to grow because of poor soil, but with such as the islanders had, their corn, oats and barley, their cattle and a good supply of fish, they managed to maintain a distinctive lifestyle.

Simplicity is an attribute which has been largely lost; making the best of what is available, yet not wholly embracing materialism. It is, fortunately, still found in the Highlands and Islands to a greater extent than might be thought possible considering outside pressures, and it is refreshing to find. Seton Gordon wrote, 'To those who understand the isles, how irresistibly do they call. Those who have sensed their serene, benign atmosphere are drawn again and again, to gaze upon the glorious sunsets, to watch the moonbeams dance upon the waves, and to hear the musical clamour of wild geese. The people, in their simplicity, dignity and charm, are a race apart. They have retained the natural refinement and courtesy that distinguished the Highlander of old.'

Returning to Oban, a letter awaited Seton from John Johnston, who wrote that he had nearly died of a strangulated hernia – 'but I was saved by the good handling of the island doctor. He pulled me through, though I suffered terribly. I am now in comfort, but must keep the springbelt on and that in itself is very annoying.'

In contrast to these weeks in the isles, on the 19th, Seton Gordon left Oban for London. He called on his publishers, Cassell, to discuss his latest book, *Land of the Hills and the Glens*. Denys Finch Hatton was home from Africa, and they met at the Carlton Hotel for breakfast. It was of considerable interest to him that his golfing partner was now a successful writer, which Seton found flattering enough to mention in his diary.

At the end of August the Gordons travelled directly to Dinnet, where several old friends had gathered. Seton and Audrey cycled around the district and on one day rode to Aboyne to see 'the parent' and spent an afternoon with him. On the 8 and 9 of September they attended the Aboyne Games and the Braemar Gathering. A curt note on Aboyne says, 'Piping not good!' At the Braemar Gathering, Seton noted, 'Talked to King and Queen, King very interested in the piping.'

Following Aboyne and Braemar, came the Northern Meeting of Pipers, with a full week of programmes. Seton fully participated and had an opportunity to meet and talk with several pipers who were either legends, or became so later. Angus MacPherson and his brother John came respectively first and second in the pibroch competition for *'My King has landed at Moidart'* and later in the week John MacDonald of Inverness played 'Mary MacLeod' and *'I Got a Kiss of the King's Hand'*.

Angus MacPherson was proprietor of the Inveran Hotel in Ross-shire. Seton Gordon was drawn by his quiet modesty and their introduction at the Northern Meeting began an association that lasted for fifty-five years. Angus MacPherson's father, Calum Mhor MacPherson, was piper to Cluny MacPherson, and was said to be one of the greatest exponents of *piobaireachd* ever. Angus himself was for seven years, from 1898 to 1905, piper to Andrew Carnegie, the Scottish-American millionaire, whose Highland seat was at Skibbo. Angus sometimes accompanied Carnegie to the United States. John MacDonald of Inverness received much of his tuition from Culum Mhor, who taught only by *Canntaireachd*, or singing the notes as a means of passing on expression. Less than two weeks after the Northern Meeting, Seton Gordon received another letter from John Johnston. In it he said:

> . . . regarding the MacPherson pipers you mention, I never met with any of them. Being on an isolated island I had not the chance of meeting people of that kind but seldom. I had the secretary of the Edinburgh Pipers' Society here a few years ago, but playing him one of my best *piobaireachds* made no impression. He had a big *piobaireachd* book with him, and of course when my playing did not measure up to that, he thought little of it. Of course he was absolutely nothing, but he held his books as gospel, when they were actually worthless further than to keep the names of certain tunes in memory.

Two other men who attended the Northern Meeting regularly were Captain Robert Wolrige Gordon of Esselmont, and Major J.P. Grant of Rothiemurchus. Of all the anecdotes that have evolved from Seton Gordon's relationships with people in the Highlands, his friendship with these two was the most intriguing. In 1927 Robert Wolrige Gordon married Joan, the younger daughter of Dame Flora Macleod of MacLeod, and one of their sons, John, is now the present MacLeod Chief. Both Wolrige Gordon and Grant came from old families with large estates. It was not the fact that Seton Gordon came from a middle-class background, but that he had taken on a mantle that was as Highland as theirs. They could trace their ancestry and land-holdings through several generations, and here was someone who had set himself up as an historian and piping expert, who had come into their midst as an equal.

Another explanation, which came from Lieutenent Colonel Iain Grant of Rothiemurchus – another great Highlander, who died in July 1987, aged 73 – is that there was some resentment over the fact that Seton Gordon did not respond to an intensive recruiting drive early in the first war for those with expertise and knowledge of mountain terrain to join the Lovat Scouts. J. P. Grant and Robert Wolrige Gordon had distinguished war records, and the latter's death in 1939 was attributed to failing health from his war wounds. When Lord Vimy was the Governor General of Canada, he went to Canada as ADC. He and Grant had no knowledge of the fact that Seton Gordon had volunteered to drive an ambulance, and was on the point of going to France when he was asked to report to the Admiralty. As well, Robert Wolrige Gordon always felt that Seton Gordon sought publicity for himself too much! Colonel Grant felt it was to Seton Gordon's credit that his good nature and friendly disposition never allowed these criticisms to affect his association with these men. It is also likely that a degree of exaggeration on these friendships has crept in.

Some sources have referred to Seton being 'careful' with money. Whether this was true or not, he was very generous in other ways and always adhered to his belief in practising true Highland hospitality. The Gordons were very generous in putting people up and helping people less fortunate than themselves. People of all levels in the Highlands were delighted to have him and Audrey, and later his second wife Betty, as guests, whether in croft or castle, because he was so entertaining. Nobody seemed to mind his erratic hours and total absorption in things around him.

Seton Gordon was also attending the Northern Meeting in an official capacity as piping correspondent to several newspapers. A diary note for Monday 20 September reads – Got *Morning Post* with my account of Northern Meeting. Very poor account in *Times* – must have a word with them!

In January 1921, Seton Gordon received Johnston's final letters. He was in his eighty-fifth year. The first expressed a wish that he would see Seton again at least once, 'before I am off the stage' and thanked him for some clothing the Gordons had sent. The letter showed how hard life was for him:

> There are four of us, and no way of earning anything, there being no work, but I hope to be able to swim through after all, and will struggle on to the utmost of our ability. Meantime I hope you will not put yourself to any trouble about me; I hate the very idea of BEGGING, with the most enthusiastic hatred, yet I know it was from extreme kindness you remember me, and appreciate it so.
>
> I have done nothing on the chanter since you were here, and I suppose shall never be able to do anything at it again. But now I must stop as it is very cold sitting to write . . .

Seton replied on the the 17th. A lecture in Aberdeen on 18 January gave him another opportunity to visit his father at the house he had bought in Pitfodels,

Seton Gordon and Major J. P. Grant of Rothiemurchus judging piobaireachd *in the 1920s*

on the western edge of the city. The next evening he lectured in Dundee, then moved on to Edinburgh where on the 20th there was an audience of 1500 people at the Synod Hall, beating by seventy the best previous. In Glasgow where he lectured to 500 and met Osgood MacKenzie again. On 29 January came Johnston's last letter:

Lieut. Seton Gordon, RNVR Glencunich, Oban.

Sir,

I was very happy to read in your letter of the 17th that you have taken to lecturing. I presage a complete success and you will become a Sir Harry Lauder yet. Your interview with the King is a very good introduction itself, and a little incident of this kind goes a long way. I AM FULLY CONFIDENT OF YOUR SUCCESS, as you are just the very man for such. Of course you are fully aware of that, but my principal reason to refer to it is to instil confidence in you. That is very necessary for anyone who appears on a public platform, and I know you realise that fully.

I had a relapse a few days ago which I was afraid I would not get over. It came on suddenly and made me quite weak. My pulse rose to over a hundred in the minute, and lasted through that night and all next day, but thank goodness I am nearly as well as ever, although considerably weaker, but no wonder at my age.

May all success attend you. Keep confident in yourself as you contain a 'mine' which when developed will carry all before it. Other people will see it, more quickly than perhaps you do yourself. At all events, I hope to see you Sir Seton, yet. With best wishes and regards,

I am Sir, yours very sincerely, John Johnston.

John Johnson of the Isle of Coll, Coast-watcher and knowledgeable piper

In *Hebridean Memories* (1923) the chapter called The Island Piper ends:

> The old piper is gone now, and there is none on Coll, or Tiree to perpetuate the old compositions he loved so well. The tunes have died with him, and some of those he played are never heard at the present day. There are those that held his piping as incorrect, but then, the playing of pibroch is ever controversial among pipers, and it is scarcely fair to be too dogmatic with certain pipe music. Each school of piping at the present day asserts that its own rendering is the correct one, and it may be that the MacCrimmon's playing of the great tunes they composed is an art which they have carried with them onto that spiritual realm beyond the western horizons of the Atlantic, '*Riogh achd fo Thuinn*' – the Kingdom Beneath the Waves.

Although Johnston was almost unschooled, he had a way with words which though quaint at times, were capable of carrying his thoughts on a subject, and showed the variety of his interests. He was not afraid to take on people about historical matters, on one occasion taking part in lengthy correspondence in the *Oban Times* on the Norse occupation of Coll. His living conditions were primitive in the extreme, amplified by his reference to being too cold to write.

There is an interesting postscript to the story of John Johnston. In February 1960, Seton Gordon received a letter from Dr Hector Maclean of Grianan, Isle of Eigg:

> Dear Seton Gordon,
>
> I have just read your book *Afoot in the Hebrides* and I was surprised and delighted to find in it your description of John Johnston, the old piper of Coll. The fact that you learned some tunes from him means that you are almost certainly the only man alive who may be able to answer a question which has for long intrigued me.

My only previous knowledge of Johnston was derived from David Glen's publication *The Music of Clan MacLean*. In the preface to this work Glen states: 'I have also to tender my special thanks to Mr John Johnston, Isle of Coll, who journeyed especially to Glasgow, in order that I might write down some of his playing, several tunes belonging to this clan which were, so far as I could learn, known only to himself, and which his ancestors had learned from the Rankins, who were hereditary pipers to the MacLeans of Coll and Duart'.

Now, the only tune in this collection which is stated to have been 'written down by the compiler from the playing of Mr John Johnston of Coll,' is called '*Cas air amhich a Thighearna Chola*' – 'MacLean of Coll putting his foot on the neck of his enemy', and it has a special footnote as follows:

> 'This tune was written down by the compiler from the playing of Mr Johnston, who played the 'G E D cadence' as given in Example 1st. The usual method of playing this cadence is given in Example 2nd'.
>
> It has always seemed to me that this footnote does not make clear whether Johnston ALWAYS played the G E D cadence as noted here; or whether he did so only in this particular tune.

From your recollection of his playing can you tell me if this was indeed his usual style of playing the G E D cadence?

Yours sincerely, Hector Maclean.

Seton Gordon replied:

Dear Hector Maclean,

Your very interesting letter arrived last night. I knew Johnston when I was coast watching in World War I.

He was temperamental and I was one of the few people he liked – he would therefore play the chanter to me but to no one else.

As you infer, his cadences were quite original. Pipers poured scorn on them but I did not. There was a strange, primitive, and haunting charm in them as he played them, rather fast, on his practice chanter, his eyes tightly closed. ALL the cadences I heard him play were in the same unorthodox form. He was over eighty at the time but his memory and grasp were unimpaired. Yours sincerely, Seton Gordon.

P.S. The only piping authority Johnston thought much of was David Glen – and perhaps also Dr Bannatyne.

In 1921, Seton Gordon was invited to join the Oxford University Expedition to Spitsbergen as official photographer. Many of his companions later became distinguished scientists and naturalists, among them Julian Huxley, Charles Elton, a pioneer ecologist who later worked in the Canadian north, and Dr Thomas Longstaff (brother of Gilbert) who became a mountaineer of international status.

The expedition members sailed from Newcastle to Tromso on 7 June, where they waited for the expedition's ship *Terningen* to sail in from Bear Island, where it had dropped seven members to do field studies, among them the Rev. Francis Jourdain, the leader. During the three or four days spent at Tromso, Seton explored the neighbouring countryside and found a tremendous variety of bird life. The *Terningen* sailed again for Bear Island, reaching it on the 24th after a rough passage. His relief was great after four days at sea. It was an old ship and not very watertight. There was water on the cabin floor, and water dripping on his head as he lay in his bunk. He was concerned for the photographic gear, which was in danger of being ruined by the damp, but when Bear Island was sighted, Seton's discomfort was forgotten: 'I shall never forget that first sighting of the island, a mile or so distant. A grey misty morning. Mist almost to the water's edge. Many Brunnich's guillemots pass us as they head to their breeding rocks.'

On the 25th the *Terningen* reached Spitsbergen. There had been a constant fog-bow ahead of the ship as they sailed north, but as the ship nosed into Ice Fjord at mid-afternoon the fog suddenly lifted to reveal a magnificent view of the island's snow clad hills:

> The wondrous beauty is not easily described. Northward on the horizon arose the snow-encrusted spires of Prince Charles Foreland, flooded with the pale light of the Arctic sun. The blue of the Arctic sky is altogether a colour by itself, but the clearness of the air is, perhaps, the most wonderful thing; distances are deceptive; faraway hills seem near, though, of a truth, ethereal things.

At 10 p.m. the *Terningen* reached Advent Bay. A valley led up from the bay to great terraces of cliffs around which large numbers of Barnacle geese flew. Seton Gordon went ashore with Tom Longstaff to explore and they came upon a colony of little auks, literally in their thousands. Seton wrote in his log:

> As we descended, grey clouds floated above the fjord, which rendered more remarkable the delicate blue of the northern sky by contrast. The whole land was pervaded with a great, a wonderful stillness, a strange inscrutable silence which is the charm of this Arctic outpost.

Next day the *Terningen* sailed to Edinburgh Island, off Prince Charles Foreland. Continuing along the coast, it anchored off Vogel Hook, the most northerly point of the Foreland. Seton Gordon's log says:

> Self, J. Brown and Paget Wilkes were landed on Vogel Hook. A wild and desolate spot it looked in the gray misty light. The headland towered grim above us, its summit wrapped in gloom and mist. It was uncanny to hear, coming from out of the mist-cap, a babel of bird voices. Streams of Brunnich's guillemots flew in from the misty spaces of the ocean. Flying higher as they approached the cliff, they disappeared in the clouds as nesting sites were reached.

The three members were to traverse a desolate stretch of level land for about seven miles and rejoin the ship at Richardson Lagoon. This land was called the Aberdeen Machair, and another Scottish touch was that it lay at the base of a range of mountains named the Sidlaw Hills. Even this late in the season, there was no likeness to a machair, and it was, to Seton Gordon's mind, more a place of inconceivable dreariness. The terrain was so treacherous that they had to retrace their steps and keep to the ice-bound shore. For several miles they waded waist-deep through a bog of half-melted snow, their feet and legs numb with cold. They came across a cluster of ancient graves, the coffins exposed, many without their lids, yet no human remains were visible. On the graves was a mass of red *saxifraga oppositifolia*. A little over a mile beyond they came across the remains of a long wrecked sloop, stranded several feet above high-water mark. At last the *Terningen* came into view and at 5 a.m. Richardson Lagoon was reached. For Seton and his colleagues it was an anxious moment:

> The ship was a mile and a half off-shore. We hailed her, fired shots, everything in our power to attract her attention. She appeared lifeless and it was not until we had waited, shivering, a full four hours by the barren shingly shore of the lagoon that we were rescued from our plight.

Despite their discomfort, ornithology was foremost in their minds. A diver which flew in and settled on the lagoon, was, after careful watching, identified as a black-throated diver, a first recording for Spitsbergen. Soon after they returned on board, the *Terningen* sailed for Liefde Bay, where Seton Gordon took ashore a hide to study turnstone and grey phalarope. The next day, with the help of Tom Longstaff, he returned to the hide and continued observation of the turnstone. One of the eggs was chipping and the parents remained close by. The cock was even bolder than before and stood confidently on a large nearby rock, repeating his high-pitched whistle. In his log the entry for 3 July says: 'Noted the difference between them, how confiding the turnstone, and how suspicious the grey phalarope.'

Other members were also engaged in activity. The mate shot an ivory gull and Tom Longstaff shot two reindeer and a long tailed skua. In answer to a question as to why, on a natural history expedition a total of four reindeer, three puffins, a seal, a long tailed skua, and an ivory gull were shot (as reported in S.G'.s log, there were possibly others as well), Charles Elton replied to the author in 1986:

> Shooting game was quite natural in those days, and our people shot very little, when you consider that a shipload of ring-seals taken to Norway often amounted to 5000 skins or more! Further, the 1921 expedition was doing serious collecting of bird-skins and eggs for museums. Fortunately attitudes have changed nowadays. But note that with complete protection, the Spitsbergen reindeer have begun to overgraze their winter lichen feed, as happened with the introduced reindeer in Alaska, which reached a peak of 100,000 or so and crashed to 20,000 from starvation. They will, therefore, have to cull the [Spitsbergen] deer.

In a 1970 radio interview, Seton Gordon spoke of the difficulty of hide work when some of his colleagues were over-zealous in collecting species. He explained, with good humour:

> Some of these chaps were very keen about shooting birds and taking eggs, and as a bird photographer I couldn't work quickly. I had to put up a hide and spend several days with the bird. Some of the others thought this was a waste of time. Once I was photographing a bird on an ice-flow. There was a shot, the bird fell over and one of the members came up to me and said 'I hope you didn't mind my doing that, but I thought it might fly away!'

Several years after the expedition, Seton Gordon told naturalist-writer R. M. Lockley that Lord Grey of Fallodon had donated a large sum of money to the expedition on the understanding that nothing would be 'molested', and that he (Seton) had afterwards dissuaded Grey from protesting in *The Times*. He was forbidden to use his pictures taken on the expedition for one year, even though he had planned to help defray costs by donating his fees.

The most northerly piece of land visited by the *Terningen* was Moffen Island, at 80 degrees, 3 mins N. The date was 8 July, and the pack ice which stretched away to the North Pole was visible only about a mile distant. Although it was the warmest day encountered so far, a fog bank lay above the ice. The island is horseshoe-shaped, enclosing a large lagoon, and at high tide is no more than 6 feet above the water at any point. On the shingle by the lagoon entrance were several Spitsbergen eiders, and some were still brooding, on primitive nests, made of their own down and drifted seaweed. Hundreds of walrus skulls were scattered along the shingly beach. In an article on Moffen Island Seton reflected, 'Great numbers of these animals used to frequent the island, but they have been exterminated. Although Spitsbergen has been alloted to Norway, the treaty has not yet [March 1922] been ratified, and the fact that the archipelago has always been, and is still, a no-man's land has been unfavourable to its wild life. Walrus, polar bear, arctic fox – all have decreased alarmingly during recent years, for no protection can be afforded them. It is greatly to be hoped that Norway, if she takes over Spitsbergen, will frame strict laws for the protection of the wild creatures.'

The water in the lagoon was so clear that the bottom could be seen several fathoms down, and three of the expedition members were tempted into its cool depths – surprisingly Seton Gordon was not one of them. He could see 'water boatmen type' beetles at various depths and shrimp-like creatures on the bottom. Drifting ice flows and a fog bank on the northern horizon made the crew anxious to weigh anchor.

As the *Terningen* sailed south-west, bound for Magdalena Bay, the strains of the pipes were heard across the still water:

> Here, 80 degrees north, with the sun warm on my fingers, I tuned up the Piob Mhor – as the bagpipe is known to the Gael – and there drifted across the Polar sea the strains of two old *piobaireachd* tunes – 'Cumha Mairi Nic Leoid'

> and 'Cumha Chaisteil Dun Naomhaig.' I have wondered since whether the Ceol Mor has ever been played so far north; I think not.
>
> It was pleasant to find that the Norwegian crew took a great interest in the national instrument of Scotland. In many ways they reminded me of the West Highlander – indeed, the latter race has much Norse blood in it – and I was often requested to play the 'sack peep,' as they pronounced it, of an evening when we had come to an anchorage for the night.

One person who did not share the Norwegians' enthusiasm for the pipes was Charles Elton, who in the 1986 correspondence said they were not always appreciated by other expedition members. He personally felt 'conspicuous' when Seton and one other, whose last name was MacDonald, started to blow their bags.

At Magdelena Bay the scenery was the most magnificent seen so far on the archipelago. Seton's log entry says:

> At the head of the bay was the great Waggon Way Glacier. The bay ended in a high ice wall extending from this great expanse of snow and ice. Overall there brooded that mysterious and inscrutable atmosphere which I had learned to associate with the wilds of Spitsbergen. It is difficult to analyse this atmosphere. It is altogether aloof. There is nothing friendly in it, yet on the other hand, nothing sinister or forbidding.

Retracing its route, on the 12 July the *Terningen* arrived at Cape Boheman in Ice Fjord. With Jourdain, Huxley and Paget Wilkes, Seton Gordon visited a Dutch mining station, from where they were taken to see a purple sandpiper's nest with four eggs. Huxley erected a hide to photograph a grey phalarope's nest, and there is in the log a plaintive note: 'Jourdain took a King eider's nest, but I was given no opportunity to photograph it!' Dr Desmond Nethersole-Thompson knew Francis Jourdain well, and when asked about the seeming rivalry between him and Seton Gordon, aside from the question of egg taking, he said 'I heard both sides of the story. Jourdain and Paget Wilkes were quick walkers, but Seton was slow and steady. They set out to photograph certain birds' nests. Seton got so far behind that they [sometimes] took the eggs before he appeared on the horizon. Naturally he was a bit peeved! Personally although Jourdain was my greatest friend in ornithology, I had quite a bit of sympathy for Seton.'

On 19 July Seton Gordon wrote:

> I think today I realised for the first time why the streams of Spitsbergen are so inconspicuous at a distance. Their waters are of an opaque yellow-brown colour which closely harmonises with the hillsides themselves. To one familiar with the Scottish hills the apparent absence of water is at first curious. One misses the white torrents of the western seaboard of Scotland. Today, it is true, Ice Fjord more closely resembled a Highland sea-loch, for across its hills there hurried soft mists, such as play about the Cuillin hills of Skye, or swirl around the cone of Hecla of South Uist; and there was in the breath of wind a softness unusual for this arctic clime.

More so than any other of Seton Gordon's notes, this one gives a clue about his feelings for the west coast of Scotland. It is possible to read into these words a longing for the Highlands and Islands. Yet when the ship made a last landfall on the 21st, only he went ashore for a last walk on the archipelago, in the 'primrose' evening light, wandering up the valley through cotton grass and arctic poppies. He stopped to watch a pair of ringed plover flying around in agitation. He was sure that there was a nest nearby, but despite a two-hour wait, it was not revealed. Although well past midsummer day, the sun was still high at midnight as he walked eastwards up the valley, spotting ptarmigan feathers, but no bird. He walked until 2 a.m. before retracing his steps. At 5 a.m. he was again on board the *Terningen*.

This walk before departing from the archipelago is another illustration of what set Seton Gordon apart. Though all the expedition members were biologists, with a more than passing interest in nature, no one else stayed up to take a last lone walk and savour the uniqueness of this northern wilderness. On 22 July, the *Terningen* sailed for Tromso, where it arrived on the 26th. The crossing was uncomfortable, made worse by sharing a cabin with Jourdain, who spent much of the time blowing rotten eggs! A highlight on the 29 July was the first sight of the moon since the end of May, and on the 31st, the first sunset in many weeks.

Reflecting on the expedition, Seton Gordon wrote:

> To a naturalist, perhaps the most remarkable thing about the birdlife of Spitsbergen is the unlikely nesting places of the seabirds. Whereas in Britain no guillemot or fulmar would nest away from the sea, here they breed far up the valleys, choosing their nesting-places even above the snowline, breeding on narrow snow-free ledges of rock. Between Ice Fjord and Hinlopen Strait, fulmars were found nesting at a distance of twenty miles from the nearest sea; yet at their Scottish nesting-grounds, the fulmars are unwilling to fly across even the most minute strip of land.

During the course of the expedition, Seton Gordon identified a total of fifty-five birds, thirty of them on Spitsbergen, and the balance on the Norwegian coast. He also identified fourty-three plants, thirty-one on Spitsbergen and the others in Norway. No time was wasted in preparing a book on the expedition, *Amid Snowy Wastes* and it was ready for publication the following year. In his log he had already begun to outline chapters.

The concerns expressed by Seton after his visit to Moffen Island had some validity. There were Acts laid down by the Norwegian Government in 1925 and 1930 aimed at giving protection to birds and animals throughout Spitsbergen (Svalbard), but they were not strengthened by Royal Decree until the 1970s. It was not until 1973 that three national parks, two nature reserves and fifteen bird sanctuaries were established. In 1974 regulations were brought in to protect cultural monuments, such as burial mounds, cairns, urns, dwelling sites, bones and other human remains. Regulations concerning the management of 'game and freshwater fish' were introduced in 1978, but Moffen Island did not become a nature reserve until 1983. The first Plant Protected Reserve, at Ossian Sars Mountain in Kongsfjorden, was not established until 1984.

CHAPTER

5

CAIN AND ABEL IN THE EYRIE

As well as working on the Spitsbergen book, in 1921 Seton Gordon produced *Wanderings of a Naturalist*. Many of the book's fourty-four chapters were taken directly, or adapted from, previously written articles, but the scope of the book embraced pre-war visits to France and wartime service in the Inner Hebrides and Ireland.

Working on two books did not prevent him from attending a number of Highland Games in August and September, staying again at Dinnet in preference to Auchintoul. A day's walking with the Prince of Wales was arranged, and at Braemar, although not yet on the judging circuit, the King talked with Seton about the pibroch competitions. King George V took a great interest in piping, though not himself a piper. He asked many questions about the tunes being played and also asked Seton Gordon how his own pipers had done in the competitions. It is not difficult to see that this would cause eyebrows to be raised, especially when others were present who would consider their knowledge at least equal, and their right to the sovereign's ear greater.

Seton still preferred to walk through the Larig at night to be present for the games in Speyside, rather than take the long way around by train via Inverness. Few other pipers or judges were willing to accompany him on the long march over a rough trail.

The end of the year saw another Christmas holiday at Alnmouth and in early January 1922 Seton and Audrey visited Viscount Grey, as Sir Edward had now become, to see the Fallodon sanctuary. Grey created the sanctuary by fencing off several acres around two ponds, the largest just under an acre in size. The list of birds successfully reared at Fallodon is impressive. British surface feeding ducks – mallard, wigeon, pintail, garganey, teal, and shoveller – all nested and reared young. British diving ducks were the tufted duck, red-headed or common pochard, red crested and white-eyed pochard. Foreign ducks included spottedbill, Carolina wood duck, Mandarin, Chiloe wigeon, Chilian pintail, Bahama pintail, Chilian teal, Brazilian teal, Jalcated duck, blue-winged teal, Japanese teal, versicolor teal and Rosy bill.

The sanctuary was started in February 1884 when Grey was sent down from Oxford for two months because of dilatory work habits. He returned in June and did well enough to earn a BA, though he never collected it. His first Oxford degree was an Honorary DCL in 1907, and he became Chancellor of the University in 1928. In 1885 he embarked upon a course of reading in history, philosophy and poetry, entirely for his own pleasure, won a seat in Parliament by a comfortable majority, and married Dorothy Widdrington.

Seton Gordon was drawn to Grey by his recognition of a kindred spirit who shared a love of nature which was for them almost beyond the realm of expression. Yet both felt compelled to try, with results that have bridged several generations. They were introduced by Ella Pease, who was one of Dorothy Grey's greatest friends. Ella was warm, unpretentious, and gifted with common sense, all of which appealed to Grey, and he regarded her as a confidante, writing letters on matters of state, such as the letter on his concern for the Kaiser. In another, sent from the United States in 1919, he wrote of his high regard for the American people, finding life in Washington more tolerable than in London.

Towards the end of April Seton and Audrey once again crossed to the Outer Isles, to see the swans on Loch a'Mhachair in South Uist, the home of almost 100 wild swans. Despite some illegal shooting in the war years, the numbers have more than doubled to the present day. At nearby Grogary, is Ormiclate Castle, which they explored, and Seton Gordon noted in his diary on 24 April, 'Where MacDonald of Clanranald left from, and his wife had a vision.' This simple statement does not adequately tell the story of MacDonald of Clanranald and the destruction of his castles.

Clanranald had been 'out' with the Earl of Dundee at Killiekrankie in 1689 and after the slaying of Dundee in the battle, he lived for a time in France, where he married Penelope MacKenzie, daughter of Colonel MacKenzie, Governor of Tangiers under Charles II. When Clanranald and his bride returned to Uist, Ormiclate was rebuilt, taking seven years. They then lived in it for seven years. Then came the rising of 1715, and Clanranald was killed at Sheriffmuir. On the night on which he died the house was burned down, through the chimney catching fire. Some days before this double tragedy the Lady Clanranald had confided to her guests that she had experienced a terrible vision, in which her eyes were dissolved in boiling water and her heart was was burnt like a glowing coal of fire.

Another Clanranald stronghold, Tioram Castle at Kinlochmoidart, was burned on the same day, on the orders of the same chief. This was done because as Clanranald set out with his clansmen, just as he had done twenty-six years before in support of James II, a strong premonition came upon him that he would not return. Fearing defeat for the Stuarts he said: 'Better that our familty seat be given to the flames than provide shelterr to those who are about to triumph over our ruin'. It is not recorded whether he discussed his premonition with Penelope, which may have been the cause of her nightmare. Neither castle was rebuilt, but Tioram is in a better state of repair than Ormaclate.

Before returning to the mainland the Gordons purchased a length of Harris Tweed woven in dark blue flecked with crotal (brown). It provided enough material for a kilt jacket and waistcoat for Seton, and a suit and two skirts for

Viscount Grey of Fallodon with tame robin, photographed by Seton Gordon in 1931. The Gordons were frequent guests at Fallodon

Audrey. While with the weaver, they learned the various steps then used in the making of the tweed. Seton Gordon noted that the final act of making the tweed is the 'waulking' or shrinking, from which comes the Hebridean waulking songs. Many of these have a primitive and haunting melody:

> Young women are usually the waulkers. They sit at a long table, at one end of which the tweed lies soaking in a tub of urine. Yard by yard it is circulated around the table. As it passes each waulker she pounds and squeezes it vigorously. Waulking is accompanied by singing of a distinctive type, the rhythm very pronounced as each person pounds the tweed with the measure of the song.

The process of making Harris Tweed has since become mechanised, though its sales increased dramatically after the Second World War, mainly to the United States. Unfortunately in recent years sales have declined because of a desire for lighter fabrics. To meet this demand producers in the Hebrides are experimenting with lighter forms of the tweed and new designs and colours are being offered.

It is fortunate that someone with such empathy and a discerning eye saw and recorded Hebridean life in the years before the Second World War. Island life had seen little change then and Gaelic was still the predominant language, but since the end of the war, many changes have come. In recent years there has been a renewed interest in preserving Gaelic as a living language, not only in Scotland, where a Gaelic business college has been started on Skye, but in some of the Maritime Provinces of Eastern Canada. Gaelic courses are now being given in Eastern Canadian Universities. At the turn of the century Gaelic speakers represented 5.1 percent of the population of Scotland. The census of 1981 showed that this was down to 1.6 percent, the majority living in the Western Isles, where 23,000 people, or 80 percent spoke Gaelic. When Seton Gordon first visited the Hebrides many people could speak no other langauge than Gaelic. It could not have been foreseen that within forty years there would be such a dramatic drop in its use. The decline in population was another factor. Many schools that had a full complement of pupils at the turn of the century were closed by the start of the Second World War. The nearest school to Seton Gordon's home, Kilmuir, had 115 pupils in 1900. In 1937 it was 80, and by 1950 only 45.

The year after Seton Gordon's death, the Western Isles Council approved a bilingual policy. Street signs are in both languages, some council meetings are held in Gaelic and council chambers are equipped with simultaneous translation facilities. Radio and television broadcasts are made in Gaelic not only in the isles, but in Inverness and Glasgow.

Although Seton Gordon was not a fluent Gaelic speaker, he had some knowledge of the language and was very interested in place names. He corresponded with Professor W.J. Watson, head of Celtic studies at Edinburgh University, throughout the 1920s and 1930s. Watson's son, James Carmichael Watson, followed his father in the position and gave up the Chair to serve as an ordinary seaman in the Royal Navy. He lost his life in action in the Mediterranean early in the Second World War.

The Gordons returned to the Outer Isles on 3 July and remained until 9 August. They journeyed north to see the summer shielings on Lewis, the only island where the practice still occurred. Seton Gordon wrote:

> How delightful it must be to set out for the moorland on a fine June day with one's dog and cattle and live simply during the two finest months of the year.
>
> It was late one evening when we reached the shielings. The air was still, and here and there across the moor the blue peat smoke from the sheilings rose into the air.
>
> The sun set, and the cows were herded in and were tethered around the dwellings. Against the setting sun could be seen the neighbours of our host driving cattle to their shielings. Here and there boys and girls were talking together, perhaps discussing the arrival of the strangers. The peat fire was fanned and we sat down to a wonderful meal, followed by piping and dancing on the rough moorland, and sweet voices sang old Gaelic airs. It was after midnight when the *ceilidh* came to an end.
>
> A shieling has two entrances and a screen is placed on the windward side, leaving one open. If the wind shifts the screen is moved to the other side, so light is always flooding in.
>
> Next morning more peats were placed on the fire and soon we were sitting down to a memorable breakfast. The breath of heather entered the room with the breeze, and outside the grass waved and nodded. This very day, shieling life would end for the year, and the children are particularly sorry to leave moorland and lochans where the moonbeams played during the short summer nights.

Although Seton Gordon paints an idyllic picture of shieling life here, much of it was borne out by Dr John Smith, Head of Microbiology at Vancouver General Hospital. Born in Lewis in 1936, in his early years he did not speak English. Smith's family was one of the last on the island to have a summer shieling, and he has strong memories of them preparing for their journey across the moors to the grazing land for the summer:

> The shieling was really a one room bothy. The outside wall was a mixture of turf and stone, two or three feet thick, the roof constructed of low quality timber in the form of a ridgepole, with joists across, overlaid with turf. A hole in the end of the roof was the chimney. The fireplace was all stone, ideally a flat piece of rock with two sides built up, where the peat was laid. We became quite skilled at adjusting the smoke outlet so that it did not blow into the interior. It was a very simple device. All you needed was a stick, as you created the chimney out of a turf which was propped up with the stick on the windward side of the chimney. This enabled the fire to draw perfectly. If the wind changed you hopped up and adjusted it again.

By 1922, Seton Gordon had visited the Outer Isles on four separate occasions, seeing shieling life in the old way. The material collected was used in his first book entirely on the islands, *Hebridean Memories*.

Seton's finances were now much better, and cheques were coming in very regularly, the largest one to date £18 from the *Scotsman*. From 1 January, to the end of March 1923 he earned £117–9–6d, and by 30 June had increased to £318–12–3d. Much of this was earned giving lectures to schools and clubs. The faithful Wolsley, mainly known as Horace but sometimes confusingly called Horatio, was still going strong, and driving from Oban to Deeside in September, Seton recorded that Horatio reached 48 m.p.h.! Although not yet on the judging circuit he was treated as more than a spectator at that year's Highland Games, and at Braemar lunched with Lord Aberdeen and his family. He noted – 'marvellous day – flight of oyster-catchers passed over games field, also golden eagle.'

Audrey took her share of lecturing, by visiting girls' prep and public schools around the country, but remained at home during the winter 1922–1923. On 16 February 1923 she gave birth to another daughter, Audrey Bridie Seton Gordon, whose second name, the one always used, came from the fact that February is Saint Bride's month. Lord Wardington, a relative of the Pease family, and Mrs MacDonald of Barguilean, accepted the responsibility of godfather and godmother to Bridie.

A happy child with a wonder for the world, and a way of expressing it, Bridie was aptly named through her father's knowledge of the feasts and festivals of the Gael. Caitriona, by this time seven years old, was much more serious and introspective, but both grew to be delightful children, of independent character, with much of their parents' love of the outdoors.

In the April following Bridie's birth, the emigrant ship *Marloch* sailed from Lochboisdale, South Uist, carrying fifty families from various parts of the Outer Isles to St John, New Brunswick. From here they travelled across Canada by train to Red Deer, Alberta. With other journalists, Seton Gordon joined the ship at Glasgow on the 14th, to witness the embarkation. He described it in *Hebridean Memories*, published later that year:

> Lochboisdale was, this April morning, the scene of yet another great departure of Islemen. Over 300 men, women and children were being embarked on the Canadian Pacific steamer *Marloch* for the Red Deer area of Alberta.
>
> Shortly after 7 a.m. she steamed slowly into South Uist, anchoring about a mile off the entrance to Lochboisdale. At noon the small steamer *Dunara Castle*, hove in sight to the southward, bringing with her 100 emigrants from Barra. There were one or two men of sixty, or thereabouts, bearded and deeply bronzed, with fine open faces; but the majority were considerably younger. Their wives and families accompanied them, anxious-faced women in head shawls of various colours, white, brown, or tartan.
>
> The *Dunara Castle*, which was acting as a tender for the *Marloch*, approached the pier to pick up the emigrants assembled there. Fully 1500

people were beside, or on the pier. Nothing like such a concourse had ever been seen on the island.

The sun shone and a piper provided cheerful music upon the pier. A freshening wind was forming wavelets on the loch. Many miles to the east, hazy and ethereal in the strong sunlight, stood Rhum with its conical peaks, and northward of it the serrated summit of the Cuillins of Skye.

Tearful farewells were heard in the Gaelic tongue – '*Beannachd leth*' (Blessings be with thee) one heard constantly spoken. Those sailing kept a smiling and cheerful face towards the land, which some of the older people were probably looking at for the last time.

A piper who was making the long overseas journey, played such animated marches as '*MacDonald of Glencoe*' and '*The Highland Wedding*', pacing up and down the after part of the vessel. On shore a second piper was playing in time with the first. The *Dunara Castle* cast off her moorings. There was a sudden fluttering of handkerchiefs. Cheer after cheer came from those on shore. Cheer after cheer was returned across the water.

Up to now, nothing but cheerful pipe music had been heard, but as the boat slipped across the waters of Lochboisdale, one of the oldest of the men who were sailing from his home, snatched his pipes from where they lay on deck at the ship's bow and played with deep feeling the mournful strains of an old Gaelic air. It seemed to voice the sorrow of that company of wanderers. The pipes were not in tune and the execution did not compare with that of the previous players, yet that sad melody will always remain in my mind, '*Cha till mi tuilleadh*' (I return no more). It was played with a heart that was heavy with sorrow.

The wind freshened and something of the emigrants' foreboding seemed to have entered the weather itself. The air was chill, the sun's rays failed to warm the heather-clad banks of the loch. A party of handsome eider drakes with their attendant ducks of silver plumage flew rapidly downwind over the loch, unmindful of the great gathering of people on shore. It was sunset before the *Marloch* sailed. In the twilight she weighed anchor and steered south to Barra Head, and then west for her far distant destination of St John, New Brunswick.

[See Appendix 1]

At about this time the Gordons moved once more, this time to Aviemore, to yet another rented house. It was the last one before purchasing their own. Aviemore is more central, with quick access to Inverness and Edinburgh by train, though not so convenient for Aberdeen and the Dee Valley.

A series of letters began from William Gordon on the question of ancestry. Seton desired to establish the correct lineage of the family and hoped that his father would provide some information on it. On 27 September he informed Seton: '. . . the crest of the Gordon of Auchintoul is given in Bollough's book as a demi-boar proper with the motto BYDAND, and the crest of Gordon of Ardmeallie (Banffshire) as a boars head erased or, with the motto BYDEBE. This seems to be the one we have assumed, rightly or wrongly.'

On 8 October he wrote again: 'I'm sorry I cannot throw any light on the crest question but I am quite content to stand by the old boar's head whether Ardmeallie or Auchintoul. In my view BYDEBE has much more of the dash about it than the milk and water BYDAND unless this word is divided into two and used in a minatory sense i.e. 'Byd! and –' (you will see what will happen to you by so doing).'

There followed several letters on the subject, and also on the Huntly (District) tartan. The final communication on the subject came in the form of a terse memo at the end of November:

> I daresay I could, if you wished it, procure a copy of the old Huntly tartan design – but is the game worth the candle! You will simply produce an ugly red tartan, which you would always have to explain was at one time the tartan of the Huntly District, but has long ago been discarded and fallen into disuse. If you have any means of getting a tartan hand woven, it appears to me that the 'Antient' Gordon would be much more attractive and effective.
>
> W. Gordon.

(Seton's cousin, John Cook, in assisting the author with clarification of these letters said: 'From these it is clear that William leaned towards the Ardmeallie descent rather than Auchintoul. It looks from the second letter as if he did so from a simple preference for the Ardmeallie motto. I agree that this is strangely lax for so precise an individual, but convenient arrangements of one's ancestry were commonplace in the nineteenth century, and searches much less rigorous than they are today.')

Seton Gordon went ahead and had a kilt made of Huntly tartan, and was joined by Robert Wolrige Gordon and the then chief of the Gordon clan, the Marquess of Huntly. The present Robert Wolrige Gordon, brother of John MacLeod of MacLeod wrote:

> When the late Lord Huntly found a pattern of the old Huntly District tartan, he, my father and Seton all wore it. In fact I cannot remember Seton in any other tartan. My father wore it shooting, so did I until my one fell apart. My brother John wears it (although he is now a MacLeod).

October and November were busy months for lectures. A list of titles covered subjects ranging from the Golden Eagle – Seabirds and Seals – the Cairngorms – the Hebrides – Scottish Islands and Outposts – Glens, Hills and Lochs – to Spitsbergen. In 1923 the locations of the lectures were Fettes, Edinburgh; Merchiston Castle School, Edinburgh; Edinburgh University Christmas Lectures; Greenock Philosophical Society; Leith Thursday Club; Glasgow Palette Club; the Bank of England Library and Literary Association, London; Alton Burn Prep School, Nairn (attended later by Alasdair Gordon and John Cook); St Hughes School, Bickley; Wellington House, Westgate on Sea.

For the modest fees received, there was a great deal of travel. Fortunately at that time there was a network of railway branch lines and a frequent train service. The slide boxes and lanterns were heavy and the journeys, by present day standards, were tiring and dirty. In the days of steam there was the acrid smell of coal smoke and wisps of it drifted into the carriages. It of course helped if lectures could be grouped, though it was not always possible and sometimes they had to return to a town to which they had already been just a few days previously to accommodate a neighbouring school. One area which proliferated in preparatory schools was the Thanet Peninsula, with at least twenty schools, most of them for boys. One of them was St Peter's Court at Broadstairs, attended by several people who recall Seton Gordon's visits, among them Captain Alwyne Farquharson of Invercauld, and Donald Bell, son of the late Follet Bell and the Hon. Pamela Bell. The Hon. Edward Adeane, one-time Personal Secretary to HRH the Prince of Wales attended nearby Wellesly House School. He recalls attending a Seton Gordon lecture on the golden eagle, and being woken up the next morning by the sound of bagpipes. Seton was playing them in the school swimming bath. Adeane hastened to add that there was no water in it at the time.

In Edinburgh he lectured to a large crowd at the Central Hall in Tolcross, and was honoured by having Sir John Lorne-Macleod, a one-time Lord Provost of the City, in the chair. Sir John later became President of the Clan MacLeod Society after Dame Flora became Chief. Three days later, on 7 March, William Gordon died suddenly while preparing to set out for the Townhouse. The *Aberdeen Press and Journal* ran a four column obituary on him under a large photograph of the portrait painted by Feddes Watt for the city in 1919.

With the passing of his father, the proceeds of the estate which included both the Pitfodels and Aboyne homes, became Seton's. It made a considerable difference to their financial position. When William Gordon's estate was settled, Seton Gordon became the owner of 'Auchintoul', the lodge at Aboyne, and 'Arnlee', the house at Pitfodels. The latter had no appeal as a family home and was sold. With the proceeds a substantial house was purchased at Granish, about a mile north of Aviemore. He named the house 'Achantoul', so he now owned two houses with essentially the same name. The Aboyne house was kept for several years. There was little incentive to sell; when at the end of the year the rates came in for the Aboyne chalet, they were £6–3–10d for the country 'birse' and £2–15–7d for the parish rates.

'Achantoul' is a stone house, built on a slight bank on the west side of the road, with a magnificent view of the Cairngorms, particularly of the Lairig Ghru pass, which it faces directly. The country to the base of the mountains is flat, and south-east in the middle distance, it is possible to make out the roof and chimneys of Drumintoul Lodge on the Rothiemurchus estate, until his death in 1987 the home of Lieutenant Colonel Iain Grant of Rothiemurchus. The question of furnishings and pictures became important, and a first contact was made with Poolewe watercolour artist, Finlay MacKinnon, specifically for paintings to hang in the new house.

Seton Gordon was now a property owner, with a permanent base in the central Highlands. Before June was finished he received his first invitation to judge piping. The occasion was the combined Seaforth and Cameron Highlanders' sports day at Nairn. Another army invitation came at the end of July to judge at the Gordon Highlanders' sports day at Fort George. Judging invitations began to come in from all quarters; in August the Crieff Gathering, Lochaber Games, and Portree Games; on 10 September for the Oban Games, where with Ronald Cheepe and Lechie Ewing he judged the competitors for march, strathspey and reel.

On 17 June, at Aviemore, Audrey gave birth to Donald Alasdair Seton Gordon. A homely diary note reads, 'D.A.S. Gordon arrived 11 a.m. after having made a preliminary announcement at 3 a.m. and again at 8 a.m. Fine dull day – warm and summery.' Alasdair's godparents were distinguished. They were Admiral Sir Arthur Farquhar, Denys Finch Hatton, and Mrs Graham Menzies of Halliburton.

With Charles Farquhar, a brother of the admiral, and another friend, General Sheppard, the Gordons took a lease on a North Uist shoot, where they stayed for the month of October. The shoot consisted chiefly of snipe ground, though it contained several lochs where brown trout could be had. One of the larger lochs contained excellent sea-trout, which swam up from the sea by way of a small peaty burn through the moor. Both Seton and Audrey had considerable success with these, though Seton lost a sea trout which the ghillie estimated at over 7 lbs. On one day, between his catch and Audrey's, they landed a total of twelve trout.

Aside from fishing, Seton and Audrey's days were filled with other interests. On one occasion they helped two very old Gaelic speaking men with their corn, and on another helped a neighbouring crofter with his harvest for an entire day. They visited an old Gaelic speaking lady in her blackhouse and took pictures of her spinning outside her door. It is interesting to compare John Smith's description of the shieling dwellers' ability to eliminate peat smoke, and Seton Gordon's word picture of this blackhouse:

> The house had no chimney, and in the centre of the room a peat fire burned, its smoke escaping through the crannies in the thick walls, through the open doors, and through the hole in the roof. In the room the blue peat smoke hung so thick that it was difficult at first to distinguish the old lady at her spinning wheel. Yet the room was spotlessly clean, and the earth floor was sprinkled with sand, carried up from the shore with much labour.
>
> She had never left the island, yet she possessed that indefinable charm and dignity which many people well endowed with this world's goods would have given half their life to acquire.

A significant ritual for many years in the islands was the 'smooring', or banking of the peat fire. Islanders kept their fires burning twenty four hours a day, but they were banked up at night. In Alexander Carmichael's *Carmina Gadelica* is an incantation for the smooring, which Seton Gordon quotes in *The Immortal Isles*. Carmichael describes the procedure, which was practised for centuries:

The ceremony of smooring the fire is symbolic, and is performed with loving care. The embers are evenly spread and formed into a circle, which is divided into three, a small 'boss' being left in the middle. A peat is laid between each section, each touching the boss. The first is laid in the name of the God of Life, the second in the name of the God of Peace, the third in the name of the God of Grace. The circle is covered with ashes sufficient to subdue but not put out the fire, in the name of the Three of Light. The heap in the centre is called the '*Tula nan Tri*', the Hearth of the Three. When the smooring is completed the woman closes her eyes, stretches her hand, and softly intones:

An Tri numh	The sacred Three
A chumhnadh	To save,
A chomhnadh,	To shield,
A chomraig	To surround
An tula,	The hearth,
An taighe,	The house,
An teaghlaich,	The household,
An oidhche,	This eve,
An nochd,	This night,
O! an oidhche,	O! this eve,
An nochd,	This night,
Agus gach oidhche	And every night,
Gach aon oidhche.	Each single night.
Amen.	Amen.

Early editions of *Carmina Gadelica* were bound in white to emphasise the spiritual nature of their contents. The volumes are divided between invocations and incantations. The invocations are prayers and blessings for different occasions – the seasons and special days such as Christmas, Hogmanay, Beltane, St Bride, Michaelmas and Hallowe'en. Invocations also include labour – under which the smooring of the fire is found, but also reaping, milking, herding, shearing, weaving, and fishing. Incantations cover both charms and spells, such as charms for bursting veins, sprains, jaundice, toothache, swollen breast, indigestion, love, thwarting, and exorcism of the evil eye.

Carmichael spent years collecting these, and was only just in time. Stories and songs were lost under the influence of narrow minded church ministers, who condemned and ridiculed the people. Often it was 'educated' young islanders who ridiculed their own relatives. Carmichael's great empathy with the people of the isles shows in his introduction to the first volume:

> During all the years that I lived and travelled among the people of the Outer Isles, I never met with incivility, never with rudeness, never with vulgarity, never with aught but courtesy. I never entered the house without the inmates offering me food, or apologising for their want of it.

Seton Gordon was influenced a great deal by the *Carmina Gadelica* and quoted from it frequently. There were other myths that Seton Gordon wrote about. Many of the *ceilidh* subjects were of fairies, fiery dogs, will o' the wisps, mermaids, serpents and assorted monsters. There were also near-human heroes, such as Cuchulainn and Fionn of the Fingalians, whose exploits between Ireland and the west of Scotland showed them to have exceptional powers. One myth which held for many years in the Inner Hebrides and parts of the mainland was the *Each Uisge* (*Ye-achh Ooshkuh*), the water-horse. The *Each Uisge* took the form of a black stallion without a mane. It would assume the human form of a handsome man, who could easily entice young maidens, whereupon they would be carried off to a peaty lochan and plunged into the murky depths, never to be seen again. As Seton Gordon came across these tales he made pages of notes in his diary memoranda and gradually they were interwoven into articles and chapters.

For the balance of 1924 he concentrated on his eighth book, *The Cairngorm Hills of Scotland*, in readiness for publication the following year. There were only five recorded lectures, two schools in Midlothian – Cargilfield and Dreghorn Castle; a talk on Spitsbergen to the Edinburgh Young Scots' Society, and a talk entitled *Hill and Glen* to both the Lanark Natural History Society, and the Architectural Association.

Now began several months of intense activity and study of a golden eagle's eyrie, which culminated in the publication of Seton Gordon's first book devoted entirely to this bird, *Days with the Golden Eagle*, published in the spring of 1927. Much of the book covers a two month period starting 10 May 1925, when a nest was discovered which contained two eggs, to 16 July when the last eaglet, a male, finally took flight. The observation was interspersed with trips to the Outer Isles and other activities, and totalled thirty-one days and 167 hours of observation.

On 10 April one of the eagles was observed soaring. Seton and Audrey made a line to where it disappeared into the trees on a hillface about a mile from where they stood. After a strenuous climb, they arrived approximately at the place where the eagle alighted. Climbing a little higher, Audrey spotted an eyrie so large that it covered the crown of the old Scots pine on which it rested. A spot was found for a hide barely 30 feet from the nest. They saw two eggs, one richly marked with red splotches and the other white, and almost unmarked.

They returned on 10 May by which time two eaglets had hatched and were about eight days old. A hide was constructed and gradually moved up. Seton took the first watch from 11:30 a.m. on the 13th. The birds had grown noticeably in those few days, and the female, stronger and more powerful as is often the case, demonstrated cruel behaviour to the young male, reigning vicious blows upon his head with her beak. Sometimes the male is killed during the first five or six weeks after hatching, and both young have been known to die when, in a chase around the nest, they topple out. During this first watch the male was attacked three times, the last one leaving him stunned. A freshly plucked grouse lay in the nest on which they fed from time to time. By the end of the day two more had been added.

The weather was cooler than usual for the season, and the only thing which made the watches bearable was the ongoing spectacle of the female eaglet's cruelty to her brother: 'She pecked him without mercy, several times driving him almost to the edge of the eyrie. Just as it seemed he must fall, she caught him with her bill and swung him back into the centre of the eyrie. The fate of the younger bird hung in the balance at this time, and since she seemed bent on killing him, we named her Cain, and her brother, Abel.'

In the late afternoon of the 20 May Seton had his first close view of the hen. The weather was warmer and the forest was filled with the scent of birch and blaeberry. At 6:20 p.m. the mother returned with a freshly caught hare which she shared with her young. As dusk approached she appeared to settle in for the night, and as it would be critical to depart when either parent bird was on the nest, Seton wondered if he would have to remain in the hide. She suddenly became alert to some far-off sound, and soared off, so that Seton hurridly left the hide and scrambled down the hill. Audrey had made their collie, Dileas, bark to distract the eagle.

The following morning Audrey entered the hide at 6:30 to be rewarded with the sight of the adult male returning with a grouse in his talons. Audrey was witnessing a rare event, as the male rarely fed the young. Though his every gesture was regal, he was smaller than his mate and lighter in colour.

At midday, Seton settled in for a long watch. The parents were absent and there was silence until one of them appeared, causing Cain to yelp loudly but it brought no food, and the adult sailed on without returning to the nest. All the time, Abel cheeped miserably. Cain crossed to her brother and as though to pass the time, aimed several blows to his 'behind'. After a few more blows he fled to the edge of the eyrie and lay down. Cain pursued him and now struck him repeatedly on his back. Tiring of this, she then tore off some grouse flesh, possibly the first time that she had fed herself.

Just after 5 p.m. the hen returned and fed Cain, while Abel lay some feet away. It at last occurred to her to feed her other offspring, and with a 'dejected mien' he took a half-dozen mouthfuls and refused more. Cain's appetite was tremendous and Seton observed:

> This gorged and satisfied eaglet looked with contempt upon poor Abel lying beside her without appetite. Once her mother gave Cain a bone, who almost choked the first time she tried to swallow it, but succeeded on the second attempt.

By 26 May, Abel looked much healthier, and it was no longer expected that he might one day be found dead, or to have disappeared from the eyrie. Cain was now growing tail and wing feathers that looked like black edging. At 1:10 p.m. the cock returned with a plucked grouse which he dropped into the nest, barely pausing in flight. Neither parents had returned when Seton left at 6:30 p.m., the eaglets showing their hunger by furious calling.

On the 28th, Seton took up his position at 11:40 a.m. It was a day of sunshine and great dark, slow-moving clouds, the surrounding peaks in turn hidden, then bathed in sunlight. Heavy rain squalls occasionally moved across the view. A fierce storm struck the hide at 1:30 p.m. and in its midst the mother eagle appeared, creating a memorable scene:

> While the storm was at its height the mother alighted then walked to the windward side of the eyrie to shelter her young. As the storm became, if possible more fierce, they lay together, happy and quiet. After a time one of them tapped upon her bill, and to this child she gave a kiss – or its equivalent.
>
> The eagle made a magnificent picture in the deep gloom, as the wind rushed through the pines and in the glen far below, the sunlight gleamed. The eyrie swayed rhythmically in the gale; the eagle's tawny plumage became matted with moisture, and from her bill the raindrops fell in a steady drip.

When finally, after a six-hour watch, Seton crawled from the hide he was so stiff and cold that he could hardly stand erect. Almost immediately another squall began, adding to his discomfort as he retuned to camp.

Observations continued until 3 June, occasionally witnessing more attacks on Abel. Seton watched one 'very painful scene':

> Cain, peevish on an empty crop, made a terrific onset upon poor Abel. It was the most determined attack I had yet seen, for she drove him mercilessly around the nest. Curiously, their mother paid no attention to the row, and flew away for some minutes. During the hen's absence, Cain behaved inexcusably. With wild cries of triumph she pursued Abel, pecking him brutally and pulling out his down and raining blows on his 'behind', his body, his head and neck. I had fears lest she should blind him.

There was now a gap of fifteen days while Seton and Audrey camped in North Uist, where they carried out a number of observations. These were used in *The Immortal Isles*, and combined with the photographs, provided material for at least two chapters. They set up camp just a few miles south of Lochmaddy, beside a loch and close to the main island road. The weather was cool and damp, but the next day turned warm and sunny, staying that way for most of the time, on several days reaching 80 degrees.

The delight of the warmth was ruined by the arrival of swarms of midges, increasing in numbers as the temperature climbed. The agony which Seton and Audrey were forced to endure was made worse by the long hours of daylight, as the insects 'danced in great dense clouds around our tent. Through the closed flaps they made their way. Sleep was permitted only by covering our heads with a towel and making a small tunnel to breath through.' The heather was home to small ticks which added to their discomfort. One morning at five o'clock they were driven from their tent by a midge swarm, and grabbing their clothing they ran around the moor swatting and waving as they tried to dress. Preparing for breakfast was impossible, so taking their food and primus they launched the boat onto a lochan and rowed to the middle where conditions were slightly better, though the kippers were coated with a layer of midge corpses.

Despite the problems, much valuable bird-watching was accomplished. On a small island near the camp a greylag goose and a grey crow had nests. The crow, a notorious robber, had not only sucked most of the eggs of the greylag, but had also robbed several other birds. Because they intended rowing to other islands in the maze of lochs in that part of the islands, a small boat had been put at their disposal. Audrey used it on the first day, while Seton, showing his imperviousness to the cold, stripped off and swam to the island. He found one young crow already fledged. In a cool wind, despite the sun's heat, he collected heather and bracken, which was placed near the nest in readiness for a hide.

Other birds were observed: black-throated divers, oyster-catchers, sandpipers, a merlin and an Arctic skua. The merlin had taken over an old hoodie's nest. The nest was built in long heather and was well-hidden as a result. The hide was placed to within 10 feet of the nest, close by a rowan tree laden with blossom, and its fragrance was appreciated in the heat of the day by whoever was on duty. The heat became so great that the bog-water was hot to the bare feet, and the hide was stifling.

Both the cock and the hen took turns on the nest, and one morning Seton reported: 'The hide was well covered but the cock merlin was suspicious, and two and a half hours went by before he returned and alighted to brood his wife's eggs, swaying in the breeze on top of the heather. What a charming picture he made – very light in plumage, dapper, and handsome. He reminded me of a diminutive fiery colonel, piercing of eye, nervy and very gallant.'

When a breeze came up to keep the midges away, Seton was in his element. On many mornings early mist reflected the rising sun. Its warmth brought out the fragrance of the heather and the flowers of the milkwort, tormentil, sundew, butterwort and lousewort were everywhere. Brilliantly coloured dragonflies darted 'like the magic lances of Mirdir above them, and in all directions were lochans with their water reflecting the sunlight.'

Audrey concentrated on observing and photographing red and black-throated divers and short-eared owls. She also took her turn at merlin and hoodies' nests. Her notes are brief:

9 June – Seton in hide 11:25. First cock came back 1:55 but very wild. The hen came and sat till I relieved Seton at 2:30. Both birds wild and suspicious and fly off when shutter goes off. Seton took 3 photos. I went in and bird came back & I took photo & she went off & did not return.

Put up hide at short-eared owl's nest & the hen never left the nest. Cock flew over and grunted at us. Sun all day from 5 a.m. to 8 p.m.

10 June – Midges awful at 6 a.m. and fog at sea. Tried merlin and short-eared owl. Owl did not come back when Seton was in but came back 8 p.m. when I was in. She alighted a few yards off and walked to the nest by a track under the heather. Brooded the young facing the hide, and quite unsuspicious. Poked the tiny one in under the bigger one. Could not nearly cover all the family. Went to sleep with one eye open. Snaps her bill to call the family and they do it also. No food in store-hole today. Father owl came over twice and they looked up at him. Left hide at 8.50 p.m. Lovely warm calm day.

> 11 June – Awful job putting up hide at hoodie's nest on island south arm of Scadavay in clouds of midges. Only one nearly full feathered young one in nest.
>
> 16 June – Staying on in hopes of getting black throated diver. Awful stormy morning, westerly gale and rain. No use for anything!

They returned to Aviemore and by 20 June were once again in the glen of Cain and Abel, who were now seven weeks old. Cain was well feathered all over while Abel still had white on his head and some down still on his body. The nest had been freshened with a green pine branch and heather. A freshly caught blue hair lay in the nest. The eaglets appeared at peace and for the first time they did wing exercises, stretching out their wings and holding them out for some time.

On this first day back at the nest Seton wrote, 'I left the hide shortly before six o'clock. As I commenced my walk down the hillside the cock was sailing high overhead in a sky of deepest blue. He hung there like an aeroplane, the sun shining full upon his golden head so that it seemed almost white. Behind him rose great hills, still carrying wellnigh unbroken winter's snow upon their upper slopes. The north wind blew chill, and the whole countryside, after weeks of drought was as dry as tinder.'

On 24 June, Seton left to judge the piping at the Highland Division's Sports Day at Grantown on Spey, where the top three pipers in pibroch were all from South Uist.

While Audrey watched in Seton's absence the cock again fed his young. Audrey described with some humour the attitude of the eaglets to this:

> Like human fathers, he did not seem to realise that his family were no longer babies and could now tear off large pieces of flesh for themselves. Cain accepted rather scornfully the tender morsels that her parent gave her, with the same tenderness that he had used when she was a chick in down. After a while Cain evidently thought she had sufficiently humoured her stupid father, and commenced to feed herself in a grown-up manner, where upon the cock complacently fed himself.

On 26 June the eaglets were asleep when Seton commenced his watch at 10:30 a.m. They lay dog-fashion, with their heads pillowed on the eyrie. A squirrel had recently been deposited in the nest. Abel unexpectedly plucked the squirrel from Cain and began to eat it. Seton expected trouble, but she merely looked surprised, and after a few minutes he noticed that for the first time the eaglets fondled each other with their bills.

Later in the day Seton wrote:

> At 4:15 p.m. I was looking out for a moment throught the opening of the hide when I saw what I at first took to be an insect against the sky. But in a second the 'insect' was seen to be the male eagle, who swooped down at a truly incredible speed. A wonderful sight, he must have been travelling at over 100

Golden Eagle taken by Seton Gordon (reproduced by kind permission of British Birds*)*

m.p.h.! It was a most wonderful thing and his descent was so swift that the impetus took him far beyond the eyrie, and he had to sweep round and sail in from the opposite direction.

On 28 June Audrey arrived at 5:40 a.m. It was now her turn to witness an unusual event. At about 9:45 a.m. the young birds suddenly became excited. The adult cock appeared, flying heavily and panting with exhaustion, carrying a roe-deer calf, minus the head and entrails, in one claw. He was barely able to raise himself to the level of the nest. The young birds clamoured as he alighted and it seemed odd to Audrey that their father ignored them and the calf, and proceeded to eat the grouse. He even offered pieces to his offspring, to their obvious disgust. Cain even tried lifting the calf. After twelve minutes the cock flew off again without feeding either himself or the eaglets on his latest prey.

On the 30th, Seton departed again for the Outer Isles for a one day excursion to the Flannan Isles with Niall Rankin. (See Appendix 2.) They were there for only one day, and spent much of the time with the principal lighthouse keeper, Thomas Middlemiss, who was himself a keen bird-watcher. A few weeks later he sent a lengthy report to Seton on birds observed in the interval.

By 3 July Seton was once again back in the hide. Conditions in the nest were deteriorating. The roe calf and game was in a state of decomposition. the nest had become dirty and uncared for, with no fresh branches or heather. The eaglets suffered agonies in the nest from the swarms of midges, and biting sand flies. They continuously rubbed their eyes against their shoulders. When the cock appeared just before 3 p.m. he found the flies intolerable and was off again within half a minute. The hen did not appear for the whole of that day.

During the next two days Seton went off again with Niall Rankin to the Cairngorms. It was as well that he returned to the eyrie on the 7th for after an uneventful watch, at 3 p.m. Cain suddenly appeared on the ground, looking very disturbed at this unexpected freedom, and disappeared from Seton's view. The reason for her freedom was that part of the nest had given way.

Abel was now alone and from now on had to fend for himself or starve. Several times during the next few days his parents were seen overhead but they made no move to descend to the nest. Abel cried pitiously, and it seemed that they were trying to entice him from the nest.

Early on the 10th Seton Gordon discovered that one of the parents had relented and Abel slept contentedly until 10:45 a.m., then for the rest of the day practised wing exercises, at one point so vigorously that he almost left the nest by accident. So engrossed was Seton in the plight of Abel that he barely acknowledged this was the day of publication for his *Cairngorm Hills of Scotland*.

By 13 July Seton was so sure that Abel had flown that he started to climb to the eyrie. He reached the level of the nest and had a fright when Abel suddenly appeared and flapped his wings in fury and indignation. Seton was afraid that he would fly off, but he did not. In *Days With the Golden Eagle* Seton Gordon described the last few days of their two-month long watch:

> From the eyrie was a glorious prospect. On Ben Alder the sun shone full upon the lingering snowfields. The lower slopes of Ben Nevis were hidden in dense white cloud, above which the higher reaches and summit of the mountain showed clear . . . I crept into the hide, being followed by a great swarm of flies and not a few clegs. It was distressing to see Abel's hunger. At 3 p.m. he made quite a good flight across the nest, and then began another frantic and hopeless search for food. When I departed at 5:35 p.m. he was the picture of misery.
>
> At last, on 16 July, after being alone for nine days, the eaglet took wing. Hunger drove him forth, and spreading his great wings, he mounted unsteadily into the air and disappeared for ever from our view.
>
> As we dismantled the hide the sky darkened and quickly two thunderstorms formed. Against the inky clouds blinding flashes of lightning followed each other in rapid succession and the rain descended in torrents. For two months or longer the eaglets would remain with their parents, sailing above the hilltops in the glow of the summer sun, or steering unflinchingly into an autumn blizzard of stinging sleet.

> But a day would come when the parents would turn upon their children with ferocity and drive them forth into the wide world to make a home for themselves in new territory.

Except for this last quotation, most of the information was gleaned from incredibly tightly packed notes – in a pocket diary measuring only 6 inches by 3 inches when closed. Audrey's notes are written in an 8 inches by 5 inches exercise book.

Before *Days with the Golden Eagle* was published, Seton wrote to various papers throughout the Highlands asking people to provide first-hand accounts of golden eagle behaviour they had witnessed. He received over sixty replies and several were included in the book. Most were from gamekeepers and stalkers, though foresters and some land-owners told of unusual incidents they had seen. There were only twelve reported cases of attacks on lambs despite these men being on the hills daily, year after year, which led Seton to conclude that lambs were taken only in exceptional circumstances.

All the letters are in Seton Gordon's papers and almost without exception are well written and legible, which says much for the schooling in the Highlands from the turn of the century onwards. Some of them told of unusual events, including fascinating stories of eagles at play. Favourite toys were a branch or bone. The bird would carry the object to a great height, and then let it drop, to retrieve it before the object hit the ground. John Ferguson of Badenoch once watched this play for over three-quarters of an hour. The bird failed to retrieve the bone only three times in forty drops.

Some correspondents had seen fights with other birds. One letter on this subject came from Alfred MacAulay of Golspie, to describe a fight between an eagle and a peregrine falcon: 'A friend and I were fishing Loch Lundie when we saw an eagle get up near us. At that moment the falcon appeared, steadied himself over the eagle and came down like a bolt. Just as we thought he was likely to strike, the eagle turned a 'cartwheel' and reached out with feet and claws for the peregrine. The eagle righted as the attacker returned and once more performed another cartwheel. He did this five or six times, then the peregrine went off and the eagle flew around us. It was a magnificent sight.'

A keeper in the north saw a stoat get the better of an attacking eagle. He watched as the bird rose high in the air, and suddenly fall back to earth. He ran quickly to the spot, just in time to see a stoat run off. The bird had a deep bite in its throat and the keeper could only surmise that it had caught the stoat, which had managed to bite the eagle's throat even as it was being lifted into the air.

Many letters gave accounts of seeing grouse and ptarmigan taken on the wing. One incident, which became the frontispiece painting by Jack Harrison, was of an eagle attacking a flight of greylag geese and taking one of the birds. Several other Harrison paintings are in the book. The original of the attack on the greylag is still in the possession of the Gordon family. Harrison spent several of his early years in British Columbia, a paradise for artists, and then took formal training at the Slade School.

CHAPTER

6

THE CUILLINS BECKON

SINCE 1914, SETON GORDON HAD BEEN TO SKYE perhaps four or five times, mainly enroute to the Outer Hebrides. He had viewed the Cuillin Hills from every possible angle, from both the mainland and the islands, but had showed no particular interest in Skye during those years.

In 1925, from 1 August to 22 November, the whole Gordon family stayed on Skye. Until 21 September they rented Tayinloan Lodge on a joint tenancy with General Sheppard. Tayinloan is north of Portree on the Dunvegan road where it skirts Loch Snizort. For many years it was in the ownership of the Hilleary family, who still live on Skye. On 21 September, the Gordons and Sheppard moved to Duntulm Lodge for the next two months. The General, or 'Genoo' as he was known to the Gordon children, was a senior officer in the West African Campaign during the First World War.

From the first day it was as though Seton Gordon had discovered a paradise whose existence had only just come into his conscious thought. Almost as soon as the family arrived there he became immersed in island life and activities. An invitation came from Dunvegan Castle to have tea with Norman MacLeod, twenty-sixth chief. He showed them the Fairy Flag, Rory Mor's Drinking Horn, and other relics of the clan. A few days later Seton and Audrey had tea with MacLeod of Skeabost whose house, now a hotel, is close by the Dunvegan turn-off from Portree.

There was a diary note: 'A good day for the Cuillins, but not very clear.' There were several similar notes in these first weeks on Skye expressing disappointment at not getting into the Cuillins. Within a short space of time Seton Gordon had climbed the higher MacLeod's Table (Helabhal Beag – 1601 feet), visited Dunvegan Head at the north end of Duirinish, attended a concert at Dunvegan and walked part way through Glen Sligachan.

On 19 August he judged at the Kyleakin Games, in all categories, and on the 25th travelled to Lochaber Games and judged there, making a note, 'A perfect day to climb the Cuillins – and had to leave the island!' On the 30 August the Gordons went for the first time to Viewfield House at Portree. Colonel 'Jock' MacDonald was then in India, tea planting. His sisters Meg, Joanna (Toonie) and Flora (Bogue) all lived at Viewfield and were very good musicians, especially on piano and clarsach (harp). Another invitation to Dunvegan followed on 4 September, and Seton recorded: 'A great day of piping with Kilberry.' Archibald Campbell of Kilberry spent many years in India where he was a Judge of the High Court of Lahore. He returned to Britain in the late 1920s and

Colonel 'Jock' and Evelyn MacDonald of Viewfield, Portree, Skye 1967

became a lecturer in Indian Law at Cambridge. He was a very keen and knowledgeable piper and became Secretary of the Music Committee of the *Piobaireachd* Society. Campbell began piping in about 1897 and kept very full notes on his tuition, in which he set down examples of the instruction he received from many of the pipers previously referred to in Seton Gordon's earlier years on Deeside. In 1905 he received three full weeks of tuition from John MacDonald of Inverness, and many more lessons from him and from others over the years. These took place during periods of leave from India, and though infrequent, were intense.

When in the late 1930s and 1940s MacDonald corresponded with Seton Gordon, he had bitter complaints about Kilberry and the *Piobaireachd* Society. MacDonald was by then an old man who resented change, and his petulance stemmed from his dissent from some of the settings which the Society's Music Committee had published in the previous twenty years.

The week after the piping with Kilberry, Seton Gordon finally climbed Bruach na Frithe, the most northerly peak of the Cuillin range, noting 'Thin mist on summit but good view.'

The next day he sailed from Dunvegan to Borreraig, site of the legendary MacCrimmon's piping college: 'No sun at Dunvegan but Cuillins in brilliant sun all afternoon.' On the last day at Tayinloan, before moving to Duntulm Lodge on 21 September, was a remark: 'From 19 August to 19 September there were only three excellent days for the Cuillins. On one of them (25 August) I was at Lochaber. On the other (11 September) on Bruach na Frithe, and the last (12 September) we missed. The last was undoubtedly the finest of the three.'

Duntulm Lodge, now the Duntulm Castle Hotel, is in Trotternish, the northern most part of Skye and is in a slight depression facing the bay and the promontory on which are the ruins of Duntulm Castle. The depression offers little protection as the bay faces north-west and receives the full fury of the frequent Atlantic gales. Nevertheless in fine weather the Outer Hebrides are seen clearly beyond Tulm Island, which is a few hundred yards offshore.

The lodge belonged to the Department of the Secretary of State for Scotland, and after the short lease in 1925 the Gordons rented it thereafter for the summer and autumn months each year, until in December 1931 they moved to Kilmuir.

The road goes no further north. From here it turns east through Kilmaluag then south to Staffin and eventually back to Portree past the Storr Rock. The island roads were then gravel tracks and extremely hard on cars, as the Gordons were to find out. Many villages were not serviced by roads at all, merely footpaths across the hills. It is a landscape of severe beauty, hills of dramatic shapes, with crags and buttresses where mist is moving and wreathing even in fine weather, the most awesome being the area known as the Quirang, above Staffin. Quirang looks like a huge rock fortress, where the atmosphere is foreboding. From Sgurr Mor (1612 feet), where a sheer cliff drops to sea-skirted moorland dotted with crofts, to Ben Dearg (1808 feet) above Portree, the high ground is golden eagle country to this day.

Once settled into Duntulm, Seton and Audrey wasted no time in exploring the Quirang, and set out on the morning of 4 October. How many times they climbed here in their years on Skye is impossible to guess, but it would be in the hundreds. That first time, Seton wrote of it:

> Quirang is a bewildering country. Huge rock-masses, deeply fissured and cracked, rise on either side. Visitors are overawed by the strangeness of the scene, especially the most remarkable feature, the Table. A mass of rock with precipitous sides, the top is like a level lawn some 80 by 30 yards in size. Its green grass is a foil to the black rock masses above.

Seton piped among the ruins of Duntulm Castle, the ancient home of MacDonald of the Isles. It is a wild spot, with the wind snatching and carrying the notes along the cliffs and across the stony moorland. A plaque erected in the castle ruins tells of the MacArthurs, who were hereditary pipers to the MacDonalds of the Isles and whose piping college was nearby at Peingown. Under the commemoration are the words:

THIG CRIOCH AIR AN T – SAOGHAL
ACH MAIRIDH GAOL IS CEOL

(the World Will End but Love and Music Endureth)

The Gordons were fast being accepted into island society and soon were at Dunvegan again and at Armadale Castle for tea, then the home of the MacDonalds of Sleat. On both occasions Seton joined in piping after tea. Another ruined castle is Dunscaith, on the opposite side of Sleat from Armadale and with a full view of the Cuillins. On 14 October, following the visit to Armadale, he spent several hours exploring the ruins, and mapping out an article for the *Glasgow Herald*.

Of all the castles on Skye, Dunscaith's history goes far beyond stories of clan warfare, to a time of legendary figures whose exploits are beyond imagination. The castle sits on a small headland, yet it took on surreal dimensions according to accounts from the distant days of the Irish warrior Cuchulainn and the Amazon-like Queen Scathach. It was said to stand on a rock of appalling height, with seven great doors and seven great windows between every two doors of them, and thrice fifty couches between every two windows of them, and thrice fifty handsome marriageable girls in scarlet cloaks and in beautiful and blue attire attending and waiting upon Sgathach.

Seton Gordon sat on a stone and in the late afternoon sunlight penned:

> An October gale sweeps across from the Cuillin, making the ocean into a smother of foam. The music of the breaking seas and the cry of the gale are in harmony beside the old ruin. There is a deep continuous roar here this autumn day from the waves that beat ceaselessly against the cliffs. Across the sea, shadows of wind-urged clouds race. In sunlight the white crests of the waves sparkle and quiver; as the clouds overshadow them the whiteness of the spray is changed instantly to pale grey, and the waters no longer smile. On the narrow ledge of the cliff an assembly of dark-plumaged shags stand, heads to wind.

The excitement of Seton Gordon's early climbs in the Cuillins were captured in articles written for the *Glasgow Herald* and the *Scotsman*. Most of these were later incorporated into the 1929 *The Charm of Skye*. He stressed that, contrary to popular belief, these hills are not just the preserve of rock climbers, and with common sense the climbing is very easy. Up to that time he had been on the summit of six peaks without once needing a rope. On an ascent of Sgurr Alasdair he was accompanied by John MacKenzie of Sconser, a fascinating figure who was the only full-time professional guide in the Cuillins. He died in 1933 well into his eighties and climbed almost to the end of his life. He took Seton up the gully known as the Great Stone Shoot, where the climb is over loose stones and at first the climber has the fear that he may be carried upon the sliding rocks to the corrie below. After a time it is realised the slope is less formidable than it appears. They reached the col and from here to the top the climb was along a narrow ridge with immense precipices on either side. There is little enough space on the summit. Dileas (Jeelus – Gaelic for Faithful), the Gordons' collie was with them and John MacKenzie believed that she was the first dog to stand on the hilltop. But she was not happy, for there was no room for her to lie down on the summit.

The family returned to Aviemore on 23 November, and before he left the island Seton filled several diary pages with notes on Skye legends and historical items: MacCrimmon legends of the silver chanter; an account of the nursemaid dropping the infant at Duntulm; and there were several quotes from *Carmina Gadelica* including the smooring incantation, and several little homilies:

> With love no harm can come. Do not forget, ever, the light that is shining ahead of you, calling on you to look ever up – and up. Feel always that we are guided and guarded in all ways by the spirit of love.

Duntulm is haunted by the ghost of Donald Gorm, one of the more unpleasant chiefs. There are also said to be the ghostly screams of his cousin Hugh, who in plotting to kill Donald Gorm, mixed up the invitations to a feast, so that the latter read of his impending murder. Hugh was put in the Duntulm dungeons where he was fed salt meat and denied any liquids. He died, raging with thirst. The ancient event of the dropped infant that Seton recorded in his diary was certainly of the stuff to cause uneasy spirits:

> The story of the nurse who dropped the baby. She was dangling it before a sea-window, pointing out the ships and galleys when suddenly the baby sprang up. She dropped him and he fell into the sea and was drowned. [Other accounts say he fell onto the rocks]*
>
> MacDonald thereupon called one, Angus, and put him in a boat without oars or sails and had the nurse tied to the stern in the water and she was dragged thus until she drowned.

*Glenelg Castle, by the Kyle Rhea narrows, held by the MacLeods of Dunvegan as far back as the thirteenth century, has a similar tale of a dropped infant.

On 1 July, 1926 the family again returned to Duntulm and settled in for their second long stay on Skye. Work continued on *The Immortal Isles* which was due for publication in the autumn. From the room he set aside for writing he had the added inspiration of seeing the hills of Harris and Lewis across the Minch and in his daily walks feeling the prevailing wind, the Grey Wind, which was the subject of the first chapter. The book's dedication was 'To Those Who Know the Grey Wind'.

Assembling his thoughts, perhaps gazing out over the Minch from the hills above Duntulm, where he often wrote, the chapter took shape:

> Far beneath the western horizon is the magic isle of Flaith-innis. One may visualise it when the setting sun dips, a ball of glowing fire, below the Atlantic, when distant St Kilda on the far horizon seems a fairy island, and when the benign Spirit of the West permeates both land and sea.
>
> Westward, too, lay Tir nan Og, the Country of the Young, and Tir fo Thuinn, that mystic land in the Atlantic depths where many wonderful spiritual beings dwelt in joy on the ocean floor that stretched radiant away and away in the light of an eternal day. And since the Grey Wind came from the west, there was held to be in it some peculiar occult essence . . .

August was the month of the Skye Gathering, which commenced on the 25th with a ball at the Royal Hotel in Portree. By 1926 the Skye Gathering brought many spectators from beyond the island. It is one of the most attractive settings for a Highland Gathering. The field is at the north end of Portree and to the south the view is bounded by the Cuillin Hills, and eastward beyond the cliffs is the Isle of Raasay.

Of all gatherings, Skye is important to pipers, especially in *piobaireachd*, where now they have a chance to compete at Dunvegan for the MacLeod Silver Chanter, the highest award in the world for *piobaireachd*. In 1926 Seton Gordon remarked that so often at Highland gatherings, when the Ceol Mor was played it was the appropriate time to discuss your latest grouse bag, or for the ladies to engage in gossip. He was impressed to see that on Skye the ladies of the well-known island families seated themselves together, where there was little chance of them being disturbed, to listen attentively to the ancient music. Competition amongst the best pipers was fierce, and regular attenders at Portree included John MacDonald of Inverness, Wullie Ross, and a piper who was at his peak in the 1920s, George MacLennan of Aberdeen. Despite having just recovered from a long and serious illness, MacLennan received a first in 1926 for his playing of *'The Lament for the Children'*.

On 9 September Seton Gordon travelled back to Deeside where he judged at Braemar with Hughie Robert and Colin Caird. He was again invited to talk to the King on the various *piobaireachd* contestants. Afterwards he walked with Robert Wolrige Gordon to Luibeg cottage, where after supper with Sandy McDonald and his family they set off over the Lairig for Aviemore. Seton recorded:

> We left Luibeg at 12:45 a.m. in pitch darkness. At about 2 a.m. rain began to fall, and we walked into mist near the pools of Dee. There was only one ptarmigan awake! Sandy had loaned his acetylene bike lamp to R.W.G. We had to catch the morning mail train at Aviemore, as he was to play at a concert that evening at Kyle. We reached Aviemore in good time – but he insisted in having a bath at the station hotel and we missed the train. R.W.G hired a car – very expensive – from Aviemore to Kyle. His piping was indifferent, and as he played, a drunken man staggered after him and put the big drone out of action.

The present Robert Wolrige Gordon had heard the story from his father, who insisted that the reason they missed the train was that Seton Gordon spent too much time trying to buy up every paper on the news-stand with pictures of himself at the previous day's Braemar Gathering. A consolation for Seton was that a few days later he received from the King's equerry a note which read:

> When the King heard the rain in the small hours of the morning, His Majesty hoped that you were enjoying yourself!'

The day following the Kyle concert he travelled over to Skye with Robert Wolrige Gordon to climb Beinn na Caillich, one of the 'Red' Cuillin hills, which sits above Broadford. Travelling from Kyle to Broadford it is the first of these hills which is seen closeby. At 2400 feet it is an easy climb, despite large areas of scree, and some very large boulders on the south side. On the summit is a large cairn which is easily visible from several miles distant. Under it, legend says that a Norse Prince lies buried.

Beinn na Caillich is of special significance because from the summit the Black Cuillin can be seen from close range, and one sees their relationship to the rest of Skye. The view is a clear 360 degrees and even the Cuillin do not prevent the whole of the Outer Islands from being seen. Weather conditions were perfect for this climb and, reaching the top at sunset, they remained by the cairn all night:

> The sudden view of the Cuillins from the crest of Beinn na Caillich is always striking, but tonight there was exceptional beauty upon this great range, the peaks in dark shadow and clear cut against the bright sky beyond.
>
> In the sinking sun Harris and Benbecula glowed; a sea of mist that filled the Minch was so ethereal that it was impossible to define its boundaries. The rocky coast of Lewis seemed to be suspended in the air. The hills of MacLeod's country took on a deep bloom, while southward, evening closed in upon Ardamurchan and Mull, upon Eigg, Rhum and Canna.
>
> The sun sank ever lower, and the western country about Loch Bracadale glowed in an aerial bath of amethyst. At last, at 10:15 p.m. the sun was gone, and the clouds alone were in its rays.
>
> Near midnight, from behind Beinn Sgriol the red rim of the moon, near the full, climbed into view and set out on its course through the silent sky. Through the night we witnessed the course of the moon as she passed slowly southward, throwing a glistening pathway across the Sound of Sleat.
>
> Shortly after one o'clock the dusk was deepest. At 4.45 a.m. the rising sun came with dramatic swiftness. From behind Beinn Bhan of Applecross, rose suddenly a single narrow ray of fire. For an instant it glowed, then was gone. And now appeared the sun's rim, flashing out fire upon a world that lay spellbound, and awakening the earth's life to activity. Soon the full orb had topped the mountain and we looked back upon the Cuillin. Peak after peak in turn caught the rosy glow of this incomparable sunrise.
>
> We eagerly greeted the sun's strengthening rays, for we were chilled by the north wind of the night hours. By seven o'clock the sun was drawing the scent from the wild thyme, the dew was leaving the grass, and the inspiring night was a memory only.

A few days after climbing Beinn na Caillich, Seton Gordon travelled to Oban to judge at the Oban Games. It was here that an amusing incident occurred that became another of his favourite stories to tell against himself. He was judging the *piobaireachd*, and was pleasantly surprised to see in the stands an elderly, distinguished looking man with thick white hair, listening with rapt attention to the piping. This was, as has been mentioned, quite rare except among other pipers. When the competition ended, Seton went over to the man and congratulated him for sitting so long to take in the classical music of the pipes. The man replied that he had no idea what he had been listening to. He had simply sat there because his son had told to remain there and not to move away until he came back!

The remaining weeks on Skye were filled with further excursions and writing, putting the finishing touches to *The Immmortal Isles,* starting to prepare for *Days with the Golden Eagle*, and even making notes in readiness for a book on Skye, with ideas for chapter headings. One of the remoter places visited was Talisker, in the western area known as Minginish. Talisker House is several miles further west than the well-known whisky distillery of the same name. The house once belonged to the MacLeods, and was traditionally occupied by the heir to the clan chief. Like Inverewe, the climate differs from its surroundings and in the sheltered garden, roses often bloom in December, as does a pale blue hydrangea. At the time of this 1926 visit, begonias and chrysanthemums were still blooming robustly. Talisker sits at the base of the hill, Preshal, which though only 1000 feet in height is, in the opinion of Seton Gordon, one of the most shapely hills on Skye.

The house has associations with Dr Samuel Johnson and James Boswell who stayed in it during their 1773 journey to the Inner Hebrides. An historical letter was written in the house in 1745, by Sir Alexander MacDonald of Sleat, while a guest of MacLeod of Talisker. It illustrates that support for Prince Charles Edward Stuart was by no means universal in the west, and some felt that those taken in by the Prince's persuasive manner were foolish. Ironically the letter was addressed to Duncan Forbes of Culloden, Lord President of the Court of Sessions:

> My Lord,
>
> Probably you'll have heard, before this reaches you, that some of your neighbours of the mainland have been mad enough to arm and join the young Adventurer mentioned in MacLeod's letter to you. Your lordship will find our conduct with regard to this unhappy scrape such as you'd wish, and such as the friendship you have always showed us, will prompt to direct.
>
> Young Clanranald is deluded, notwithstanding his assurances to us lately; and, what is more astonishing, Lochiel's prudence has quite forsaken him. You know too much of Glengarry not to know that he'd easily be led to be of the Party; but, as far as I can learn, he has not lately been with them . . .
>
> Whenever these rash men meet with a check it's more than probable they'll endeavour to retire to their islands; how we ought to behave in that event we expect to know from your lordship. Their force, even in that case must be very considerable to be repelled with batons; and we have no other arms in any quantities. I pledge MacLeod in writing for him myself. I now come to tell you, what you must surely know, that I am most faithfully, my lord, your most obedient humble servant, Alex. MacDonald.
>
> Talisker, 11 August 1745.

In writing *The Immortal Isles* and later, *The Charm of Skye*, Seton Gordon was constantly researching historical facts on the Highlands and Islands. He read not only *Carmina Gadelica* but Martin's and Pennant's accounts of their journeys in about 1695 and 1774 respectively, and those of Johnson and Boswell. Because Johnson and Boswell were closer to the aftermath of Culloden, their chronicles give a truer picture of the effect this had on the Highlands than most travellers were able to supply. Seton Gordon quoted all of them extensively.

Johnson and Boswell toured the Highlands in 1773, and witnessed the restrictions imposed after the defeat of Charles Edward Stuart. The banning of Highland dress and music lasted from 1746 to 1782. When the proscription was lifted, too much time had elapsed to rekindle the old spirit, too many clanspeople had died, either at Culloden or in the wave of butchery and torture that came after it. The English army of occupation was aided by the newly formed Highland Regiments, officered by people who remained on the side of the Crown.

Unfortunately, before too many years passed, something equally insidious happened. Sheep came to be seen as the economic salvation of the new generation of chiefs, many of them born outside Scotland following the aftermath of Culloden. They cleared the land to make way for the sheep, removing hundreds of families from their crofts. Most accepted passage across the seas, or moved to shanty towns around Glasgow. There were some instances of sympathetic treatment, but as a period it has been considered the blackest in the history of the Highlands. Seton Gordon wrote of it as that reprehensible policy.

In the autumn of 1926 came the publication of *The Immortal Isles*. Finlay MacKinnon, whose paintings were chosen for Achantoul, provided watercolour plates and pencil sketch headpieces for the beginning of each chapter. Three years later he was commissioned to illustrate *The Charm of Skye*.

One of those who complimented Seton Gordon on his new book was his father-in-law, Howard Pease, who wrote on the 15th November:

> . . . You have captured well the strange, sweet, pensive charm and melancholy of the Hebridean Isles. I loved being reminded of Grogary and Balranald and Griminish. I wished to be able to see again the Monach light, Haskier, the sunset light on St Kilda and the utmost west.
>
> Your photographs are of course splendid – never saw better ones; the raven and the hoodies seem quite human. I send you both my congratulations and hope it will prove your best seller. Shall look out for the press notices. With love to all, I am, yours affect'y, Howard Pease.

The family again began preparing for their third summer on Skye, and were on their way by 1 July 1927. Not many days passed before Seton Gordon was once again in the Cuillins, making the climb to Loch Coire a' Ghrunnda, 2400 feet above sea level.

A letter from Paris had arrived when he returned to Duntulm Lodge. It was perhaps one of the most unusual pieces of fanmail ever sent to him:

> Dear Mr Gordon,
>
> If you are a busy man you will not even read these lines. If a vain man it may please you to be flattered. If a cynic you will simply toss the letter across the breakfast table saying, 'What fools women are to be sure!' But if you are simply a sympathetic soul, with a little inward smile you will say, 'I understand, I have known such moments'.

Whooper Swan at the nest taken by Seton Gordon (reproduced by kind permission of British Birds*)*

Yes, fancy from the heart of busy Paris comes a yearning and a nostalgic sigh for the misty loveliness of your Loch a' Machair of Uist.

Your article in *Cornhill* [magazine] appeared last September, but I got the number in December. Life seemed gloomy and I was lonely, when I happened on your article. Immediately something awoke within me and after reading it I sat for hours by the firelight musing and smiling, for verily I had come to the land of Uist.

I could see your wild swans. I could hear the wind moaning and whistling. The salt dampness of the air was on my hands. Then the scene shifted and it was a crisp spring day, the machair all green and studded with flowers. The song of the birds was in great competition with the buzzing of the bees and the rustling of myriads of tiny insects, and my souls said 'Tis good, let us build a tabernacle here'.

> The lark is singing! Oh, why am I imprisoned in a wee apartment on the fifth storey of an old house overlooking the Seine?
>
> The fire burns low, my vision fades, but never completely. Every now and then when the restless spirit seems to sleep, I can conjure up the atmosphere, the landscape, people it with birds and fill it with a thousand calling notes.
>
> So I would thank you for the beautiful country you have revealed to me – a country of dreams. I have just come back from the sunny skies of Italy and its blue waters, but I ran once more to my *Cornhill* to read again your article. Thank you, thank you, for my wandering in the land of fairies.
>
> Gratefully yours, Alice Stuart Whyte.

Cornhill is, alas, a magazine which ceased publication many years ago, but a chapter in *The Immortal Isles* tells of Loch a' Machair, one of the lochs bordering the almost continuous machair along the western seaboard of the island. Alice Stuart Whyte's vision was not strictly accurate. The machair would not have regained its full greenness by spring, and the 'myriads of insects' would, fortunately, not be out in force. However, such a strong vision should be allowed some poetic licence.

This was the third summer spent on Skye and Seton Gordon's enjoyment was reflected in his articles and books, particularly *The Charm of Skye* which he now commenced work on. In late summer the Gordons joined their neighbours to take part in the harvest. It was a family effort, and to take advantage of the fine October weather of 1927, an early start was made each day. The crofters left their houses as soon as the sun was warm enough to dispel the dew.

Most of the corn had been harvested and the concentration was on oats and hay. Everything was done by hand, and the men were skilled with the scythe. The women and older children bound the oats into sheaves. The hay was raked up and taken by cart to the yard of a small thatched cottage almost hidden by the stacks of peat, and corn. A brief rest to eat a midday meal, and the crofters, anxious not to lose the fine weather, continued with the harvest.

One of their neighbours had completed his harvest and all was secure against the winter gales, the stacks roped and held down with large stones. To celebrate, the crofter followed the harvest traditions which still then lingered in Trotternish. Seton and Audrey were invited to the house after the work was completed for the day:

> With the harvest ended, at night there is the old observance of drinking the 'stapag', a dish of thick churned cream, into which oatmeal has been dropped. A peat fire glows. The crofter and his wife are charming hosts. She is refined and gentle voiced. He is the best type of islesman – strong, self reliant and courteous. Two pipers play in turn while the 'stapag' is being drunk. From the bay shine the lights of a herring drifter lying at her nets.

In the memoranda at the end of the diary more poems and inspirational sayings were quoted. One of the more whimsical entries was under the title Bridie's Prayer:

> Please good fairies take care of Bridie
> and help her to be a good girl,
> and take the bad fairies out of Bridie's tum tum!

By May 1928 they were again on the island. Seton went off to stay at Glen Brittle Lodge for ten days and made several trips into the Cuillins. One night he spent on the shores of Loch Coruisk, cooking a meal over a fire of rowan wood. These hills had without doubt cast a spell him, for he wrote:

> There are days (and this is one of them) when the Cuillin are alive with benign spiritual forces; when the hill silence tells of many wonderful things; when hill, sky, and ocean glow with life and energy.

He climbed Sgurr nan Eag, which rises straight from the Sound of Soay to just over 3000 feet. Below him was the island of that name, seeming very close in the clear twilight. The crossing from Glen Brittle is around the point of Rubh an Dunain, where the full sweep of the Cuillins can be seen. At its narrowest the Sound is only half a mile wide.

To cross to the island without prior arrangement, a visitor had to walk over the moor between Rubh an Dunain and the Cuillins, then light a smoky fire to attract attention. An answering fire would be lit to tell him that a boat would soon cross. Before leaving Glen Brittle, Seton Gordon put the method to a test. The first time he tried, he could not get a sufficient volume of smoke. The weather turned wet and it was several days before he succeeded, after finding an area of old heather, from which a blue smoke soon rose. Seton watched its effect on the island:

> In a few minutes a thin column of smoke came from the island, and a boat put out. As I landed upon Soay, the scent of the birches greeted us and oyster-catchers called shrilly. The people of the island again showed their hospitality. They are crofters but many also fish for lobster. The houses are well built, with slate roofs.

On the north side of the island is a natural harbour and there Seton Gordon found a delightful scene, birches growing down to the tide and below them a carpet of hyacinths, primroses and violets. He saw the 'cas chrom' in use on one of the crofts. A plough-shaped spade worked by hand, it was the traditional ploughing tool for hundreds of years throughout the Highlands. Though an unwieldy tool in the hands of an amateur, a skilled user could work fast with it.

Soon after an came invitation from MacLeod's factor, John MacKenzie, to sail out to Soay of the St Kilda group. They remained for almost a week and as well as Hirta, landings were made on several of the neighbouring islands. The vessel that transported them was the faithful Islands ship, *Dunara Castle*. One of the first hills climbed by Seton was Conachair. Beyond South Uist the Cuillin could be seen and for the first time he had a reciprocal view across the expanse of ocean and islands. Reaching the clifftop, he looked over the greatest precipice in the British Isles. Twelve hundred feet below, the Atlantic swell beat against the base of this massive cliff. Gaining the summit, the clustered houses of the village lay 1400 feet below, and in the bay the steamer lay at anchor. Seton wrote in his diary:

> That evening as I sat in the church I could hear the deep music of the unresting swell upon outpost cliffs, blending in harmony with the cadences of Gaelic psalms sung fervently by an earnest and simple congregation.
>
> Half an hour after midnight, with the ending of the Day of Rest, the unloading of the *Dunara Castle* began.

An expedition was planned to the neighbouring island of Boreray. There was quite an air of excitement in the village, as the men prepared for the voyage. Seton was sure that on St Kilda dogs outnumbered the people. The morning of the boat launching was accompanied by shouting, arguing and much gesticulating by the crew. There was little or no discipline, and each man had his own ideas of what should be done.

When Martin Martin visited the island, he had noted that the men were excellent swimmers, but Seton Gordon saw no one take to the water in the week that he was there. Boreray was four miles north of the main island and as they rowed, the occasional burst of 'Ho ro' was shouted in unison to assist the timing of the strong pulling. He thought how appropriate the setting was to hear an 'iorram' or Gaelic rowing song. After questioning the crew it was discovered that one of them, Finlay MacQuien, had in his early days sung an iorram, but neither the imploring of John MacKenzie, or the coaxing and teasing of the other boatmen would peruade him to try, and so they continued the long pull in the heavy boat with the periodic shouts of 'Ho ro, ho ro'.

As they neared the island, Seton wondered how a landing was to be made, and commented that to anyone but a St Kildan a landing would have been impossible. The skipper gave an order 'Boots off', and all the men removed their boots and each pulled on a thick pair of socks over the ones they already wore. When they were within a few feet of the rocks, the most agile member of the crew sprang on to the nearest one, poised for a second while he regained his balance, and then climbed nimbly to a broad ledge. He carried the end of a rope, and while he braced himself, the rest of the people in the boat used it in turn to jump and balance themselves against the pull from above them. They climbed to a grassy slope where thousands of puffin nested.

Boreray's cliffs were as precipitous as those of Hirta, and from the highest point Seton looked down on Stac an Armuinn. He calculated that the gannets on Hirta nested to a height of 1050 feet, which he thought was a record for nesting gannets in Britain.

Next morning a freshening south-east wind brought uneasy seas, but it did not keep him from visiting Soay, the namesake of the island in the shadow of the Cuillins. Soay of St Kilda is close to the north-west coast of Hirta and when they arrived after a rough crossing, Seton thought that a more inhospitable coast could not be imagined. The boat was rowed in amongst grey seals, until a narrow, rocky peninsula was reached. The men again replaced their boots with thick socks, and the most skilled rock climber leaped ashore, followed by the others. A rope was passed around beneath the arms of the visitors and they were dragged ignominiously up the smooth seaweed-covered rocks, too quickly to establish any foothold during the ascent. The party then set about climbing at least 100 feet of sheer cliff. The visitors were all roped during this 100 feet of formidable climbing. Above each one was a St Kildan, who took the strain during the worst part of the climb.

The high point of the island was 1225 feet, and while the men went about their work Seton climbed to the summit. The sky was only partially covered with clouds, and where they reflected on the surface of the Atlantic it created pools of palest pink. The clear air had given way to haze and the Outer Isles were barely visible. Below him, sheep clung to ledges so narrow that it seemed impossible that they could return to safety.

He surveyed this lonely island group which within two years would be deserted by the men with whom he climbed.

Seton Gordon's pursuit of history continued, particularly on that of Trotternish. He was fortunate that several records and documents exist to show the turbulent history of the promontory. It has been referred to as the granary of Skye because of the fertility of the soil, and for that reason, as early as the thirteenth and fourteenth centuries there was rival claims between the MacDonalds and the MacLeods.

In *The Charm of Skye* there is a reference to MacFarlane's Geographical Collection, Volume II, in which is a description of Trotternish, written in about 1545: '. . . It is a most pleasant, profitabl and most fertill Countrey both of corne and abundances of milk. Duntalme the cheiff place of residence belonging to McDonald is built upon a rock 200 fathom above the sea. The Lord or Superior therof is Donald Gorme McDonald of Sleitt. The inhabitants of this Island are much addicted to swimming, wherin they are verie expert. They are great lovers of Musick.'

The flight of Prince Charles Edward Stuart after Culloden is, in itself, a heroic tale and Trotternish people played an important part in the story. Flora MacDonald was at the time visiting relatives in South Uist, and when approached was reluctant to help his escape, but as no better way could be found, she agreed to take him in the disguise of her Irish maid. Her stepfather, Captain Hugh MacDonald, was in Uist at the time commanding a company of militia sent to search out the Prince. It is obvious where his true sympathies lay, because he actually wrote the letter which would provide an alibi for the Prince in the event of the party being caught, addressed to his wife on Skye:

> I have sent your daughter from this country lest she should be frightened with the troops lying here. She has got one, Betty Burke, an Irish girl, who, as she tells me is a good spinster [spinner] . . .

After leaving South Uist the small party made a perilous crossing of the Minch in a violent storm. A landing was attempted close to Vaternish Point, but being fired upon by MacLeod militia, the boat put out again and eventually landed below Monkstadt House (sometimes called Mugstot), the home of Flora's uncle, Sir Alexander MacDonald of Sleat. The landing place is known as the 'Prince's Strand'. Seton Gordon visited there in 1928:

> On the September day when I stood upon the Prince's Strand the sea was calm and blue. In the fields the crofters were reaping their oats or 'curing' their hay. Meadowsweet and scabious were flowering beside the shore, and the blue of the field gentian blended with the purple of the last blossoms of the knapweed. Across Loch Snizort rose the Ascrib Isles. Beyond the Minch were seen faintly the hills of Uist and Harris. For the residence of a great Highland family, Monkstadt House was small, and cannot be compared in appearance or situation to Duntulm Castle, which was still standing at that time.

Time has not served Monksdadt House well. It is now a ruin, although enough still stands to see that it was of interesting design. The present owners of the property hope to restore it, together with the outlying buildings.

The Prince and Flora MacDonald were escorted by MacDonald of Kingsburgh, a kinsman, to his house when it was discovered that loyalist troops were in the vicinity of Monksdadt. Kingsburgh is several miles further south, and the next day the Prince was taken to Portree, where he took leave of Flora MacDonald to cross to the mainland and await his final departure from Scottish soil.

Flora married Allan MacDonald, Kingsburgh's son and heir, and they went to America where Allan and two of their sons fought in the War of Independence as officers in the Royal Highland Immigrant Regiment. Allan and one son were captured, but all returned to Trotternish where they resumed farming. Flora died in 1790 and is buried at Kilmuir, close to Seton Gordon's house at Upper Duntuilm. Dr Samuel Johnson was destined to have the last word on Flora MacDonald. His words used to describe her after their meeting in 1773, are now on the large memorial cross above her grave: 'Her name will be mentioned in history, and if courage and fidelity be virtues, mentioned with honour.' Dr Johnson also described her as a woman of middle stature, soft features, gentle manners, and elegant appearance.

The present Kingsburgh House is in a sad state of repair, and as the house is privately owned, it is not within the power of the authorities to do anything about it. It is a great pity when it is a link to a moment in Scotland's history.

Trotternish holds numerous tales of the past when men were tortured on a whim, sometimes over trivial matters – if they earned the ire of a chief or laird. Beside Duntulm Castle is a hill called 'Cnoc a' Rola' – the Hill of the Rolling. Culprits who had been judged by the chief were brought here from 'Cnoc an Ceartais' the Knoll of Justice, where he had tried them. In his hands lay the power of life or death. They were placed in nail-studded barrels and rolled down the Cnoc a' Rola. If they survived this torture they were held to be innocent of the crime.

For the first time in Seton Gordon's memoranda, 1928 included details of total earnings for the year. It was £515–6–0d – £103–12–0d for royalties, and £411–14–0d for articles. While not a fortune, when related to average earnings at that time, supplemented by the rent from Aboyne and help with the children's school fees from Audrey's parents, it was sufficient to provide a very comfortable lifestyle.

South of Skye are the islands of Rhum, Eigg, Canna and Muck. Rhum is the largest and has mountains in excess of 2500 feet. As one approaches the coast along the 'Road to the Isles' it is Rhum and Eigg which stand out. Eigg has a large rock pinnacle, or sgurr, which rises to almost 1300 feet and changes shape according to the angle from which it is viewed.

In June 1929 the Gordons landed on Eigg, where Seton was pleased to find an abundance of *Dryas octopetala*, the first that he had seen since leaving Spitsbergen. They also found there dog roses, cushion pink, wild honeysuckle, crimson orchis, yellow iris and trefoil. On the island's west side, by the white 'singing sands' at Laig, is one of the finest machairs he had seen. From the Bay of Laig the mountains of Rhum fill the entire westerly view, like a mirror image of the Skye Cuillins to the north.

A massacre took place on Eigg in 1577. It was a direct result of clan enmity between MacLeod of Harris and MacDonald of Clanranald. Several families were suffocated in a cave, the number of victims being put at 395. MacLeod of Harris had led several galleys filled with his clansmen to maraud the people of Eigg; they had taken shelter in a well-hidden cave. After three days in hiding, one of the men went to see if the MacLeods had departed. The galleys were sailing away, but the man was not cautious enough, and was spotted from the boats. His footsteps were traced in the freshly fallen snow, leading back to the cave. Using thatch from a nearby cottage MacLeod ordered the fire to be lit, but not before he had prayed for several hours that the wind would direct the smoke away from the cave, in which case he would spare the victims. It did not, and the families died. Their bones remained undisturbed until recent times, when they were reverently interred. Sir Reginald MacLeod of Macleod, twenty-seventh Chief, actually slept in the cave as a young man. He told his daughter Flora, who became twenty-eighth Chief, that he saw the bones of these people still lying as they had died. He said it was very moving to see how they lay in families, some with children, and some with older family members.

All this happened during the chieftainship of Alasdair Crotach, the hunchback, who is buried at Rodil church, and it was one of the bloodiest periods in the Clan MacLeod's history.

Another incident of suffocating enemies in a cave occurred almost fifty years after the Eigg massacre. This time it was after the Campbells had sacked the MacIain's Mingarry Castle near the village of Kilchoan on Ardnamurchan. Seton Gordon did not have an opportunity to visit Mingarry until 1933.

On the ferry ride back to Skye, Bridie came out with a quaint question – 'Dadkins, is this a different world from Aviemore?'

When *The Charm of Skye* was published, Seton Gordon received several interesting letters of praise. One was from Norman MacLeod of MacLeod, who wrote the Foreword to the book. On receiving his copy he sent this letter of thanks:

> Dear Seton Gordon,
>
> Thank you very much for your kind present of your book. It is the first present in recognition of my ninetieth birthday that I have received. I wish I could read it myself, of course I can get it read to me, but that is not quite the same thing. I hope the book will go well.
>
> You have got it out at the right time. It seems very well got up and they tell me the illustrations are very good. My wife read the review in the *Oban Times* which I thought very good.
>
> Glad Skye weather is nice . . . my daughter is going to Dunvegan Cottage about the end of the month. You will probably see her at Portree. My brother Reginald can't get away till August. Glad to hear Skye piping is improving. Again, thankyou.
>
> Yours sincerely, Norman MacLeod of MacLeod.

Anxious to be in the Cuillins again, Seton left Sligachan one evening in mid-July to climb Sgurr Alasdair. His intention was to remain in the Cuillins past midnight. The day had been one of the warmest for many years, and away to the west thunder clouds were approaching from the Minch. Glen Sligachan was still in sunshine when he set out, but with each minute the light decreased, yet he carried on. It resulted in one of the finest pieces his pen produced. It appears in a chapter of *Islands of the West* called *The Hill Silence*:

> One summer evening the silence of the Cuillin was shattered by a furious thunderstorm. I was in Coire Lagan that night. The day had been one of great heat and at evening a spirit of silence brooded over the Cuillin. As I crossed the corrie the growl of distant thunder was heard from the direction of Rhum. As dusk settled in the corrie the thunder approached quickly. Sgurr Dearg, Sgurr an Banachdich, Sgurr Alasdair – all stood with the darkness of night upon them before its time. Seaward the air was now thick with driving rain. Among the rocks an increasing south wind played.
>
> Beneath an overhanging boulder I lay awaiting the coming of the storm. The clouds now approached more slowly, and the moon sailed into view from behind the rocks of Sgurr Sgumban. She moved, an orb of glowing bronze, serenely across the velvet starless sky like some friendly beacon. A thunder-cloud crept slowly, relentlessly, across her face. Distant sheet lightning played upon the horizon and it was not long before the thunderstorm drew near. Momently the lighting flickered more brightly, but the bursting of the storm over Coire Lagan at midnight was dramatic in its swiftness. The dusk of a summer's night changed quickly to the blackness of a midwinter's evening. This pall was suddenly rent by a blinding flash. The lightning appeared to strike Sgurr Alasdair. A glowing halo for a moment surrounded the hilltop. Almost on the instant came the thunder, followed within a second by a

second report as Sgurr Dearg threw back on the pulsating night the echo of that fearsome peal. Flash succeeded flash, peal succeeded peal. The sky glowed. The corrie was illuminated so that each stone was clear. Once forked lightning sped across the heavens from behind Sgurr Dearg. Quivering and changing colour like some living creature the lightning hastened across the sky. It was as though some mighty being had struck the rocks with a stupendous hammer, causing the sparks to fly.

As the storm continued and heavy rain added its soft music to the tumult in the sky, it was interesting to watch the flashes and record their colour. Some were a pale green, others a warm reddish tint. They flickered about Sgurr Alasdair; they played nobly about Sgurr Dearg. The spectacle was of a sublime grandeur which no pen can adequately describe. The eyes were blinded, and the ears deafened, by the storm's intensity. Then at length the sky brightened, the peals of thunder no longer rolled, the rain ceased, a soft dusk replaced the darkness. When the storm passed the air remained warm as before.

At sunrise, when I left the corrie, the wild thyme flowered and on the grass, short cropped by mountain sheep, the tormentil spread a yellow carpet. The perfume of the bell heather scented the fresh, rain washed air. The hill silence had returned.

CHAPTER

7

SKYE ROAD IMPROVEMENTS

In the years since he began judging the piping at Highland games, Seton Gordon had occasionally met Prime Minister Ramsay MacDonald, who liked to attend them when not kept in London on state business. He had a house, 'The Hillocks', at Lossiemouth, originally built for his mother. Mrs Sheila Lochhead, MacDonald's youngest daughter, writing of the friendship that grew between Seton and her father said, 'He was anxious that I should get to know Seton a bit, and took me with him sometimes when they were meeting. They seemed so content with each other.'

The Gordons were concerned with the state of the roads on Skye, or in some cases the lack of them, not for selfish reasons, but because of the plight of the crofters, many of whom were cut off by lack of access. It occurred to them that MacDonald, with his Highland background might be sympathetic to the crofters' plight and Seton wrote to draw the matter to the Prime Minister's attention. This first letter was written partly on 7 August 1929, to encourage him to see for himself:

> I do not know whether you have sufficient time for a holiday in Skye. If you have, I should be glad if you would come and stay with us. Skye has many needs but I feel that what some of the poorer crofters need above all are roads – many of them have no roads at all to their houses, and the women are compelled to go far across the wet bogs in winter, to the nearest road.
>
> But I am not writing a letter of complaint – and it would be a great pleasure to my wife and to me if you could find time to come even for a couple of days and see something of the island, and perhaps the Cuillin also! Yours very truly, Seton Gordon.

Ramsay MacDonald replied on August 9, from 10 Downing Street:

> Dear Mr Seton Gordon,
>
> I am so glad to hear from you. I owe many letters of thanks for the pleasure you have given me. Nothing would give me greater pleasure than to accept your invitation to go to Skye once more and be under your roof.
>
> But I cannot. I have to be in Geneva (Skye is far better) on 1 September and then it looks as if I might have to go to America.

As to the roads, I have already given instructions that road development in our West Highlands must be examined without delay and I shall now repeat these instructions as regards Skye specifically. But goodness, the machinery of men, as well as the mills of God grind slowly. I get impatient.

Yrs Sincerely, J.R. MacDonald.

P.S. I took the liberty of advising my son who is in the House of Commons, and a devoted lover of birds to write to you for information about the golden eagle before I got your letter.

MacDonald's party had been swept to power on 30 May of that year because of Stanley Baldwin's inability to turn around the growing numbers of the unemployed, especially in the north. Coming from an impoverished background, MacDonald was drawn to the fledgling labour movement at an early age. He was reared by his grandmother, while his mother sought such work as she could get. As soon as he was old enough he went south, and soon held memberships in the Social Democratic Foundation, the Fabian Society, and the Independent Labour Party. A turning point in MacDonald's life came with his marriage in 1896 to Margaret Gladstone, daughter of a chemistry professor. Margaret shared her new husband's belief in social change and became intensively involved in the growing labour movement.

They had six children. The youngest, David, died of diphtheria on 3 February 1910. Margaret never got over her grief, and the by the next year her remarkable strength and endurance gave out. In July 1911 she developed blood poisoning and died on 8 September, aged 41. It was her wish that her husband should write down their life together. *Margaret Ethel MacDonald* was published a few months later, and received glowing reviews. The Rt. Hon. C.F.G. Masterman described it as 'One of the most moving short biographies in the language'.

The remaining five children, Alastair, Ishbel, Malcolm, Joan and Sheila were placed in the care of a housekeeper, but MacDonald jealously guarded time spent with them, and they grew up to become self-reliant individuals, Ishbel taking her mother's place as hostess when her father became Prime Minister. As they grew older he took them on walks in the Highlands, often strenuous and always sleeping rough.

This was the appeal of Seton Gordon and his writing. It answered a longing for wild places which he could not escape to as much as he would have liked. MacDonald's work schedule was horrendous, and is well illustrated in the letters. His life was in total contrast and sometimes, when he replied to a letter which gave a tantalising glimpse of Seton Gordon's freedom his frustration showed, though it was usually couched with humour. MacDonald sympathised with the Skye crofters and their need for improved access to the townships and in early September, as a result of the Prime Minister's personal intervention, Seton Gordon received a letter from the Scottish Office. Though pointing out that nine out of thirty-one roads approved earlier were already under construction, the letter ended:

> The work is still proceeding, and the question of construction of further roads will no doubt arise when the present scheme is completed. I do not think I can do better than suggest that if you have any particular township roads in mind, you bring them to the notice of the District committee. Yours faithfully, Wm Adamson.

In mid August the Gordons spent several days at Dunvegan Castle as a guest of MacLeod, and he took them by boat to Borreraig, the site of the MacCrimmon piping college. In *The Charm of Skye* there are five chapters on the MacLeods and their lands. Dunvegan vies with Glamis for the reputation of being the oldest inhabited castle in Scotland. What is not in dispute is that the MacLeods have inhabited their castle for over 700 years. Its origins go back to Norse times, but the present building has parts that were erected in the eleventh century. The Fairy Tower dates from 1490. The castle also has a moat surrounding it except for the seaward side, where there is a sea-gate.

The principal clan treasures are the 'Fairy Flag', the speckled pipes, and Rory Mor's Drinking Horn. The flag held such power that if unfurled on three occasions when disaster threatened the clan would be victorious. Should it be unfurled when there was no danger, a curse would come upon the clan. It was used twice in time of need but the third time there was no danger, and the curse came to pass. This resulted in the fulfilment of a prophecy on the fate of the clan, made by Coinneach Odhar, a Lewis seer, in about 1600. The prophecy foretold the accidental death of the fourth Norman, heir to Norman, twenty-third chief, while he served in the navy; that in the space of a few years there would be no MacLeod lairds on the estate, and it would diminish in size. The last part of the prophecy spelled more hope by saying in a far distant time another Iain Breac would arise who would 'redeem the estates, and raise the power and honour of the house of MacLeod to a higher flood than ever'.

In 1799, to satisfy the curiosity of a visitor, the business manager to the chief broke open the chest in which the flag was kept. They found it inside a box of scented wood. Soon after, the news came that the fourth Norman had been killed at sea. The number of MacLeod tacksmen [minor lairds] on the estate gradually reduced. The prophecy was not, after all, fulfilled. The next Iain Breac was killed in the First World War, on 17th April 1915, leaving no male heir in direct descent.

One legend of the flag's origin states that it was given to the fourth chief, Iain Keir, who died in 1390. He married a fairy wife, and after twenty years she pined to go back to her people. Seton Gordon tells the story in this way:

> For twenty years they lived in happiness at Dunvegan; then came to the fairy a longing to return to her own people, which she was powerless to fight. She told all to MacLeod, and with hearts heavy with sorrow the two left the castle, walking until they reached a small burn, where the fairy left him. Her parting gift was the Fairy Flag. The place where they parted is still known as the Fairy Bridge.

Sir Reginald MacLeod, afraid that the flag would crumble with age, took it to Mr Allan Wace of the Victoria and Albert Museum, an expert on ancient textiles. He mounted it on fine cloth and framed it. Wace advised Sir Reginald that the silk had come from either Syria or Rhodes, and that the darns were made centuries ago in the Middle East. He offered the opinion that it could well have been a saint's shirt or vestment. Dame Flora loved to repeat the end of the conversation. Sir Reginald insisted: 'Mr Wace, I know that my ancestor married a fairy and it was given to him by the fairies'. With great diplomacy Wace answered, 'Sir Reginald, I bow to your better knowledge!'

Rory Mor's Drinking Horn is from the horn of a bull killed by Malcolm, the third chief. A tradition grew, honoured by John, the present chief, to drink a hornful of claret (one and three-quarter bottles), at either coming of age, or on obtaining the chieftainship. John wisely practised by building up gradually until he could manage a similar quantity of wine.

It was during Rory Mor's time (1595–1626) that the MacCrimmon pipers came to prominence, though their origins go back beyond this. His piper, Donald Mor MacCrimmon, composed 'MacLeod's Welcome' (*Failte nam Leodach*). Donald Mor's son, Patrick Mor was the composer of 'Lament for Rory Mor' after the chief's death in 1626. Another of his compositions was 'Lament for the Children', after he lost six of his seven sons in an epidemic. The survivor was, fortunately another exponent of *piobaireachd*, Patrick Og. Two of Patrick Og's sons, Malcolm and Donald Ban carried on the gift bestowed on the MacCrimmon family. Donald Ban is thought to have composed the lament heard by Seton Gordon from the pipes of the old man at Lochboisdale – '*Cha till MacCruimein*' (MacCrimmon will not Return).

The beginning of the MacCrimmon legend was the entrusting of a silver chanter to Iain Og by a fairy woman. It was called '*Sionnsair Airgoidna Mna Sithe*' – the Silver Chanter of the Fairy Woman. One version says the fairy warned him never to swear at the chanter or it would disappear. The decline of the MacCrimmons was attributed to one of the later pipers forgetting himself in a moment of anger, and the chanter being whisked away for ever. Seton Gordon's favourite *piobaireachd*, *'I Got a Kiss of the King's Hand'*, was possibly composed by a MacCrimmon. The doubt comes over the spelling of the piper's name, which is sometimes given as MacGurmen, or M'Gyurmen. When Charles II inspected the army at Torwood near Stirling a competition between the assembled pipers was proposed, but none would compete against MacGurman, 'the Earl of Sutherland's domestick'. All the pipers had removed their bonnets, except MacGurman, and the King asked, 'What society is this?' He was told, 'Sir, you are our King, and yonder old man is the Prince of Pipers'. The King called him forward and offered his hand to kiss, and MacGurman composed '*Fouris Pooge I spoge I Rhi*' (I Got a Kiss of the King's Hand). Seton Gordon believed that it MacGurman was a mis-spelling of MacCrimmon.

After he had judged at the Oban Games, Seton and Audrey stopped to explore Loch Shiel and Kinlochmoidart. Today there is a road to Kinlochmoidart, commencing at Lochailort, on the road from Fort William to Mallaig, though it was not constructed until after 1960. Mrs Cameron-Head of Inverailort, an Inverness

County Councillor worked tirelessly for fifteen years to convince the authorities of the need for it. Her husband Francis, the late laird, was one of Seton Gordon's closest friends and it was an area that they explored many times together.

The road from Fort William to Mallaig was then little more than a gravel lane, but it provided access to one of the most romantic and beautiful areas in the west Highlands. At Glenfinnan the road dips towards the head of Loch Shiel. Close to the water's edge stands a large monument with a life-size figure of a Highlander at the top, built to commemorate the raising of the Jacobite Standard on 19 August, 1745 when Prince Charles Edward Stuart met the first of the clans that supported his bid to take the Crown.

There is no better location in the Highlands for such a stirring occasion. Mountains rise on each side of the loch and are mirrored in the water. From Glenfinnan the loch recedes to the south-west and the light changes dramatically throughout the day. A wooded island in the middle distance provides a focus. It is one of those rare places where poor weather serves to enhance, even when the rain and mist allows only the dimmest outline of a mountain shoulder.

Seton Gordon once said that the Jacobites' attempt to retake the throne came within a measurable distance of succeeding. This in itself is remarkable when it came so close to not even starting. In *Highways and Byways of the West Highlands* he shows that Sir Alexander MacDonald and MacLeod were not the only ones to have doubts. The man who has over the years epitomised one of the most ardent supporters of the Prince was the 'Gentle Lochiel', Donald Cameron, nineteenth chief. Seton Gordon pointed out how close Lochiel came to spurning him:

> On his way to meet the Prince at Borrodale, Lochiel called on his brother, John Cameron of Fassiefern, and said that as the Prince had arrived in Scotland with neither money, nor troops, nor arms, it would be folly to be concerned in the affair. John agreed, but advised him to go no further, suggesting that Lochiel should send a letter to the Prince. He said, 'Brother, I know you better than you know yourself, and if this Prince sets eyes on you he will make you do whatever he pleases'.

He was right. Lochiel, after he met the Prince, felt that he could not stand aside, and placed himself and his clan at the disposal of Charles Edward Stuart. From Borrodale a small group escorted the Prince to Loch Moidart, and after passing the ruined Tioram Castle, he was brought to the estuary of Loch Shiel. He was rowed its length in the company of twenty-five followers. At Glenfinnan only two men came forward to greet him, MacDonald of Glenaladale whose lands were on the north side of the loch, and the elderly Gordon of Glenbuchat in Aberdeenshire, a veteran of the Jacobite rising of 1715. Each had a few men with him.

Two hours passed before the sound of distant pipes were heard and into the glen marched Cameron of Lochiel leading approximately 700 to 800 men. MacDonald of Clanranald led approximately 400. MacDonald of Keppoch was the last to arrive with a company estimated at between 300 to 500. These variations

Seton Gordon with film director Michael Powell at the 200th anniversary of raising the Jacobite Standard, Glenfinnan, August 19 1945 (by kind permission of Mr Brodrick Haldane)

from key eyewitnesses suggests little attempt to take an accurate count. Later they were joined by MacLeod of Raasay and a few followers. His chief, MacLeod of MacLeod, had refused to leave Dunvegan. When the march south began, Charles Edward Stuart had approximately 1400 men behind him.

The inscription on the monument suggests that it stands on the precise spot where the Standard was raised. It is now fairly certain that this is not the case. In the late 1970s a shepherd was burning grass on a knoll several hundred yards away on the hillside, close to where the railway now runs. The burn exposed an almost flat rock face and on it was carved the name of Prince Charles Edward Stuart and the names of the clans that were present. Several historians, including Seton Gordon, had thought it more probable that the Standard was raised on a knoll rather than the beach and this find gave credence to their belief.

One of those who believed the raising was elsewhere was Donald B. MacCulloch, author of *Romantic Lochaber*. He believed the words 'on this spot' to be figurative and to mean the glen. The monument was erected at the expense of Alexander MacDonald of Glenaladale who died in Edinburgh at the age of twenty-eight in 1815, before it was completed. The inscription was by Dr Donald Maclean of Ardnamurchan, and it is possible that Glenaladale never lived to give final approval. In support of MacCulloch's assertion, Volume IX of the *Miscellany of the Scottish History Society* has an eyewitness account of the event, possibly written by the youthful Clanranald:

> On the 19 August at about seven in the morning the P. set out for Glenfinnan. At about three of the clock thereafter Lochiel arrived with 600 men, and about two hours thereafter HRH ordered his Standard to be carried to the other side of the river Finnan where it was displayed, which was done by the D. of Athole [actually the Marquis of Tullibardine, Atholl's son] carrying it, and 100 of Clanranald's men with himself at their head escorting it.

MacCulloch contributed a paper in 1963 to the '45 Association in which he gave all the information he had collected to that time relating to the Standard raising. Most of it supported evidence that Tullibardine took his stand on a small knoll.

In Appendix III to *Romantic Lochaber* MacCulloch wrote: 'The evidence given in my paper to the '45 Association received the following commendation from Mr Seton Gordon, the well-known authority on many Highland subjects:

> You must have taken a great deal of trouble in gathering all this information, and we members of the '45 Association are very grateful to you. I have read your article several times and am impressed by the clearness with which you make your points. I think you have been very modest in the assessment of your evidence. You have, to my mind, made it clear that the small knoll which you describe is the actual site where the Standard was raised, and I highly approve of your article.

Iain Thornber, a knowledgeable Highland historian, who has helped immeasurably in researching this book, wrote in a November 1987 letter on Glenfinnan: 'I first heard of this controversy when, as a boy, I overheard two old men discussing it at Glenfinnan. I did not know it then but later discovered that the two 'old men' were in fact Seton Gordon and Francis Cameron-Head! I was only six or seven at the time, so I feel I have a head start in this – call it fate – to carry on solving the riddle.' (The August 1988 edition of *Scots Magazine* has an article by Iain Thornber on this inscribed rock.)

When Seton Gordon first saw Glenfinnan such knowledge was a few years away, and in Audrey's company he continued down the loch to Kinlochmoidart. Castle Tioram, which they saw next day, stands on a knoll beside Loch Moidart and at first glance appears whole, an illusion created by the good condition of the four overhanging corner turrets. Toiram dates back to the fourteenth century and was always a Clanranald stronghold. Mention has already been made of his premonition, and it is interesting to speculate whether in 1745 the Prince was told of the tragedy by the young Clanranald who accompanied him.

In the ruined castle, Seton and Audrey saw the remains of the kitchen and its beehive oven. In the massive castle walls the marks of the beams show that the ceilings were low. Also shown to them was a piece of one of the old beams, cut from resinous pine, which made the task of firing Castle Toiram all the easier.

Before they returned to Aviemore, the ninety-year-old Norman MacLeod of MacLeod died, and his eighty-five-year old brother Sir Reginald MacLeod became the twenty-seventh chief. By an entail of 1866, the heir to Dunvegan could be the eldest daughter of the last surviving brother. Thus with the death of Iain Breac in 1915, Sir Reginald's daughter, Flora, became a candidate. She did not become the official heir, however, until 1934 after the death of her uncle, Cannon Roderick MacLeod. After the funeral of Norman, Seton Gordon received a warm letter of thanks from Sir Reginald for securing the services of Angus and Malcolm MacPherson to be the official pipers. The letter suggests that in fact he played a bigger part in the arrangements than simply getting the agreement of the MacPhersons:

> 6 November 1929.
>
> Dear Seton,
>
> I can hardly say how grateful I am for your wonderful kindness. It was an immense matter getting the Macphersons to play the Lament for Rory Mhor in the old Keep, and as well the Lament for the Children was superbly grand and affecting. The pipers playing as the procession moved with the constant silent change of bearers, the hundreds of friends of all classes present to show their affection, undeterred by the storms of wind and rain and sleet, were almost overwhelming, and you were the moving spirit in so much. No one who was present will ever forget, and from my heart I thank you.
>
> Yours very sincerely and gratefully,
>
> Reginald MacLeod of MacLeod.

The MacPhersons returned to Duntulm with Seton where they spent several days before going home. While at Duntulm, Angus composed a pipe tune which he called, *Salute to Seton Gordon*. The copy in Seton's papers is inscribed,

> This *piobaireachd* was composed by me after a visit to the home of my ancestors, the Isle of Skye. The occasion being the funeral of the chief of the MacLeods at Dunvegan, at which my son Malcolm and myself played the pipes together.
>
> Mr Seton Gordon himself being a *piobaireachd* player of wonderful taste and sentiment, it may truly be recorded that on this occasion the old MacCrimmon spirit was once again played near to the cradle of its origin.
>
> To commemorate a special occasion,
>
> Signed respectfully, Angus MacPherson.

On the last day of November Ramsay MacDonald wrote again, this time from Chequers:

Dear Mr Seton Gordon,

Since I wrote to you my little cobble has been whirling madly . . . I put in a note to the Scottish Office about Skye roads, and now will do so again.

Do be careful lest you hand yourself over to mechanically minded engineers who are at enmity with the soul, in giving yourself roads. One day I hope to set foot on Skye once more and see how you are doing. My youngest daughter tramped it last Autumn and loved it.

As you have had warnings that, in spite of the scent of wild thyme, the winter approaches I cannot, alas, do what I used to do. But I would like, more than I can tell you, to stand once more on the Cuillins and look around me.

Yours very sincerely, J. Ramsay MacDonald.

1929 ended with the family back in Aviemore, where Seton gave attention to their finances. His total earnings for the year was £423–10–9d, of which £104–2–6d came from lectures. The balance was from articles and royalties. There was a mortgage of £700 on the Aviemore house, but the rates were only £3–12–9d. Income tax was £7–0–0. During the year Horace did exactly 4000 miles. When it is considered that most of this motoring was in the west and central Highlands, it gives an indication of the amount of travel undertaken for research, bird-watching, and piping.

During January and the first part of February Seton remained in Aviemore, fishing some of the tributaries of the Spey and Loch an Eilean. Before heading south to give a series of lectures, he made a brief return to the west coast. This produced a most unusual diary entry, which showed beyond a shadow of doubt how his feelings for the west had crystallised, and for him there was no other place to live:

14 Feb. A sense of well being pervades me.

It was after a long journey eastward to the Highlands lying east of the Highland line, that on returning to the west, I realised with swift gratitude the sea spell, or perhaps I should say the spell of the ocean at the pleasant lands that go to meet her by Garve and Achnasheen. The sullen rain had swept the sodden moors. The trees were leafless, Nature was cold. Then, as the train dropped down to the western seaboard, I chanced to look out of the carriage window. What a transformation met my gaze. The sky was a deeper blue, the whitened dome of a shapely hill caught the noon-tide sun. There was a glowing warmth on the moor – colour was everywhere. A sense of well-being pervades me. It was the uplift of the spirit – very wonderful – the more inspiring was that it was totally unexpected.

This led me to think that going from the west was made worthwhile, however irksome that journey had been. The joy with which the traveller greeted the homelands of the west on his return. There is storm and wind, but there is colour everywhere, in the vast cumulus clouds, in the wind-torn waters, where white crested waves dance joyfully. I feel I have come home. The things I loved have been restored to me – fully.

It may have been this moment when a decision was made to make Skye his permanent home. During the coming year enquiries were made about purchasing Duntulm Lodge from the Department of the Secretary of State for Scotland and when it was found that the Department would not sell, a search was made for another house. Audrey gave tacit consent to the idea, but never totally shared Seton's enthusiasm for Skye. According to Alasdair Gordon, his mother referred to it as a 'wet desert'. Nevertheless, she dutifully made her home there, and gave her all to it, joining committees in the pursuit of improved social services on the island, and fully supporting Seton in his bid to improve the roads.

Although he enjoyed his own company, many of Seton's walks in the Highlands and Islands were taken with a companion, but seldom more than one. Unlike his contemporaries who wrote about the west of Scotland, he preferred a single companion who could share his appreciation, to the company of a babbling group.

Two men who entered Seton's life in the early 1930s, and shared many outings were Francis Cameron-Head of Inverailort, and Viscount David Fincastle. He had seen Cameron-Head intermittently through the years and, according to the guest-book had visited Inverailort as early as 1911. It was not until now that a closer association developed. Both men shared a consuming love of the Highlands; both played the pipes and had an equal knowledge of *piobaireachd*. Cameron-Head's widowed mother was a dominant factor in his life for many years, until his marriage to Lucretia ('Putchi') Farrell in 1942. In common with Seton, Cameron-Head was a Fellow of the Zoological Society and an ardent member of the Royal Scottish Pipers' Society and the '45 Association. He had attended Balliol College, Oxford where he studied law, and was called to the Bar, Inner Temple, in 1923.

Viscount Fincastle's father was the Earl of Dunmore, VC who had a home on Sleat, very close to Armadale Castle, and this is how Seton became acquainted with the family. Fincastle joined the Territorial Battalion of the Cameron Highlanders and received his commission in 1927. Because of his love for the Outer Isles he was attached to the Island Company, which he later commanded. The MacDonalds of Sleat still occupied Armadale Castle at that time, and Hamish MacDonald, although still at Eton, came under Seton Gordon's spell and was another frequent companion on hill walks and at piping occasions. Like Viscount Fincastle, Hamish joined the 4th Territorial Battalion of the Cameron Highlanders and was commissioned Second Lieutenant in the Skye Company in November 1930. He also died in the war. Lady Marjorie Stirling, Viscount David Fincastle's sister, remembers Hamish as a charming and gentle person, much quieter than his brother Alasdair, who succeeded to the Chieftainship in 1951. The direct succession was broken when the Hon. Godfrey MacDonald of Sleat, father of Alasdair and Hamish, was killed in February 1915 while serving in the Scots Guards.

When Seton went south in February 1930 he lectured at Eton, where he took the opportunity to pipe with Hamish. Among other places where he lectured on this tour were: Oakfield, his old prep school, Cambridge University, and the

Royal Institute. There were sixteen lectures and the most important was to raise funds for the Gaelic Society of London and the London Highland Club. The first intimation was a note to Ramsay MacDonald from Aviemore:

> . . . If you find yourself with an hour to spare on 19 February, I hope you will come to support my lecture, and incidentally the Societies for which it is given.
>
> You will see that Sir Edward Grey is kind enough to preside, and I hope we may have the pipes also. I enclose a leaflet.
>
> If you can come, will you propose a vote of thanks to the ladies who have worked so hard for the lecture?

A reply from 10 Downing Street advised that the Prime Minister's time was uncertain, though he invited Seton Gordon to lunch on the 19th. MacDonald was unable to attend the lecture, but in thanking him for lunch, Seton pressed another invitation on him to come to Skye for Easter – and there were further enquiries about the Conista road.

In August 1930, the whole population of St Kilda was removed and resettled in the west Highlands. Despite his lifelong interest in these islands, Seton Gordon did not go to witness the evacuation, but he was at Oban to see them disembark. In *Afoot in the Hebrides* he mentioned the St Kildans' aversion to the kilt. As they came off the gangway, one of the assembly there to meet them was a Gaelic speaker who always wore Highland dress. He greeted one old man, who after thanking him lowered his voice and said, 'Are you not ashamed, you who have the Gaelic, to be wearing that indecent dress?'

Seton was again in the Cuillins for a September climb of Sgurr nan Gillean, the impressive hill with a notched summit which forms the background to Glen Sligachan. In the Glen is the renowned Sligachan Inn, from where over the years many climbers, some of international fame, have set out for a day's climbing in these incomparable hills. Glen Sligachan is inseparable from the Cuillins and there are few people who can resist its spell. Many writers have given their impressions of Glen Sligachan, their sense, not always of love, but of awe, among them Alexander Smith in his *Summer on Skye*, H.V. Morton in *In Search of Scotland*, and Alasdair Alpin MacGregor in *Over the Sea to Skye*. It is interesting to read some of their impressions compared to those of Seton Gordon. Describing Sligachan and the Cuillin in 1857, Smith wrote:

> Glen Sligachan is wild and desolate beyond conception. As in many other parts of Skye, the scenery curiously repels you, and drives you in on yourself . . . Their utter movelessness, the austere silence, daunt you.

In 1929 H.V. Morton published *In Search of Scotland*. In it he described arriving at Sligachan too late at night to see his surroundings, and his reaction the next morning when he saw the Cuillins for the first time:

> Imagine Wagner's 'Ride of the Valkyries' frozen in stone and hung up like a

> colossal screen against the sky. Their scarred ravines and towering spires of rock never look the same for very long, now blue, now grey, now silver, sometimes seeming to retreat or to advance, but always drenched in mystery and terror. . . . Skye is outside normal experience and stands alone, one of Nature's supreme experiments in atmosphere.

Alasdair Alpin MacGregor also wrote several books on the west of Scotland. *Over the Sea to Skye* was written in 1926 and in a sub-chapter called *The Wildness of Glen Sligachan* describes his thoughts while hiking through the glen:

> On my last journey through Glen Sligachan, in mist and driving rain I climbed above Loch a' Choire Riabhaich to the ridge known as Drumhain. The wildness of the scene around Drumhain I shall never forget. Marsco, Trodhu, Blaven, Sgurr Alasdair at the four cardinal points of the compass fill one with a sense of magnitude and desolation that is sometimes depressing, nay, appalling. Below, Loch Scaviag rolled furiously before a driven gale, and Coruisk bore a sullen countenance . . .

For one place to capture the minds of these men, and for them to describe it in such terms, shows that they have caught the essence of Skye. It explains why such words as 'magic' and 'dream' can be used side by side with 'appalling', 'fearful', 'mystery' and 'terror'.

Yet Seton Gordon embraced, and saw in a totally different way, things that Smith, Morton and MacGregor mentioned with an awe bordering on fear. How different from his revelling in the thunderstorm in the heart of the Cuillins. How different from his diary entry for 2 September 1930:

> On Sgurr nan Gillean found azelea procumbans in two places – did not know it grew in the Cuillin. Blaven was almost as blue as the sky, and Marsco glowed pink at sunset. Gradually mist slipped over all the tops except Sgurr nan Giliean – fine moonset over Vaternish.

On every occasion, he felt only beneficence from these peaks. Someone else whose love of the Cuillins equalled Seton Gordon's was international mountain climber and chemistry professor, Norman Collie. This intellectual man, who named over thirty peaks in the Canadian Rockies, returned to the Cuillins regularly. He always took John MacKenzie of Sconsor as his companion, the Cuillin guide with whom Seton had first ascended Sgurr Alasdair. A strong bond developed between these two men, so different in background and intellect. Collie ended his days at Sligachan, and died there on 1 November 1942, at the age of 83. He outlived MacKenzie by nine years, and asked that he be buried next to his friend in the churchyard at Struan, on Loch Harport.

Despite having climbed almost every mountain range in the world, Norman Collie's first and last love was the Cuillin Hills. There is no record of a meeting with Seton Gordon, but it is almost inevitable that their paths crossed, so much time did they both spend in them. Spiritually they were very close, and Collie's diary descriptions of the Cuillin are remarkably akin to those of Seton.

On 12 September Seton Gordon arrived at Inverailort House, for an outing with Francis Cameron-Head. From here they set out on the long walk to Loch Moidart, and the island of Shona Beag.

It was late afternoon when they arrived and the tide was at a low ebb, so they were able to walk across the channel to the island, to call on Dr MacVicar, a direct descendent of the MacDonalds of Kinlochmoidart. His house held a collection of Raeburns and many relics of the '45. Dr. MacVicar showed his visitors a bagpipe given to his ancestor in 1790 by a Macintyre of Uldary, the last hereditary piper to Clanranald, just before he emigrated to America. It was played at the Battle of Bannockburn, and an unusual feature was an extra hole, below the 'low G' hole. It was said to have been added on the advice of a fairy who said that the extra hole would guarantee music, the like of which had not been heard before.

John Macintyre, hereditary piper to Clanranald, composed *'My King has Landed at Moidart'* in 1745 when the Prince arrived there from Loch nan Uamh. Seton Gordon recalled that tune as he held these ancient pipes, the mouthpiece being four-sided and not rounded as in bagpipes of recent times.

When they left the house, dusk was falling and the tide had risen so that it was necessary to be rowed across the channel where a few hours before they had walked. The road to Lochailort was at the time many years away, and Seton captured a feeling of the country of Moidart when the only means of traversing it was by ancient tracks:

> We had a long way before us, across the hills to Glenuig, and thence along the shores of Loch Ailort. I saw on my walk that evening, many cairns built beside the path. Some were of great age, a few were almost new. They marked the resting-places of those who carried the mortal remains of their loved ones from the shore of Loch Ailort to the sacred Eilean Fhionain on Loch Shiel. The path climbs heathery slopes, and looks down upon the clachan of Glenuig and the waters of Loch Ailort.
>
> Dusk had fallen as we passed through Glenuig. Blue peat smoke rose slowly from the houses. From the west came the flashes of the small lighthouse on Eigg, and the hills of Rhum grew fainter in the deepening gloom as we made our way towards the welcoming lights of Inverailort.

Before road construction began, Seton Gordon received a letter from John Gibson, secretary of the Advisory Panel on the Highlands and Islands, St Andrew's House, Edinburgh, in May 1959 asking his advice on the origins of this track:

> I am writing to ask if you can throw any light on the history of the bridle track which runs from Inverailort to Kinlochmoidart, through Glenuig. Lord Cameron, of the Highland Panel walked along part of this track and expressed

> great interest in its history. Mr Iain Hilleary has suggested that we consult you since you know the area so well.
>
> Consideration is being given to the possibility of constructing a road to link South Moidart with the Fort William-Mallaig road. The community at Glenuig is also falling off in numbers and is not likely to remain in existence for very long unless a road is built. The South Moidart and Ardnamurchan people have also made their views known to the Panel that the development of the tourist trade is bound up with this road.
>
> What impressed us was that long sections of the track are built of solid blocks of stone. Culverts of solid stone construction have also been built at very considerable labour. There are no records of the building of this track, although it is thought to have been in existence at the time of the '45. There are, too, the funeral cairns between Glenuig and Kinlochmoidart. Some of these, I understand are very old and should be preserved.
>
> It may be that this track is only unique in that most others of this type have have been built over by modern roads.
>
> I know that the opening up of Moidart is bound to cause some regret but if it has to come we must ensure that links with the past, such as the more spectacular bits of this track are kept.

It is difficult to realise that this road is so recent. It does not intrude too much on the landscape and is narrow. When road construction finally started, after the lobbying efforts of Mrs 'Puchi' Cameron-Head, her husband Francis had died. He would have appreciated the concern shown for the funeral markers which he and Seton Gordon had examined on their way home from Shona Beag. Great care was taken in the siting of the road, many of the cairns were left in place, and those that had to be moved were relocated as close as possible to their original positions.

Seton Gordon was eager to arrange a lecture on behalf of the MacDonalds' Baby Clinic and reminded the Prime Minister of this in March 1931. The clinic was a project started years earlier by Margaret MacDonald, and Ishbel had taken over its upkeep. She had also taken over as hostess at 10 Downing Street, long before her twenty-first birthday. The clinic was the first of its kind, and eventually became a hospital specialising in infant care. The lecture did not take place until early the following year. The reply was in a humourous vein, but it served to emphasise the pressures of MacDonald's job:

> I really think I must prohibit you from writing any more of these bewitching letters about your voyaging and your weather! Think of the cruelty you do me, doomed to get up at 6.30 in the morning to a foggy day, and to sit here at the House of Commons until at least 11 o'clock in the evening, doing drudgery work which a wise man like yourself despises. Your letters to me are like revolutionary and seditious literature which evil minded communists distribute in barracks and for which they get sentenced quite properly to months and months imprisonment! . . .

The wheels of government were turning and a significant step in the confirmation of the Conista road took place in early May. Ramsay MacDonald's letter on this event has not survived but it produced the following reaction at Duntulm:

> 14 May 1931.
>
> Dear Prime Minister,
>
> Your letter arrived here yesterday morning. My wife and I went over to Conista forthwith . . . It would have cheered you to have seen its effect on the good folk there. In one of the houses there was an old blind woman nursing a baby by the fire. She had no English and held our hands & refused to let us go.
>
> If the new road gets under way this summer I think you must come here & meet some of your friends you have made by helping them in their simple lives.
>
> I heard from Viscount Grey in Switzerland. He is undergoing a last remedy cure for his eyesight & wrote in a rather depressed state. He misses more than anything being away from his birds at Fallodon at this season of the year – I hope he may get good out of it all. Again thank you so much for your kind help & the trouble you have taken. Yours very sincerely, Seton Gordon.

The news of Viscount Grey's worsening eyesight was received just prior to writing to the Prime Minister:

> My visit to the Swiss occulist has left me with a dreary prospect. He says I must go into his clinic as soon as possible for eight weeks. I am going on 24 April. I shall be back by 20 June, but I shall have missed nearly all the singing of the birds and the greater part of the breeding season of my waterfowl. I feel crushed . . .

Skye was soon to be the Gordon family's permanent place of residence. Early in 1931 an agreement was signed to buy the Kilmuir manse, also known as the Lodge of Osmigarry. The Gordons wished to be near to watch the renovations and the building of an extension, so they remained at Duntulm Lodge to 19 December, when the move was made to Upper Duntuilm, as their new house was to be called, with an 'i' inserted.

It is a large stone house, standing a few hundred yards off the main road around Trotternish, two miles south of the lodge which they had rented in recent years. With the manse came the glebe of 70 acres. The Kilmuir cemetery where Flora MacDonald lies buried is just to the north, and the large monument on her grave is visible from the house.

A sad note was recorded on 1 July, the death of their collie Dileas. Seton wrote: 'Dileas went away from us today. We are both very sad. We buried her body beside the gate – where she had often listened for Horace'. A few days later he wrote another inspirational line: 'God has written his name in the Heavens with stars, on the Earth with flowers'.

In *A Highland Year*, he spoke of Dileas and her successor, Dara:

> Dileas was a black and white collie, lightly built and swift of foot. She was our constant, most devoted companion for many years, a remarkable dog in many ways. Dara is a philosopher and her appetite never fails. Dileas had a more sad nature, and the sight of a suitcase being packed used to cause her grave disquiet until she realised that she was to accompany us on the journey. She knew by name each member of the family, and when told to go to any particular one did so without hesitation. A dog can be a great friend and companion – almost one's greatest friend and companion in some respects.
>
> At last our beloved Dileas fell sick. Each morning, like Dara, she was accustomed to accompany me to the sea for a swim. That morning she came with me a short distance, then turned sorrowfully back. She knew that she was shortly going out on that long journey which would separate her from those she loved. She had sat in hides with us as we watched the golden eagle; she had listened to the lovesong of the greenshank and had accompanied us in the tracks of a hill blizzard, and beneath the hot summer sun. Her life had been bound closely to ours and now she knew she was going to an unknown land, far from us both. Her look of sadness and despair remains with me still. That day I had to be from home, but my wife remained with Dileas. In the afternoon I knew there was sadness in my home, and knowing this I was ready for the news I received when I returned.
>
> That night we wrapped our beloved Dileas in her faded tartan rug, which had been her bed for many years, and when we had dug her grave we laid her to rest in it and built a cairn of stones over her body. I write 'body' advisedly, for I am sure that dogs, like human beings, are not extinguished by the great experience called Death, but go on to the world yonder which holds the spirit forms of trees and flowers, rivers, lakes and seas, birds and animals, and all those beings that we see in their material form on this earth. And so perhaps we shall some day find Dileas again.

In a letter to the Prime Minister after the death of Air Minister Lord Thompson in the October 1930 R101 airship disaster, Seton expressed much the same thoughts:

> Life is at best short and uncertain and, did we think that personality ended with earthly death, would often seem meaningless. But we know that personality survives and may come again to us from the unknown just as surely as if those we knew and loved were standing beside us in the flesh.
>
> We do not know what their work is over yonder, what occupies them but we do know that at times, in the rush of the wind, in the turmoil of the storm-pressed ocean, they come to us with good tidings, and thereafter we take up life again refreshed.

This expressed belief in an afterlife which comes through in so much of his writing, did not suggest a purely Christian concept of Heaven, but more of the Celtic idea of a life beyond. To Seton it applied as much to animals as to humans, as each of his much loved dogs died. The references to Tir nan Og and

Their Majesties King George VI and Queen Elizabeth as Duke and Duchess of York at Upper Duntuilm, September 1933. (Reproduced by kind permission of HM Queen Mother)

other spirit places would to some, particularly to strict Presbyterians, be sacrilegious, but he managed to endow the idea with a simplicity which embraced his entire range of feelings, for the natural world, for the vastness of the ocean beyond the Outer Isles, and for mysteries beyond the sunset.

An invitation to a Royal Garden Party was received. It was to be held at Holyrood Palace, Edinburgh on 9 July. Seton and Audrey went south to attend it despite their sorrow over the loss of Dileas. His diary entry for that day said:

> King very friendly – said he was framing my golden eagle picture for his own room at Balmoral. A big thunderstorm when the party was half way through!

It was here that Seton had a conversation with a woman, which became another story he liked to tell against himself. She came up to him and said 'Aren't you Mr Seton Gordon?' Feeling pleased at being recognised, he said 'Yes I am'. The woman then said she had a sister who suffered from insomnia, and she had bought her a Seton Gordon book to read at bedtime, ending with the statement, 'Since then she barely gets into more than a few pages and goes straight off to sleep!'

One person absent from Holyrood was the Prime Minister, and on the 14th he wrote on another matter for which Seton Gordon had been lobbying, a suitable honour for John MacDonald of Inverness:

> Private and Confidential.
>
> My Dear Seton Gordon,
> I was very glad to have your letter though Holyrood was quite impossible for me.
> As to John MacDonald – I do not quite know what sort of honour would be appropriate. If he would promise to walk up and down the House of Lords every afternoon playing some martial air, I might make him a Peer, but I am afraid that the days when that would be appropriate are over. The minor honours of the British Empire, like the OBE, would probably not be appreciated by him. If I could do anything within reason and in artistic keeping with the man and his work, I would do it with great pleasure.
> With kind regards, I am yours very sincerely, J. R. MacDonald.

In the autumn the Gordons purchased their second collie, Dara, who, like Dileas, became a faithful companion for many years. The renovations and addition were progressing at Kilmuir, and they hoped to be settled in by Christmas, but their request was granted to continue living at Duntulm Lodge beyond 31 October. Despite Seton's preoccupation with the new house, he wrote again to Ramsay MacDonald offering to distribute information on the newly elected National Government and suggesting that he should come to Skye to address a meeting.

It was a time of great stress for Ramsay MacDonald. By the summer of 1931 it was obvious that the Labour government was no more capable of finding solutions to the depression than the one it replaced, with two and a half million out of work. MacDonald had offered his resignation to the King in August, resulting in a constitutional impasse. George V ended it by requesting that he form a National Government.

When the votes were counted, the election gave the National Government a majority, though it was heavily weighted towards Conservatives. MacDonald remained nominally Prime Minister of the coalition. With a naval mutiny at Invergordon over a proposed reduction of pay, and Great Britain coming off the gold standard, it is unlikely that MacDonald had much time to dream of Skye.

On 19 December, the family moved into Upper Duntuilm. With royalties of £372–12–8d and earnings for articles and school lectures of £195–15–0d, Seton's total for the year was £568–7–8d. The faithful 'Horace' was driven a total of 3156 miles.

CHAPTER

8

HIGHWAYS, BYWAYS AND A NEW FRIENDSHIP

THE EXPOSURE OF UPPER DUNTUILM, although further from the sea than Duntulm Lodge, was as great because it was higher, 300 feet above sea level. There was no windbreak of trees or bushes and there was some trial and error before suitable ones could be found that would take the gales and the salt-damp air. Nevertheless they persevered and Upper Duntuilm became home to Seton and Audrey, and subsequently for Seton and his second wife Betty, until his death in 1977. The house was equipped with radiator central heating throughout, but when Ronald Lockley and his wife stayed a few years after the Gordons had moved in, he said that they preferred to burn peat and use paraffin lamps which 'give an old-fashioned shadowy light at night, in keeping with the Isle of Skye'.

Seton had further to walk each morning to take a swim, but he continued this practice, to the amazement of his new neighbours. Dara soon learned to enjoy these outings, and they discovered a natural rock pool with about 15 feet of water at high tide. This ritual took place almost daily until the early 1940s:

> On a frosty winter's morning it was sometimes Dara and sometimes it was I who took the first icy plunge. Those were cold swims in the half-light when all the earth to the tide mark was frozen iron-hard and when there was ice even on the rock pools where the sea anenomes were torpid from the cold, but the splendour of the rising sun upon the snow-clad hills of the Outer Hebrides on our return journey was an ample reward for that cold walk and swim. Sometimes in rough winter weather one had to time the plunge into the pool so as to be able to climb out during a momentary lessening in the fury of the waves. Dara, I discovered, watched the far-out oncoming waves as carefully as I did and if she saw a distant wave of unusual size, even sometime before it approached the shore and broke, she could not be induced into the water.

Seton and Audrey went south as usual early in 1932 to give their school lectures and while in London Seton gave a joint lecture with Viscount Grey to the English Speaking Union. Great care had been taken in selecting the pictures of the Fallodon ducks with Viscount Grey, and because of his blindness Lord Grey had to memorise the order in which they came. Seton's job was to point out the salient features of each slide while Grey described them.

Ramsay MacDonald was at this time also having acute eye problems. He was suffering from glaucoma and eventually had an operation to relieve the pressure. His doctor ordered complete rest, and in offering sympathy Seton Gordon revealed his thoughts on deafness compared to blindness:

> I hope you will take a bit of a rest now, and remember that good men are scarce.
>
> Sight is an even more precious thing than hearing – I've lost a good deal of my hearing – it would be pleasant to hear the birds as I used to, but sight is a more precious gift.
>
> I am wondering where the lecture for the Clinic is to be held, and whether your daughter has got any leaflets I could send to people? . . .

The Prime Minister replied on 22 February:

> I have just had yours of the 17th. Ishbel is writing to you about the lecture. This trouble of mine has played havoc with my engagements, and your proposed lunch also falls in the uncertain days. Everything is so unfortunate and I am rather sick of it. However we must try to meet somehow.

The lecture in aid of Ishbel MacDonald's Clinic took place as arranged, on the 14 March at 5:30 p.m. in the state drawing room of 10 Downing Street. Ramsay MacDonald hastened from the House of Commons to introduce Seton Gordon. The next day Ishbel MacDonald sent a letter of thanks and informed Seton that 126 people had attended and a total of £91–1–6d was raised.

Each time Ramsay MacDonald wrote to Seton Gordon expressing a wish to be among the Cuillin of Skye, it was no idle statement. He found comfort in the hills, and the family holidays in Scotland were vital to his mental and physical well-being. He wrote to a supporter, 'I have been a day and a night in the hills in wild weather. It soothes me, & being able to tramp over miles of wet heather & to sleep in a bed of wet stuff & get up as fresh as a daisy to see the sun, & wash in roaring torrents of icy water, makes me feel that there may be some kick left yet. The heather and pine woods never smelt sweeter . . . We lay down under shelter of a great boulder. No king in his feather bed was ever happier. We were alone amongst the clouds, the companions of the storm and the rushing water'.

In another context, the tragedy of Ramsay MacDonald was that his vision of peace was one which at that time most people could not share or fully comprehend. He had attained the Prime Minister's office yet he never fully recovered from his revulsion of the events between 1914 and 1918. By 1932 he no longer headed a strong party and had to be content with overseeing an unsatisfactory compromise.

When Macmillan asked Seton Gordon to write *Highways and Byways in the West Highlands* and later, *Highways and Byways in the Central Highlands*, the publisher commissioned Sir David Young Cameron to provide the illustrations. He was a man of great spirituality, and writing of 'D.Y'. as he liked to be called, Seton Gordon said,

> My friendship with D.Y. began when, unknown to me, Macmillan the publishers asked him to illustrate one of my books. I knew him first through the medium of letters His life's quest, his life's ideal was Beauty, but not for himself alone. He was happy when through the medium of his art, others were able to share it. From him I received many cherished letters. I soon learnt that in each one I could expect a gem of thought, a flash of inspiration.

D.Y'.s style was quite different from that of either MacKinnon or Harrison. His illustrations were in muted tones and the faintest curved lines and washes gave a satisfying impression of distant cumulus cloud above exquisitely drawn mountains. There were great pools of light and deep shadows on the landscape for dramatisation. (See Appendix 3)

To prepare for this new commission, Seton and Audrey began to visit islands and areas where they had not yet been. In July 1932 they did a tour down the coast as far as Arran. While exploring Colonsay, Jura and Islay, Seton spent much of the time talking to old families on these islands and gleaned a considerable amount of folklore from them. While on Islay the Gordons stayed for a few days with the factor to Morrison of Islay, James MacKillop, and his wife Grace. MacKillop was a skilled piper. A letter from Grace MacKillop following the visit showed the 'awe' which was beginning to be attached to Seton Gordon. In it she said: 'It was a great pleasure seeing you both here. I don't mind confessing I was a little nervous, but I can honestly say that we have never had nicer, or easier visitors and to have met you both has been a great happiness we shall never forget'.

James MacKillop wrote a letter as well, and it is the one that Alistair Campsie referred to and extensively quoted in his *The MacCrimmon Legend*. It dealt exclusively with the MacCrimmon speckled pipe, and was a personal letter to Seton Gordon. Since at the time there was no controversy over the MacCrimmon legend, there was no reason why it should not have remained so. It was, according to Campsie, not made public until 1968 by the, as he called it, 'self-styled' Glasgow College of Piping. He wrote: 'But in 1968 it had already been 'revealed' that James MacKillop may have eventually realised he was the victim of a piping confidence trick, symptomatic of the times'. The letter, written on 16 September 1932 reads:

> Dear Seton Gordon,
>
> Many thanks for your letter. It is a long time since I made the pilgrimage to Dunvegan with the late General Thomason and Colin Cameron, and I fear some of the details may have escaped my memory, but I shall try to recall as much as possible.
>
> The reason why nothing is stated regarding the chanter on the *Piob Bhreac* is that we were doubtful about it. The chanter was brought to us at

Dunvegan. It was said to have belonged to the MacCrimmons and was broken and cracked. I was given it on condition that I sent a new Henderson chanter to replace it, which I did. I got Peter Henderson of Glasgow, to bind up the broken chanter with silver rings, and fit it with a new sole, and later on when I managed after long negotiations to secure the drone tops of the *Piob Bhreac*, I decided to complete the set of pipes, and return them to Dunvegan along with the repaired chanter.

The drone tops are genuine. They had been in the hands of a Skye family of MacPhersons for a long time, and the man I got them from was a pipe-major in the Royal Scots, Donald Ewen MacPherson. He was a well-known piper about thirty years ago, and I always liked him and admired him for his pluck and courage, tho' he always had a weakness for the 'mountain dew' which was largely responsible for my being able to secure the drone tops, otherwise they would probably have been in Canada with MacPherson, as I understand he is there now, and I hope doing well.

It was through the late Peter Henderson of Glasgow, and the late J. MacDougall-Gillies, that I negotiated with MacPherson about the drone tops, and both were most helpful. MacPherson was at first unwilling to part with them and said it would bring a curse on his family, and that he would forever be disgraced.

The negotiations lasted about two years and would not I think have been concluded if poor MacPherson had not got into troubles financial. He owed Peter Henderson quite a lot of money, which I agreed to pay on condition that I got the drone tops of the *Piob Bhreac*.

The late Peter Henderson was a splendid craftsman and it was entirely due to his skill that the lower parts of the drones were so successfully copied from the original, and the set completed. I kept the pipes for some time and used to play them, but considered the rightful place for them was Dunvegan, so I sent them to the late MacLeod.

As you know, the *Piob Bhreac* was a well known set of MacCrimmon pipes, *breac* meaning spotted, speckled, chequered, piebald; *bhreac* exactly describes the drone tops, with their variety of rings.

I had heard about the *Piob Bhreac* long before I knew MacPherson had them. The late MacLeod very kindly let me have the two-drone pipes on loan, and I got a new bag fitted and tried them out with the old General, MacDougall-Gillies, Peter Henderson and others. I am sorry to say that we were not greatly impressed with them. I dont know anything about the history of the chanter . . .

I hope you will both find your way back to Islay again very soon.

With kindest rememberances from both of us.

Yours very sincerely, James MacKillop.

General Thomason died in 1911, so the events described were indeed 'a long time ago', as MacKillop stated.

Achnacarry was the location for the Gaelic Mod in October of 1932. The

Prime Minister attended in the company of Seton Gordon. The following day he wrote to Ramsay MacDonald from the castle, to say how pleased he was to have spent several hours in his company, '. . . This is a line to tell you how glad I was to see you yesterday – I think it was quite the most pleasant moment of the Mod to me when I saw your face. I wish you had been there again today, although I think yesterday was more enjoyable . . . you have made many friends in Lochaber'.

While at Achnacarry he made notes for a chapter of *Highways and Byways of the West Highlands*, called 'Lochiel's Country'. He described it as perhaps the most romantic district in all the western Highlands. Of all Highland clans, the Camerons of Lochiel are one of the most noteworthy and Seton Gordon became as fascinated by this clan as he had been with the MacLeods. The chiefs have a direct and unbroken lineage for generations past, and many were outstanding leaders. The present chief, Sir Donald Hamish Cameron of Lochiel, like his father, saw active service, though instead of the Cameron Highlanders it was with the Lovat Scouts in the Second World War. The next two generations are assured, through his son, Donald, Younger of Lochiel and his grandson, also Donald.

Although no clan can completely escape censure for the behaviour of its chiefs at the time of the Clearances, the Camerons were far from being the worst. The family also had its share of suffering from the '45 and its aftermath. Sir Donald's forbear, the 'Gentle Lochiel', was severely wounded at Culloden and was carried back to Achnacarry, where he went into hiding. He watched as Cumberland's troops ransacked the house before burning it. His lands were confiscated and he fled to France, where he died in 1748. Two of his brothers who also fought on the side of the Prince, Alexander, a priest, and Archibald, a medical doctor, were executed. Another brother, Ewen, although at Culloden, fared better and was banished to the West Indies where he became a merchant. He returned to Scotland and became a burgess of the City of Glasgow.

One of the darker periods of Cameron history came with the restoration of their lands in 1784, coinciding with the lifting of the proscription on the wearing of Highland dress and playing the pipes. The chieftainship had passed to a fifteen year old, another Donald, grandson of the Gentle Lochiel. He first visited his lands in 1790 when he came of age. Brought up in France and a stranger to his clan, he used eviction and the sale of land to pay off debts accrued, and to build a new castle. He died in 1832 with Achnacarry unfinished. However, a succession of responsible chiefs has brought prosperity to Lochiel's lands. The Castle sits beside Loch Arkaig, and the short Arkaig River passes by before draining into Loch Lochy. The surrounding hills are dominated by Ben Nevis to the south. The castle, actually a very comfortable and well appointed home, holds many relics of those far-off days.

Of particular interest to Seton Gordon was a silver flask given to the Gentle Lochiel by Prince Charles Edward. An inscription reads, 'Snuff Box or Dram Cup, while skulking in ye Highlands, given by him to Lochiel AD 1747, at Paris'. Hung on a wall is the clan banner, rescued after Culloden. Near the castle stands an avenue of beeches, in which at one end the trees are planted evenly spaced, and further along are close together. The reason for this is that Lochiel had been planting them when he went to meet the Prince to dissuade him from a 'reckless enterprise' and thought he would soon return to complete the task. The remaining trees grew where they had been temporarily set in the ground.

Describing his visit in a letter to Professor Watson, Seton Gordon wrote:

> Francis Cameron-Head and I had an interesting time . . . after climbing Beinn Fhada we returned to Achnacarry, passing through Glendessary. We looked down on Loch Nevis, and saw the three cairns on the watershed marking the marches of Lochiel, Lovat, and Glengarry.
>
> We passed two drovers at the bealach [pass] driving two beasts across from Nevis to the Fort William sales, and by the lochan at 1000 feet we found a little heap of sea mussel shells!

The present Lochiel was kind enough to write about the meaning of these romantic names, and said: 'The derivation of Arkaig is obscure but Glen Kaig, after which it is named, probably means Glen of the Dark River. Glendessary is derived from the Gaelic and means the Glen of the South Shieling. Loch Eil is also derived from the Gaelic, for the Loch of the Glint of Sunlight'.

A plaintive diary note on October 21, 1932 reads: 'Sulisda. Horace's Last Journey. Back Axle broke and he was towed home by MacLeod lorry'. Horace (or Horatio), manufactured in 1909, had finally given up. It was impossible to have the back axle repaired or replaced without a wide search for parts. Horace was buried at Upper Duntuilm and the gipsies took the brass. When one thinks of the restorations accomplished today on vintage cars and the ability of car enthusiasts to keep them running, it is a shame to think that buried at Kilmuir is a 1909 Wolseley. This car did well over 100,000 miles in its twenty seven years on the road, mainly on gravel.

The Gordons celebrated their first anniversary at Upper Duntuilm on 19 December. The previous day, at Kilmuir, Margaret and Hector MacDonald had a son born to them. He was christened Jonathan. As he grew he became increasingly under Seton Gordon's influence and they had almost daily contact for forty-five years. Jonathan looks back upon this time as a rare privilege.

After living at Upper Duntuilm for a year it became imperative for Seton and Audrey to establish a windbreak. The wind there is relentless and they had not found any species of tree that stood a chance of growing to a reasonable size. Advice was sought on the wind resisting power of various species and it was found that trees without tap roots were the only ones with any chance of surviving because two or three feet down was a thick layer of clay. Both the common spruce and the Sitka spruce stood up well to the frequent gales. It took twelve years to establish a belt of healthy trees to shield the house. Seton wrote, 'We were in the curious position of having excellent soil, and yet being unable to take advantage of it. Our vegetable garden is perhaps the most exposed in the British Isles. It is on the 300 foot contour line, and even though surrounded by a stone wall 6 or 8 feet high, there is little protection'. The kitchen garden, is now, alas, completely overgrown.

From 1932 on, a small herd of sheep was maintained, as well as from six to ten cows. The main crops were potatoes and oats. Near the main road is a blackhouse, now part of a crofting museum, and here for many years lived their farm hand, John Graham. Nearer to Duntulm Lodge was the MacQueen croft. Mary MacQueen became nanny to the younger Gordon children. Her reliability gave Seton and Audrey the freedom that they desired for their frequent trips away. A number of governesses were employed until the younger children went away to school.

Before the end of the year Seton was approached by his publisher, Cassell to produce another book for publication in the spring of 1933. He chose as a provisional title, *Peaceful Days*. The book was published with the title *Islands of the West* and he thought it one of his best books. It contained a chapter called 'Peaceful Days' and also 'Hill Silence'. Other chapters dealt with various Celtic festivals such as Hogmanay, Beltane, and St Bride.

Edward Grey wrote from Bath, where he went to take another form of eye treatment. Whatever it consisted of, the treatment did not work, nor, obviously had his earlier visit to Switzerland. He cannot be faulted for perhaps 'clutching at straws' in an effort to have his sight restored: 'I have no improvement in my sight, but I think the treatment I am taking here is on the right lines and I may try more of it later on, though I am now so blind and helpless that a sister has come to live with with me and help me'. (This was the last letter written in Grey's own hand. The remaining few were written by his sister and signed by him.)

It was not until March 1933 that a decision was made on a replacement for Horace. The car selected was a Lancia, a totally different class of vehicle. The price no doubt influenced Seton, as he purchased it second hand for £250, barely a third of the original price. It was given the name 'Grey Wind' and a Simplex Car Registry was kept up daily for as long as he owned the car. It was a rather grand hard-cover daily journal with two pages for each month, including a log with a line for each day, and a place for noting petrol, tyres and general maintenance expenses. It provided an accurate record of his movements around Scotland. Most entries reveal the reason for each journey, so it was part diary, although much briefer.

All the Gordon cars were serviced at Macrae and Dick of Inverness, and a retired mechanic remembers the Lancia well. Only the then foreman, Malcolm Reid, was allowed to work on it. The present managing director, Francis Hamilton, recalled that it was rather outstanding for its time, with independent front suspension comprising of telescopic springs while the engine had an overhead camshaft with offset cylinders. He said, 'It was a beautiful car and painted dark blue with a grey leather interior'. One correspondent referred to it as 'draughty and uncomfortable' but did acknowledge that Seton was very proud of it.

In Mid-April, Seton and Audrey visited Ardnamurchan, one of the remoter parts of the Highlands and roadless at that time. In 1933 the only direct access was by mail boat from Oban to Kilchoan via Tobermory. There were a number of hill-tracks from here to the clachans straddled across the peninsula. During

Betty Gordon, Seton's second wife, at Upper Duntuilm, Skye

his naval patrol days Seton frequently visited Kilchoan and Ardnamurchan Point, the most westerly place on the Scottish mainland. On the south shore of Ardnamurchan, a few miles before the point, is the castle of Mingarry. It belonged to one of the more uncommon clans, the MacIains, who had links with Clanranald. Ardnamurchan was held by the MacIains, who were as warlike as any of the neighbouring clans, but in 1624 the Campbells proved too much for them. A Campbell force sacked the castle and devastated the surrounding area. A band of escaping MacIains fled to the north side of Ardnamurchan and found sanctuary in a cave. A tragedy ensued remarkably similar to the one which occurred on Eigg forty-seven years earlier. It was described in *Highways and Byways of the West Highlands*:

> No echoing voices of men are heard today within the thick walls of Mingarry, and the stout galleys which rowed out from the castle have long since crumbled to dust. The massacre cave, which is now known as '*Uaimh Chloinn Iain*', the Cave of the MacIain's, is close to the sea, on a raised shelf. Below the cave the moss grows green and untrodden. Much driftwood lies upon the rocky shore here, and on the morning when I visited the cave, a flock of eider ducks were courting a little way out to sea. As I stood beside the cave four wild geese passed above it, gliding easily on the breeze. The Cuillin became less clear; grey showers of snow descended upon them, though on Ardnamurchan the sun still shone.

Mingarry is now on private land, but the ruins are much as Seton Gordon saw them. The keep is plainer than that of Tioram, but the arrangement of the inner walls suggests it was once a complex structure. Seen on a day of angry seas and racing clouds that throw great shafts of fast moving sunlight onto the hills of Ardnamurchan, it embodies the magic of the Highlands.

During the late summer of 1933, two events of importance took place on Skye. The first was in August when the MacCrimmon Cairn at Borreraig was unveiled by MacLeod, and the second was a tour of Skye by the Duke and Duchess of York. In May Seton Gordon wrote to Ramsay MacDonald to advise him of the first, and to tell of the simple things that gave him so much pleasure. Quite possibly it made the Prime Minister wonder why he spent so much time on the affairs of men, all the while resisting temptation to retreat once and for all to his home at Lossiemouth:

> I have just been listening on the wireless to your account of your America visit, and as you spoke the sunset glow was over the hills of Harris & a warm southerly breeze was ruffling the Minch. It is now almost 9:30 and still broad daylight.
>
> I have been out all day with the lobster fishers & have been watching the gannets plunge beneath the blue waters of the sea, in brilliant sun, and have seen little parties of migrating swallows.
>
> There is to be a ceremony in Skye on 3 August when MacLeod is to unveil the memorial cairn to the MacCrimmons, greatest pipers of all time – I should like you to be there. We should be very glad to put you up if you could get away . . .

The Prime Minister replied:

> How much do I wish that instead of meeting Cabinet Ministers I could meet lobster fishers in Skye! I should love to be with you at the cairn, and have made a note in my diary. Whether I can get away, however, is another question, because it is not only the House of Commons but the International Economic Conference that I have to keep my hand on this summer and autumn.
>
> We are all suffering from an evil which I have been preaching for years – that the economic mechanism of the world is most unreliable and that we have been living on the turning out of a machine which was never anything but ramshackle and uncertain.

Edward Grey dictated his last letter to Seton Gordon on 20 July. A few days before, Grey had put an end to the life of one of his favourite birds, a twenty-two year old Eider drake, who, like himself, was quite blind. His last letter said:

> Your account of the eagle and merlin is very interesting, and I am glad your book has been well reviewed.
>
> As to my ducks, I cannot see, but I am told there are several young

> widgeon, of which two will feed from me. Some young tufted ducks of which five will feed from the hand, five young crested pochards, of which four will also feed from the hand . . .
>
> My robin still takes mealworms every day in order to feed the second brood, but he does not introduce them to us.

Ramsay MacDonald sent a last-minute note to say: 'I have kept the MacCrimmon date of 3 August for a long time in my diary, but alas! At the last moment I have to sacrifice it.'

> I have made a note of the Lochaber Gathering, but again I am not really master of my movements. If, however it is within the bounds of possibility I should like very much to turn up. With all my best wishes & regrets that we are not to meet at Dunvegan, yours sincerely, J. R. M.

The Borreraig cairn was built of natural rock in the shape of a large 'beehive'. The inscription reads:

The Memorial Cairn of the MacCrimmons, of whom ten
generations were the hereditary Pipers of MacLeod,
and who were renowned as Composers, Performers and
Instructors of the Classical Music of the Bagpipe.

> Near to this spot stood the MacCrimmon School of Music. 1500–1800.

Sir Reginald MacLeod of MacLeod, twenty-seventh chief, unveiled the bronze plaque on which was the inscription. The two pipers honoured to play at the ceremony were John MacDonald of Inverness and Robert Reid.

In his speech MacLeod asked, 'Who were the MacCrimmons? Their origin is lost in the mists of antiquity, but for nearly 300 years, from 1500 to 1800, they were hereditary pipers to the MacLeods, and recognised authorities on pipe music in Scotland; eminent as composers, eminent as players, eminent as teachers. Wonderful, was it not, that for three centuries this family should have occupied the land on which we stand, in hereditary right, in full view of Dunvegan Castle, the home of the chiefs they served. Their work as teachers was in no way casual; on the contrary, admission to their college was formal, and seven years apprenticeship was required. . . . What men the MacCrimmons must have been to attract students from all over the Highlands to this wild spot, 60 miles from the mainland, in an island roadless and very difficult of access in those early years'.

The tunes heard that day were part of the MacCrimmon legend. The two pipers played *'I got a kiss of the King's Hand'*, *'Lament for the Children'* and *'MacCrimmon's Sweetheart'*. Seton Gordon was accompanied at Borreraig by the poet Charles Cammell who, to commemorate the cairn ceremony wrote 'Pibroch Voices'. It was published in *The Scotsman* (See Appendix 4). If the

Borreraig site did not even have the most scanty remains of a building, as claimed by Campsie and others before him, it has since fulfilled its fame as a Mecca for pipers with the 'silver chanter' competitions held every year.

Only six weeks after the Borreraig unveiling, MacLeod was host to the Duke and Duchess of York, who toured Skye from 11 September to the 15th. Seton and Audrey, as well as attending the ball at Dunvegan, received a visit from the Royal couple. A letter to Inverailort describing these events, was not to Francis, but to his mother, Christian Cameron-Head. In great excitement Seton told her:

> My Dear Mrs Cameron-Head,
>
> I did not write before to thank you for your kind hospitality, as I wanted to tell you about the Royal visit.
>
> The Duke and Duchess came to see us yesterday afternoon, and were very informal and friendly and liked our Prince Charlie portrait and the stone fireplace in my study. Dara, our collie took a great liking for the Duke and constantly licked his hand and so we think (tell Francis) a new *piobaireachd* ought to be composed called 'I Got a Lick of the Prince's Hand'.
>
> The dance at Dunvegan last night was most successful and nearly everyone wore the kilt. Lochiel was in great form. There was one Foursome, danced to the pipes and I danced with the Duchess of York. There were two Eightsomes, the Flowers of Edinburgh, the Dashing White Sergeant, Inverness Country Dance, Petronella, and others. It was over at 1 a.m.
>
> The Viewfield MacDonalds played excellently. And now to thank you for a very happy visit, in beautiful weather. It was pleasant to walk again with Francis, and I hope we may have another expedition soon?
>
> I was glad, too, to see you so much better than in the early spring, and I greatly enjoyed playing the pipes in that golden sunlight. Yours very sincerely, Seton Gordon.

Christian Cameron-Head was a formidable figure to some, especially to the young. Caitriona Macdonald-Lockhart remembers attending a ball at Inverailort and described her standing at the door looking very severe, wearing a long tartan skirt, a huge blue cloak and a yachting cap.

Another visitor to Inverailort at that time was Colonel Dermid Bingham, who now lives near Victoria, British Columbia. He trained as a surgeon in Edinburgh and had a distinguished medical career. His association with the Highlands was interrupted for some years when in 1937 he received a Rockefeller research grant and went to the University of Michigan. He attended several balls at Inverailort before 1937. He recalled that Christian Cameron-Head was very strong-willed and could not easily be dissuaded from a course of action, even if it turned out not to be in her best interests.

Colonel Bingham was also a frequent visitor to Duntulm Lodge in the 1920s and made several climbs in the Cuillin with Seton. He was a member of the Scottish Pipers' Society and the Pibroch Society and took part in the piping sessions at Inverailort, where he remembered the large number of servants before the war. He said that as well as playing the pipes, Francis Cameron-

Head was a Highland dancer. It is only in recent years that one sees more female Highland dancers than men at gatherings, and there was a time when it was an exclusively male interest. It is therefore not surprising that with his great love of Highland traditions Francis was a dancer.

In the interval between the Borreraig ceremony and the Duke and Duchess of York arriving on Skye, Edward Grey died. A memorial service was held in Westminster Abbey, though the one at Embleton village church, close to Fallodon and attended only by friends and neighbours, was a more intimate gathering. In his sermon, the vicar, the Rev. R.B. Dawson said: 'For us who lived beside him and encountered him on our daily walks, he had the unmistakable qualities of greatness'. Grey's life was a triumph over adversity, and his biographer, G.M. Trevelyan wrote:

> He was indeed one whom fortune loved and hated out of the common measure. All that he enjoyed so intensely and suffered so profoundly, all that he undertook and endured and performed, operating on a mind and body of unusual strength, made him a nobler man every year he lived. His face, in youth beaked and bright-eyed like a hawk's, became like that of the king of birds. Men spoke of his 'sad eagle eyes'. At the close of his life all who were sensitive to the touch of greatness felt it in his presence.

Seton Gordon had also referred to Grey's greatness, but he was better qualified to write on Grey as a naturalist, which he did in an article decribing their long friendship, 'Viscount Grey of Fallodon – Nature Lover':

> Grey the statesman is likely to pass into history as one of the greatest Englishmen of all time: Edward Grey the naturalist is a figure that is less widely known. No one who visited Fallodon failed to be impressed by the atmosphere of the place where the calm and kindly presence of its owner radiated goodwill towards all living creatures. The study window was open from morning to night, so that a squirrel guest could enter the room whenever it felt inclined to do so and feed on the bowl of nuts that was already on the desk. Titmice flew freely about the room, and in the spring of 1933 a robin was in the habit of singing its full song when perched on Lord Grey's head.
>
> My last morning at Fallodon was memorable. It was in March, 1933 and the sun shone brightly as we walked round the upper pond to the famous white seat where Lord Grey sat down and I stood on the path a few yards away. I had long wished to see, and to photograph, a mandarin drake fly up and alight on Edward Grey's head, but I had never been present at the right moment. It was my last morning at Fallodon, and I had to leave after lunch.
>
> A little time later a mandarin drake swam into our view, climbed the bank and after looking intently at Lord Grey, flew into the air and landed on his head. Standing on this remarkable perch the mandarin actually began to display. Two more mandarin drakes flew up and alighted on the back of the seat – one on either side of him. The picture was remarkable and beautiful. The spring sun shone full upon the rich plumage of the three mandarin

drakes as they stood motionless as though on guard, one on the statesman's head and one on either side of him. They were without fear or uneasiness and one of the drakes actually closed his eyes and dozed for a brief space. All the time the friendly figure on the seat did not move, and the only moment when the mandarins showed uneasiness was when the shutter of my camera clicked.

The birds were his constant friends and companions and to the last days of his life gave him deep pleasure. The sanctuary at Fallodon remains, but he who, like Saint Francis of old, was the presiding genius of the place is gone.

Throughout December, engagements were being booked for the 1934 lecture series and Seton wrote to the Prime Minister as soon as most of the dates were confirmed: 'You asked me to let you know when I would be south. I expect to be in London from 20 February for three weeks and am writing to you to ask if you can keep a day free to lunch with me? I hope you will be able to do this. I have a certain number of lectures to give in, and around London during my time there . . .'

There was an immediate reply:

> You have again struck me at a most unfortunate time, every day being heavily mortgaged. I have suggested to Ishbel, however, that she should ask you to join a little semi-official lunch which we are giving here on Thursday, 1 March, at one o'clock, and I should be delighted if that date would suit you.
>
> Most unfortunately the night of your lecture finds me hopelessly engaged. Yours always sincerely, R. J. M.

Perhaps this letter, more than any other, shows the relationship between Ramsay MacDonald and Seton Gordon. There was mutual liking and respect, but the nature of their lives was far apart. Ramsay MacDonald's commitments to his party, to the House of Commons, were such that it finally began to affect his health. He governed a coalition in which a majority were from the opposition, and this put him in an unenviable position. Accused of stalling, even on key issues such as urban renewal, it would be almost impossible to get agreement from such a diverse Cabinet. MacDonald had less than a year left in office before Stanley Baldwin took over once more.

Seton Gordon's life was one of calmness and serenity, by contrast to MacDonald. Why was he so persistent with his friendship? Others would have given up trying to meet or to make engagements which were inevitably cancelled. Ramsay MacDonald tried where possible to help the friendship flourish, as indicated by an invitation to this semi-official luncheon. How many long walks they were able to take together in simple companionship will never be known, but it is poignant that this was the original basis of their long contact with each other.

The younger Gordon children were away at prep school by 1934, Bridie at Crofton Grange, Buntingford, and Alasdair at Alton Burn, near Nairn. Caitriona was now eighteen and had left her school, The Grange, at Totteridge in Hertfortshire and for a time worked at a stables in Rickmansworth. She sometimes accompanied her father on hikes in the Cuillins and in the Highlands. She recalled one climb in Glen Shiel to hear if the snow bunting sang at all during the night: 'It was a long walk to the top, probably 3000 feet. We spent the night sitting on a rock waiting for the snow bunting. I had to do the listening as my father would not have heard it. About 4 a.m. it was very cold and rather wet and how glad I was when he suggested that we go down and make breakfast by the car. The porridge, made on a primus stove, was particularly good that morning. We never heard the snow bunting!'

Caitriona and Bridie particularly emphasise the great contribution made to their lives by their mother. Caitriona mentioned one area in which her mother played a key role, and this was in developing their photographs:

> I remember very well at home after supper, she often worked late at night, developing, printing and enlarging their photographs in her 'dark' room, no modern short cuts and ready made equipment then. She enlarged and mounted each photograph carefully and beautifully, for several exhibitions, both in this country and abroad.
>
> As well as helping with the photography and proofing my father's books, she was for many years on the District Council, and also found time to be a Guider, including running several Girl Guide camps. She was always ready to help people in times of trouble, especially the 1920s and 1930s when times were bad for so many. We often had a tramp sleeping in the stable and there was always eggs, bacon and tea for them in the morning .

Caitriona also mentioned her parent's efforts to have roads built and to raise money to help replace fishing boats destroyed in a particularly fierce gale. There were several fundraising *ceilidhs* to help poor children who often went to school with bare feet or inadequate clothing, so that they could have hot food and drink provided at school.

One group of people helped by Audrey Gordon were weavers from Harris who were settled at Port-na-long. They had no method of selling their tweed and were badly off, and for many years she collected their patterns, suggesting different colours or weights of tweed to them. She then sent samples to friends throughout Britain and took orders from them.

If Seton kept meticulous records for the car, the same must be said for his wife's farm records. In 1934, egg production was almost 5000 of which their household used over 4000. This included a live-in couple and the farm hand, John Graham, a great character who had constant battles with Seton Gordon. After the first couple of years, the value of food used at Upper Duntuilm more than offset the cost of running the farm. Almost the total production of milk and butter was used by themselves. By 1935 they were selling cattle. Feedstuff for all the animals and poultry, plus bills for the blacksmith, vet and bull service was £50–4–0d against a total value of £123 for livestock and poultry sold. John Graham was paid £1–15–0d per week, plus the blackhouse, (now part of Jonathan MacDonald's croft museum).

The years from 1932 to 1939 must surely have seemed 'golden' to Seton

Gordon. During that time a pattern of activity was established. Travels to the mainland to judge or to lecture, according to the time of the year; visits to Inverailort and the company of Francis Cameron-Head; journeys to Lochmore, the Highland home of the Duke of Westminster, or to the Outer Hebrides with Viscount David Fincastle. There were many piping sessions with David, Hamish MacDonald, John MacDonald of Inverness, and Kilberry. Piping lessons were begun by Alasdair under John MacDonald. The glebe land was gradually improved and production increased, to Audrey's credit.

The Gordons were frequently at Dunvegan, Armadale, Viewfield or Edinbane, the home of Edward Hilleary. When he was a young man, Edward was cut off by his wealthy family when he came down from Cambridge and started a laundry in London. The White Heather Laundry became hugely successful and eventually obtained a Royal Warrant. He had several sons, and one of them, Iain, shared a passion for the Highlands, and, like his father, ran a successful business in London which allowed him the freedom to indulge it.

Edward Hilleary's wife was a native of Skye who could trace her family roots over 500 years. Her ancestors included Flora MacDonald and Neil MacLeod of Gesto. Kenneth MacLeod, one of her most illustrious ancestors, made a fortune in India and returned to Skye where he purchased the three MacLeod estates of Skeabost, Greshornish and Gesto. One of Iain's sons, Ruaraidh, has in his possession the original manuscript of Neil MacLeod of Gesto's interpretation of the MacCrimmon notation. Iain Hilleary bought Tayinloan Lodge shortly before the start of the second war and created an outstanding garden, now unfortunately let go.

Edward Hilleary was asked by the government to write a report on economic conditions in the Highlands, which was published in 1938 as the 'Hilleary Report' and led to the formation of the Highland Panel, the forerunner of the Highland and Islands Development Board.

Seton and Audrey made one of their rare trips abroad when in July 1934 they received an all-expenses-paid invitation to the Scoto-Breton Festival of Roscoff in Finestere, Brittany. Seton was asked to demonstrate the *piobreachd* and other pipe-music. The Festival is mentioned in Seton Gordon's diary as a 'Picturesque pageant showing the landing of the little Queen Mary Stuart at Roscoff in 1548. Prince C. E. Stuart arrived here after sailing from Loch nam Uamh – what must the feelings of the Prince, Lochiel, and Dr Cameron must have been when they arrived on 16 September in 1746?'

The Gordons crossed to the Isle de Batz, off the Breton coast and he gave a chapter to it in *Afoot in Wild Places*. They spent several days on the island, where at the time 1200 people lived. The main industry was seaweed harvesting, which by this time had died out in the Hebrides.

Soon after they returned to Upper Duntuilm, Audrey had an attack of appendicitis and was taken to St Margaret's Nursing Home in Inverness for convalescence. Even while Seton was visiting her he wrote to the Prime Minister on paper bearing the home's letterhead. In a two page letter he gave four lines to Audrey and her condition, which was fortunately good, and he said 'I think they are quite pleased with her progress'. He also wrote:

Pipe-Major Robert Brown and Francis Cameron-Head (by kind permission of Mr Broderick Haldane)

> I think you will be interested to know that John MacDonald is going to play a *piobaireachd* for Empire listeners from Edinburgh on the night of 25 October.
>
> The broadcast is on shortwave at twenty-five minutes past midnight. I am sure he would appreciate a message from you if you had a minute to send one to the Edinburgh studio.

The reply from MacDonald pleased Seton Gordon – 'I should like very much to hear the music. You can tell him that I will certainly do my best to be one of his listeners; I can assure him from my recent visits to Eastern Canada and Newfoundland that he will have an enthusiastic Highland audience there'.

This broadcast was the second time that Seton Gordon had introduced John MacDonald to Empire listeners, but on this occasion it was distinguished by an unfortunate slip-up by the announcer. They were accompanied to the studio by Hamish MacDonald of Sleat, and the poet Charles Cammell. Again Seton introduced thc piper, as well as giving the history of each tune before it was played. It is a story he told many times:

> I had to give a brief description of the tunes he would play, so John and I arrived at the studio just after midnight with Hamish MacDonald and Charles Cammell. When the red light went up, the announcer, perhaps wearied by the labours of the day and knowing little or nothing of the man he was to introduce, made a bad start by telling Empire listeners that they would 'now

hear Piper MacLeod'. This mistake would have had an adverse effect on most musicians, yet with John it was otherwise, and in the hot and stuffy studio, within a chalked circle marked 'piper' he played that great composition *'The Massacre of Glen Coe'*. As variation followed variation, the intricate grace notes were played to perfection, so that the studio was filled with a flood of harmony, with a rippling as of waves on the seashore. A tribute to his playing that night I recall. Charles Cammell after a time rose from his seat in the studio and, with his hands shading his eyes, paced slowly after the piper, as though joined to him by an invisible thread, for he was held fast in the spell of that master playing.

As we walked home in the early hours of the morning I ventured to say to the announcer, 'It was a pity you did not get his name right'. It was a mild remark, yet when he had left us John turned to me and said, 'It was a pity you said that, it might have hurt his feelings!'

With the number of piping events that Seton Gordon attended, both small and large, from church or village halls to large gatherings it was inevitable that incidents would occur along the way, most of them amusing. Some were related to his increasing deafness. One happened when lecturing to a church society at which it was arranged that a well-known piper would play following the chairman's opening remarks. Unknown to Seton the chairman immediately called upon a member of the audience to say a prayer. Before he could comply, in all innocence Seton, in a very loud voice called for a tune. He noticed some embarrassment but was not aware of the cause until later, 'for the piper at once rose and played of his best'. Later Seton told the story to Cosmo Lang, Archbishop of Canterbury, who asked, 'Did the piper win?'

Another incident happened at a Highland concert at which the chairman proclaimed that it would open with a tune by a certain piper (whose skill was not rated too highly). As Seton described it, 'he had scarcely taken the pipes from their box when one of the audience with more vigour than taste, yelled at the top of his voice "Sit doon ye –". At once the chairman was on his feet and called out in a stern and disapproving voice "Who called the piper a –?" Came another voice in broad Scots, "Fa caa'd the – a piper?" (Who called the – a piper?)

One of Jonathan MacDonald's favourite stories was the occasion when Seton Gordon was returning to the island on the Armadale ferry. He was wearing his favourite old, very patched kilt and because the day was blustery he also wore an old mac. He went to the foredeck and began to play the pipes. A woman approached and dropped two shillings into his mac pocket. He continued playing and afterwards went up to her and thanked her graciously.

Seton sometimes stayed with Deeside headkeeper Donald McDonald on the Invercauld estate. Once, he was playing the pipes outside, but the midges were so bad that Donald said he had better come indoors. There was a passageway at the back of the cottage with a sloping ceiling. In one direction the angle of the drones matched the slope, so instead of turning around he marched backwards when he came to the end of the passage.

CHAPTER
9

FROM THE HIGHLANDS TO A WELSH ISLAND

Despite the number of requests for road upgrading sent by Seton Gordon to the Prime Minister, in February 1935 he sent another report. This was on the state of two side roads between Kilmuir and the headland of Ru Bornesketag, both within sight of Upper Duntuilm. It affected thirty-three crofting families and he advised MacDonald that repeated petitions by the crofters to the Board of Agriculture, County Council, the local MP and the Secretary for Scotland had had no results. The report ended: 'The people of Kilvester and Bornesketag humbly petition the Prime Minister to come to their aid, remembering what his influence did for the making of the Conista road'.

As Ramsay MacDonald wrote earlier, 'the machinery of men and the mills of God grind slowly'. It took almost a year, but finally the government relented and a letter from the Ministry of Transport gave the good news that Skye roads would receive special attention. Commencing the following year, a programme involving 137 miles of road would begin, at a total cost of £324,660.

Readers of Seton Gordon's books and articles would have no idea that he lobbied so hard for his crofter neighbours. His words spoke of an idyll that was essentially true, yet separate from the practicalities of everyday living. It was so with *Highways and Byways of the West Highlands* when it was published in April 1935. Its scope and detail was enhanced by Seton Gordon's unique descriptive style and D.Y. Cameron's illustrations, even though the artist was disappointed with the final result. He wrote on 6 May 'I wish the drawings were equal to the writing. They are very badly reproduced. I am not at all pleased'.

'D.Y'. was unnecessarily critical of his own work. The reviews were good and the letters of praise to Seton Gordon thought the drawings complimented the text admirably, with the artist's dramatic use of light and shade. The Sgurr of Eigg, Glen Coe, and Glen Sligachan were singled out for special mention. Professor Watson wrote, especially for the book, 'Hints on Gaelic Pronunciation' and a 'Glossary of Place-Name Elements, Norse and Gaelic'. The book was reprinted in June of the same year, with a third printing in 1949.

Seton Gordon's last letter to Ramsay MacDonald while he was still in office was written at the end of May. He had sent a copy of *Highways and Byways of the West Highlands* and the Prime Minister was reading it, 'not as a tour de

Force, but in sips'. Seton's letter offered another invitation to Skye, but MacDonald was unable to even contemplate resting at his house in Lossiemouth, though he was grateful for Seton's letter with its 'breath of air of Skye and glimpses of the Hebrides'.

The pressures on him, leading up to his resignation in June 1935, were enormous. His health and mental capacity were giving cause for concern and it became clear that the Prime Minister could no longer continue. After Cabinet reconstruction, he surrendered the seals of office to Stanley Baldwin on 7 June. However, there remained the question of his constituency at Seaham, and instead of retiring from Parliament he was determined to fight the next election as a backbencher.

Despite the assistance offered by the government to upgrade the roads on Skye, there were other problems facing the crofters, highlighted in a *Scotsman* article on 19 July, 1935:

> The hardship experienced by Skye crofters because of the crop failure in 1934 was voiced at a large meeting in the Parish of Bracadale on the weekend. Not since the time of the land league has there been such a large meeting in the district.
>
> Recently a petition was made to the Department of Agriculture for Scotland seeking a rent reduction to assist them in their plight. The Department, however, refused to make any reduction and the crofters have now directed an appeal to the Secretary of State for Scotland and to Members of Parliament.
>
> The crofters find themselves in very low circumstances and unable to pay rent. They feel that their labours of the last ten years count for nothing, and have vowed to fight this matter to the utmost.
>
> Arrangements are being made to hold meetings in other districts in order to present a united protest.

The parish of Bracadale was then represented on the County Council by Flora MacLeod. Following the death of her husband Hubert in 1933, Flora left London where she had served on the Chelsea Borough Council, and as Chair of the Chelsea Branch of the League of Nations Union. Settling on Skye, she stood for the Inverness County Council and was the first-ever woman elected, as district councillor for Bracadale. When her uncle Cannon Roderick MacLeod died in 1934, she became heir to Dunvegan and changed her name to Flora, Mrs MacLeod of MacLeod. In the next few years she served on the Health and Education committees, as well as the County Nursing Association Board, and opened an egg-grading station and a tweed-making industry close to Dunvegan. With her concern for the well-being of her crofter neighbours it is quite certain that Flora MacLeod became embroiled in their representations.

Unfortunately the eighty-eight-year-old Sir Reginald was ailing, and on 20 August the Chief died. Ten days previously his granddaughter Joan Wolrige Gordon, younger daughter of Flora, gave birth to twins. They were christened John and Patrick. Thus for those ten days three Chiefs of MacLeod were alive,

Reginald, Flora and John, whose installation came after Flora's death in November 1976.

Sir Reginald's funeral had all the pomp of Norman's in 1929. Pipe-Major Robert Reid was asked to play at Dunvegan Castle, and later at the graveside. He was delayed, and rather than hold up the proceedings, Seton Gordon played at the castle, *'MacCrimmon will not Return'*. The Pipe-Major was in time to play at the graveside the MacCrimmon *piobaireachd 'Lament for the Children'*.

Once more Seton Gordon had come to the rescue at a MacLeod Chief's funeral, and a few days later received a letter of thanks from Flora:

> Dunvegan Castle.
> August 24th, 1935.
>
> Dear Seton,
>
> I do want to thank you warmly for the friendship you have shown me these sad days. How good that you were here with your pipes to play some portion of that glorious pibroch before my father left his home for the last time, when Pipe-Major Reid failed to arrive. I would have liked to thank you today but it was not possible.
>
> I thought everything passed in perfect dignity and beauty and just as my father would have wished, and it was good to know that he was honoured and loved.
>
> Please give my love to Audrey. I hope you will both come over soon and we can have a quiet talk.
>
> Thank you warmly again. Yours ever, Flora MacLeod of MacLeod.

In that summer, Seton Gordon published one of his few books not connected with the west of Scotland, *Seagulls in London*. The purpose was to describe such well known gulls as the black-headed, common, herring and black-backed on the lakes, rivers and reservoirs in and around London. The photographs, not all of them taken by the author, are in sepia and there is one of Seton Gordon standing on the bridge in St James's Park, dressed most unusually in a suit, dark overcoat and Anthony Eden hat, feeding the gulls. He had spent time in London regularly in late winter and early spring for several years, and a favourite walk was through St James's Park. Here he had an opportunity to watch not only the common birds of the garden, but to observe the habits of gulls in an unusual setting:

> I have watched gulls in the London parks on cold winter days and on March mornings when the breath of spring was in the air; when the waters were held fast by the ice and when the almond trees and the crocuses were flowering, but there is one day that stands out in my memory. It was a February afternoon in 1933 when a blizzard struck London. I passed through St James's Park at the height of the storm. Heavy snow was driving almost horizontally before a bitter east wind, and with the intensity of an Arctic blizzard. I did not see one single person abroad in the park, and for that afternoon at least the gulls had to go hungry.

Seton Gordon in Hyde Park 1930s – an unusual mode of dress for him

An amusing misunderstanding arose over the title of the book, and Seton Gordon told the story, to the great appreciation of the audience, while undulging in a bit of repartee with Colonel Jock MacDonald at a Portree lecture in the 1970s.

Colonel Jock chaired the evening, and Iain MacFadyen played the *piobaireachds* that Seton described. In his introduction Jock said

> Ladies and Gentleman, you have all heard of Mr Seton Gordon, because to begin with, he's a great bird man. I mean feathered birds, not the other variety. You are only interested in feathered birds isn't that right, Seton? Anyhow, Mr Gordon is going to give a talk tonight, and he has a vast knowledge of piping, classical piping, and has been playing the pipes for seventy years. I have been playing for about sixty-five years and I can't play yet! . . . There is nobody better qualified than Mr Gordon to talk about the pipes and piping. Ladies and Gentlemen, Mr Seton Gordon!

When Seton stood up he said:

> I was rather amused about Colonel Jock mentioning the birds, the human birds, because many years ago I wrote a book which was called *Seagulls in London*. Gulls were very numerous in the London parks in winter and early spring, and I was asked to write this book, and when it came out a friend of mine asked what the book was about and I told her it was about the "gulls" of London. She looked rather surprised and said, "I didn't know you wrote about that sort of thing" and I said "Oh yes, I've written many books about it!" And she asked again, "What did you say the title was?" and I repeated it. That was a long time ago, but Jock's remarks brought it back to my mind. [*Voice in audience* – "The gulls or the girls?"] 'Tonight at anyrate we are going to talk about something more interesting than the gulls (or the girls) of London . . .

In complete contrast to the London parks, Seton and Audrey were anxious to photograph an Atlantic seal nursery, in preparation for his next book, *Thirty Years of Nature Photography*. In the autumn of 1935 they arranged for a motor-drifter to call for them when conditions were favourable. The journey called for a crossing of the Minch, out through the Sound of Harris, and then into the open Atlantic to the seal rocks.

A telegram informed them to be ready for pick-up in Duntulm Bay at 5:30 a.m. the following morning, and before dawn they rowed their small boat out to the drifter to be taken on board. They watched the eastern sky lighten and the mainland hills take on a dark outline. As the stars paled an ominous bank of clouds began to build in the south-west.

The wind began to shift and increase in strength, and soon the drifter began to respond to a rising sea. Full daylight showed an angry sea and a leaden sky which hid the Outer Isles. The waves increased and with no place for them below deck, Seton and Audrey were drenched with spray. Four hours later they begged to be landed at Rodel, on Harris, exhausted as they were with cold and seasickness.

A landing could not safely be undertaken there and the boat made for the open sea again. Seton realised that the only hope now was to land on Berneray in the Sound of Harris, where there were some protective bays on the east side of the island. Though used to the discomfort of hides in all weathers, this was a new experience. Only by huddling together, and once in a while sipping at a bottle of whisky, did they endure the crossing. Fortunately it was possible to land on Berneray and the inhabitants were surprised to see them come ashore in such weather.

It was a two mile walk to their lodgings, but there a hospitable welcome was given them. The next day was calmer, though dull, and the boat hove in close at 8 a.m. with their smaller one in tow. It was a two hour passage to the island, and a swell began to build but it remained calm, though some time was spent rowing backwards and forwards to find the best landing place:

> Only one who has experienced it can know the might of the Atlantic swell; our boat was lifted like a cockleshell and we risked disaster if it had been dashed on the rocks.
>
> At last a landing was made. When, in the afternoon we came to re-embark we found the swell had increased, and the boat had a narrow escape from being swamped.

Following another night on Berneray the wind had risen by the next morning and as a re-crossing of the Minch in the motor-drifter was impossible, a decision was made to return to Skye by the mail boat from Lochmaddy, on North Uist. They hired an ancient Ford car to convey them to Lochmaddy, where after a short night's sleep, the mail boat was boarded at 5 a.m. From here Seton and Audrey were taken to Harris, from where they were assured a cargo steamer would shortly sail for Skye, but more disappointments were in store. They landed at Tarbert in Harris, believing that in two hours the cargo steamer would land them at Uig, but at the last moment a change in her normal route dashed their hopes and they had to await the mail boat to board her again, returning to Lochmaddy once more before crossing to Dunvegan. It was late evening and the only way to complete the journey was by hired car. On the way to Upper Duntuilm they had four punctures. Seton, in summing up their journey said:

> Thus the trip, which could have been completed in fine weather in a single day, lasted six full days and throughout was full of adventure and excitement. My wife had the misery of toothache as well, and during our enforced wait at Tarbert had made the double journey of fifty miles by bus to Stornoway to have the offending tooth extracted.

The photographs taken on this excursion for *Thirty Years of Nature Photography* are of the highest quality. In this same year Seton and Audrey were awarded a certificate of merit at an international exhibition of nature photography.

The 1935 general election was called for 14 November, and Ramsay MacDonald's opponent was 'Manny' Shinwell, then only in his mid-forties and a tough campaigner. Shinwell received 38,380 votes to MacDonald's 17,882. Malcolm MacDonald was also defeated by 15,000 votes.

There were so many expresssions of condolence sent on the loss of his seat, among them one from Seton Gordon, that cards were printed to thank people. However, neither father or son were out of the House of Commons for long. The death of Noel Skelton, re-elected as Unionist MP for Scottish Universities, and an elevation to the peerage of Sir Ian MacPherson, National Liberal MP for Ross and Cromarty, allowed both to seek re-election as National Government candidates. The by-elections were to be within a week of each other in early February 1936. Seton wrote to offer his good wishes for the forthcoming campaign:

> . . . I am a graduate of Oxford so cannot I fear do much to help you, but it will be a happy day for me to see you elected and able once more to take your place in the Government.
>
> Good men are scarce, and you deserve the good wishes of all for your hard work for the Empire during the last few years. '*Bliadhua Mhath Ur Dhuibh!*' . . .

While preparations were being made for the by-elections, George V died on 20 January 1936, at Sandringham. When, in February, the result of the first by-election was announced, Ramsay MacDonald was returned with 16,393 votes, double those of the Scottish Nationalist candidate. The moment the news reached Upper Duntuilm a note was on its way:

> Monday, 6.15 p.m.
>
> My Dear Ramsay MacDonald,
>
> This minute the result of your fine victory has been announced on the wireless and my wife and I send you our hearty and friendly congratulations. You have had a magnificent majority and it will hearten Malcolm in his Ross-

shire fight, in which we all hope he may be successful. [Malcolm was returned with a 3000 vote margin.]

I hope there may be chance of our meeting soon. I expect to be in London for some engagements from 21 Friday for a fortnight or more. Will you be free on 22 Saturday? The Piping Society of London will hold their annual competition at the London Scottish Regiment headquarters at Buckingham Gate on that day, & special trains are bringing pipers from Glasgow, Edinburgh, Aberdeen and Dundee. I have been asked to be one of the judges & I know everyone would be delighted if you could look in.

Yours always most sincerely . . .

Once again there was uncertainty about Ramsay MacDonald's plans. He wrote to say that the piping competition sounded 'most attractive and as far as I know I am free from official work, so have made an entry in my diary and hope to be able to keep it'. His secretary, Rose, sent a note on the same day to ask at what time the event took place so that she could remind him in good time. She was advised that the morning might be the best time, but Seton Gordon pressed for an answer – 'I should like to know if I could say at approx. what time Mr Ramsay MacDonald hopes to come, so perhaps you could ring up Mayfair – and leave a message?'

By the 18th, Rose was expressing doubts, warning that attendance would have to be a last moment decision. Whether MacDonald made the event is not recorded, but the correspondence provides yet another example of Seton Gordon being blissfully unaware of the complexities faced by a man who only two weeks before had been returned to Parliament after a massive defeat, and who still held the office of Lord President of the Privy Council.

Whether the ex-Prime-Minister still had any influence on road construction or not, a letter on Skye roads was received from the Minister of Transport himself, advising not only the spending of £324,660 but that 'Under the Crofter Committee Scheme there is an expectation of £4 million in five years. There will be 10 feet carriageways, with raised grass verges 4 inches above the road to prevent cars passing except at fixed passing places. One of the grass verges will be 4 feet wide and will provide a safe refuge for pedestrians. Yours faithfully, L. Hore-Belisha.'

Driving the remnants of the quaint Skye roads today, from Uig to Portree, and from Armadale to just south of Broadford, it is amusing to think that they were actually designed. The local people are skilful in timing it so that they do not have to stop at one of the 'passing places' when a car is seen approaching from the opposite direction. It also says much for the government's faith in Skye drivers that a mere 4 inch grass verge would stop them from illegally passing if they were in a hurry. For visitors, to this day, a rare lesson is provided in old fashioned courtesy and co-operation, which all seem to enjoy.

There was correspondence and outings with Francis Cameron-Head in the summer. Seton Gordon wrote to him about a possible connection between Somerled, the first Lord of the Isles, and a cave near Ardgour. A reply from Cameron-Head just after the turn of the year shows his shared enthusiasm for historical detail, his keenness to examine the cave – and his wit, but there was no reference to the cave in any of Seton's subsequent books, so it is likely that the connection was never proven:

> I am most thrilled to hear of Somerled's cave. It seems to have a very strong *prima facie* case in favour of it. One thing appears to me remarkable – & that is the tradition that a certain cave was Somerled's has survived until now . . .
>
> But the discovery is one of the very greatest interest – especially as the continued existence of the Gaelic civilisation is in perhaps as critical a state as it was in Somerled's own time. And Somerled has this advantage over us – that he could at least count upon his own people being loyal to themselves & to his & their traditions (which we scarcely can today).
>
> Perhaps the cave may come in useful as accommodation for the Gaelic Summer School – or even solve the vexed question of the Celtic College!
>
> But, seriously, it is well worth investigation . . .

Seton Gordon wrote next to Sir Godfrey Thomas, Edward VIII's Deputy Private Secretary, to advise him that Alexander MacLean, a local centenarian, was approaching his 103rd birthday, and asked if the King would send a telegram. The following correspondence ensued:*

*This exchange of letters was reproduced with the gracious permission of Her Majesty the Queen.

> Buckingham Palace,
> 21st July 1936.
>
> Dear Mr Gordon,
>
> Thank you for your letter about Alexander MacLean. It seems quite clear from what you say that the old man must be at least 103 years old and a message of congratulations will be sent to him from the King on 12 August if you let us know nearer the date that he is still alive and well.
>
> Yours sincerely,
>
> Godfrey Thomas.

> Buckingham Palace
> 27th August 1936.
>
> Dear Mr Gordon,
>
> Thank you for your letter of 24 August. I am sorry to hear that after all the trouble we took between us that old Alexander MacLean thought at first the King's congratulatory message was a practical joke!
>
> Still if he keeps it under his pillow and won't let even the Minister see it, it has evidently given the old man a certain amount of pleasure.
>
> Yours sincerely,
>
> Godfrey Thomas.

During their frequent trips away, the Gordons left Upper Duntuilm in the hands of the farm labourer, John Graham. He was with them for many years, and even after he retired, lived in the area. English was not one of John's strong points and he could not always get his point across as he would like to. When he tried to be blunt it often came out quite differently from what he intended to say. He did not always see eye to eye with Seton, and over the years some amusing incidents came about as a result.

Jonathan MacDonald was by now becoming aware of Seton Gordon, although still very young. His mother occasionally did housework for Audrey and they lived less than a mile from Upper Duntuilm. He would occasionally be taken up to the house, and the tall, kilted figure, who frequently played the pipes, made quite an impression on him. He was also aware of his unusual neighbour going down past the crofts, followed by the collie Dara, for their early morning swim. Interviewed on the BBC Highland programme, *What a Life* Jonathan said:

> I remember him very well indeed in my very early years when I was just a little boy, going down past the old croft every single morning to take his dip just below the township. I can visualise him right now as he used to go in his waterproof coat and his wellingtons with his trunks on, going down past the house. We used to be quite amazed at how he would dive from the cliff right into the open sea, followed by Dara.

As he grew older, Jonathan heard their neighbours chuckling as they recounted the latest exchange between John Graham and his master:

> John had his battles with Seton. He was quite illiterate, and he wasn't terribly good with his English or his grammar. Whatever happened, John went straight to the heart of the matter; he did not beat about the bush and he often went to see Seton and blamed him for this or that wrong. It produced a lot of humorous occasions, John trying to interpret his own point of view, and Seton trying to tell John as he saw it.
>
> John lived in the blackhouse which is now a part of my museum. He left the Gordons for a while and went to work on the County Council on the road schemes. Then he came back and worked for them until he retired.
>
> There was a woman working at the house, and she had some strange quirks. She took things out of the house and hid them. One of these was a very nice clock that was in the lounge. Seton was sure that she would not do anything like that, but John was convinced that the woman took it. He said to Audrey, 'Well, I think we had better go down and have a look in the fields to see if she put anything down there'. So they went down and right at the bottom Audrey stumbled over the clock hidden in a clump of grass. John's remark was, 'Well, I'm pleased you got him!'

Each autumn everyone would pitch in to bring in the hay, and one year Seton was helping, perhaps a bit absent mindedly. Jonathan recalled the scene as John Graham began to lose patience:

> They were making the stacks this day, and Seton had other things on his

> mind. He went up to the top of the stack, and then came down the ladder. John would have to go up and redo what Seton had done. After a time, John eventually stopped Seton coming down the ladder and said, 'Now if you be up there you be up there, but if you be down here you be down here!' Audrey was a very generous person and always tried to help local people. There was one family who were very poor and she sent over some milk from her Jersey cows. John was inclined to look at things very materially, and said, 'Surely you are not going to send any milk to the —— this week'. When he was told that they needed it, he replied, 'Remember, you won't send the —— to the sale!'

During the early part of 1936 Seton Gordon put the finishing touches to *Thirty Years of Nature Photography* and a new book was in preparation for release the following year, to be called *Afoot in Wild Places*. In the late summer and autumn of 1936, he sailed to some of the smaller and remoter islands of both the Inner and Outer Hebrides to be included in this book, some of them for the first time. Among them were Taransay, located just west of Harris; Scarpa, just to the north-west; Berneray, between North Uist and Harris; Hasker, which was a two-hour sail west of North Uist; Vatersay, very close to the south shore of Barra, and Canna, the most westerly of the islands immediately below Skye.

On Vatersay there were fifty-eight holdings and all the crofters were of the Catholic faith. They had settled at the turn of the century from Barra, Mingulay and Pabbay. There were only three houses that were thatched, and the others were found to be surprisingly modern for the period.

One of the few references to Seton's Gealic is mentioned here: 'On the machair I found an old man herding cows. This veteran, the oldest man on the island, was unable to speak English, and was besides very hard of hearing; but my halting and indifferent Gealic, shouted into his ear, enabled us to converse for a time while his cows cropped the short green grass, where the wild pansies opened yellow flowers and the milkwort held to the sun their flower heads of deep blue'.

1936 ended with the abdication crisis, and Seton noted in his diary on 10 December, 'The King announced that he would abdicate – mild & half a gale S.W'. The following day he wrote, 'The King abdicates. Duke of York is King George VI – very dark and rainy morning – wind shifted 10 a.m. from W. to N. – faired up before sunset'.

It was years since he had last seen the abdicated King, and there had been no correspondence other than the indirect letters on the Skye centenarian. This was not the last exchange between them, though they were old men when it finally took place.

Ramsay MacDonald sided with Stanley Baldwin and the majority of Cabinet members against Edward's morganatic marriage to Wallis Simpson. He at last decided to resign, though he continued to preside over the Coronation Committee. George VI was crowned on 12 May 1937. On 27 May MacDonald had an audience with the new King. The next day Baldwin tendered the government's resignation, and Ramsay MacDonald was no longer a minister. With ties to

Golden Eagle and chick taken by Seton Gordon (reproduced by kind permission of British Birds*)*

London cut, he wisely headed for Lossiemouth where he spent most of the summer. There were several exchanges of notes with Seton Gordon and promises to meet during the Highland Games season.

A busy year lay ahead for Seton, who was working on two books for publication in 1937, the previously mentioned *Afoot in Wild Places* and *Edward Grey of Fallodon and his Birds*, a small volume, but a simple tribute to the memory of his late friend.

During the winter of 1936–37, there had been an exceptional storm, coupled with a high tide which smashed dozens of fishing boats on the Trotternish coast. Seton and Audrey were determined to help their neighbours, and as well as organising *ceilidhs* and concerts they launched an appeal through the *Times* and the *Scotsman*. This brought in £1300, sufficient to replace several boats. In their gratitude the local fishermen named three of the boats, *Audrey*, *Caitriona* and *Bridie*. There was also the question of a breakwater at Camusmore to help prevent damage from further storms. Seton used his influence to lobby for this and in February, a letter of thanks was written by neighbour John Nicolson, which showed how effective this petitioning was:

> Dear Sir,
> I write to inform you that again your efforts on behalf of the fishermen and on behalf of the whole of Kilmuir has come to a satisfactory ending.
> I have great pleasure in telling you that the breakwater at Camusmore is going in. A final survey took place on 12 February.
> I think things are working wonderfully by your influence and it is sure to put an end to the disagreements, which are already settling down, as I thought.
> Please show this letter to Mrs Gordon, as I am anxious she should see it also, and may good luck be always on your trail.
> Yours sincerely, John Nicolson.

Seton was invited by Macmillan to write another book in the *Highways and Byways* series, this time on the central Highlands. In early March 1937 there were two letters from Sir 'D.Y'. on the project. Macmillan had asked him to provide the illustrations once more. He wrote: 'I find difficulty in knowing what to do. The landscape is very wide – I am not young and cannot climb mountains, and yet would like to take a part'.

In the second letter he said,

> . . . Scotland is a paradise of beauty these days – yesterday I had to visit the Gareloch and never remember such intense loveliness and such colour, unknown and un-dreamt by Sassenachs, and they never come north at this season . . . If I do undertake this new work I shall insist on better reproduction, as I hide my face when anyone praises the last things in the midst of your fascinating writings.

After complaining that for him the first book was not a financial success, he went on to say,

> Of course the pleasures were great, but life is expensive and new taxes will make it more so. However, I really wish to be associated with you in these new books – will there be writing and drawing I wonder, in the next world we travel towards?
> With best regards, Yrs, D.Y.C.

The letters show an interesting mix of practicality and other-worldliness. Although he did produce the drawings for *Highways and Byways of the Central Highlands* the war intervened in its publication, and D.Y. had died before it was published in 1948.

Dotterel taken by Seton Gordon (reproduced by kind permission of British Birds*)*

Accompanied by Audrey, Seton Gordon visited Wales for the first time, to spend time on the island of Skokholm. On it lived nature writer R.M. Lockley and his artist wife, Doris. They had restored the island's ruined farmhouse some years before and made it their permanent home. Writing of Skokholm some time later in the *Manchester Guardian*, Seton started by praising the work of nature writers, the BBC nature programmes and the influence of the Boy Scout and Girl Guide movement. In praising nature writers he included one of the most intriguing, Grey Owl, who rose to prominence in the 1930s, and whose books on the Canadian wilderness thrilled thousands of readers:

> We owe a debt of gratitude to men like Grey Owl, who by books and lectures brought to many a home a love of wild creatures. Here, R.M. Lockley has taught many people to know and love wild nature. This well-known author and his wife live on the small grassy island of Skokholm, off the coast of Wales. In spring, summer and autumn he welcomes nature lovers who assist him in his work of ringing birds.

Describing this May journey to the Welsh island, located between the entrance to Milford Haven and Skomer Island, Seton Gordon told of their thrill as the boat approached Skokholm:

> The weather was unsettled, and after meeting stormy seas off St Anne's Head we rounded the promontory and saw above the waves, the island of Skokholm rising from the ocean. As we approached it we saw fields of wild hyacinths, of a more lovely blue than the sky, and a small homely house standing on a sunny slope. We ran in beneath the cliff, landed at a stone jetty, and climbed up to the house, to take our host and hostess unawares, for they had not expected us to cross with seas still running high.
>
> We were impressed by their tireless enthusiasm, especially Doris, who as well as assisting with the daily chores, helps her husband in his research, illustrates his books and, like him, seemed to do with a couple of hours' sleep each night. During the day the bird traps were visited and any migrants in them ringed and released. At night, by torchlight we caught and ringed some of the thousands of shearwaters which nest on Skokholm then released them into the darkness. It is a grand life the Lockleys lead, and his writing creates a clear picture of island life to his readers who are less fortunately situated than himself.

The Lockleys were forced to abandon their island when war broke out only two years later, because of its dangerous situation in the approaches to Milford Haven. After the war their work was taken over by the West Wales Trust for Nature Conservancy, now the Dyfed Wildlife Trust, and the island continues as a reserve.

It was a coincidence that while they were on Skokholm, after having introduced the island by talking about the influence of naturalists, and naming Grey Owl, a letter was on its way to Skye from him. His home was then Beaver Lodge, in Prince Albert National Park, Saskatchewan. He had just returned there after a lecture tour in Britain, where among one of his avid audiences were Seton and Audrey. He was received by the Royal Family, also ardent admirers of this Canadian Indian, who wore buckskin clothing and a single feather in his braided hair, looking every inch the classical North American Indian. It was a letter of thanks for a signed copy of *Thirty Years of Nature Photography*:

> 19th May, 1937.
>
> Dear Seton Gordon,
>
> At last, being home again, I find your magnificant volume in front of me.

> Not usually given to superlatives, I can only call the whole thing superb. The photography I have never seen equalled and to get those wild creatures in exactly the pose that portrays them to such advantage, naturally and all unconscious of the operator, must I know only too well have entailed long hours, days, or even weeks of unremitting toil and monumental patience. They portray a skill not only in the art of picture taking, but in the art of hunting without a gun, for a permanent record of wildlife in its natural environment.
>
> Any fool can shoot a patch of hair or a bunch of feathers, but it takes skill, address, and sometimes no little courage in the accomplishment of such work as you have produced. To get all those creatures live, alert, poised for instant flight – boy, what a thrill is there!
>
> The Eagles, not only on account of their excellent pictures, but also because of the birds' significance to the Indian in his symbolism, interests me particularly. Will you please thank Mrs Gordon for her part in this wonderful gift.
>
> In sincere gratitude and with every good wish from both my wife and myself, I remain brother, your friend,
>
> Grey Owl (Wa-Sha-Quon-Asin).

Starting with *The Men of the Last Frontier*, published in 1931, to *Pilgrims of the Wild* (1935) and *Tales of an Empty Cabin* (1936), Grey Owl's books were published in Britain. Because of their success in portraying the Canadian wilderness, his books were read as avidly in Britain as the poetry collections of Robert Service had been several years earlier. Grey Owl, or Wa-Sha-Quon-Asin (Ojibway for 'He who walks by night'), is now acknowledged as one of Canada's earliest conservationists. His second wife, Anahareo, was descended from Iroquois chiefs, though until she met Grey Owl she had forsaken her native ways. After his death in 1938 she continued the protection of beavers, and in her later years lived in the town of Kamloops in central British Columbia. In 1983, shortly before she died, Anahareo was awarded the Order of Canada for her contribution to conservation.

The true story of Grey Owl emerged after his death. He was Archibald Belaney, brought up in Hastings by two maiden aunts and educated at Hastings Grammar School. He went to Canada, becoming a successful backwoodsman, canoeist and trapper. He was at one time appointed Assistant Chief Ranger in the Missisauga Forest Reserve, but eventually went back to the freedom of the northern woods. After more years of trapping he became sickened with killing, and encouraged by Anahareo, founded his beaver sanctuary. He claimed to be a half-breed, who was adopted by the Ojibways. The truth of his early life palls into insignificance compared to his contribution in awakening people to the vanishing wilderness.

A few months after the Gordons' visit to Skokholm, the Lockleys were invited to Upper Duntuilm. Living on a small island, they were true economists and when, driving on the narrow Skye roads in darkness they hit first a rabbit, then a hare, R.M. picked them up to use 'for the pot'. Arriving at the house they found that Seton was giving a piping lesson in his study and Audrey was in the kitchen. The Lockleys let themselves in and made their way through the dimly-lit hall, rabbit, hare and all. Seton got up to welcome them, at the same time putting on the hall light, where to the visitors' horror, a trail of blood led across the carpet!

This misfortune did not mar the visit, and Ronald Lockley has memories of a trip out to the Ascrib Islands in one of the boats that Seton and Audrey were instrumental in obtaining for local fishermen after their boats were was smashed.

With the approach of the Highland Gathering season, Seton began receiving invitations to judge. He was in doubt about the Gordon Castle Gathering, as accommodation was uncertain, though it would provide an opportunity to meet Ramsay MacDonald. A few days later a card was received from Lossiemouth and a reply was posted on the same day:

> Many thanks for your card which arrived this morning – just as I was wondering about Gordon Castle.
>
> Yes they have asked me to judge again, but I have not decided yet as the castle is let and the Duchess cannot put me up this year.
>
> I thought perhaps if our mutual friend John MacDonald were to be in Inverness I might stay with him – but I have not heard from him yet.

Regrettably, he and Ramsay MacDonald could not find each other, and their last opportunity to meet was lost. MacDonald and his youngest daughter, Sheila, sailed for South America a few months later, and he died en route. Seton Gordon's last letter, sent in mid-August, included in it an invitation to Skye, like his first one in August 1929:

> How kind of you to write that very nice letter! I too looked everywhere for you before you left, but Dr Simpson, who was judging the piping with me had brought me from Inverness and as he had to be back early we left at 4.30 p.m.
>
> I was sorry we had no opportunity for a talk. It is difficult at these gatherings.
>
> Is there any chance of you coming over to Skye in the autumn? We should be very glad to see you and you would find much to interest you I know. We could meet you at Portree if you came by steamer.

On the 17 November a letter, edged in black, arrived at Upper Duntuilm from Malcolm MacDonald:

> Upper Frognal Lodge,
> Hampstead, N.W.3.
>
> Dear Mr. Seton Gordon,
>
> Thankyou very much for your kind letter of sympathy. It is indeed a bitter sorrow that my father is not to come back from South America restored in health and vigour, as we had hoped.

> He always felt a great regard for you, and I know that he enjoyed your meetings together. My brother and sisters had already decided to find a piper who would play the 'Flowers of the Forest' in the churchyard at Spynie when we take my father there at the end of next week. I am most grateful to you for your suggestions as to pipers. I will discuss this with brother and sisters, and will perhaps send you a telegram later on asking you to get in touch with them. Yours sincerely, Malcolm MacDonald

Ramsay MacDonald's body was brought home in the cruiser, HMS *Apollo*, and arrived in Devonport on 25 November. The next day, following a public funeral service at Westminster Abbey and then cremation, his ashes were taken by train to Lossiemouth. At Spynie churchyard, they were placed alongside Margaret's ashes as Pipe-Major Robert Reid of the Highland Light Infantry played *'The Flowers of the Forest'.*

On 6 December, Ella Pease died, so severing the Gordons' last connection with the Northumberland coast. A September letter from her gave no indication of any health problem. She made mention of Seton's most recent book: 'Your book on Edward Grey is delightfully done and has been a great pleasure to read . . . I am so glad you have done it in the way you have. I think that it must have been a pleasure to write, and a labour of love'.

Ella was a countrywoman with an uncomplicated view of life, and a wisdom which shone through the pages of her letters. This was amplified in her obituary, which said, ' Her work in public, social, and charitable spheres had endeared Miss Pease to many friends and made her name a household word in the county'.

1937 had been a successful year for Seton Gordon. With his two latest books plus articles, it was one of his best ever finanancially, with an income of almost £800. Rainfall at Upper Duntuilm for the second year hovered at just over 40 inches and for the first time, hours of sunshine were recorded – 1213.6. 'Grey Wind' had covered slightly fewer miles at 5080. There was international recognition for Seton and Audrey, with a diploma from the Paris Exhibition des Arts et des Techniques.

In late January 1938 Caitriona departed for Germany where she stayed for two months with a family named Uhrmeister, in the Berlin suburb of Zehlendorf. Only Brigitte, the daughter, spoke English. The remarkable thing about Caitriona's letters is that in a mere two months in Berlin, she saw all the evidence of Germany's new power lust which would again lead to war. In one letter she wrote:

> Sunday, about 7 p.m. went to the Wilhelmplatz – a HUGE square with fine buildings all round, to see the march past of the party, the fifth anniversary. Over 6000 marched past Hitler and a few other importants standing on a balcony. TREMENDOUS crowd and v. fine sight with all the flags and floodlighting and a fine night. Each of the party carried a flaming torch and [there was] a banner at the head of each brigade. Brigitte and I stood on stools and every few minutes the crowd swayed and very nearly many times

> we were lying on top of the people, terribly hard to keep on the stool! But two kind young men held on to us. Great fun and v. interesting. Frau and Herr U. were there too, and then we drove about Berlin and saw them marching in various places, with more floodlighting.

In further letters, all full of excitement about attending dances, balls, visits to the ballet, museums and art galleries, Caitriona mentioned other events which perhaps she did not fully comprehend at the time. In March she wrote: 'Last night and today there is great excitement about Austria. The Uhrmeisters were up till 2 a.m. last night listening to the wireless from Vienna. Today all the houses have their swastikas out and now after dark, many have candles in their windows. For most of the day the crowds have been cheering, and speeches from Vienna were heard on the wireless'.

On 19 March she wrote to say the she had watched Hitler's return from Austria, while she again stood on a stool in the Wilhelmplatz. There were crowds everywhere. In her last letter on the 25 March she told of going to Potsdam where, 'In the evening the troops did a parade with torches and played various tunes for an hour. It was lovely, v. calm warm night'.

It was agreed that Brigitte would visit Skye later in the year, and Caitriona was anxious to take her around the Highlands. In the opinion of her mother, Caitriona came back 'a proper little Nazi' and Audrey saw to it that she came to her senses as quickly as possible.

A series of letter exchanges began with John MacDonald of Inverness. They give a good indication of his thoughts on the state of piping from then into the early war years, and on the changes which the war brought about in the piping fraternity. The first letter, on 21 March, 1938 was from South Uist, where he had gone to tutor pipers. With his encouragement, South Uist had produced first-class pipers who competed on the mainland, yet the South Uist Gathering was too small to attract pipers from outside the islands. Recalling the times when he judged there with John MacDonald, Seton Gordon said that the Gathering was 'delightful in its simplicity'.

After the war he wrote that the results of MacDonald's teaching were still evident in South Uist. He also praised the Catholic church, which he said had done more to encourage piping than the Protestant churches. In MacDonald's March 1938 letter he refers to Robert Brown and Robert Nicoll, the 'Two Bobs'. Both were promising pipers from the Balmoral estate who would soon gain distinction through their playing.

Seton Gordon and Jack Harrison spent two weeks in July touring Iceland. At Reykjavik they found an English speaking driver with an American Ford eight-cylinder car. The man, Simon, proved to be an agreeable and tireless companion during the 1200 mile journey around the country. They were especially glad of his presence when they discovered the road conditions. There were no tarmac roads in Iceland then, and little solid foundation under those that existed. Sometimes a stony stream bed was the only path to follow before again finding the next primitive stretch of road.

One of their early stops was the fishing port of Akureyri where close by the town was a lake fringed by birch trees. Here several tents were set up. Amusingly, in his diary Seton made a note on Icelandic girls akin to Colonel Jock's leg-pull. He would have had good reason to accuse Seton of an interest in 'human birds' on this occasion:

> Around the lake were small tents which contrasted pleasantly with the green of the birches – Icelandic girls were camping here. The girls of Iceland are most attractive and goodlooking. They are in appearance clean and healthy – and make up is seldom seen. I should say that they are the most attractive girls I have seen – many of them are very fair haired and have beautiful colouring which is heightened by the suntanned look. One girl is wearing a crown of seathrift in her hair. They wear long and wide very becoming trousers.

Many stops were made before returning to Reykjavik and a few unusual events occurred. Driving on one rutted section, made more difficult by heavy fog, a golden plover suddenly rose in front of the car. Walking back to the spot Seton found a nest containing four eggs actually on the road. It had so far survived despite the fact that car wheels had to pass within a foot of it.

Standing beside the waterfall at Gullfoss, they looked into a huge chasm, where opaque glacier water thundered into the gorge. Seton commented, 'There is sensed beside this cauldron a strong, primitive power, as though the ages have rolled back and one is standing deep in the past'.

On another day Seton and Harrison were rewarded by the sight of some inhabitants in the hinterland fording a river as they took their sheep and ponies to pasture. Horsemen, cracking whips and shouting loudly, drove their flocks into the water, the air full of bleating cries. Seton watched them as the assembly moved away from the far bank and noted: 'The sheep and ponies spread out over the hillside, climbing, and moving slowly towards the bleak pass with its large snowdrifts'.

At Geysir, their last stop before returning to Reykjavik, Seton watched throughout the night from his window: 'The north sky is aflame with crimson clouds, and sunset merges into sunrise with no appreciable decrease in the daylight in between. Through the hours of the night the steam from the boiling springs drifted on the cold north-east wind current low over the ground, and the calls of redshank sounded from the boggy land beside the river'.

While Seton was away, Audrey was having an exhausting time. She took Alasdair south to Stowe, his new school, where Audrey had tea with the headmaster. She liked the school very much and thought the boys were very polite. Returning to Upper Duntuilm, she had only just unpacked when two men came to arrange installation of an underground electric cable. In readiness she had a group of young people digging the trench at sixpence a yard. While all this was going on Audrey did the washing, prepared the weather report and cleaned out both sheds and the loft in readiness for the electrical insallation. She was also keeping watch on a merlin's nest with four young birds in it.

Despite all this she had time to think about Seton and even rang up the

Meteorological Office to get the Iceland weather forecast. It painted a gloomy picture. In a note to Seton she told him it predicted: 'gales and depressions in every direction for the next three days, so I felt very sad for poor Seton. . . . Must end now and do washing. Much hope sea calmer now & less swell. Hope very much Seton happy. Thinking much of him. All love from Audrey'.

CHAPTER

10

WAR LOOMS ONCE MORE

SOON AFTER SETON GORDON RETURNED from Iceland he headed for Deeside to judge the *piobaireachd* at Aboyne and Braemar. The tradition of the Balmoral house party's visit to the Braemar Gathering continued under King George VI. By now Robert Brown and Robert Nicoll were being recognised as outstanding pipers. They competed in the 1938 Braemar Gathering, where Seton was judging. Later the King asked Seton what he thought of his pipers. In *A Highland Year*, Seton recounted the conversation:

> I happened to know how greatly Brown and Nicol wished to have a course of tuition under John MacDonald, and answered that both were good but would be even better if it could be arranged for John MacDonald to teach them. The King replied that he wasn't sure if he could spare Brown, who had trapped 3000 rabbits the previous winter. Greatly daring, I replied, 'Well sir, I would rather have a piper who had been under John MacDonald than a man who trapped 3000 rabbits'.
>
> The King said, 'I will see that they go to John MacDonald'. That was the beginning of the tuition both Brown and Nicol received under John MacDonald, and I am sure no pipers more deeply appreciated the privilege of the tuition.

According to MacDonald's letters the King agreed that the 'Balmoral boys' should be absent for two weeks early in January for tuition from him. In the same class was Pipe-Major Donald MacLennen and Lance-Corporal Donald MacLeod of the Seaforth Highlanders, an outstanding piper, who, by 1942 had became Pipe-Major in a newly raised Battalion.

In a letter dated 11 September, 1938 John MacDonald continued his theme on the declining state of *piobaireachd*, and there were very few letters in which it was not mentioned. He blamed the *Piobaireachd* Society for the supposed decline in standard of playing:

> I am pleased to note that you have been doing so much playing lately. It is nice to know that the grand old music is not being neglected, as I am afraid

> that it is in great danger of going out. I am quite justified in saying that the Piobaireachd Society is helping it on its way to a great extent.

In another letter he accused the Society of altering the tunes they published, but 'as there are not many left who can corroborate what I say it is not worth my while worrying about it'. Only a few months later he wrote, 'bagpipe playing is on the downward grade and our grand old instrument is fast becoming a mish-mash more than a musical instrument'. He did not think too much of the playing at Braemar that year and had heard that it was not much better at the Skye Gathering, although he expressed some satisfaction with the standard at Oban a few days before.

It is hard to understand why Seton Gordon sometimes echoed John MacDonald's opinions on the state of pibroch. There were, at that time, many younger pipers coming along whose expertise was beyond question; the MacFadyen brothers, Iain and John, Seamus MacNiell and Donald MacLeod, to name a few.

Was Seton Gordon exaggerating when he said of John MacDonald:

> In him are combined perfect fingering, perfect timing and beautiful expression, the whole producing a rare and very lovely harmony that thrills the senses. It is the hallmark of genius that it should all sound so simple – the listener feels there is no reason why he should not go home and do the same thing himself. When John MacDonald ends his playing days, something rare and precious will be lost.

The familiar pattern of life in the Highlands continued through the summer and autumn despite the disquieting international scene and government priority to increase the strength of the Territorial Army. Viscount Fincastle was the senior captain in the 4th (Territorial) Battalion, Queen's Own Cameron Highlanders and in command of the Island Company. The Officers' mess had other distinguished members. The Commanding Officer was the Earl of Cawdor, the Adjutant was Captain Derek Lang, who became the youngest CO in the Cameron Highlanders and ended a long army career as General Officer Commanding Scotland. Lieutenant Raymond Burton was a Scottish Hockey International and taught both Alasdair Gordon and John Cook at Alton Burn preparatory school.

Work continued on the central Highlands book, with much travelling and writing in preparation. Seton was well aware of the international situation, and on a visit to Rannoch on 27 September from Fincastle House, where he and Caitriona were staying, he noted that on this day, Prime Minister Neville Chamberlain broadcast a message to Britain and the Empire, having returned from a meeting with Hitler on the question of ceding Sudetenland from Czechoslovakia. He also saw in Rannoch, policemen distributing gas masks, 'the constables talked quietly one to another, as though they could scarcely credit this menace of imminent war'.

On Wednesday 28th, Seton and Caitriona spent the day in Glasgow, after catching an early train from Perth. He thought the international events of that day so important that he made a special note of them, stating, 'The following are my impressions of that day, when in the morning war seemed unavoidable and when hope dramatically arose late in the afternoon:'

> We left Fincastle House on a dark, misty morning. Early as it was, there were little groups on the road as we passed through Dunkeld and other villages. The workmen as they bicycled to work, the postmen on their rounds – all looked serious.
>
> We had breakfast on the train. Everyone was very solemn, and one woman, reading the morning paper, was in tears. We took a bus from Buchanan Street out to the Exhibition, and here people seemed to be trying to forget the approaching tumult, yet even in the midst of fun and good humour, were seen sad eyed women reading the papers.
>
> Caitriona and I went to the Mod in the afternoon and as we listened, I felt the atmosphere 'lighten'. I did not then know what had happened until I saw over someone's shoulder the welcome news in an evening paper that Neville Chamberlain had made an announcement in the House of Commons. He told the Members that Mussolini had persuaded Hitler to join a four power conference. Chamberlain would return to Munich the next morning.
>
> As we travelled to the station that evening it was remarkable to see the changed expressions in the faces of fellow-passengers. Buoyancy and happiness had replaced anxiety and foreboding. It had been a long and memorable day, and we had seen the war cloud miraculously lift when it appeared about to overwhelm Europe and perhaps the world.

(Fincastle House house stands to the west of the Pass of Killiecrankie, and oddly, has no direct connection with the Fincastle family. Though the Fincastles are descended from the Atholl Murrays through the Earldom of Dunmore, the land was never deeded over. It came into the possession of a branch of the Stewarts and the present owner, Richard Barbour of Bonskeid, is descended from John Stewart of Bonskeid who became master of the house after the '45.)

Several letters were exchanged with Sir D.Y. Cameron. He was concerned over the size of the area to be covered in the proposed Central Highland book, and thought it should be expanded to two volumes. They met at Kippen in November to discuss the book, and afterwards 'D.Y'. wrote offering 'warm thanks for your visit and talks and piping. May we share some of the great scenes together – though I cannot alas climb mountains with you'.

For a man of great spirituality and concern for peace Cameron again showed a poor opinion of people south of the border: '. . . I hope the lectures are a success and that you are quickening the Sassenach's imagination and revealing to him that London is not first and last and is really a most inconvenient distance from the Centre of Life and Work – which is, of course, north of the Tweed'.

When the book was published, Seton Gordon acknowledged that his almost constant companion as he had explored each area, had been Francis Cameron-

Seton Gordon fishing the Shin – 1920s

Head. In October and November of 1938 they concentrated on the country of Rob Roy, from Lochearn to Aberfoyle and Inversnaid.

Less than a mile north of Inversnaid is a cave where, according to tradition, Rob Roy hid for a time after his house was burned by troops. It was only by the perseverance of Cameron-Head that the cave was located. He then descended 'with determination into its dark depths'. There was at the time an old wooden ladder to help reach the cave floor, and Seton noted his companion showed considerable agility while descending it.

At Loch Earn the late Major 'Jock' Stewart of Ardvorlich, a brother-in-law of the present Lochiel, gave Seton considerable help. Ardvorlich and its 7000 acres have been in the Stewart family for 400 years, and some aspects of its history are among the bloodiest in the Highlands. Ardvorlich is on the south side of the loch, bordering a large wild area which includes Glen Artney and Ben Vorlich, 3224 feet. Not all of the deeds directly concerned the Stewarts, but with the MacGregors as neighbours it would not have been easy for them to remain on the sidelines for too long.

Seton and Francis Cameron-Head climbed Ben Vorlich with Major Stewart. After a sunny start the weather closed in as they neared the summit and hours later were glad to be back at the house where, he recalled ' that evening when the fire burned cheerfully on the hearth in the old house of Ardvorlich and the moon showed fitfully through the storm wrack, the piper tuned his pipes and played a pibroch of the past, telling of the days when broken men haunted these hills, and when human life may have been of small account, but Highland hospitality was strong'.

Still in the possession of the Stewart family, and seen by Seton and Francis on that long-ago visit is the Clach Dhearg, the Red Stone, said to have had miraculous properties. If the stone was dipped in a pail of water and moved three times sunwise around it, the water then had healing powers for ailing cattle. People came great distances to take back water to their cattle into which the stone had been dipped.

On Friday 2 December, Seton had the honour of presiding at the Glasgow–Skye Association Gathering, with 2500 people present.

By 31 December 1938, 'Grey Wind' had travelled a total of 34,577 miles since it was purchased in late 1932, almost all of it on rough Highland roads. The Upper Duntuilm rain gauge showed 64.03 inches and sunshine was recorded at 1143 hours.

In mid-January 1939, Seton Gordon drove to Sleat for a day of piping with David Fincastle at Ostaig, the Fincastle's Skye home. David had composed a march, which Seton considered to be 'not at all bad'. Even as they played the pipes together, with the hills of the mainland prominent across the Sound of Sleat, events were taking place in Europe which within a few months would lead to the mobilisation of all Territorial units. The Captain, Viscount David Fincastle, 'Dubbie', as he was affectionately known to his friends, would lead his Island company to the continent. Hamish MacDonald, who had embarked on a law career and was an advocate, still served in the Skye Company. He joined the 5th Battalion upon mobilisation, which did not go overseas until later.

Seton and Dubbie had enjoyed many days of fishing together, but one which they shared in South Uist stood out in Seton's memory. It was at the Houghmore Bridge pool and was fondly recalled in *Afoot in the Hebrides*:

Lord Fincastle decided to fish the loch, but as the neap tides were on, and

> the river was low, the salmon and sea-trout were unable to ascend the river beyond the bridge pool. I preferred to try my luck there, and found it crowded with sea-trout.
>
> That morning only the slightest ripple disturbed the surface of the water. I began to fish at the tail of the pool, which was literally alive with fish. At my first cast I hooked a sea trout and saw a grisle leap high out of the water. The trout took with remarkable freedom, and sometimes I played two fish at once. Then the breeze dropped, and the ripple disappeared. I stopped fishing until a small shower, drifting in from the Atlantic, caused the breeze to freshen once more.
>
> I had landed a 3 lb trout, and was playing another when the tide entered the pool. The trout ceased to take, and I stood on the bridge and watched their behaviour as the cold Atlantic current replaced the relatively warm fresh water. The fish swam in shoals restlessly round the pool, sometimes turning on their silvery sides, so that a momentary flash of colour could be seen. The fish were of all sizes, some of them 5 lbs or 6 lbs, some fat 3-pounders. I was continuously playing fish that morning, and when David Fincastle, returned from the loch at lunchtime he greeted me with the remark, 'I am afraid there is nothing doing today; I have not seen or risen a single fish in the loch'. He then looked over the bridge, and I shall not readily forget the surprised look on his face when he saw thirty-six silvery sea-trout laid out in a row on the sand. I do not claim to be an expert fisherman, but I have found that I am the only person who has an affection for the Bridge Pool.

The following day Seton and Dubbie climbed Beinn Mhor. On its slopes the heather was in bloom and below them the crofters were cutting their peats. Now, with war threatening and the likelihood of general mobilisation at any time, it was pleasant to share memories as they talked at Ostaig.

On 15 March the Germans began their occupation of Czechoslovakia. With so many promises broken, the Prime Minister at last saw through Hitler. With words that had a familiar ring, on 31 March he said in the House of Commons, '. . . in the event of any action which clearly threatened Polish independence . . . His Majesty's Government would feel themselves bound at once to lend all possible support to the Polish Government. They have given an assurance to this effect'.

Leslie Hore-Belisha, who a few years earlier had written to Seton Gordon about Skye road improvements, was now Secretary of State for War. On 27 April he introduced limited conscription and ordered the Territorial Army be brought to full strength.

When the order came to increase the size of the Territorial Army, Adjutant Derek Lang accompanied 'Dubbie' Fincastle to the Outer Hebrides where they began recruiting. Through David Fincastle's influence they recruited greater numbers than anywhere else in the 4th's recruitment area. Writing of this recruiting drive in April 1988, General Sir Derek Lang said, 'We had instructions to open up Harris, which was 4th Battalion territory, but up to that point we had no Territorials there. Dubbie made full use of his family feudal connections and in no time we had mustered over fifty men'.

In 1938 Viscount Fincastle had married the Hon. Pamela Herman-Hodge, elder daughter of Baron Wyfold, whose Highland home was Dalness House in Glen Etive. On 3 April, while her husband was busily recruiting in the Outer Hebrides, Viscountess Fincastle gave birth to a son, christened John Alexander Murray.

By the second week of May, Seton Gordon and Francis Cameron-Head were again in the Central Highlands enjoying an outing to Glen Charnaig in glorious weather. En route they examined Rob Roy's grave and the site of his house near Loch Voil. By noon they had reached the head of the glen and around them the view opened up:

> We came in sight of a vast country of hills, glens and lochs, all of them sunlit. Ben Lawers, Ben Dorain, Ben Nevis – each one distinct. We heard the croaking of ptarmigan and the 'chacking' of a wheatear as we crossed the stony slopes of the spur of Stob Inneoin. We lunched beside a lochan near which was a peat-stained snowfield. Overhead a raven sailed, the sun glinting on his dark plumage as he dived joyously from a giddy height. The smoke of hill fires rose from the slopes near Loch Lomond.

Seton received a communication from Buckingham Palace in June 1939 to advise him that the CBE had been conferred upon him. It was for services to natural history and literature. With eighteen books published there were two more in preparation, the central Highlands book and *In Search of Northern Birds*, to be published in 1941. The investiture did not take place until early the following year, by which time the country was embroiled in the confused early months of the war.

There were many similarities between the summer of 1939 to that of 1914. Then, Lord Hankey talked of the swiftness of events in those final weeks before the First World War began, and the belief almost to the last moment that war could be averted. On 3 August, 1939, Sir Thomas Inskip, Minister of Defence Co-ordination, said, 'War today is not only NOT inevitable but is unlikely. The Government have good reason for saying that'.

At 9 a.m. on 3 September the British Ambassador, Sir Nevile Henderson, was instructed to present an ultimatum to the German Government which informed them that if no satisfactory reply was received to Britain's note requesting withdrawal of military forces, war would be declared at 11 a.m.

In a diary note on Sunday, 3 September, Seton Gordon wrote, 'It is now 10.55 a.m. and in 5 minutes we will know whether we are at peace or at war. 11 a.m. It is not peace, but war! Let us hope it may be short. Lovely day – 72 deg'.

> 4 September – Went down to Coast Guard to see about defence work. Heard that *Athenia* had been torpedoed last night with considerable loss of life. [The 13,500 ton *Athenia*, outward bound, was torpedoed and sank, with the loss of 112 lives, 28 of them American citizens – the German U-boat menace was once again a reality.]

8 September – When I was weeding, the tame robin came up again. Its red breast is now complete.

17 September – Ark Royal passed with six destroyers. Six or so planes took off – a fine sight. Russia invaded Poland.

Before this first month of the war was over, the Gordons had a visitor, the film director, Michael Powell. His 1938 release, *The Edge of the World* had inspired Audrey to try her hand at script writing. The storyline in his film was based on the evacuation of St Kilda, dramatised into a conflict between two of the island's families. Audrey's script had a more mystic touch, drawn from the Hebrides rich folklore. Powell was sufficiently impressed that he wrote to thank Audrey. When they read that his next film, *The Spy in Black* was to be filmed in the Orkneys, the Gordons got in touch and invited him to Skye.

In his 1986 autobiography, *A Life in Movies*, Powell recalled a delightful picture of life at Upper Duntuilm. He describes the meeting at Portree with Seton, Audrey and Dara, with whom he 'shook paws' and the journey to the north of the island, where at the house he met Caitriona and Bridie. They had been busy preparing a Highland welcome, a traditional high tea of hot scones, eggs, tea from a huge old teapot – and whisky. Of his meeting with the girls he said, 'They had expected somebody awe-inspiring and truculent, but they looked me over and decided I would do. I returned the compliment'.

Skye was not yet a closed area and the Gordons took their guest to all parts of the island. They scrambled on the lower slopes of the Cuillins, climbed the higher MacLeod's Table and visited Talisker.

Michael Powell had collected most of Seton's books over the years and was impressed with his 'lovely old-fashioned photographs' but the visit to Skye made him aware of Seton's uniqueness. Recalling that time, Powell wrote, 'Nothing that moved on the hill escaped his attention. To walk with him was an education. Every sound and sight was interpreted by him immediately . . . Now that he has gone, I feel, when I am on the hills, deaf, dumb and blind'.

Audrey's script was never used, because the timing was wrong, but a friendship was born which became stronger over the years. Michael Powell returned to London, taking with him a shepherd's crook with a carved ram's horn top, a present from Seton which he treasured until the end of his equally long life.

The war gradually made its impact on the lives of Skye men and women. Seton continued his diary notes:

30 September – To Kilmuir for gas masks.

3 October – Red aurora over N. Uist – crimson to zenith with two pale bands crossing.

5 October – Wrote 'Peace on the Hills'.

6 October – Captain Buchanan called, appointed me coast-watcher.

During this period Seton Gordon's diary was filled with descriptions of cloud

Biddlesden Manor, with Betty Gordon and film producer Michael Powell conversing on lawn

and light effects, as though he absorbed the beauty to assuage the horrors being reported on the Polish offensive. This period of the war was coined by Neville Chamberlain, 'the twilight war'. There was no air action between Britain, France and Germany other than reconnaissance flights and the armies on the western front were static. At sea, however, several ships were sunk, beginning with the *Athenia*.

Members of the British Expeditionary Force were dispatched to France the day after war was declared, and by this time all Territorial regiments were fully mobilised. The 51st Highland Division, which included the 4th Battalion, Cameron Highanders, was moved to Aldershot but did not leave Britain until February 1940. It is doubtful if Viscount Fincastle had an opportunity for any last fishing expeditions with Seton.

While the tempo of the war increased, a young boy in Aberdeenshire was more concerned with natural history and the influence of Seton Gordon's books on his growing interest in bird-watching. He posted a letter to Upper Duntuilm on 15 October, and could not have dreamt as he reached up to the letterbox what he had set in motion. It was not an ordinary letter. Interspersed among the writing were six small diagrams, four across the middle of the page, one above, and one at the bottom. They were simply, but boldly drawn. The first was of a golden eagle and its nest (it said, 2000 feet up), the next was of the Larig Ghru, then, a deer, a lizard, a ptarmigan, and the last showed a kilted figure with a cromack and binocular case against three mountain peaks.

The letter said:

Old Bank house Turriff
Aberdeenshire.

15.10.39.

Dear Mr Seton Gordon

I would like to go through the Larig Ghru from Aviemore to Braemar which is 22½ miles. But I have never done it. I have never seen a golden Eagle. I wear a kilt, I am getting your book, The Cairngorm hills of Scotland for my birthday. I have been at the Chest of dee, and the white bridge, and Climb-ed Sgorr mor 2,666. I saw a big herd of deer between Inverey and the Linn of Dee. I have been at the Colonels bed, and Loch Bulig, and Derry lodge. I like to fish, I read your book, Afoot in wild places. And I like the pictures they were very nice. Especially the one of you climbing Bruach na frithe in early April. I would like very much to climb Lochnagar. I am only nine years old. Do you think I will manage. I would be very happy if I could climb it.

from Adam Watson.

Golden Eagle and Nest 2000 feet up.

Larig Ghru.

DEEr.

Lizard

ptarmigan.

The 1939 letter from Adam Watson that began his long friendship with Seton Gordon

The letter struck a sympathetic chord in Seton Gordon. It must surely have called to mind his own early awakening to nature at a similar age. He replied within the week. Adam Watson quoted the letter in his Foreword to the reprint of the *The Immortal Isles* in 1979, two years after Seton Gordon's death. The reply said:

> Dear Adam,
> I was very glad to see your nicely written letter and the interesting pictures you drew. It was clever of you to draw Lairig Ghru so that I could recognise it at once.
> It is a fine thing for you to have a love of the hills because on the hills you find yourself near grand and beautiful things, and as you grow older you will love them more and more.
> I think you could manage to climb Lochnagar. Our daughter Caitriona climbed Braeriach with me when she was eight. When she reached the Wells of Dee she was rather disappointed with them as she thought she would see a big river like the Dee is, lower down.
> You must write to me again after you climb Lochnagar. I am sending you two photographs, Your friend Seton Gordon.

In the Foreword, Watson recalls the moment which led him to write his letter to Skye. He was eight years old and while one day browsing in the Ballater library he found in the shelves, *The Cairngorm Hills of Scotland*. It made a lasting impression:

> Books are one of the pinnacles of human culture and achievement. Few things can have a more revolutionary effect on the attitudes and beliefs of young minds in a receptive mood. That was so for me, with Seton Gordon's books. Only perhaps twice in a lifetime may a brief event, such as a glance at a book, or a sudden union of two like minds, become a clear turning point which transforms the rest of one's life . . . From then on I saw Scotland, its wild life, weather, skies, people and culture, with this different eye. Others whom I know had a spark lit in them by Seton Gordon's writings, and went on to become naturalists and writers themselves. And others unborn will have this magic in future.

Dr Watson, who in 1990 retired from his post as Senior Principal Scientific Officer at the Institute of Terrestrial Ecology, did not expect a reply from 'such a busy man' and was surprised by the immediate response. Over the next few years, until they met, all his letters to Seton Gordon contained notes of bird and weather observations. From the age of thirteen, Watson kept systematic records of his nature observations.

Seton and Audrey stayed with D.Y. Cameron at Kippen for a few days. In a follow-up note after their return to Skye, D.Y. showed his despair of the world:

> . . . your visit was a thrill and an inspiration because no one else I know

> carries me back so to earlier days, when the world was not mechanised and vulgarised and so brutal. How much you do to turn the thoughts to nature and the spirit indwelling – and away from what so drags and depresses in our day.
>
> I am glad you are safe again in your sea-girt wilderness, where heather fires burn and the snowdrops whisper with the welcome voice of spring. Are they prophetic of what is coming, and peace [is] near at hand?
>
> I find work difficult under present world conditions. Romance and dream and the deep spirit of poetry seem baffled and crushed. War and politics and cruelty darken all the land and destroy happiness – so essential for art.
>
> You must feel likewise, but we must rest in hope and be not afraid of good tidings. My love to you and gratitude & best regards to your partner in life . . . D.Y.C.

Seton Gordon once again became a coast-watcher, Francis Cameron-Head was commissioned as a Home Guard officer and Inverailort House was requisitioned by Combined Operations. Because of his coast-watching and war-related activities, Seton was not as inconvenienced by wartime travel restrictions as most people living in the west of Scotland. Even so, he experienced a few amusing situations:

> The identity card of each railway passenger was carefully scrutinised by the Security Officer at Mallaig before they were permitted to board the train. On one occasion I was travelling on the engine foot-plate for a special purpose and was issued a railway permit from Mallaig to Glasgow. I made myself conspicuous on the engine when we stopped at Corpach, but even then had difficulty in attracting the attention of the military. At last a sergeant saw me and, full of suspicion, he hurried to the engine. I gave him the ticket which passed me through the area, but he was still doubtful, and to the amusement of the engine crew, went to consult his officer, who had plainly not been on an engine before and the oil and smoke deterred him.
>
> He was just on the point of pulling himself into the cab when the fireman, apparently innocently, released a jet of boiling steam about his feet. I thought I would further surprise him by warmly shaking hands with him – my hands at the time being black with grease. He was obliged to agree that my papers were in order. As he climbed down, the driver, who had viewed the proceedings with disapproval, released another jet of steam, causing the man to leap several inches in fright. When he looked back, the driver and fireman were both engrossed in their tasks.

A regulation was in effect that no telescope or binoculars could be carried without special permission, either on the coast or in the Hebrides. This posed problems for stalkers, and once the deer controller was apprehended upon returning from a count on Rhum because he displayed his spotting scope. Another example of what Seton Gordon called 'spy mania' took place on Aviemore station when the Registrar-General for Scotland alighted from the train to enjoy a day's hiking. He brought out his map to study it and was immediately accosted by the stationmaster who only released him when proper identity was provided.

Officers of the Lovat Scouts carry a stalking glass as a part of their uniform, but this did not impress a duty officer on Mallaig pier when he apprehended a Lovat Scout captain who was crossing to Skye on leave. When the Scout asked 'What am I to do with it?' it took a few moments for the answer. He was finally advised, 'Put it in your suitcase!'

Seton Gordon's old friend Sir Malcolm Barclay-Harvey was far away from the frustrations of wartime Britain. In 1939 he was appointed Governor of South Australia. His wife, Margaret, had died of peritonitis in 1936 and the year before his appointment he married Lady Muriel Liddell-Grainger, a daughter of the Earl of Lindsey.

Barclay-Harvey's successful political career as Unionist Member of Parliament for Kincardineshire and West Aberdeenshire, culminated in the Australian appointment. He was a popular Governor and got on well with the Australians and their informal lifestyle. They appreciated his love of trains and he had a locomotive named after him, which he sometimes drove. When he left in 1944 the metal number plate (520) was presented to him.

The Germans began their major offensive and invaded France, Holland, Belgium and Luxembourg. The British Army took the brunt of the fighting in the spring of 1940, as the Allied armies crumbled. A withdrawl to Dunkirk was put into effect, as the only solution to save the British Expeditionary Force. In nine days 338,226 men were evacuated back to Britain from the beaches.

The 51st Highland Division was performing a rearguard action near Abbeville on a front which extended for 16 miles. Viscount Fincastle's B Company was engaged in an attempt to retake a position. An intense mortar bombardment met them and Viscount Fincastle was wounded in both legs, but continued in command of his company until so weakened from loss of blood that he was removed to a dressing station. He was killed when it received a direct hit. B Company lost over seventy men and the Battalion's losses were 250 men in this one action.

News of David Fincastle's death did not reach Seton Gordon until 18 June just as he and Audrey were setting out through Glen Sligachan to Camusunary. It was a beautiful June day and Seton felt David's spirit accompanying them, on what had been one of his favourite walks. Seton wrote:

> . . . It seemed fantastic in this country of peace and beauty that scenes of madness should be even then occurring across the sea. Throughout the night at intervals oyster-catchers called beside the tide. The machair was green; along the shore yellow sedum flowered profusely to the edge of the pale sands. Blaven and the Black Cuillin rose in beauty, their hard outlines softened in the early morning light. As we watched, a cloud, small and ethereal, formed in the corrie of Garsven. So thin and diaphanous was this fair weather cloud that it failed to hide the rocks behind it from view. It rested there lightly, without movement, suffused by the sun, then, as stealthily as it had grown, it diminished in size and vanished.

Seton Gordon wrote an appreciation in the *Scotsman* in which as well as making mention of David Fincastle's love of the Hebrides and its people, he mentioned among those who would miss him was – 'his wise collie, Marsco, who was his friend and companion on many a walk'.

As a means of ensuring that the Highland spirit would live on in the face of this blow, the 9th Highland Division, which included the 5th Battalion, Cameron Highlanders, was renumbered the 51st. Those that escaped from France were remustered to this Division, which in 1942 fought with distinction in North Africa.

Throughout 1940 there were also several letters from Bridie, who had left Crofton Grange and at the age of seventeen and joined the Women's Land Army. Her first posting, in January, was to a farm at Bucksburn, close to Aberdeen, for a period of training. She was having some difficulty adjusting to life with girls whose language was coarser than she was used to, but she was a hard worker and did not mind long hours, getting up at 5.30 a.m. The food was plain, but served in huge quantities.

By the end of February Bridie was at Inverlochy Castle, north-east of Fort William, working for Lord and Lady Abinger. Writing to Audrey, who was suffering from an attack of lumbago which was severe enough to keep her in bed, she described it as a very grand place and wrote:

> I have a very large room with a fire in it every night and they have marvellous food served in nothing but silver dishes and lots of wine etc! They are both very nice.
>
> . . . My job is to work the steriliser, look after a boiler, milk four cows, look after calves and young stock and a few odd jobs. It is not hard work but very long hours.

In August Bridie returned to Aberdeen. Ardtannes Farm was at Inverurie and owned by Major and Mrs Kirkcaldy, who treated Bridie with great kindness. They lived in a very old house with a huge open fireplace in the kitchen, with long chains to hang pots over the flames. In an amusing letter Bridie described conditions on the farm:

> The Grieve is very nice and so is his wife. They tell the cook that they cannot understand why I am doing such dirty work when I am a lady! The dear old 'wifie' tries to make me wear gloves, she thinks I will spoil my hands. There are quite a lot of men working on the farm but only the married ones talk to me – the others are oh so shy! All the animals are very well treated, the Grieve takes a great interest in them. The work is perhaps a little harder than Inverlochy but I like it . . .

Alasdair was home for the summer and helping with the harvest. He was in the sixth-form at Stowe and was a sergeant in the OTC. He had received instruction in small arms during the spring and was working towards his Certificate 'A'. There were interesting touches of wartime economy measures even in his letters: 'I am afraid I will not be able to make that butter as there are no measurements and I am not very sure if I will be able to manage the roller'. He was still playing his pipes regularly and was giving lessons to some of the other pupils.

A letter from Francis Cameron-Head brought into focus a problem which the war had brought to many of Britain's larger homes if they were requisitioned for military use:

> You heard, I suppose of how the soldiers behaved at Achnacarry.
>
> The Sergeants' and Officers' messes broke each other's windows, including the big plate window of the drawing room and dining rooms. They appear to have pillaged the house and we are all furious about it. The damage done at Inverailort pales by comparison. There will, I hope, be a court martial about it, and I hope they put it across them.
>
> Yours ever, Francis.

In the course of a training exercise later in the war some of the ancient pines at Achnacarry were burned. People can be very forgiving in a war about 'youthful pranks', but when one considers that Donald Walter Cameron of Lochiel had fought in the first war and his sons were serving in the second, wanton damage to a lovely and historic house is inexcusable.

Inverailort fared badly, but for different reasons. Had Francis' mother been properly advised she would have offered the house as soon as war was declared. It might then have been used by the Department of Health, perhaps to house evacuees, or some other benign purpose. Instead it was taken over by Combined Operations. She was in London when the house was requisitioned, and by the time she arrived at Inverailort the furniture was already being removed with many of the drawers still full even as they were taken out. Everything was placed in an old church, taken over for storage, together with the contents of other houses. Consequently it was not possible to prove that woodworm was absent before they were placed there. Some of the Inverailort furniture was smashed on the way when a huge pothole was encountered. It was used to place in the hole.

The legacy of dry rot in the expropriated homes was equally hard to prove. At Inverailort the whole of the upstairs floors were covered in heavy duty linoleum, and the Surgeon Commander, nicknamed 'Pemican Pete', had a fetish for 'swabbing the decks'. The water was constantly seeping under the lino. With no ventilation the dry rot began and by the time the house was derequisitioned the damage was done. Compensation, when it was paid out, was based on 1939 values. The smoking room, which was used as an office, had a very beautiful 'fleur-de-lys' wallpaper. In recounting their fight with the war office after 1945, Mrs 'Putchi' Cameron-Head said, 'when people were bored they must have thrown ink-wells at one wall because it was covered in ink. It was not possible to replace it, and we were offered £10. The hall floors are of parquet, and the reason they are loose is that they were completely ruined with water, and never polished'. In one room, she came across a sergeant removing a fireplace tile. When asked what was going on he said it was to go towards a collection of tiles for his own fireplace after the war from houses where he had been stationed.

Mrs Cameron-Head showed her generosity of spirit when she said: 'You can't fault them when they were doing a job. The St. Nazaire raid men were chosen from here. You can't expect people in the middle of a war – risking their lives – to take their boots off every time they walked in. I think they are honourable battle scars'.

Francis and his mother moved to Dunain House, near Inverness. Francis was unfit for active service, but was commissioned into the 2nd Inverness-shire Battalion of the Home Guard and soon attained the rank of Major. His mother died on Easter Day 1940. (One legacy left from the war is that the doors at Inverailort House still have on them, picked out in white lettering, the function of each room while it was occupied by Combined Operations: Wren's Quarters, Captain's Office, General Office, etc.)

1941 was an uneventful year for Seton Gordon. A letter was received in February from John MacDonald. It contained news of Brown and Nicol who were now both Pipe-Majors. There was a direct mention of Alasdair Gordon's piping:

> I am pleased to see Alasdair is keeping up his piping. He was playing very well when I last heard him at Inverness. He was, I think, rather overdoing it with grace notes, particularly the D Grace note in his marches, but that was how he was taught and the fault was not his doing.

Alasdair was in his last year at Stowe, and during the summer there were several visits to the Cuillin Hills with his father. Another expedition, in October, was taken with Caitriona to Beinn Edra, via Glen Conan, and became an article, '*Peace in the Isles*':

> Skye is at war, yet one has only to go to the hills to pass beyond the breath of war and on that bright October morning, peace might have returned to the world.
>
> Caitriona and I, when we reached high ground looked back to the sunlit waters of Uig Bay. Summer flowers were still in blossom, and on dry stony knolls was a second bloom of bell heather. Here and there were blue sprays of milkwort and eyebright, and the button-like flowers of scabious. On the higher slopes of Beinn Edra we saw rosettes of *saxifraga stellaris*, still green and fresh. High in the air, against a dark cloud, five ravens soared.
>
> At a height of 1500 feet above the sea we reached the watershed, at the edge of the dark wall of rock which divides, for many miles, the north wing of Skye. When we reached the cairn on Beinn Edra, several plants of *silene acaulis* had a second bloom on them.
>
> Sun and shade alternated on the Cuillin range and through a gap between Marsco and Sgurr na Stri, we could see the faint cone of Ben More on the Isle of Mull 80 miles to the south. As we made our way to the low ground, the sun

> shone with soft violet light on the summit of Beinn Edra, and when the last rays left the hilltop, Glen Conon became a place of twilight. Cold dew settled on the grass as night approached, and on the far north-west horizon, the cone of Boreray rose from a serene, peaceful sky that was suffused with bars of softest pink.

By the end of 1941, the war had reached a critical stage. While Seton Gordon reflected on the peace which blessed the Western Isles, the 7 December attack on Pearl Harbor by Japan now made the conflict worldwide. Soon the men of Skye and the Outer Isles who had joined the Highland regiments would be sailing for the Far East to fight in the jungles of South-East Asia.

Paper shortages cut the production of journals and magazines, and those that kept going were reduced in size. Difficulties in travel meant cutting back on visits to schools, and many of the prep schools in the critical area of south-east England were evacuated to remoter areas of the country. All this had a dire effect on Seton Gordon's income, though no concern was expressed in his notes. Earnings for 1941 from lectures and writing was down to £140–17–6d. The November release of *In Search of Northern Birds* was too late to improve his income for that year.

CHAPTER

11

NATURE TALKS FOR THE ARMED FORCES

EARLY IN THE WAR it had occurred to Seton Gordon that his considerable experience with weather observation might be of assistance to the Air Ministry's Meteorological Office and in August 1941 he wrote to offer his services. On 27 January, 1942, he received news that his offer was accepted:

> . . . In the normal course of events, there is no case for an additional station at Duntuilm. I mean that if you were not already there, it would not be necessary to establish another station over and above those already in place.
>
> I think nevertheless that your observations could be really useful because, as you indicated, you have had a long experience in making them and are well-qualified to observe and report features of weather which are of the greatest importance, namely, visibility and height of the cloud base. If you could make three short reports each day it would be useful to the Officer who receives them and would be made available to others who are directly concerned with the meteorological conditions in the West of Scotland . . .
>
> Arrangements will be made so that your messages may receive the necessary priority.
>
> Yours faithfully, N. K. Johnson.

A follow-up letter from Group Captain Turner, RAF, Dungallon House, Oban, confirmed that the times would be, 07.45, 11.45 and 15.45 GMT, from April 6. Although it could not have always been convenient, the reports were sent regularly, and continued after the war was over.

Caitriona joined the FANYs (First Aid Nursing Yeomanry) early in the war and served as a driver. She was stationed at Cameron Barracks, Inverness, and drove officers to and from the various military locations in the Highlands, Fort George, Gairloch, Aberdeen and others. While at Inverness, Caitriona met Simon Macdonald-Lockhart of the Lee, an officer in the Lovat Scouts, who were then stationed a few miles away at Beauly. Eventually Simon proposed to her and Caitriona accepted. They were married in St Mary's Cathedral, Edinburgh, on 28 February 1942. The weather was bitterly cold in Scotland, and her father almost missed the wedding. He was at Pitlochry and a diary note for that day said '. . . Desperate job to get to wedding – all ice bound – caught train by ten seconds at Pitlochry'.

Simon Macdonald-Lockhart was born at Largie Castle in Argyll, opposite the Isle of Gigha. The castle was demolished after the Second World War, as its condition was so bad that repairs were out of the question. Simon became heir to the extensive Lee and Carnwath Estate after the death, in war, of his older brother. The estate centres on Newholm, near Dunsyre, at the foot of the Pentland Hill of the same name, and about 8 miles north-east of Carnwath.

In early March Adam Watson, now twelve, sent another letter in which he told of his latest enterprise:

> I am writing a book about the Cairngorms, Rothiemurchus and Mar called *My Mountains* and hope to get it published. I have put a few pictures in it and photographs. I have written twenty chapters. There are twenty-five pictures and photographs. But publishing is difficult just now, so I will likely have to wait a good while, if I get it done. I have so far done 36,400 words in the twenty chapters. I think I will do about 50,000.
>
> This summer I shall climb Braeriach (my favourite mountain), Cairngorm, and maybe Sgoran Dubh. A few days ago I saw about a dozen snipes rising from a field near Turriff. Do snipes come as many as that? I was surprised to see them . . .
>
> Here is a list of the chapters I have done and will do: . . .
>
> With Good Wishes From Your Friend, Adam.

There follows a list of twenty-five chapters, listed in Roman numerals, mostly of mountain or glen names, but included are some original titles such as *The Great Moss*, *Three Hills as Outposts of the Western Cairngorms*, *A Walk up Glen Dee in April* and *Stand Fast Craigellachie!* There is also an index listed.

Enclosed with the letter were more bold sketches. Although some of the chapter titles bear a resemblance to what his mentor might have chosen, the young Watson proved that he had the tenacity necessary to become a published writer. He now has several hundred papers to his credit. A recent book, co-authored with Elizabeth Allan, is *The Place Names of Upper Deeside*, published in 1984. Approximately twenty-five accompanying photographs were all taken by Watson.

Someone else put pen to paper that same spring. With help and encouragement from Seton Gordon, John MacDonald of Inverness published his reminiscences in the *Oban Times* in April 1942. It stated that he was a pupil of Calum Mor MacPherson, and like Calum's son, Angus, came from a distinguished piping background. He had a long association with army piping, which he was always striving to improve. His greatest recognition came in 1909 when he was asked to become instructor at the new Army School of Piping at Inverness, a position held by him until 1921.

MacDonald then became instructor to the Pibroch Society. The quality of his playing was recognised in the number of Clasps he won at the Northern Meeting. Between 1903 and 1934 he won seven. Four of them were won when he was over sixty. He was also Honorary Piper to Kings George V, Edward VIII and George VI.

From John MacDonald comes a picture of Calum Mor MacPherson as tutor and his method of teaching. It is a scene which will never be repeated: 'Each morning Calum used to play jigs on the chanter before breakfast. I can see him now, with his old jacket and his leather sporran, sitting on his stool while the porridge was being brought to the boil. After breakfast he would take his barrow to the peat moss, cut a turf, and build up the fire with wet peat for the day. He would then sit down beside me, remove all music books, then sing in his own *Canntaireachd* the ground and different variations of the particular *piobaireachd* he wished me to learn'.

The Gordons travelled to Fort Augustus on 9 June, for the marriage of Francis Cameron-Head to Lucretia Pauline Rebecca Ann Farrell. The wedding took place at the Abbey Church and Seton was best man. There were many young serving officers at the wedding, some of them from Inverailort, and a contingent of Lovat Scouts, including Iain Grant, the younger, of Rothiemurchus. Seton's diary note was brief:

> Francis and Putchi married at Fort Augustus. Salmon and Champagne. Chauffeur blotto! A successful wedding, many guests.

Francis Cameron-Head had proposed to Lucretia Farrell in a truly romantic Highland setting, on an islet of Loch Eilt, but she would not accept until they were back on 'dry land!' A second proposal at Fort Augustus was successful. After their marriage Seton addressed the new Mrs Cameron-Head of Inverailort as 'Putchaidh' – a word he elaborated from her childhood name Putchi. Her father called her 'Michelin' (after the tyre man), because as a very young child Luctretia was chubby. The closest she manage to say, sounded like 'Putchi' and the name stuck.

Tall and slim with a most beautiful speaking voice which time has not diminished, 'Putchi' Cameron-Head became a Red Cross ambulance driver. Later in the war she had an executive post with the Board of Agriculture. Following their marriage the Cameron-Heads went to live at Dunain Park, where they stayed until allowed to return to Inverailort.

Seton later stayed at Dunain Park, following up with a note of thanks to his hostess:

> Dear Putchaidh,
>
> I found that there has been terrible weather here, so the harvest prospects are not cheerful and much of the hay is still uncut. It must be the same all over the west, I hear from Mull that much of the feeding stuff has already been lost . . .
>
> Now I must thank you both very sincerely for my pleasant time with you.

Dr Adam Watson, Seton Gordon's protégé, taken in 1986 at the Institute for Terrestrial Ecology, Banchory

Francis is a fortunate man to have found so capable and charming a wife and I can see that you will be both be very happy.

Every good wish to you both, Seton.

By autumn the news was filled with the success of the Battle of El Alamein, but on Skye there was a growing concern for the fate of Hamish MacDonald, by now a Captain with the 5th Battalion, Cameron Highlanders in North Africa.

The 5th Battalion was part of the reformed 51st Highland Division, who, with divisions from Australia, New Zealand and South Africa, were chosen to form the main attack force at El Alamein, one of the decisive battles of the North African campaign. The attack began on 23 October and by 3 November the enemy were in full retreat and General von Thoma, Commander of the Afrika Korps, was a prisoner.

On the 14 November John MacDonald wrote to Seton, 'I heard today that Hamish MacDonald is missing. I do hope he is safe'. By the 24th there is a note in Seton's diary, 'Lochiel and Alasdair [MacDonald of Sleat] think there is little chance of Hamish being alive – think he was blown up by a mine. John MacDonald played a pibroch composed for Hamish, whose mother thought he was 'too good for this world'.'

It was subsequently learned that Hamish had died on 22 October while carrying out a reconnaissance before the start of the battle. He had set out on his mission on the night of the 22nd, accompanied by Corporal Fleming, and was killed by shell-fire. Fleming was taken prisoner and this is why news of what happened was not immediately available. In the opinion of General Makgill-Crichton, a brother officer in the pre-war Territorial Army, and a member of the 51st Division staff at the time of El Alamein, it is unlikely that Hamish was blown-up by a mine, as the Germans at that time did not use anti-personnel mines and he thought a man as slight as Hamish would not set have off an anti-tank mine.

Even as the battle of El Alamein was raging, Seton was in Sutherland fishing. The lodge was at 600 feet with clear views to Skye. There were some memorable images; his most rewarding one was the sight of a skein of whooper swans flying slowly north-east against the wind. Seton thought this wind, which had prevailed during their long flight had carried them farther south than they intended before making their landfall on the Scottish coast.

Such images were far removed from the battles then taking place in many theatres of war. Like Seton's observations of the merlins on the moors above Otterburn in 1914, they served as a reminder of nature's eternal flow in the midst of man's folly.

Seton Gordon was in touch with the War Office on another matter in addition to weather reporting. He offered his services to go around the various stations to lecture on birds and coastal mammals. This was gladly accepted and he began in the spring of 1942 with a lecture at RAF Oban. It was the first of dozens given during the remaining war years to various armed forces audiences.

Seton Gordon's next lecture series was given on board naval ships in the Orkneys, and he was flown there in a two-seater fighter plane of the Fleet Air

Arm. He gave talks to the crews of the flagship, *King George V*, the *Norfolk*, *Cumberland* and the *Tyne*. Although he also lectured to army units, his main military contact during the war years was with the Edinburgh Castle School of Piping, when Pipe-Major Ross was its Director. A pupil with a strong memory of one of those visits is Pipe-Major James MacMillan of Burnaby, a suburb of Vancouver, British Columbia. He is now a distinguished tutor of piping on Canada's west coast.

In 1943 MacMillan was a corporal piper in the Canadian Scottish. Born in Scotland, at Campbelltown in 1911, he emigrated to Canada with his parents when very young. He began to learn the pipes at the age of nine and at seventeen joined the Canadian Scottish as a boy piper, where he made such good progress that in 1936 he was sent to the unveiling of the Vimy Ridge Memorial and met the Prince of Wales. A few months after war was declared he arrived in Britain with the Canadian Scottish and spent two years at Aldershot from where, in January 1943 he was selected to go on a piping course to Edinburgh Castle.

On 13 February, James MacMillan and five others in the school were selected to play for Seton Gordon. The others were Edmond Esson of the Canadian Seaforths, Peter Denham of the King's Own Scottish Borderers, John Low of the Black Watch, Pipe-Major Albert Woods of the Royal Irish Fusiliers and Peter Bain of the Scots Guards. After playing a number of marches, slow airs, strathspeys and reels, each one was asked to play a pibroch. While Seton Gordon sat by the fire, listening attentively, MacMillan played *'MacLeod of Raasay'*.

The guest made a few comments to each of the pipers in turn, and at 5:15 p.m., Ross poured a dram, and after further conversation, Seton Gordon left. James MacMillan recalls him saying that there is far more to piping than nimble fingers. Although the meeting took place forty-five years ago as I write, the Pipe-Major has a clear memory of it.

Less than a month after the session at Edinburgh Castle, on 9 March, Seton and Audrey became grandparents for the first time, when Caitriona gave birth to a baby girl, christened Susan. Caitriona left the FANY and with Simon overseas, first in the Faroes and then Italy, she divided her time between Duntuilm and Largie, where Simon's mother lived in a cottage on the Largie estate.

Shortly after Susan's birth, Alasdair came home from Cambridge, his last vacation before joining the army. Many coastal stretches around the British Isles were completely inaccessible because of barbed wire and concrete anti-tank traps, but on Skye, although there were travel restrictions, the beaches were not cut off to local people. Seton and Alasdair were able to enjoy an idyllic day fishing for codlings and flounders. The day, after months of wild weather, was calm and sunny. Seton noted some of the difficulties encountered with their fishing:

> Setting a small line involves considerable labour. Lug-worms have to be dug in the sand at low tide, and in the Isle of Skye sandy shores are few and far between. Several hundred hooks have to be baited and the line set a quarter of a mile offshore, preferably on a rising tide. We returned after sunset to the shore. A strong, gusty wind had sprung up from the east, buffeting the shags

Seton Gordon taken in the Cairngorms, a few months before he died, by Adam Watson

> as they fought their way home to their roosting island. To lift the line under these conditions was no easy task, for the wind threatened to sweep the boat off its course as it was rowed slowly above the line, one of us rowing, the other lifting the hooks. From the darkening waters, flounders and codlings gradually emerged and were hauled over the side until a fair-sized collection of fish lay at the bottom of the boat. It was a stiff row to the shore, for the wind was contrary and in the swell a landing was not too easy.

Alasdair was in the University OTC and in a letter to his parents he described his adventures with various army vehicles, particularly a motor bike:

> . . . Thank you very much for all the things you bought in London for me. So far only two things from Selfridges have come. The saucepan is fine for making the morning porridge in, and the frying pan is just as good without a handle, as I can either leave it on until it gets cold, or take it off with a cloth. My neighbours all think that the Scots are a hardy race, and that I take it off the fire with my fingers!
>
> Last Wednesday I had an adventurous time risking my neck scorching around the country with a crash helmet on a motor cycle. Yesterday morning we did a part of the assault course, which was relatively easy . . .
>
> I played the pipes in my rooms until 11 p.m. last night, and as I wasn't lynched I am beginning to pluck up a little courage, and even agreed to pipe for the Cambridge Reel Society . . .

On 8 July Alasdair reported to the Scots Guards armoured depot at Pirbright. He was selected for a commission, having proved his mettle in cadets and OTC at school and university. During the war, Sandhurst Royal Military College was used by armoured regiments and Alasdair took his officer training there.

With severe petrol rationing, Seton and Audrey were forced to use public transport more and more. Journeying to Aberdeenshire after the severe late snowstorms of May 1943, they set out by taking the local bus to Portree. Upon reaching Upper Deeside they set out to climb Lochnagar. In the course of the climb they passed a stony knoll on the edge of a snowfield, recently enlarged by the blizzard. It was 28 May and Seton recorded that it was forty years almost to the day when he passed that spot and found his first ptarmigan's nest, leading to the sending of a telegram to Richard Kearton. He expressed concern for what he found:

> The stock of ptarmigan has greatly decreased since then. Whereas I was accustomed to seeing twenty or thirty pairs of ptarmigan, I now found only two pairs. Foxes were increasing, because so many stalkers and keepers were serving in the army. All through the Highlands, grouse and ptarmigan and, more important, increasing numbers of lambs were being killed.

Seton had other reasons to be in the Cairngorms during the war years. Because of the rough mountain terrain the Cairngorms were used for military training exercises, especially as in winter they provided some of the best snow conditions found in the British Isles. Lord Rowallan, who in 1945 became Chief Scout, raised a battalion of the Royal Scots Fusiliers, which he led through the BEF Campaign, despite a severe leg wound from the first war. By 1943 he was in charge of training officer cadets and quickly realised the benefits of mountain training. He set up a camp in the Cairngorms for this purpose and asked Seton Gordon to assist him by taking some of them to the high tops. This led to several outings with these young men.

Many other soldiers were sent to the area for training. On one occasion Seton was almost swept from a forest path by a troop of mounted Indian horsemen 'galloping furiously, crouched on their horses and balancing skilfully on the sharp bends, their black beards streaming in the wind'.

There were many Norwegian ski-troops, who found the terrain and conditions on the high tops particularly suitable for training. Seton recalled that on one of the outings with officer cadets, it very nearly caused strained relations when they drove up to the Norwegian headquarters and were told by an irate officer that they had no business to be there.

Seton's summer was divided between fishing and piping at Invershin with Angus MacPherson and working in the garden and fields at Upper Duntuilm. In mid-September he gave several lectures to forces' bases and ships, ending with a visit to Balmoral where the Lovat Scouts pipers played for the King.

There was still an occasional letter from D.Y. Cameron and one which awaited him upon his return from the lectures, began:

> Your notes always carry me off on Eagles' Wings to the great places. The name Seton Gordon spells romance to so many of our countrymen. Your speaking and your writing are joy to hosts unknown to you.
>
> So glad you like my jottings. You are most welcome to any of the drawings and it would be a great pleasure to hand them over to you. Macmillan asked me to keep them beside me till the book is published.

This letter from Sir D.Y. with its inspirational tone came at a most fortunate time for Seton. An upheaval was about to take place in his life which would upset his pattern for the next three years. The goverment was anxious to recruit people with a background in science, no matter how 'rusty' they might be, to work on projects of importance in the war effort. Because of her background in biology, Audrey was recruited and asked to join a group of scientists at the laboratories of Burroughs Wellcome in Beckenham, Kent. She left Skye in early December and commenced work on the 10th.

Although she had an honours degree in biology, Audrey had not done any laboratory work since leaving Lady Margaret Hall, but it was obviously felt that she was an ideal candidate and would be able to quickly pick up the required knowledge. The main thrust of the work conducted here was to come up with new forms of treatment for tetanus, gangrene and other problems which might afflict soldiers wounded in battle.

Several academic scientists left their university posts to work at Beckenham, and returned to academia after the war. On her first day she commented in her diary 'Historic Day! Two interviews with Attwood [Dept head] and just spoke to the big chief [Miss Barr, senior scientist of the Immunology Department]'. Lodgings were found in Albermarle Road, Beckenham, not far from the laboratory, to which she moved on 23 December. It was not a good time to live in London. Within a few months the V1s would start, and the following September the V2 rockets began to fall.

Aside from the worry of Audrey being in London, the separation imposed a considerable strain on Seton, though food had never been a concern for him and he could get by on very little. It was fortunate that Caitriona was available to stay for long periods at Upper Duntuilm.

From her notes, Audrey enjoyed life at Beckenham, doing such ordinary things as going to the cinema and taking meals with her new colleagues. Even so she did not neglect the opportunity to study local bird populations, and fortunately she had a few colleagues who were keen ornithologists.

One of them, Dr Albert Woiwod, still lives in Beckenham. In 1944 he was a young science graduate who joined Borroughs Wellcome about the same time as Audrey. He was one of the bird-watching group and remembers that having an 'expert' arrive in their midst made a great impression on them. The laboratories were located on the Park Langley estate and the mansion itself still survives. The estate provided many opportunities for bird-watching with its great variety of garden birds. There were even foxes in the vicinity. Dr Woiwod particularly remembers visits to the nest of a nuthatch with Audrey, and a group paid a visit to Knole Park near Sevenoaks where long-tailed tits were studied.

Most of the research staff belonged to the Association of Scientific Workers and Audrey was asked to give a lecture on the golden eagle. Seton sent down her slides and a hall was booked. The lecture was greatly appreciated and led to others at the local public library.

The laboratory manufactured sera and vaccines. There was tetanus toxoid for servicemen going overseas. Another was yellow fever vaccine, and research was conducted into new chemical approaches for the cure of gangrene and gas gangrene. Diphtheria was another concern of the researchers. Dr Woiwod described the method of procuring the agent for all of this vital work. There were 700 horses kept in stables and from each one two litres of blood was drawn daily from their jugular, with no resulting harm to the animals. The separated blood became the agent on which the experiments were done. It was essential that the horses were well cared for and accurate records kept on each one. It occurred to Audrey that it was a job which Bridie might like, and early in 1944 she joined her mother at Beckenham.

A letter on 29 December from Archibald Sinclair of the Air Ministry confirmed more lectures for Seton Gordon with RAF Coastal Command:

> I am delighted to hear that you are prepared to give natural history talks to west coast units of the RAF. I passed this information on to Coastal

> Command who control the units in that area and they will, I know, be very glad to hear it for they were most disappointed when you were prevented by illness from lecturing before.
>
> At the same time I think I should warn you that we now have fewer stations in the area than we had before and in particular we are no longer manning a number of isolated stations that we hoped you might visit as we felt that your talks might be of most value to men stationed in such surroundings.

A letter arrived just before Christmas from Sir Malcolm Barclay-Harvey, in his fourth year as Governor of South Australia. He missed life on Deeside and Seton's companionship on walks, but inevitably he warmed to his favourite subject, Engine No. 520:

> . . . my chief joy at the moment is the new engine I am going to see tomorrow, which should be very interesting. They have named it after me so I take an almost parental interest! I have been on a good many engines out here and one of the most thrilling experiences is to stand on the engine of the Melbourne Express. There are several long gradients of 1 in 45. and to be going all out on one of those is a grand experience!

The letter from his old friend was one of the few things to cheer Seton Gordon that Christmas. Audrey's new job would not permit the time needed to return all the way to Skye and back, and in any case, the tribulations of wartime Christmas rail travel would have been enough to daunt anyone. Alasdair was in the army and Bridie still on the other side of Scotland. However, it is quite certain that Seton would not have been neglected by his friends in Skye, and Dara was still there to keep him company. He was also working on his second wartime book, *A Higland Year* to be published in May 1944.

Final plans were made for lectures to RAF, Coastal Command personnel. The first one in 1944 was on Benbecula where on 29 February, he stayed as a guest of Group Captain Albert de Gruyther, DFC, the Station Commander. De Gruyther recalls an incident during the visit which has remained in his memory. It was some years since Seton had been on that island, though he had regularly stayed on the neighbouring islands of North and South Uist. When last on Benbecula he had watched red-necked phalaropes by a lochan, and he wrote about them in *Wanderings of a Naturalist* and how he had found a chick suffering from the cold. He took it to a neighbouring croft and warmed it by the fire before returning it to its parents. Writing in January 1986, Group Captain de Gruyther said:

> I knew of Seton Gordon through his articles so I was pleased when told that he was to visit Benbecula. I was asked to give him what help I could and in his few days on the island I took him around in my car. One jaunt I remember and often recall was for him to discover whether the red-necked phalarope still nested on the island. He had an idea where he had seen it before and we got as near as we could in the car. Then it was marsh or bog. He took off his

> shoes and socks, girded his kilt up around his middle and waded out up to his thighs. He then wandered around a bit before returning. 'No' he said as he drew near, 'It's gone'. He then continued, reflectively, 'Of course, it was about twenty-one years ago'. He stayed with us a couple of days and then I flew him to Tiree.

The rationale behind these lectures, given at the request of the Education Branch, Coastal Command, was twofold. There was the immediate concern of recreation for personnel of all ranks, so that they could learn to identify various plants and birds, making their off-duty time more interesting. The other was for the benefit of air-crew, who were subject to long flights over the Atlantic. To break the monotony and give them something to take their eyes off the ocean while scanning for submarines, a knowledge of seabirds and their behaviour would help to keep them alert.

The reception that he received on Tiree was as warm as that on Benbecula, but he may have been surprised at the response to the notice on the Squadron bulletin board a few days before. Flight Lieutenant Ken Harper, then with 518 (Met.) Squadron remembers the occasion very well, and also some of the remarks made when the announcement went up – 'The only birds I am interested in are the non-feathered variety!' – 'I'd rather have a fat roast pheasant!' – 'O'h well, there's nothing else to do on this bloody island!' Ken Harper described the evening of the lecture:

> However, on that night the NAAFI was packed and Seton Gordon held everyone spellbound for nearly two hours and at the end of his talk we gave him a standing ovation, which is a measure of the way in which he held everyone's interest.

Seton discovered that only one of his Tiree coast-watchers of the 1914–18 war was still living. It was John MacDonald of Sandaig, and the station commander, Group Captain Jeoffrey Fairtlough, took Seton by car to see him at his home at the extreme south-west end of the island. Tiree was covered in several inches of snow and they had not gone more than three miles when a large snowdrift blocked the road, making it necessary to complete the journey on foot. Arriving at the croft, Seton had a grand reunion with his old coast-watcher:

> We found John and his sister Flora in their small thatched house, looking out to the lonely lighthouse on Skerryvore. It had not changed, nor had an absence of twenty-five years lessened the warmth of our welcome. John, who had spent his life on the island, told me that he had seen heavier snowfalls, but had not seen one accompanied by so strong a wind – or drifts of such a depth as covered parts of the island.
>
> Not far from Sandaig lies Loch a'Phuill, a sandy loch which is the home of magnificent trout. A number of whooper swans were riding majestically on the windswept waters.

Group Captain Fairtlough now lives at Ballybrittas in Eire, and he not only confirmed the circumstances of the visit to John MacDonald but added some anecdotes of his own:

> I found Seton Gordon to be a most charming man. He stayed with my wife and I several times during 1944 and spent some time in the mess. I remember he was very deaf, so had to be roared at a good deal – very exhausting!
>
> I recall the day we went to see John MacDonald, and had to walk the last part because of heavy snow. We passed a loch on which were some swans. He crouched behind a rock and focused his telescope on them. This took some time. A very strong wind was blowing directly up his kilt as I was kneeling beside him. He turned to me and said 'I do hope you are not too cold'. Of course, even in my greatcoat I was frozen but I didn't say so!

Another officer who served under Group Captain Fairtlough was Flight-Observer Peter Rackliff. Writing in response to a request for his recollections of these wartime lectures, he gave some valuable information in recreating the activities of the meteorology squadron:

> . . . We did not see many birds in the open ocean, but I think this was mainly due to lack of time and opportunity. We were kept busy taking observations and encoding them every 50 miles along the track, and also going down to sea-level at every fourth positon for a set of low-level observations. The most important of these was the sea-level pressure. Also the navigator had to feed us with continuous wind measurements. The W/Ops transmitted coded messages to Group at frequent intervals.

There were other lectures at RAF stations, but these two illustrate Seton Gordon's almost total imperviousness to cold and discomfort, yet he was by this time fifty-eight years old.

April must have seemed a long time coming to Adam Watson, but at last after four years of correspondence, on the 12th he cycled from Ballater to Crathie to meet Seton Gordon. Audrey was on leave from Beckenham and Adam met them at the house once owned by Florence Paul. Seton's aunt had died in November 1942, but her house was unsold and he had the use of it. The old housekeeper was still there and gave Adam a copy of Florence's book *Sketches of Deeside*, published in 1931. Adam recollected:

> I remember the intense excitement that I had when cycling to Crathie to meet him for the first time, at the age of thirteen. Next day we went for a long walk on the hill on a fine April day, and he showed me the first golden eagles' eyries I had ever seen, and told me of others. Knowing how garrulous and boastful schoolboys can be, he was right to warn me of the dangers that the eagles would face if I told all my friends about the exciting things I had been doing. I kept his trust. Only a few days later, I saw my first occupied eyrie,

> whose location he had told me. This started me on the eagle observations I have continued ever since.

Recalling that meeting, Adam said:

> The thing that first struck me about him was his extraordinary voice, because I knew he had been brought up on Deeside and I'm an Aberdeenshire 'loon' [lad] myself. I was expecting that he would have some Aberdeenshire accent, but he'd none. Later I discovered he had been educated privately. The other thing that struck me about him was his dress. Most people that I had seen using the kilt up to then had worn it at church or at weddings, or ceremonial occasions, but he wore it all the time. Not only that, it was obvious that he had worn it a long time because there was lots of patches on it. I can remember every detail of that evening and the next day.

A week later Adam saw his first golden eagle chick, and it is still one of the earliest hatches he has known. The date was 15 April, 1944 and he wrote:

> When the trees had begun to get more sparse, I suddenly saw a huge bird sailing on motionless pinions above – it looked like a large blanket driven before the wind – a handsome golden eagle. A soft drizzle commenced, sweeping down the wild corrie to the south. Slowly I crept along the rocks, and having approached to within 10 yards of the tree, I suddenly had a magnificent view – one I shall never forget in all my life, of a beautiful golden eagle stretching its wings and sailing off the eyrie close to me.

This ecstatic note was written the day after his fourteenth birthday. He wrote in great excitement to Upper Duntuilm and on 30 April, Seton Gordon replied:

> Dear Adam, well done!
>
> I wish I had been with you. But you took a risk in putting the eagle off twice. She is very apt to desert, so I am glad you saw her go back. Keep the eyrie dark: do not tell any of your friends about it. You will I am sure realise your responsibility – there are few people I would have entrusted with the secret.
>
> The most remarkable thing is that you saw a young bird. Are you absolutely certain? Why I ask is that I have never known a young eagle hatch before 29 April, and as you saw the eaglet on 15 April that is a record by two weeks. The eagle broods for thrity-five to fourty-two days, so you see how early that must have been to sit. I am very glad that there is at least one eyrie occupied. I have not seen a single used eyrie this spring. I went up to one near here yesterday but saw no trace of the birds. I saw a golden plover's scrape and a fox quite near – I am afraid he was after lamb . . .
>
> We saw no curlews on the Lecht, but of course we had not much time. Dara sends her love.
>
> Your friend, Seton Gordon.

Watson's sighting of the eaglet appears as a record for early hatching in Seton Gordon's 1955 *The Golden Eagle – King of Birds*, as is the sighting of the first flight of the young bird on 5 July. He has, however, recorded earlier flights since.

In May, *A Highland Year* was completed, though it was not published until later in the year. The book has a chapter for each month of the year, starting with October and ending with September. The text moves from one year to another and from one event to another, with the month as the only tenuous connecting thread. It was, in a way, a daring approach, and few people could have brought it off. The fact that it worked can be seen in the reviews, which were almost 'rave'.

There were twenty-two reviews ranging from major newspapers to the larger provincials and most critics marvelled at this ability to cover so much ground. F. Fraser Darling paid a compliment, even though lamenting the lack of source material, when he wrote in *Nature*:

> Mr. Seton Gordon is one of the few men of education who have been content to live their life in the Highlands rather than earn what many would consider to be an easier and better living elsewhere. The result is that, being a lifelong observer, he knows more about the natural history of a remote region than anyone else. He has preferred to diffuse his wide knowledge in the form of popular books rather than as systematic papers, a fact for which many general readers are undoubtedly grateful. We of a younger generation of workers may be sorry that he does not give us a compendium or source-book which he alone could write and which would preserve for us the great variety of knowledge which his sensitive, enquiring mind has gathered. Nevertheless, it is a book written graciously, one which in the opinion of the reviewer stands out as Seton Gordon's best.

6 June, 1944 was 'D Day'. Alasdair did not go overseas until several months later, when he had his share of action. Now mainly on his own at Upper Duntuilm, Seton, as always, followed his own devices and his everyday life did not alter perceptibly. An echo of loneliness might be read into a June letter to Francis Cameron-Head:

> Dear Francis,
>
> This day two years ago you took a grand step forward: you chose one of the best and kindest people I know for a helpmate through life and it is I that am glad you have been so blessed. These are dark times and to have a wife who thinks alike in these times lightens one's load.
>
> Life is a curious thing and one has years of happiness and years of spiritual sadness, when one is apparently alone, and out of touch with those near to one. This is the trial of the soul and strengthens it.
>
> Well, Francis, it was good to see you again, and it is good to think that you and I think alike about ethical, or shall I say, spiritual values.
>
> All good wishes and thank you for your hospitality. Seton.

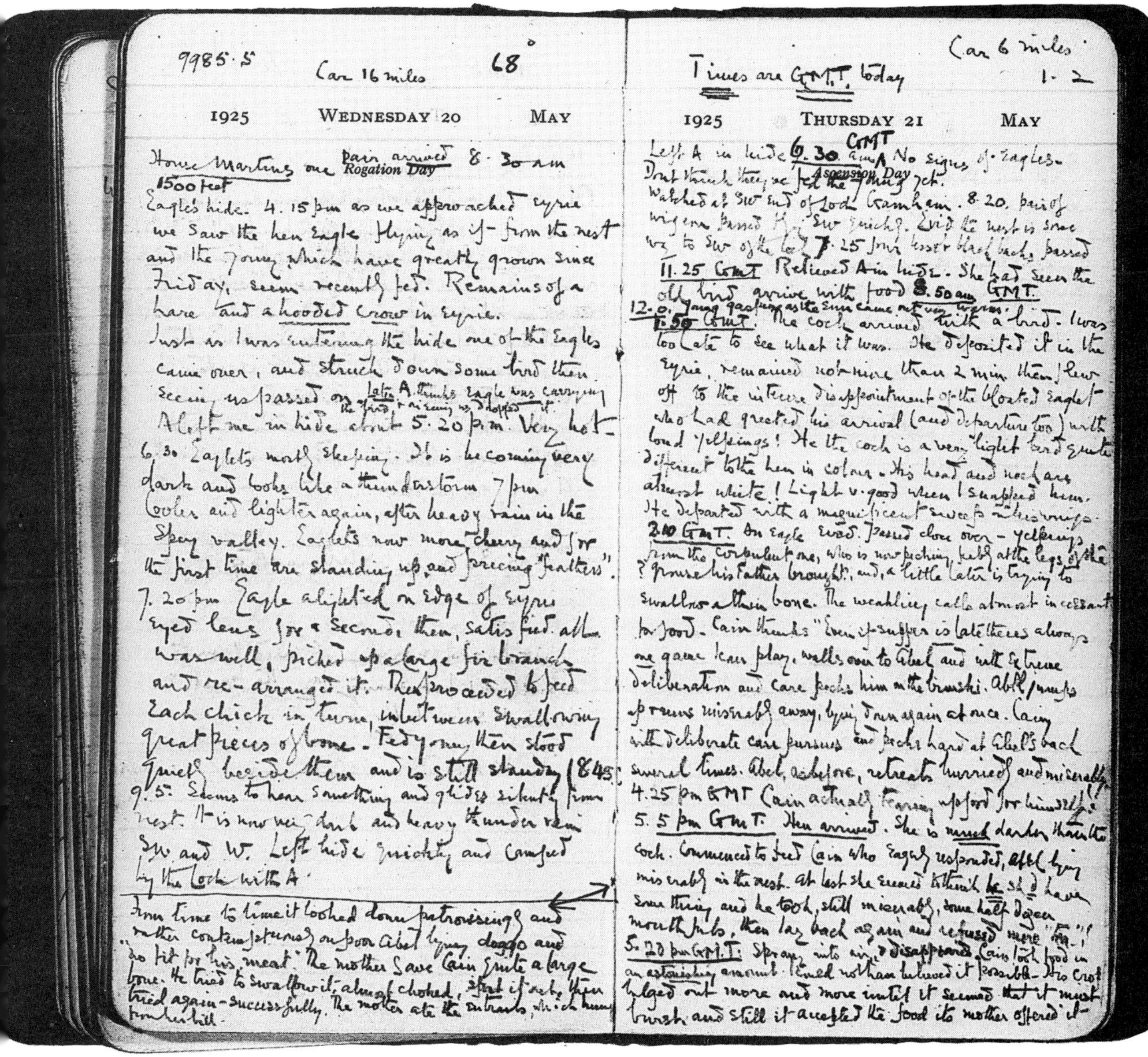

Part of Seton Gordon's 1925 golden eagle watching diary notes – actual size of writing

A few days later, on 13 June, the first V1 'doodlebugs' fell on London and it must have given considerable concern to Seton. At that time three members of his family were there. Audrey and Bridie were in Beckenham, and Alasdair at Wellington Barracks. Four V1s were launched on this date and Bethnal Green was the first place to receive a direct hit causing death. On the morning of Sunday 18 June, Alasdair had just returned to the Barracks after visiting his mother. In the nearby Guards Chapel a service was taking place at which were gathered a large number of distinguished officers of the Brigade. A few moments after he entered the mess Alasdair heard a loud explosion closeby. The

Chapel had received a direct hit and many of the 200 people at the service were killed or maimed.

In the meantime, Seton had his own brush with danger. Dara was almost thirteen, and still able to enjoy outings. In late June, Seton took her north by train to visit Lochmore Lodge, the estate of Bend Or, Duke of Westminster. On the morning of 5 July they were taken back to Lairg station for the return to Skye via Inverness. After winding around the Cromarty and Dornoch Firths the railway line takes another large loop from Lairg to the east towards the coast at Golspie. Arriving at Lairg, Seton became very concerned about Dara, who showed signs of illness. There was a vet at Rogart, a small village halfway towards Golspie. The first train to get them there was a goods train, which was due to arrive shortly. It was agreed that they could travel with the guards, and they climbed into the van. What happened next showed Seton Gordon's coolness and quick thinking. It was summarised on a sheet of paper found with his notes:

> We joined the guards at the rear of the train and as we began to climb slowly up the gradient away from the station there was a terrific jolt. One of the guards shouted, 'We're away, we're away in two places!' We began to run back down the gradient as the rest of the train disappeared. As the van gathered speed down the slope I was asked, 'Can you jump?' Knowing that the collie was ill, it would be quite impossible for her to make it, and it was because of her that this unusual journey was being undertaken. I was therefore reluctant to move. The guards disappeared and Dara and I were left alone in the runaway van.
>
> The line is straight here and I saw ahead the level-crossing gates at Lairg barring the way. My train-driving on Deeside came back to me and I at once thought of the handbrake. I was thankful to find that it was not fully applied and exerted all my strength to apply it harder. The speed was being checked but we must crash into the gates. I hung on against the impact which came with the noise of two sharp explosions at half second intervals. The van carried the gates like matchwood.
>
> Lairg station was until that moment deserted. The crash brought people out in an instant and I saw a porter run at top speed to the signal box.
>
> I did not know that the points were set against us. My intent was to stop the van on the level stretch of line which extends from Lairg to the top of the Invershin gradient. I realised that if I did not, there would be no hope of avoiding a bad accident, as I knew the mail train was following the goods. Gradually the brake power began to work and finally brought us to a stop. The first person to run down the line was the porter. He was considerably distressed and when I told what I had done he thought the extra braking power had made the difference in permitting him to run and throw the points in my favour.

There was now no way of getting Dara to the vet at Rogart, but she lived for some time after this incident, so was not unduly affected by her adventure.

On 8 September, the first two V2 rockets landed on London. The first at Chiswick and the second at Epping. In the seven months before the launch area was overrun, 1300 were fired against London, causing 2724 deaths and injuring 6467. Beckenham had its share of V1 and V2s. On another occasion when Alasdair was staying there a rocket landed close enough to cause the house to shake violently. After Alasdair had left for France, Audrey recorded in her diary: '28 October – A near miss 8 a.m. this morning by V2.'

On the continent the army had moved through France into Holland, with Paris liberated several weeks before. The Guards Armoured Division, which was Alasdair Gordon's destination, was in action on the Wilhelmina Canal. Alasdair went first to a Reinforcement Holding Unit from where he wrote on the 16 November. Before crossing the Channel on a landing craft, during the long wait he piped for about two hours on deck – 'while the men danced reels etc., until an angry captain crawled on deck and said he was trying to sleep'. After describing the train journey through France, he finished: 'How are you and Bridie? I do hope the V2s keep their distance. Don't worry if you don't get letters regularly, as we've still got a lot of moving to do and the mail is erratic'. A second letter in December talked of the tedium of waiting in a 'small, smoke-laden mess while the rain pours down outside'.

Audrey stayed at Beckenham for Christmas and had a festive lunch with her colleagues. Seton remained at home, struggling with the farm as well. He sent a list of improvements which he proposed to do, or have attended to, but his heart was not in it and it is doubtful if they were all accomplished. His income had suffered deeply by the fifth year of the war, lectures brought in only £34–5–0d and writing £241–10–0d. Royalties from *A Highland Year* did not start to come in until 1945.

The war was in its final months and the Allied Generals and politicians were pleased with its progress. The advance on the Rhine was underway and the 'Big Three' had met at Yalta in February. In the belief that the war was progressing so well, there was too much euphoria to fully acknowledge then the problems of dividing Europe when the victory was complete. But to thousands of men and women their small part in the war effort, whether in the tedium of an armament factory or the dangers of the frontline, was of greater moment than the dialogue of their leaders. With the sublimeness of the young, many American soldiers and airmen hoped that they would get to Europe before the fighting ceased. Among them was an aircrew newly assigned to a B17 Flying Fortress just off the production line. With great anticipation they were given orders to fly to Britain.

On Saturday, 3 March, they were part of a tragedy which shattered the peace of Trotternish to which Seton Gordon had referred early in the war. Oddly, the event had its roots many years earlier, when Annie MacPhee of Duntulm had a dream. She died in 1960 only a month short of her 100th birthday, so she was already a mature woman when, in about 1900, she had this premonition of some terrible, yet unspecified happening.

On the very trail, through Glen Conan, that Seton and Caitriona had climbed on that sunny October day in 1941, Annie saw in her dream, a slowly moving line of lights, which wound its way down to the village of Uig, from Beinn Edra. A sense of overwhelming sadness filled the air. Over the years the impact of the dream lessened, but she never forgot it.

Seton had talked of lingering on Beinn Edra in sunshine 'watching the beauty of land and sea'. Now in the lowering clouds on a March afternoon, bringing premature dusk to the hilltop, the scene was set.

The B17 Flying Fortress was approaching Lewis and the crew saw the Outer Hebrides below them. It would be impossible to estimate the number of planes that had made this journey before them, but it was in the thousands, all to join in bombing the last strategic targets of the war; the rocket launching pads at Peenemunde and the few remaining arms factories of the crumbling German war machine.

Skye loomed ahead across the Minch. Cloud was thickening and to stay under it the pilot lost height, levelling off at 800 feet. Below the cloud was the narrow northern tip of the island with barely 3 miles of undulating peatbog before the sheer cliffs of Sgurr Mhor disappeared under the canopy. Would an experienced eye have read the land more closely? Did their maps tell them that as they flew over Balmaqueen and Flodigarry that just to starboard of them the long ridge of Trotternish began?

The plane flew past the Quirang, but the crew could not see it. Seconds later they were over Staffin, where the crofters looked up as the huge plane roared in from the north before disappearing into the cloud. What error of map-reading made the pilot veer to starboard at this moment? Were their maps so inadequate that there was no foretelling of the mountains hidden in the mist?

The roar of engines still echoed back from the unseen Quirang and before it had faded, came another, terrible sound – a sharp cracking explosion. The noise bounced from hill to hill and a red glow came from under the cloud canopy as it spread down the hill-face towards the village of Marishader. The slight turn had taken the plane into the face of Beinn Edra, only 30 feet below the crest. The impact hurled some of the wreckage across the summit where it continued until momentum was lost in the rock strewn slope of the less steep west side.

It was Sunday before plans were in place to bring the remains of the crew down, and it was dusk before the task was completed. A flickering line of lanterns moved slowly down the glen. The war had come to Skye, nine young American airmen were dead, and Annie MacPhee's dream had been fulfilled.

In *Afoot in the Hebrides* Seton Gordon did not mention the dream though he said: 'Superstition dies hard in the Isles, and when in 1945, a Flying Fortress crashed on Beinn Edra, some blamed it on the wiles of Colann gun Cheann, the Headless Spectre. Until noon the weather was clear, then mist closed in on the hills. All day the giant planes flew over Skye. The weather experts had not forecast the shallow low front which brought the cloud over the ridge in the afternoon. This aircraft may have come down to take bearings; when it set course for Beinn Edra, shrouded in mist, those who saw it realised that it could scarcely clear the top and less than a minute afterwards there was a tremendous crash. For the crew, death had been instantaneous'.

Alasdair Gordon's regiment, the 3rd Battalion, Scots Guards, was in action twice during the Rhine crossing. In the first his tank was hit and things were 'very hot' so he gave the order to bale out. He said that it was even hotter outside, as the Germans were using *Nebelwerfer* or 'moaning minnies' – 'rocket mortars which make a blood-curdling moaning noise as they come at you. However, apart from a bit of a shaking we all got away all right'.

Two days later, Alasdair commanded the leading troop in an attack on the small town of Winnekendonk. While crossing a wide open piece of ground a troop of anti-tank guns opened up and his tank was hit five times in quick succession but not one shell pierced, although the turret was immovable and the engine was put out of action. The tank on his right caught fire and the crew were machine gunned as they tried to get out. Alasdair used his 'local smoke' which for a short time gives a very thick smoke screen – waited for it to thicken up, and gave the order to abandon tank. In a letter describing the action, Alasdair wrote: 'By this time the third tank of the troop had abandoned their tank and gone for cover. I got out of the tank quicker than I thought possible, and lay down by the bogies while Spandau bullets went over. I crawled to a ditch beside the road and my crew got into a slit trench which I had overlooked. Later on when things had died down a bit we took the troop corporal's tank and went on to the objective'.

Alasdair received a slight wound in April. It sent him to hospital, followed by several weeks convalescence, but he recovered sufficiently to have leave when Bridie married in early summer. Her groom was Hugh Prettejohn, and Alasdair was best man.

At midnight on 8 May, 1945, the war in Europe ended. In the Far East it continued until 12 September when after the dropping of two atom bombs the Japanese forces surrendered unconditionally.

Audrey continued in her job until July 1946 and Alasdair remained in the army until 1947, with a promotion to captain and a staff posting to Vienna. He never returned to Cambridge.

CHAPTER

12

PEACE RETURNS BUT THE OLD HIGHLAND WAYS ARE GONE

THE END OF THE EUROPEAN WAR meant freedom to travel the Highlands once more without restriction, but the old way of life was gone, except for one or two families of tremendous wealth. People were reluctant to return to 'service' as a means of livelihood after the war. There was also the fact of crippling death duties and surtax, which dug deeply into the income of land-owning families throughout Britain. The number of servants and estate workers diminished and estate owners took on more of the day-to-day physical work themselves. Many of the people who were themselves in service, and remained so, regretted the new order of things. They saw nothing wrong in 'knowing their place' – it had maintained order and stability for centuries. Others, however, thought the change was for the better, including some of the very people who had in the past benefitted from a position of privilege – Labour Party Members of Parliament who had gone to the best public schools or who were themselves titled.

A far-reaching outcome was the election of a Labour Government, the massive defeat of Winston Churchill taking everyone by surprise, including Churchill himself. In a letter written from Germany at the end of July 1945, Alasdair wrote:

> . . . All the officers here are very depressed by the Election results, and even the most Bolshie men are a little overwhelmed by the terrific majority – Burroughs Wellcome will soon be nationalised!

In England and Wales, land-use studies during the war continued to examine greenbelt policy and plotted national park locations, while in Scotland planning concentrated instead on the more pragmatic issue of selecting rivers and lochs for hydro-electric schemes. Seton Gordon was aware that feasibility studies had been done in several parts of the Highlands and with the war over, there was determination to follow through with as many of them as possible. The North of Scotland Hydro-Electric Board came into being on 5 August, 1943 and its engineers wasted no time in surveying the Highlands for potential hydro-electric sites. They estimated that there were 102 rivers and lochs on which it was feasible to build, and these would produce 6273 million units of electricity annually. A grid of transmission lines to carry the power was also planned.

One of the typescript items found in Seton Gordon's papers showed his fears for many of the glens earmarked. He wrote it in 1944 and true to his prophecy, as soon as the war ended, the Hydro-Electric Board began construction. The first station to open was at the Falls of Morar in 1948, and it blanketed the Falls for only 750 kilowatts of production. Seton's paper called for a close examination of their impact, especially where historical sites or areas of outstanding natural beauty might be affected. It was entitled 'Harnessing Highland Lochs'. He forecast that the four most immediate Highland Hydro-Electric Schemes were those of Loch Sloy in the Lomond area, Loch Alsh at the gateway to Skye, Loch Morar, in the romantic Prince Charlie country, and lastly what has been named the Tummel-Garry scheme, in the Pitlochry district of the central Highlands. On this last project he wrote:

> The scheme which has aroused the greatest storm of criticism, because it is a great tourist area, with Pitlochry as its centre is the Tummel-Garry project. The Falls of Bruar will disappear, Pitlochry will lose its riverside walks, golf course, bowling green and other amenities which bring tourists to the district. Lastly, the level of Loch Tummel will be raised and several miles of arable land will be submerged. The loch will be doubled in length by the projected 70 foot dam. A 55 foot dam at Pitlochry would inundate the land as far as the historic Pass of Killiecrankie, and come close up to the Falls of Tummel.
>
> It may be said that certain beauty spots in Scotland should be sacrificed, when beauty must give place to utility. But there should be some objection at a time when everything is being done to attract tourists to the Highlands after the war, and [yet] a great tourist centre is to suffer irreparable injury.

By 1948, when he again wrote on the subject, many of Seton Gordon's predictions were now fact. The scale of dam construction accomplished in a mere three years showed how determined the Board was to push ahead before any effective opposition to its policies could be organised. Writing in that year on the Pitlochry area he said:

> One of the most beautiful reaches of the Tummel, Faskally, has been inundated, for the dam extends as far as the Falls of Tummel. The sandpipers still arrive in mid-April from the south. They may adapt to the changed surroundings and will perhaps nest on the shores of the dam, but the shingle beds and fields where the oyster-catchers have nested will be flooded and displace the birds. The dippers, too, will be evicted. The trees on the Tummel banks are being felled, in the beauty of their summer foliage.

A fact that has become evident the world over, and one that a naturalist might be forgiven for failing to anticipate, is that people are attracted to hydro-electric schemes: 500,000 people a year visit the Clunie dam at Strath-Tummel, and a further 60,000 pass through the Hydro Exhibition Centre at Pitlochry.

Some say that the dams have enhanced the area, and the Falls of Bruar were not inundated as Seton Gordon feared. Once the project was completed and landscaped many walks were replaced, especially by Loch Faskally. It is difficult to argue with the number of visitors to the Clunie Dam, but having come to admire the scenic wonders of the Highlands, it is a pity that people are more easily sidetracked by huge power projects than by the activities of oyster-catchers and sandpipers.

In 1945, however, the dam had yet to be built and a more pressing concern for Francis Cameron-Head and Seton was the 200th Anniversary of the raising of the Jacobite Standard at Glenfinnan. They were determined to mark the occasion. The Cameron-Heads had only just returned to Inverailort where a shock awaited them when they saw the condition of the house.

Severe rationing was still in force, but despite this a house party was planned for the whole weekend. The anniversary date was Sunday, 19 August, and the celebrations began with a dance on the Friday night, a Saturday night *ceilidh* followed by the Sunday ceremony, with more dancing and entertainment on Sunday evening. Mrs Cameron-Head, recalling that year said, 'At the end of the war, up here, people talked as though Prince Charlie was about to come around the corner, and the traditions were very much alive. The music and Highland hospitality was very much a part of life and it is really sad how over the years it has been eroded'.

She was still in uniform, but took two weeks' leave to prepare for the event. While cleaning the house from top to bottom a large quantity of soap was found in a cupboard, a legacy from the wartime Surgeon Commander, and a precious commodity then. The bars were cut into smaller pieces and placed in each bedroom. The damage caused by the Commander's excesses with water were at that time being negotiated with the government.

In the *Highlands of Scotland* after describing the Prince's arrival at the head of the loch in 1745, Seton Gordon wrote of the bicentenary:

> Let us now go forward two hundred years to that day of August, in the year 1945, when the raising of the Prince's Standard was commemorated at an impressive ceremony. The Second World War was just ended, yet an astonishingly large number arrived by car, bus and train. Glenfinnan has the reputation of being one of the wettest places in the Highlands, but on that day there was not a cloud in the sky, and the sun shone with great power. Some of those who were there were the direct descendants of those of the leading figures of the '45. Sir Donald Cameron of Lochiel spoke of his ancestor, without whose aid Prince Charlie would have been unknown to the present generation.
>
> When the Marquis of Tullibardine [Duke of Atholl], the descendant of the Marquis who had unfurled the Royal Standard 200 years before, mounted the platform and, putting on his bonnet with its prominent white cockade, said

Seton Gordon and Francis Cameron-Head firmly believed that the Jacobite Standard was raised on a knoll and not where the monument stands. In an Aug. 1988 Scot's Magazine article, historian Iain Thornber told how as a boy he overheard Seton Gordon and Francis Cameron-Head discussing the controversy at Glenfinnan

that it was the very one his ancestor had worn at the ceremony of 1745, the imagination of the assembly was fired and there was a stir among the press, both British and American, and for the moment the dropping of the atomic bombs on Hiroshima and Nagasaki only days before were forgotten.

This latest example of man's inhumanity must surely have had a profound effect upon the sensitive spirit of D.Y. Cameron. He had reached eighty years of age in June 1945 and was still lecturing on art. He wrote to Seton, 'I have been in many places, speaking and advising about kirks, etc. and more journeys are to come before I say farewell to these things and see my coracle waiting on the sands'. In September he wrote again, 'Next week I go to speak at Evensong in the great St John's church of Perth, on the Church and Art. This is instead of the usual sermon'.

The engagement was on Sunday 16 September. Seton Gordon later wrote in an obituary, 'He carried out his sermon, returned to his hotel, had a heart attack, and swiftly saw his coracle waiting on the sands of eternity. Thus passed a great Scotsman, a great Christian, a brilliant artist, and a great and humble man'.

Few people today reveal their thoughts with such an outpouring of emotion, yet to the end D.Y. Cameron wanted to believe in the innate goodness of man. In one of his last notes to Seton Gordon he wrote, 'How great man can be, how glorious and altogether beautiful, and then to what dark depths he can descend as we see him in Europe today'.

In the obituary Seton Gordon wrote: 'Sir D.Y. Cameron's long life was dedicated to the task of opening the hearts and minds of men to the true grandeur of art. His letters contained inspiring thoughts to raise the mind to the sun-glow above the storm and clouds on the horizon. His was a glowing personality which radiated the goodness and love that were ever his quest'.

The pattern of Seton Gordon's life did not alter immeasurably after the war; there were still many outings to come with Francis Cameron-Head and other friends, though in a letter to Francis the following year he professed to be dispirited. Audrey was asked to stay on with Burroughs Wellcome for a few extra months, and did not return to Skye until the middle of 1946.

Those who had lost loved ones now concentrated on rebuilding their lives. Pamela, Countess of Dunmore, embarked on a happy second marriage with Captain Follett Bell. John, Viscount Fincastle and Earl of Dunmore, was now six years old, and like his father destined for prep school at St Peter's Court, Broadstairs, and Eton. Hamish MacDonald had not married, but his memory would be carried by his mother, Helen, and those friends who had shared his gentle presence before his death.

As Seton's sixtieth birthday approached in 1946, his health continued to be excellent and there was no appreciable diminishing of energy. Walking was still his preferred method of travel and no matter what human companions he walked with, he was never without a dog for company. It is not easy to follow the succession that came into the lives of Seton and Audrey during and after the war. They acquired a Dandie Dinmont, Ninag, but it died of hard-pad in the late 1940s and was replaced with a Cairn terrier, Morag. At some time just after the war ended, Dara succumbed and was replaced by a new companion named Dugie, their third collie.

It was a walk with Dugie in the spring of his sixtieth birthday that led to his and Audrey's eight years of observation of one pair of golden eagles. It also led to his second book on this bird. He had been aware of their presence since 1942 when they took over a disused eyrie on the cliffs above the 'dark lochan which is reputed to be the home of the "*each uisge*" or water-horse'. It was not until

1946 that the eagles were seen to show signs of nest building and so he counted the eight years from that season.

Seton was impressed by the devotion of this pair and it fascinated him through the years of his observation. He had not seen another pair so regular in their 'change-over' on the nest when brooding. It was the male's attentiveness that he found particularly interesting, and his willingness to brood the eggs. One day, he witnessed a thrilling aerial display. It began with a raven unwisely trying to out-manoeuvre the male eagle. The raven was first seen high above the loch in pursuit of the eagle, flying as hard as it could. When the eagle reached the cliff it was joined by his mate. They immediately soared to 4000 feet, then the male closed his wings and dropped headlong until about 1000 feet off the ground. He then changed position and continued feet first with legs outstretched as though to alight. Seton then realised that he was engaged in a mock attack on his mate, who at that moment came from behind a hill. The raven by this time had given up harassing the eagles, having been flown to a standstill.

On 24 June, Seton had an opportunity for an unusual, if fleeting, view of the eyrie. He was invited by the RAF on a flight by Sunderland flyingboat to visit Rockall. This was a 'thank you' from the air force for the lectures he had given at various bases during the war. As they circled over Duntulm, the plane passed over the eyrie, but he did not see either bird.

Colonel Jock MacDonald had recently returned to Skye and had taken up permanent residence at Viewfield. He arranged to have a small boat put at Seton's disposal to get him out to the plane. With uncertain weather conditions in the area, the flight could not be confirmed until the last moment. Seton was very excited about the trip and recorded it in great detail for Audrey.

> It had rained hard all night and was still raining heavily with thick mist. Conditions seemed hopeless, but when I went down for the milk pails at 08:00 the wind had veered west, the rain had ceased, and the Outer Isles were showing. At Snizort I picked up Colin Campbell of Kingsburgh, who wanted to see me start. Arrived at Portree simultaneously with the Sunderland's first appearance. Jock Viewfield was there, so he, Colin and I, with a wee boy to row, went out. When we got alongside I asked if my companions could come along. They at once agreed, so we three climbed on board.
>
> The captain, Squadron Leader Evison, said that the plane was entirely at my disposal for the day. At last airborne, we saw ahead of us all the Outer Isles. The weather by then was fine – wind West 5. We flew low above the north end of Loch Snizort. I was given the co-pilot's seat and there I remained for five hours without moving. When we reached our house they said they would take photographs and we circled round. I saw Morag standing outside and John and Dugie. We did not SEEM very low but the staff thought we would take the chimneys away and rushed out for safety!

Seton described the next few hours, as they flew over the great precipices of Boreray with their colonies of gannets, puffins and guillemots, watching the flocks of kittiwakes rise off Rockall as they passed over. He then continued:

> We set course for North Uist. We were now very low, as the skipper had taken the controls, and our speed seemed tremendous, for the wind was now stronger and with us. We passed over the white sand and green machair at Balranald, where a big herd of cattle were feeding. We passed over the sea pool of Balranald where we used to fish. Balranald and its outbuilding fell astern, and now we were over a loch with a grassy island, possibly the black-throated diver's loch. We put up a heron which struggled away against the wind. I felt like an eagle rushing against the sky; never had I felt so greatly the feeling of speed, for we must have been flying at a height of less than 100 feet – almost like being in a high-powered car.
>
> Then we were over the Minch and in ten minutes circled over Raasay, and made a perfect landing. We had covered 700 miles. Jock was given a blanket and had a sleep in the wardroom!
>
> When I looked at Shillay, Hasker and Balranald, and on the return flight looked on Hecla and Beinn Mor, just as we used to see them from Grogary, and the lochs of North Uist, I thought how many wonderful places we had seen together over a long time, and now I was having a vision of them all at once, all in sunshine and clear and smiling, as we used to see them long ago at their best. I thought, too, what a lovely island North Uist was, more happy than Skye, the light stronger; the grass a brighter green.

Seton also wrote to Francis Cameron-Head and told him all about the flight, but at the end of the letter a more serious note was struck when referring to their 'expeditions':

> Could you come to Iona with me? What good expeditions we have had in the past! I look back on them with great pleasure and you have helped me enormously in writing those books – indeed I think you helped me more than anyone.
>
> Then came those dark war years when the powers of evil flooded the Earth and one's values were changed. Even now I think one has not the same interest in those simple pleasures as one had – at all events I am finding it hard to write my book on the Hebrides – and if you CAN spare the time for an expedition or two, you will be helping me very much indeed.

He ended on a poignant note, 'I think Audrey will be back in July – for a bit anyway'. There were many other references to the joy that Seton got out of their journeys to look at historical sites or artifacts, but none where it is so clearly stated his need of Francis Cameron-Head's friendship and companionship. He may also have had an unexpressed apprehension over the fact that Audrey would soon leave Burroughs Wellcome and return to Upper Duntuilm. She had by no means forsaken her interest in natural history and as recently as 8 May, had given another lecture on the golden eagle at Beckenham public library. She

Audrey Gordon with Morag, the Cairn terrier, early 1950s

had, however, been away for two-and-a-half-years, living an altogether different life style, and on 15 July would leave her colleagues to return to the comparative isolation and often indifferent weather of Skye. Seton need not have worried, for Audrey settled in to the old life and soon picked up the threads of their long friendships on the island and mainland.

At the same time that Audrey returned, Alasdair came home on leave. It was already arranged that Seton was to go to Lochboisdale to judge the first post-war Games, and Alasdair went with him. A letter from John MacDonald of Inverness just beforehand warned Seton that he would not find the same standard of *Piobaireached* that they were familiar with in pre-war days, though he thought the trip might revive Alasdair's piping enthusiasm. MacDonald did not feel like making the journey himself, saying: 'I have had to put off judging at several places including Newtonmore, Pitlochry, Nairn, etc., which is very disappointing'.

A new Highland Gathering was about to take place for the first time. After the success of the Glenfinnan bicentenary in 1945, Francis Cameron-Head saw the possibility of an annual Gathering, to take place each August. The setting is magnificent, with adequate room at the head of the loch by the monument for the erection of tents and platforms, and there is a large grassy area for field sports.

The first Glenfinnan Gathering took place on Wednesday, 21 August and despite being midweek it drew a good crowd. Francis Cameron-Head was well pleased and he resolved that it would continue. One of the distinguished guests was Cameron of Lochiel, and after his death in 1951, the new Lochiel, Sir Donald Hamish Cameron, twenty-sixth Chief, began an almost unbroken attendance record. Each year he introduces the honorary Chief of the Day. Norman MacRae retired as piper to Lochiel in 1946 and was the last full-time piper to the chief.

Piping was of prime importance as far as Francis and Seton were concerned. Despite John MacDonald's continuing dire predictions, there were still many first-class pipers living in Scotland to attract to the Gathering, and when the invitation went out they responded enthusiastically. For several years the MacFadyen brothers, Seamus MacNeill, the MacPhersons, father and son, John MacLelland, Donald MacLeod, Donald MacGillivray, and others played at Glenfinnan.

Arrangements were made to cross to Iona with Francis Cameron-Head in the first week of November. The tourists had departed and the island once again had a sense of isolation, a wonderful time for two dedicated historians to explore it. Comfortable quarters were found at Triagh Mor, and after a meal they set out in full moonlight to explore the island, walking to the northern end in quiet companionship. Seton had visited Iona many times during the early years of the First World War and in the early 1930s when researching for his *Highways and Byways* book. By 1947 tourism was beginning to make itself felt, part of the reason for the success of the recent first Glenfinnan Gathering. Iona was always a tourist destination; to some it was considered a pilgrimage, with its deep religious association. St Columba arrived in a currach in 563 AD with twelve followers and, in Seton's words, 'Ever since that far off day this small island has been illustrious, not only in Britain and Europe but throughout the world'.

Iona Abbey was built by Reginald, Lord of the Isles, in 1203, and was largely rebuilt in the late fifteenth and early sixteenth century. Restoration of the Abbey was already underway during Seton's First World War visits, following the presentation of the site in 1900 by the eighth Duke of Argyll to the Church of Scotland. Public subscription allowed work to commence in about 1902 and by 1905 the nave was completed. After 1938, work on the Abbey and its buildings was done by a group called the Iona Community, founded that year by the Rev. Dr George F. MacLeod, MC, DD, now Lord MacLeod of Fuinary. Members are drawn from every walk of life, and from such diverse demoninatations as the Church of Scotland, the Roman Catholic Church, Greek Orthodox Church and the Society of Friends. (See Appendix 5)

A pair of Greenshanks at the nest. (Reproduced by kind permission of British Birds*)*

The first full year of peace brought at least some relaxing of wartime economy measures. Journals and magazines became thicker again and newspapers had more room for general articles now that war news had ceased to occupy so much space. Unfortunately, some journals did not survive the war, thus shrinking the market for freelance writers. However, the principal Scottish newspapers, together with *Country Life*, the *Scots Magazine*, *The Field*, and *Scottish Field* eagerly continued taking Seton's pieces. This, together with the books yet to come, provided an income which allowed the Gordons to continue much as they had done before the war. Their only son had survived the war, despite some 'close shaves' in the closing stages, and so had their son-in-law, Simon Macdonald-Lockhart, after service in Italy. He was now master of the Lee and Carnwath Estate, a large task, which after taking forestry and land management courses, he entered into with enthusiasm. After her marriage to Hugh Prettejohn, Bridie settled in South Wales, where he farmed, and her visits to Skye were infrequent.

'Grey Wind' was replaced with Aunt Florence's Wolsely, a much more comfortable car, even if less dashing, and Audrey had her own Austin Countryman. She took her share of watching the eyrie which Seton had discovered, and also became active in Civil Defence matters, which frequently took her off the island for meetings. Seton's expeditions with Francis helped to restore some of the faith he had lost during the turmoil of the war.

Watching the eagles was also a balm to Seton's spirits and they received several visits from him during January 1947. He began corresponding with people in different parts of the world, so that he built a global perspective of the golden eagle. One correspondent was naturalist Roy Bedichek of Texas USA, who sent him a copy of the *American Farm Journal* of January, 1947. It dealt with the slaughter of the golden eagle over Texas. J. O. Casparis of Brewster County, Texas, shot down 1867 golden eagles using a light airplane in 1945–46. He was employed by West Texas sheep men, and each ranch payed him $100 a year to keep the range free of predatory birds. The bald eagle – the emblem of the USA was not included in the kills, as it does not prey on larger animals. One rancher lost 500 lambs in 60 days. Another found the skeletons of 25 antelope fawns in a nest. Casparis shot most of the birds at altitudes of 100 to 300 feet after putting his plane into a dive. His weapon was a 12 gauge sawn-off shot gun. He said: 'The trick is to pick up the gun, aim and fire (which takes both hands) and then grab control of the plane while it is still in the air'. He estimated that he had killed 8300 birds in five years.

At the same time Seton Gordon was also corresponding with Francis Cameron-Head on the subject of Charles Edward Stuart's escape. He mentioned the cave near Borrodale House in which the Prince was thought to have hidden for some time before sailing for France. Another letter referred to the 'cage' on Ben Alder, where Cluny MacPherson lived for part of the time while he was in hiding after Culloden, before escaping to France. According to contemporary accounts the Prince spent some time there. The letter also confirmed that very preliminary discussion had taken place on an idea of Cameron-Head's to establish as closely as possible the spot from where the Prince departed the Scottish mainland for the last time:

> I have been looking up my books about Borodale. It is more or less agreed that the Prince sailed from Loch nan Uamh at 1 a.m., 28 September, 1746, and that he waited at Borodale for stragglers. *Argyll and the '45*, without quoting an authority, gives the names of the French ships as *Heureux* and *Prince de Conte*.
>
> There's no mention in the *Lyon in Mourning* of a cave, but in John

Mackinnon's narrative he says – 'That part of the shore towards Borodale is a rocky precipice, so steep that some parts of it are almost perpendicular. In a cleft between two rocks of said precipice, there is a bothy, or hut, so artfully contrived with the grassy side of the turf outward, that it exactly represents a natural green hue. Here the Prince was concealed'.

I did not realise that Cluny came all the way with the Prince, and that he was preparing an underground hut on Ben Alder to be the Prince's winter quarters in case the ships did not come. We ought to go to see Cluny's cage on Ben Alder before it is too late? Perhaps we could go from Corrour. Andy MacLaren, the stalker, might know of it. Seton.

After beginning it at least nine years before, *Highways and Byways of the Central Highlands* was at last published in 1948. The only advantage to this long delay was time allowed to gather extra material, examples being the Ben Alder 'cage' and the ancient Invernahaven battle between the Camerons, Davidsons and MacIntoshs. Although there was a later edition of *Highways and Byways of the Western Highlands* (1949), there is only a brief reference to the cave at Loch nan Uamh. It was the much later *Highland Days* (1963), which had a full account of the cave.

The expedition to Ben Alder took place in early June. On 29 May, Seton received news that he had been accepted as a Serving Brother of the Venerable Order of the Hospital of St John of Jerusalem. Both Francis Cameron-Head and Malcolm Barclay-Harvey were members. The Order has its roots in the twelfth century, when a hospice was created for pilgrims to Jerusalem and run by the Knights of St John (See Appendix 6). With this added bond in their friendship, Seton and Francis set off for Cluny's Cage.

Long after his defeat, the Prince still held hopes of obtaining support from France and returning for yet another campaign, but it was a vain hope. After their escape to the continent he secured the command of a French regiment for Lochiel, though the chief's preference was to 'share in the fate of the people I have undone, and if they must be sacrificed, to die along with them. It is the only way I can free myself of the reproach of their blood'.

The loyalty shown by Lochiel and Cluny exemplifies the spirit surrounding the whole of the '45 episode. Both men had suffered grievous losses, their houses burned and their clans scattered. Yet they were overjoyed to see their Prince again at the cage. All the eyewitnesses to the Prince's wanderings say that it was his finest period. There were no displays of the petulance or sulking that had sometimes marred his behaviour during the campaign.

The Prince was taken to the cage, so called because of its construction, described in the *The Lyon in Mourning*:

> . . . it being of a round, or rather oval shape, and the whole thatched or covered with foge [foliage]. This whole fabric hung as it were by a large tree, which reclined from the one end all along the roof to the other, and which gave it the name of the cage. The cage was no larger than to hold six or seven persons.

After a few days here, Charles was escorted back to Loch nan Uamh by Donald MacPherson and Cameron of Clunes. They stopped one night close by Lochiel's burned-out house at Achnacarry. At Loch nan Uamh, the French ships were seen to be flying British flags. When they sailed, the Prince was accompanied by Lochiel, Archibald Cameron and, according to a contemporary account, twenty-seven 'gentlemen' and 107 men of common rank. Cluny did not sail with the Prince. He chose to remain a further nine years, taking his chance with his people and perhaps hoping for a pardon. With no sign of it coming, he escaped to France in 1755, where he died within the year. At least 100 clansmen knew of Cluny's whereabouts, yet despite a reward of £1000 and an unremitting search by government troops he evaded capture.

The last serious Jacobite plan to retake the throne came in 1752. Archibald Cameron returned to Scotland and here was to meet James Keith, the Earl of Marischal's brother, scheduled to arrive with a strong Swedish force. The plot had been leaked to the British Government and on 23 March, 1753, Archibald Cameron was arrested and tried for his part in the '45. His wife petitioned George II and the only result was not the clemency that she desired, but a slight lessening of her husband's suffering. The King ordered that he should be hanged, without being cut down and drawn and quartered until he was dead. It was the last drawing and quartering to take place in Britain.

Charles was now powerless and from this point there is little to admire about him in his final years. He died in Rome on 31 January, 1788. It was a sad ending to a cause whose flame still burns to this day. Through the late 1940s to the mid-1950s it occupied a great deal of the time and energy of two men in late middle age who sought to find and visit the sites of triumph and of later disaster.

The Northern Meeting began again following the end of the war, and many of John MacDonald's pupils were foremost among the men who competed. In the autumn of 1947, the competitors gathered at Inverness. John MacDonald was not well enough to go, and thus missed one of his pupils winning the gold medal for his playing of 'Glengarry's March'. It was Donald MacLeod and, contrary as ever, when he wrote to Seton Gordon at the end of the year, MacDonald had little good to say about the Northern Meeting and did not even mention MacLeod's triumph.

Whatever concern MacDonald was still expressing for the overall standard of piping, Seton now had a piping enthusiast as a close friend on Skye, with opportunities for weekly sessions. A few months after the war ended, the island welcomed back one of its own sons, Colonel John MacKinnon MacDonald, Colonel 'Jock' as he became affectionately known. He returned to Viewfield House, which had been cared for by his sisters during his years abroad. With Jock back on Skye permanently he soon began to spend hours in Seton's company. Jock was a knowledgeable piper, but modest about his own playing.

A small man in stature, he had a life filled with interest. He was a true Skyeman, who spoke Gaelic, and before going on to Fettes had attended Portree School, not far from his home. He was a natural athlete and gymnast and at Fettes was on the rugby 1st XV and the cricket XI. His skill at rugby was such that in 1911 he played for Scotland against Wales, but a knee injury later finished his rugby career.

In the first war Jock was commissioned into the Cameron Highlanders. He was sent to the Middle East and seconded to the Persian Rifles. One of his great adventures was being ordered to capture Shah Ahmad, who was sympathetic to Germany. When the Shah was captured by his Persian soldiers, Jock was only just in time to prevent the women and children in the Shah's entourage from being executed.

In 1917 Jock was sent to Russia on a training mission and was there when the Revolution broke out. Somewhere along the way, he was awarded the Order of St Stanislav. By the time he arrived on Skye forty years later he could not remember why he had received it, but suggested that it might have been the prize for a record consumption of vodka. Another legendary story about his time in the Middle East, is that before he had fully recovered from a major operation, still on the danger list, he discharged himself from hospital. As he left an orderly presented him with an already completed death certificate. The man insisted on marking it 'cancelled'.

Between the wars Jock became a tea planter in Assam. He married in 1935; his bride, Evelyn, was an auxiliary nurse and proved to be a character in her own right. She insists that she nearly married the wrong man, because their best man, perhaps nervous and not quite knowing the correct place to stand, came up on the side where she expected Jock to be. She is very forthright and does not suffer fools gladly, but is immensely kind. When the Second World War began, Jock joined the Indian Army and commanded a construction unit on the Burma Road.

When they finally returned to Skye, to their magnificent home, it was necessary to produce an income. Looking at all the possibilities, they decided to turn Viewfield into a hotel. The house was in many ways suited for this purpose, with several bedrooms and bathrooms. In the early days they could afford to hire only a small staff and much of the work was done by themselves.

Some of the early American visitors may have found Viewfield different from the increasing luxury of North American hotels, but if they wanted a true Highland experience, they had found it. Their host was a Highland gentleman with a long pedigree. He had a great sense of fun and the guests were sometimes greeted by the Colonel himself, along with his tame owl, who sat so still that many thought the bird was stuffed until it winked. Jock played the pipes and entertained them with his anecdotes. It was not too many years before the fame of Viewfield House Private Hotel spread far beyond the Highlands and an early booking became more imperative each year.

As the success of the hotel grew, the MacDonalds became more and more self-sufficient, growing their own vegetables and raising livestock, including pigs. Jock made a very sensible arrangement with other Portree hotels to collect their left-over food to use as swill. For this purpose he bought a tractor and trailer. News filtered back from one hotel that an American guest complained that the only man she saw on Skye wearing a kilt was driving a 'garbage truck' (dust cart). It was Colonel Jock collecting his pig swill!

On trips to Portree, Seton often called in at Viewfield for a piping session with Colonel Jock. Piping was their common interest and Jock never went on walking expeditions with Seton and Francis Cameron-Head, but there were several occasions when the three got together to pipe. Evelyn MacDonald's most vivid memory of Seton is that he was a 'colourful figure' because of the shirts he wore, which often contrasted with his jacket and the tartan of his kilt. She described one late summer evening around 1948 when they were piping in the garden at Viewfield and the midges were particularly bad:

> I always remember him piping on the lawn in his wonderful 'get-up'. The midges were simply frightful. Jock lit a charcoal brazier and put it beside Seton, who walked up and down looming through the smoke looking exactly like Mephistopheles in the underworld playing the pipes, because of these spumes of smoke everywhere, with Seton's moustache adding to the effect, striding up and down. The music sounded lovely, but the sight was rather extraordinary! He used to come here nearly every Friday when Audrey went shopping. He and Jock used to pipe for hours.

Jonathan MacDonald was sixteen years old in 1948. Seton held this serious young man in high regard. After leaving Kilmuir school, he became an apprentice weaver with the Highland Home Industries and became very skilled on the loom. Jonathan was also developing a good voice, concentrating on Gaelic music and often went with Seton to Highland Games and Mods, especially the Skye Gathering. Here they listened to the pibroch competitions. These would start early in the evening before the games commenced and go on till 2 a.m. Seton sometimes took other local men and Jonathan recalls his reaction if these extra passengers smoked. They were made to sit in the back and often on the late night return rides the roof would be opened to add to their discomfort.

Alasdair Gordon had left the army and was happy to spend several months on Skye. Also enjoying his first few months of civilian life was Iain Hilleary's son, Ruaraidh. Another son, Alasdair, lost his life while on active in service in Palestine. The time spent on Skye was not without adventure for Ruaraidh Hilleary and Alasdair Gordon. Iain Hilleary's other son, Ewan, went into the fishing business, and in 1947 purchased a fishing boat which he moored in Loch Greshornish. It broke loose in a gale and was wrecked beyond repair despite two rescue attempts.

With the insurance money he purchased another boat in Ullapool. Alasdair Gordon and Ruaraidh sailed the boat back to Skye, but not before a prolonged storm hit the west coast. After a wait they put out, but it was rougher than anticipated and shelter was found in the Summer Isles. Finally a run was made for Skye. One of them had to nurse the temperamental engine, going into the hull to do so. They 'drew lots' and Ruaraidh lost, so had to go below, where the filter needed cleaning all to often. While Alasdair steered, his friend occasionally came up for air, looking greener each time. It was a relief to reach Loch Snizort and calmer seas.

Ruaraidh stayed in the Highlands, exept for a brief time in Rhodesia. He later started a Territorial Squadron of the SAS in Dundee. Soon after their adventure, Alasdair Gordon took a business management course in London. He joined Jardine Mathieson and spent several years in various Asian offices.

Whatever frustrations Seton Gordon endured through the delays in waiting for *Highways and Byways of the Central Highlands* to be published, when it finally came out in 1948 the timing was excellent. The Highlands were being rediscovered and the demand for information increasing. Hiking was also on the increase and young people were beginning to arrive from Commonwealth countries to tramp the Highlands. Youth Hostels were filled with people eager to hike in neighbouring glens. The kilt was a favourite form of dress for men hikers and tartan skirts for women. Highland and Island hostels were all the more colourful for it. Many people camped in less accessible places for a few days and then moved to a hostel. One was opened in Glen Brittle, where before the war Seton often saw as many as eight or nine tents pitched at the base of the Cuillins.

In 1949 both *Highways and Byways* books were reprinted. Seton was also writing *Afoot in the Hebrides* for Country Life Books. It was the one over which he had complained to Francis Cameron-Head of the difficulty in finding inspiration, though one would never know this from reading the book.

In the first month of the new year Seton developed bronchitis, his second attack in twelve months. This caused John MacDonald of Inverness to remark about it in a letter. MacDonald was, however, far more concerned about the recent publication of Campbell of Kilberry's book, *The Kilberry Book of Ceol Mor*, which contained some of the controversial *Piobaireachd* Society settings referred to at the beginning of Chapter 6:

> Yes, I have a copy of Kilberry's book and in my opinion it is the beginning of the end of our traditional *piobaireachd* playing as handed down to us. I certainly do not agree with any of his comments on the Camerons or Gillies, and I have had so much to do with him before he went to India and since his return that I am almost justified in saying he is untruthful.
>
> I will have something unpleasant to say to him when I read his book, and I am not continuing teaching the tunes for this year's competitions as written by the *Piobaireachd* Society. I am too old now to adopt the modern ideas of piob. and am quite happy to keep what I got from the old pipers. Kilberry has completely shorn the 'Vaunting' of its traditional beauty. I will not say more until I have an opportunity of a personal talk with you.

After so many years as a private document *The Kilberry Book of Ceol Mor* was produced when several leading members of the *Piobaireach* Society thought the notes deserved to be published.

It was evidently small consolation to MacDonald that Archibald Campbell wrote a warm letter to him just before sending the book. A copy of the letter, dated 15 December, 1948, was kindly offered for inclusion by Kilberry's son, James Campbell:

> My Dear MacDonald,
> I hope, in few days time, to send to you a present of a copy of a book, which is being issued by the *Piobaireachd* Society and which at long last has been printed.
> There are 114 tunes, the largest collection ever published except *Ceol Mor*. I hope that pipers will find this useful, in these days when practically all pipe music is out of print. I daresay that there are details on which people will disagree with me, but on the whole I think I have given a fair representation of what has been considered orthodox playing in our time.
> Anyhow there is no fancy alteration of the music, or airing of theories of my own.
> The longish introduction may possibly interest people who are always asking to have it explained to them what *piobaireachd* music is.
> Such as it is, it carries with it my warmest thanks for all the help which you have given to me in trying to learn *piobaireachd*, for which I have always felt and shall always feel grateful.
> Yours sincerely, Archibald Campbell.

Commenting on John MacDonald's letter, James Campbell wrote recently:

> His letter must have been written in a fit of pique. He and my father were to some extent rivals in the business of received wisdom, but their differences were trifling in comparison with the vast area of common ground. This particular criticsm was, I fancy, caused by the setting for competition the previous year (1948) of *'The Vaunting'*. There was, in that tune, a rather trivial divergence of opinion on the timing of a few bars, but it was something on which MacDonald held strong views. When his letter was written he had had very little time to form a view of the Kilberry book as a whole. My father's letter, which John MacDonald kept, and which reached me after his death, is also an indication of the generally cordial terms of their association'.

In 1984, James Campbell, wrote *Sidelights on the Kilberry Book of Ceol Mor*. Referring to his father's private, unpublished opinions on those pipers who gave tuition, in the preface he provides a succinct explanation of why differences still rage over styles and settings of classical pipe music:

> All players of *piobaireachd* have a God by whom they swear. And it was out of no disrespect to MacDougall Gillies and John MacDonald that they were placed respectively second and third in this particular pecking order. Neither of these legendary figures lack their own priests who may well not share the view of Sandy Cameron as top man . . .
> A devoted disciple is not necessarily a precise imitator, and I venture to doubt if John MacDonald played everything 'as he got it' from various Camerons or MacPhersons; if MacDougall Gillies played everything 'as he got it' from Sandy or Keith Cameron. . . . what is here published [in the original book] is not put forward as a guide to what is 'right' or 'wrong'. Its value lies

> in its stamp of authenticity as a record of what was taught by particular people at a particular moment of time at the beginning of this century. And such value is not lessened by the reflection that other people, and indeed the same people, may have taught differently at other times.

By spring, each year, both Seton Gordon and Francis Cameron-Head began to think of Lochmore, and 1949 was no different. The attraction was the warmth and hospitality of its owner, Bend Or, Duke of Westminster. It was customary for them to go without their wives, perhaps because, as Mrs Cameron-Head indicated, they enjoyed themselves more without the presence of herself and Audrey. It may have been the 'clubby' atmosphere that the Duke liked to provide. Hugh Richard Arthur Grosvenor, second Duke and fourth Marquess of Westminster, was a wonderful host, whose primary concern was that his guests should be happy. The nickname Bend Or was given him by his grandfather, when his colt of the same name won the Derby in 1880, the year after Hugh Richard Arthur was born.

Although very wealthy, he had simple personal tastes and a boyish enthusiasm which he maintained to the end of his life. He also had a deep appreciation of the wonderful scenery which surrounded his 100,000 acre Sutherlandshire estate. Bend Or's staff were treated with the same consideration with which he treated his guests and Seton witnessed this camaraderie on many occasions. He described the Duke as a man who encouraged independent thought and was not upset if one of his staff challenged him or spoke his mind. He also enjoyed entering into harmless jokes and often Seton would be asked to pipe beneath the window of a tardy guest early in the morning. It says much for the Duke's democratic spirit that there were as many commoners among his guests each year as titled people, judging from Seton's comments over the years. The Duke hated writing letters and used the medium of telegrams to communicate with friends. He also disliked having his photograph taken, so few are in existence.

Like Edward Grey, the Duke's attraction to Seton Gordon was his own interest in wildlife, especially of the Reay Forest and its rivers and lochs. He loved to fish the Laxford and spent many a happy summer evening there, sometimes until after midnight. Seton said of him: 'He was the very spirit of that wild and rugged country of the North-West Highlands, and no one was held in so great a degree of affection and respect by deerstalker, shepherd or estate worker. Many is the story one heard of his kindliness and consideration'.

The greatest attraction at Lochmore was the fishing, not only on the Laxford and the more northerly Dionard, but on the many lochs which abound throughout the Reay Forest. Almost all of Seton's fishing anecdotes refer to the rivers and pools of the north in Ross and Cromarty, Sutherland and Caithness; The Oykell, Cassley, Helmsdale and the Shin, with piping sessions on its bank.

One frequent companion was keeper John Scobie, and in June 1949 on an outing to Loch Stack, Seton's considerable reputation as a fisherman suffered when he failed to make a catch. Bend Or was on the Laxford, but because the river was low he was unlikely to get a bite. He was leaving for London the next morning and was anxious to take a salmon with him. Despite several hours on the loch, fishing into the small hours, Seton failed to live up to his reputation and returned to the lodge empty handed.

Seton and Audrey left for their first trip to Switzerland on 20 June. The day before their departure disaster struck one of Seton's oldest fiends. The Inveran Hotel, where Angus MacPherson and his wife Alice had been proprietors for thirty-five years, was burned to the ground. Despite the best efforts of the Dornoch, Golspie and Tain fire brigades, little was left of the structure. Angus lost many irreplacable heirlooms and trophies in the fire. Among the few things saved were the old family pipes made in 1800 which his father had played. Sustained by friends, MacPherson slowly recovered from the shock, though he never returned to the hotel business.

One of the attractions of the Gordons' first visit to Switzerland was to see at close quarters the Alpine swift. It was a surprise to find that despite the bird's name, high in the the Alps it was the common swift which was most in evidence. Above the 5000 foot level the alpine swift was rarely present. Three birds were seen with which they were unacquainted, the Alpine chough, snowfinch and the water-pipit. A tree familiar to Seton from his pre-first war visit to the Alpes Maritimes, was the *Pinus cembra*. There was a profusion of alpine flowers, some of them familiar from his Spitzbergen visit and some found in Scotland. Seton noted that because of damage by collectors, the edelweiss was protected by the Swiss government, prohibiting them from gathering it. One plant which intrigued them was the Alpine forget-me-not, named by the Swiss as the 'Hound of Heaven'.

Fortunately after their return to Skye the brilliant weather continued and day after day the heat brought out the fragrance of the wild plants as they made their way towards the eagles' cliff. The eaglet was well-grown and had begun wing exercises. The afternoon of Sunday, 17 July was the last time that Seton saw the eaglet in the nest, where it fed on a newly killed rabbit. (See Appendix 7)

The health of John MacDonald of Inverness was not improving and he was unable to attend any of the 1949 pibroch events, though in a September letter he wrote that he was still giving lessons to Pipe-Majors Brown, Nicol, MacRae, MacLeod and MacGillivray, in readiness for the Aboyne and Braemar Games, where Seton Gordon was to be one of the judges.

A look at the Aboyne programme for 1949, where Nicol was first in *piobaireachd*, shows a veritable 'Who's Who' of Seton Gordon's friends and acquaintances. In the list of directors are named Sir Malcolm Barclay-Harvey of Dinnet; Gordon Duncan Esq. of the Lady Wood Lodge, who had remained in Aboyne; Robert Wolrige Gordon Esq., of Esselmont; also judging the pibroch was Angus MacPherson of Invershin.

On Deeside that year, following the death of his grandfather, Captain Alwyne Arthur Compton, MC, at the age of twenty-nine, assumed the name Farquharson, and was recognised by Lord Lyon King of Arms as Laird of Invercauld and Chief of the name Farquharson and Head of Clan. Compton became a third forename. The new Chief was educated at Eton and Magdalen College, Oxford, and during the war served with distinction in the Royal Scots Greys, in Palestine, North Africa, Italy and France, where he was wounded. He was promoted to captain in 1943 and awarded the MC in 1944.

The Castle of Invercauld is two miles east of Braemar and lies on the north side of the Ballater to Braemar road. Though not as large as Balmoral, it compliments its surroundings, situated on a slight rise close to the Dee, with wooded hills and rock outcrops on both sides of the valley. As well as assuming the clan chieftainship, in 1949 Alwyne Farquharson also married Frances Lovell Oldham of Seattle, Washington, USA.

Frances Farquharson had a successful career in journalism, which began when she first came to Europe as a young woman. She visited Paris, Rome and London. From these cities she wrote a column for a Seattle newspaper, *European Letters* and went on to become fashion editor of *Vogue*, then for *Harper's Bazaar*, eventually editing the London edition. For one so gifted, the transition to becoming the wife of a Highland chief was not too daunting, even though his possessions include two castles, Invercauld and Braemar, as well Torloisk, a farm on Mull. The combined land area is more than 200,000 acres. During the shooting season the Farquharsons entertain groups who come to enjoy a week on the moors with their guns. They are happy to pay for the privilege of staying under the roof of a Highland chief with all the tradition and romance that goes with it.

Seton Gordon had visited Invercauld occasionally, but after the new chief was installed he became a frequent and welcome guest. Alwyne Farquharson took part in the typical pursuits of a major Deeside landowner, grouse shooting and deer-stalking, but he also enjoys a simple walk in the hills, particularly with someone as knowledgeable as Seton. Often, when at Invercauld, an outing was arranged into the Cairngorms, though Seton was just as content to spend time with his old Deeside friends or play the pipes in the castle grounds.

By January 1950, Seton was into his fourth year of watching the Trotternish eagles, and actually witnessed them mating. He knew that courtship can begin in January and continue until May, and mating can take place at any time during this period. A heavy snowstorm had passed over northern Skye in the second week and the snow remained for several days. When Seton left home early one morning it was an almost cloudless day and the air was incredibly clear, the lochan showing dark against the unbroken snow around it. When he reached the cliff, both birds were soaring above their ledge:

> One of the eagles had a mind to alight on top of the cliff but the snow, drifted on the ridge to a depth of several feet, was too heavy. The eagle, still airborne, was now attacked by a pair of ravens; after the ravens had left him he did succeed in making a landing. Here, after a few seconds, he began to beat his wings as though he were mating the female; yet there was no sign of a second bird. When the eagle took wing, I was surprised to see his mate rise, a few seconds afterwards, from the same spot. The deep cup she had made in the snow had entirely hidden her from my sight, and the male had been mating

> her when his wings had been violently agitated. This was almost exactly six weeks before the egg was laid.

February 1950 was a month of almost continuous storm. On the 13th Seton wrote to Francis Cameron-Head, 'A hurricane 9 a.m. Had to take weather observations on my hands and knees! NEVER before!!!'

In the spring there was more correspondence with Buckingham Palace. By the sixth year the Glenfinnan Gathering had a secure place in the Highland calendar. Seton wrote to Martin Charteris (now Lord Charteris of Amisfield), Private Secretary to Her Royal Highness, the Princess Elizabeth. He asked, on behalf of the Glenfinnan Gathering directors, if she would honour them by becoming patron of the Gathering. The reply stated that owing to the very great number of similar requests, Her Royal Highness was forced to refuse them all as it was unfair to make an exception. The letter expressed Her Royal Highness's thanks for 'this kind suggestion' and her hope for the Gathering's great success. In the acknowledgment Charteris also wrote:

> I am very glad to hear that a new book is soon to be published. Nobody writes so well about the Hebrides as you do, and it will be delightful for all of us who love the Hebrides to have another book on them. [*Afoot in the Hebrides* – See Appendix 8]

Whatever disappointment Seton might have felt that his idea had not come to fruition, he was philosophical about it. He happily continued to watch the eyrie and on 2 June, a busy day for both he and Audrey, an early start was made to the cliffs, but there was no sign of the eagles. After a quick return to Upper Duntuilm they left for Kyle where in the evening Seton presided at the Mod concert there. Instead of leaving for home immediately he and Audrey went to the railway station and when the late train from Lairg arrived they met Morag, the Cairn puppy who was to replace Ninag. Morag was a gift from one of the Lochmore ghillies, Donald Falconer.

When Seton next set out for the eyrie the midges, unfortunately, were out in force. Climbing to the eyrie, he was again rewarded with the sight of all three birds together. Dugie, the collie was asleep and seemed not to care about the midges, but his master could hardly keep still, so intense were they. As he watched though, a dramatic scene unfolded:

> A black thunder cloud formed behind the eagles' rock and soon came torrential rain, through which sunrays slanted. The air stayed warm and before the intensity of the rain blotted out the rock I could see the family group of golden eagles still perched against the skyline. After the first heavy shower the female ruffled her feathers, and I could see the down floating from them. That evening, when the storm passed, there were salmon-tinted cumulonimbus clouds high above the eagles' rock.

> 2 September was the last occasion when he saw the young bird close to the

eyrie. Below him were a few lambs and the young eagle suddenly rose and made a 'playful swoop' at one of them, making it bound away in total surprise. The bird seemed, in Seton's words, 'evidently pleased with itself'.

Afoot in the Hebrides, published by Country Life Ltd., was in the hands of the reviewers by September. One of the threads which was common to the reviews was its fairness in describing the Hebrideans. A book which had been published only a short time before had been harshly critical of them. It came from someone who had, over the same period that Seton wrote, professed a love of the Hebrides. Not one of the reviewers mentioned the book by name or its author, though parodying a popular novel, one jokingly referred to it as 'No Orchids for the Outlandish!' All of them thought that Seton Gordon had done much to redress the balance.

The *Weekly Scotsman* reviewer was forthright in his condemnation of the other book:

> The stir created by a recent book on the Western Isles lends special interest to the appearance of the long awaited *Afoot in the Hebrides* by Seton Gordon. Readers familiar with his writings will not expect from this volume any of the criticisms of the island folk which roused them to vehement reply . . .
>
> Mr. Gordon has written one of the most generous surveys of the area yet published for the general reader. The whole book is enriched by the author's references to a past more stirring and romantic than that of any other circumscribed area in Britain.

While enjoying the knowledge that sales of his new book were brisk, Seton Gordon was part of a group arranging a benefit for Angus MacPherson. Those with memories of the Inveran Hotel before the fire were easily persuaded to contribute. 19 December was the date selected for a luncheon at the Invershin Station Hotel, to make the presentation. Angus was given an 18-carat gold watch and chain, inscribed: 'To Angus MacPherson from the tenants of the River Shin and their friends in appreciation of the many happy days spent in his company on the banks of the River Shin'. His wife was given a George III era silver tea-set.

The day before the event turned cold throughout the north and heavy snow began to fall. Seton Gordon got there only by remarkable persistence and a desire not to let his old friend down. In a later note to Francis Cameron-Head, who had gone to Rome over the Christmas season, he told of his journey to Invershin:

> It took me thirty-one hours to reach Invershin, starting here at 6 a.m. Monday 18th for Angus MacPherson's presentation. The early bus never got into Portree because of ice. I went in the afternoon and hired to Kyleakin. Caught the 6 a.m. to Dingwall and had a desperate journey from there as the train was two and a half hours late and so would have missed the presentation by two hours. The road was a sheet of ice everywhere.

But Seton arrived in time. Of all the people expected, only a handful missed the event because of the storm. It was arranged that Seton would make the speech of appreciation to Angus and his wife. He said:

> Those of us who were fortunate enough to have fished the Shin, and have stayed with Angus MacPherson and his good lady, nobly and indefatigably assisted by daughter-in-law Joy, have some of the most pleasant memories of their life to look back on. It was a tragedy that – and I say it deliberately – the most hospitable family in the Highlands should have had their home burnt over their heads last summer. They met disaster with the cheerfulness and resignation one would have expected of them, but only those of us who have been welcomed and cared for in their unique manner can understand how hard the loss must have been.
>
> No man knows the Shin like Angus. No man is so skilled a fisherman. No less skilled is he as a piper, so that here one had the best of angling, the best of hospitality, and the best of piping. Those days at Inveran stand out in my life. It is a long journey from Skye to the Shin, but at the end of that journey there was always a meal set, always a tune on the pipes Each of us has our memories and favourite time of the year. In these beautiful surroundings, Angus MacPherson, his wife and family lived for thirty-five years. It is not saying too much that for those gathered here, and for their many absent friends, they cannot be replaced

While Francis Cameron-Head was in Italy, an event took place which made headline news for several weeks. On Christmas Day, a group of Scottish Nationalist students removed the Stone of Scone from Westminster Abbey. It was brilliantly executed and took the authorities completely by surprise. The '*Liath Fail*', or Stone of Destiny, in their opinion rightly belonged to Scotland. The incident also served to demonstrate the puckish sense of humour of the Duke of Westminster.

In another note to Cameron-Head in the New Year, Seton wrote:

> A bad business about the *Liath Fail*. I had a wire from the Duke of Westminster last night wishing us a Happy New Year. It began: 'Think you ought to send Stone back!' I pictured Scotland Yard ringing up our local constable!! . . .

CHAPTER

13

DAME FLORA'S FAME SPREADS; THE '45 REBELLION COMMEMORATED

THE NEXT DECADE brought changes to Seton Gordon's life, with the death of several friends and loved ones. John Graham, no doubt with an eye to earning more money, left the employ of the Gordons to work on road maintenance. He came back several years later, and stayed until retirement.

A plethora of new agricultural pesticides and insecticides were brought into use and it was not too long before disturbing decreases in wild bird and animal life were noticed. A similar pattern was developing in Europe and North America. In early 1951, however, Seton Gordon's immediate concern was the fate of the Trotternish eagles and their production of young for that year.

The previous November he had watched the parents as they chose their nesting site for the coming year, deciding upon the 1949 eyrie. The first observation for 1951 took place on 16 February and again Seton was fortunate to see another mating. This time there was no snow and he first spotted the male by the nesting rock. The bird rose, 'sailing indolently in spirals, gradually gaining height'. He then began a long glide on motionless wings, alighting by the female on a grassy slope. He immediately sprang on her back and mated her, with wings beating rapidly. They then stood together for several minutes before the female launched herself into an aerial display. She rejoined her mate and they once more stood side by side, wings touching.

Seton witnessed, for only the second time in his life, an attack on a lamb. On 25 April, he saw one of the eagles sail across a grassy slope to where a number of sheep, many of them small lambs were feeding. The eagle checked its flight, dropped suddenly, seized one of the smaller lambs and flew about 80 yards with it. The ewe did not immediately realise what had happened, but she finally ran down the slope towards them. As she drew closer the eagle flew with the lamb to the edge of a small cliff, where it made a leisurely meal of the victim before returning to the eyrie. Seton noted, 'It seemed that this flight was made to acquaint her mate with what had happened, for it left again almost at once and flew very fast back to where the lamb was'.

The post that day brought a letter from Francis Cameron-Head in which he invited Seton to be Chief of the 1951 Glenfinnan Games. He replied: 'I am very much touched by your letter asking me to be Chief of the Gathering, and I gratefully accept. I am touched, too, that you should think I have done a little towards making it a true Highland meeting . . .'

Seton and Audrey spent several days in late May travelling around Holland's bird sanctuaries but were back on Skye by 1 June for Skye Week. Iain Hilleary was chairman of the newly formed Skye Council of Social Services. In his programme message he said:

> It is once again my privilege to offer a special welcome to all visitors to Skye Week. Last year, with the emphasis on its call to Skye people wherever they might be, and particularly those of MacLeod descent, it was launched as a week of entertainment for all of those coming to the Island.

Entertainment was not the sole purpose of the Skye Council of Social Service. It was created in 1950 to represent aspects of island life. Committees were set up to study transportation, agriculture, tourism, social welfare and fishing. The Council's mandate was to assist in finding solutions to economic problems in this remote part of Great Britain.

Although at the time it was not visualised, the 1951 Skye Week would make an impact which caused tourist numbers to explode within a few years, and to rocket Dame Flora MacLeod to world fame. An American writer, Robert J. Reynolds, arrived on the island to write an article on the event for the National Geographic Magazine. Published in July of the following year, in it Reynolds captured the tempo of Skye life and the spirit of Skye Week, with comments on the pace of life, the erratic bus schedules, and Skye hospitality. Under a sub-heading 'MacLeod of MacLeod' he told his readers of a 'cherished invitation' from Flora, Mrs MacLeod of MacLeod, to stay at Dunvegan Castle. Colour photographs included one of the Dunvegan garden party with Iain Hilleary, Seton Gordon and Colonel Jock conversing on the lawn.

Before leaving the island Reynolds visited Upper Duntuilm:

> North of Kilmuir I came to the home of Seton Gordon, author of many books on Skye and the Hebrides. Over tea he told me that Skye was being uncommonly kind to me. 'I've been going over sun records I keep for the Air Ministry,' he said. 'We've had 136 hours these first ten days of June, with no rainfall whatever. That's the best weather we've had on Skye [for this period] since 1931'. We gazed out for a while from Gordon's window at one of Skye's astounding sunsets. Across the broad water spread the long chain of the Outer Isles.

The fine weather which had lasted through June and early July, broke about the 7th and gave way to rain and mist. It was not until the 12th that Seton went to the nest. As he watched, the eaglet began prolonged wing exercises. Five days later it had made a first flight and it was two months before Seton set eyes on the young bird again.

The Glenfinnan Games now took place on the nearest Saturday to 19 August, to accommodate the increasing tourists coming through the area. In 1951 it was on 18 August. House parties for the Gathering are a tradition at Inverailort and continue to this day. Despite the fact that rationing was still in place, it did not prevent the Cameron-Heads from being wonderful hosts and ensuring that their guests had a memorable time. There were formal dinners on both Friday and Saturday evenings and a large tent at the Gathering field where VIPs and house-guests were fed during the day itself.

That year Seton was Chief of the Day. Whoever had this honour led the march to the Gathering in the company of Francis Cameron-Head and immediately behind the pipers. It is still customary for the Chief of the Day to make the opening speech following an introduction. The dais on which this takes place is in the large field to the west of the monument and is used for the Highland dancing competitions. Encircling the site are the mountains, and Loch Shiel constantly draws the eye to its ever changing moods.

In his introduction, Francis Cameron-Head paid tribute to Seton's contribution to Highland history, and particularly his knowledge of the '45 and the lands through which the Prince travelled to reach Glenfinnan. Seton, of all those invited to open the Gathering since its beginning six years before, had a greater sense of occasion because he had written so prolifically on the area and could call upon a rich store of historical information. He had also been a part of the Gathering's development from its first year. Seton Gordon was, at that time of the Gathering, putting the finishing touches to his last major book. *The Highlands of Scotland* was published at the end of the year as part of the County Book series by Robert Hale of London. It was one of fifty-six books covering the entire British Isles. The General Editor was naturalist Brian Vesey-Fitzgerald.

Each of the twenty-five *Highlands of Scotland* reviewers whose comments were clipped by Romeike and Curtice Ltd., was familiar with Seton Gordon's work, and the reviews had a greater variety of opinions than for any previous book. Although the overriding theme was one of praise, Diana Leatham, writing in the *Church of England News*, made some strange comments about the modern Highlander as well:

> Mr Gordon is a fortunate man. A Highlander himself, he has been in love with the Highlands for over forty years. His life has been spent studying the birds and flowers, experiencing the unearthly best and fearsome worst of the climate . . .
>
> Mr Gordon is a romantic, more interested in the past than in the future . . . of course, the Highlander of today, though he is a magnificent fighter, is no longer cruel. Yet I think it is a pity that Mr Gordon has not tempered his praise with some account of the heartbreaking charm, plausibility, sloth and unreliability among Highland workers. What signifies their continued loyalty

> to their chiefs when their attitude to work wrecks so many schemes for bettering conditions among the hills they purport to love?

Diana Leatham had not yet finished:

> Whether Mr Gordon's manner will appeal to the young I do not know. But I do know that if you know the Highlands he can bring back to you the delicious smell of bog myrtle and of young birch leaves in the sun; the sound of the waves and waterfalls, the sights such as I happen to find among the most satisfying in the world – cushions of papery sea-pinks flourishing on granite rocks against a translucent background of green and purple sea.

A strange mixture of praise and scorn!

The reviewer for the *South Wales Post* was fellow naturalist R. M. Lockley. After saying that it was a book which all lovers of mountains should possess, Lockley ended his review:

> It is extremely difficult to stop the drift to the towns . . . Mr Gordon, however, is not one of these deserters. Born and reared in the rude weather of his splendid Highlands, he remains there on a wild treeless headland which is his home on Skye, staunch to the brave people who cling indigenously to their infertile soil, and which in summer provide the facilities for the soft Sassenachs who come trooping to the north to see wild beauty so well described in this book.

As though to give weight to this compliment, in November and December, Seton spent more time watching the eyrie than he had during those months in previous years. On 27 November, during a week of storm, Seton left the house in late afternoon as the gale whipped around the corners of the building. The day had been one of mixed cloud, sun and squalls, but now, as the sun moved west the rain promised to hold off for some time. As he struggled to the cliffs the birds were coming in, intent on roosting early, in such comfort as they could find, but the male had difficulty in finding shelter. The wind continued to buffet the cliffs. Clouds came in fragments across the Minch and Seton watched as the bird strove to master the fury of the wind:

> He came in, but swung round and flew downwind for about a mile, travelling higher and higher and then began a spectacular glide against the gale. His wings were half-closed and made very thin and narrow, giving the appearance of a gigantic peregrine falcon. Again he travelled about a mile eastward, then rose to 3000 feet or more in a very short time. The slow, steady approach was repeated, rocking when the down-draught was reached, then he dropped to the nest. As I struggled home, I was almost blown down by the force of the gusts of that severe gale.

The days were growing shorter and the eagles roosted as early as three-thirty on some days. On 1 December, Seton noted, 'The eagles at dusk made a spectacular appearance out of a black storm-cloud, diving one after the other to the cliff and the roosting ledges, and reaching them as the storm broke. Suddenly from a dove-grey cumulus cloud to the north came a brilliant lightning flash. Thunder, this winter evening, pealed, and lightning lighted the eagles to their roost'. There was a cryptic note at the end of his diary: 'thirty-eight visits to eyrie in 1951 – walked 228 miles'.

In May of the following year the Gordons accepted an invitation to stay with the Farquharsons. Although Seton had been to the Castle of Invercauld a number of times since the installation of the new chief, this was Audrey's first visit. Their arrival produced one more vintage Seton story of his timekeeping – and of Audrey's stoicism – recounted by Alwyne Farquharson:

> I had never met Audrey before and was not at the house when they arrived. Frances came around the corner and saw a rather forlorn looking lady sitting on a suitcase. She went up to her and said, 'Who might you be?' The answer was 'I'm Mrs Gordon'. Frances at once realised that she was Seton's wife and brought her into the house. She asked, 'Where is Seton?' Well, he had gone, as he always did, to Bob Brown's at Balmoral to do some piping. It happened to be a time of the year when we were particularly busy, and Seton being quite unconscious of time was not thinking about dinner. He probably had a sandwich with Bob Brown. The dinner wore on. There were a lot of people smartly dressed and I can still see Seton walking into the room – it must have been well on through dinner by then, and he had his telescope around his shoulder and his bagpipes under his arm, and was completely dazed to see so many people in the room!

Another incident which happened about this time, was related by the late Colonel Iain Grant, who was then the Younger of Rothiemurchus. Seton and Audrey were on their way to Inverness and stopped for tea at Drumintoul Lodge, where Iain Grant lived. Like his father, Iain had a distinguished war record and also served in the Lovat Scouts. He had grown up with Seton as a part of his life and through the years had taken up many of the same interests, especially piping and ornithology. There was perhaps more of a closeness than was established between Seton and the elder Rothiemurchus, though Iain was only thirty-eight at the time of this visit.

With his mind very much on his Trotternish eagles it was a thrill for Seton to see, as they rounded a bend on a particularly bad stretch east of Kyle of Lochalsh, two golden eagles fly low over the car. Colonel Grant described what happened when Seton spotted them:

> Seton's obsessive keenness on birds, which to a large extent I share, sometimes led to alarming situations, especially when driving. On one occasion in the early 1950s, he and Audrey arrived here for tea and almost before he got out of his car, he told us of the marvellous sight of two golden eagles which they spotted on a narrow and dangerous piece of road between Kyle and

> Inverness. What actually happened was that the two wheels of the car went over the edge of the road overlooking a steep ravine, with Audrey in the passenger seat. Some slides for a lecture were in the back and he was most upset at the thought of losing them. It was only his weight which kept the car from going off the road. They were eventually rescued by two passing lorry drivers. Thinking of Audrey's ordeal I said 'I hope she is none the worse' and his reply was, 'Oh, no – nothing wrong with either bird, I saw them flying away beautifully over the hills of Kintail'. As you know, he was deaf, and I shouted at him, 'It's Audrey I am concerned about, not the eagles'. I could see she was still a bit shaken, so I offered her a glass of brandy, whereon Seton replied, 'No thanks, I never take strong drink'. After shouting again that it was not he who was offered the drink, I eventually persuaded her to join me in a small brandy. When they left us after tea, I expressed the fervent hope that he would not see any more golden eagles on the rest of the journey.

It was after returning from Invercauld that Seton became aware of something unusual in the eagles' behaviour. At the end of the first week the male twice left his brooding and the hen did not take over, even though she was closeby. Once they flew away together. One day she flew over to the previous year's nest and alighted, something she had never done during the nesting season. There was at first no reason to doubt that an eaglet had hatched, until by the 15th, when he judged that they should be looking after the young bird they were both flying idly back and forth across the cliff.

It was not until well into June that Seton had an opportunity to 'spy' the eyrie carefully. The light was good and he could see no sign of a young bird, nor any 'whitewash' below the eyrie, as there should have been with a youngster in the nest. The nearby ravens' nest held four fully-fledged young in it by now.

Throughout the years of watching he had always avoided approaching their eyries too closely, but now convinced that it was empty he climbed to the top of the rock. He wrote:

> When I looked across at the eyrie it was obvious that either the egg had not hatched or some mischance had befallen the eaglet while it was still very young; it is possible that it was carried off by a raven during the absence of its parents, though it seems more likely that the egg never hatched.
>
> The raven brood were soaring on the wind, but the golden eagles had gone. For the first time in seven years the June sky was empty of those dark forms which usually sailed so steadily above me. A breast-feather, downy and delicate on the grass below, recalled to me her dignified and stately presence. I then knew how much the eagles meant to me, and how much pleasure they had given me during my years of watching, and I hoped that they might avoid poison, trap and gun, and next season might return and nest once more on their dark rock.

Whether the mishap to the egg was a forerunner of the growing pesticide

Seton Gordon, Captain Alwyne Farquharson of Invercauld and Francis Cameron-Head of Inverailort at the Glenfinnan Gathering – 1956 (by kind permission of Mr Brodrick Haldane)

problem, or just a coincidence it is hard to tell. The evidence against the agricultural use of these chemicals was mounting, especially DDT.

Seton reported in 1952 of infertile eagles' eggs in Sutherland and in the Canton of Berne, Switzerland, where he was in touch with the Swiss ornithologist Carl Stemmler. Soon other problems would give cause for alarm. In several species egg shells became so thin they could not be sustained and broke under the weight of the sitting hen. He was also in correspondence with a network of naturalists in various parts of Europe and North America; Professor Rowan of the University of Alberta Zoology Department, and American naturalists Maurice Broun and Roy Bedichek. Broun wrote: 'In America we squander our animal and bird resources, then when a few individuals remain, we pitch into deep lamentations and place the species concerned on a pedestal, as an object lesson'.

Information was still being received at Upper Duntuilm on the fate of the golden eagle in the State of Texas. Indications were that it was faring no better than when Casparis reported his activities in 1947. Having heard of two more pilots engaged in the same business, Seton Gordon wrote directly to one of them, William Hargus of Big Bend Flying Services, Marathon, Texas and received a courteous and frank letter in return:

> Dear Sir,
>
> I was very glad to get your letter of 1 March. I kill about 200 eagles a year. The highest I have ever chased one to kill it was 11,000 feet. I am sure they go to 20,000 feet without much trouble. The height depends upon the thermals and the mountain currents.
>
> Here the birds are of two types. The Golden Brown Eagle (known as the Mexican Eagle), and the American Eagle (the Bald Eagle) which is the biggest of the two types of bird. The biggest Eagle I have killed had a 7 feet 4 inch wing span. I am sure I have killed bigger ones but could not recover them. I would say that the larger birds of the American species sometimes may reach a wingspan of 8 feet 6 inches. A pair of Eagles when nesting will kill up to 4 to 6 lambs a day.
>
> Yours sincerely, William W. Hargus.

Another item sent to Upper Duntuilm was an article from the US *Cavalier* magazine, written by yet another Texas flyer named F. 'Mike' McMichael. It was called *I Fly Against Eagles*. McMichael's proud boast was that in 2800 'eagle flying hours' he shot down 512 birds. His record was nine in one day.

Bedichek told Seton of a slim ray of hope. Big Bend National Park, 708,000 acres of mixed terrain, desert, mountain, forest and river was created in 1944. It is in the heart of golden eagle country – giving protection so long as they remain within the park boundary. When James Fisher visited the park with American naturalist Roger Tory Peterson in 1953 they saw no golden eagles, although they learned that there was once three pairs in the park. They were aware of the number of eagles killed in recent years, and referring to the exploits of McMichael and Hargus, Fisher wrote: 'They have killed more eagles than exist in all of Scotland!'

In 1989, Park Naturalist Robert Rothe reported that there is now a small stable population of golden eagles at Big Bend, but no eyrie locations are known to the rangers. Peregrine falcons have also made a comeback in the park. The golden eagle was placed under Federal protection in 1972 and it ceased to be shot out of the air.

Doctor David Boag, a student under Professor Rowan, is now a senior member of the department, and has produced papers on the feeding habits of the golden eagle in the Rocky Mountains. He has also worked with Adam Watson at Banchory. He reported in 1988 that the golden eagle is doing well in the Rocky Mountains, on both sides of the border. Regular winter counts have been made for the past 25 years and the populations are stable. Ray De Marche of the British Columbia Fish and Wildlife Branch recalls a time when in Assiniboine Park in the southern Rocky Mountains of British Columbia, it was customary to offer a reward of $50 to any local person who shot the greatest number of golden eagles in a season.

The Glenfinnan Gathering in 1952 was held on 16 August and two weeks later a letter was posted to Balmoral with news of its success, and also mentioning the Portree Games. It elicited a reply from the Queen's Private Secretary:

> My Dear Seton,
>
> The Queen was very interested to hear of the success of the Glenfinnan Gathering and the other news you sent in your letter of 31 August.
>
> I hope you are keeping well and I hope also that you were not one of the spectators stung by wasps at the Portree Games!
>
> Yours ever, Martin Charteris.

It was such letters as this which, arriving at Duntuilm (or even other places where he was staying), with the E II R crest in the corner, that were mentioned by Seton's friends as they recalled his devotion and respect for members of the Royal Family. The letter does however, serve to show Her Majesty's genuine interest in Highland affairs. Her love of Highland tradition too, is very strong, and includes one started by Queen Victoria and repeated by every reigning Monarch since – to have one of her pipers play for fifteen minutes while she breakfasts.

Pipe-Majors Robert Brown and Robert Nicol were then still her pipers at Balmoral, just as they had been to the late King. Both still served as ghillies on the Balmoral estate. They assisted on the river and on the stalking ground in the deer forest. A special attachment was growing between four year old Prince Charles and Robert Brown. It was Brown who taught His Royal Highness to fish and, as he grew older, the finer points of stalking. Whenever Seton Gordon came to Deeside, he could be counted on to meet them for a piping session at Balmoral, as he did again at the end of October, this time without Audrey but with Morag the young Cairn terrier for company.

Seton was a happier man because his fervent wish had come true, before he left for Deeside the Trotternish eagles had returned. They had escaped the gun, trap and poison. Hardly daring to hope, yet knowing that another nesting season was about to start, Seton went to his usual spot and scanned the cliffs and buttresses with his field glass. To his great joy he picked them out in the area of the 1951 eyrie. They had mysteriously been away from that area for more than four months. When he visited the site on Boxing Day they had moved to the 1952 eyrie and were repairing it.

On 24 January, 1953, in spring-like weather, nest building was continuing. Seton Gordon entered into his last year of watching the eyrie. On 10 March he saw the laying of an egg and the first change-over about twenty hours later. Over three seasons the egg laying had a variation of only three days. In 1953 there was again only one offspring, and it was reared successfully after hatching on 20 April.

His intense interest in the eagles did not prevent Seton Gordon from having contact with his neighbours and there existed a warm rapport with them. They were used to his kilted figure walking past their crofts at all hours, sometimes going to the moor, or striding along the road to Duntulm Castle or Rubha Hunish point. Across the fields at the rear of the house was the croft of a newly married couple, Donald and Mary MacArthur. Donald was a piper of considerable skill, and he soon joined in piping sessions with Seton. Donald and Mary's wedding was distinguished by the presence of both Seton Gordon and Pipe-Major Robert Reid to pipe for them.

Jonathan MacDonald was proving his resourcefulness by opening up his own craft shop, Kilmuir Crafts, which he still co-owns with his sister. Duntulm Lodge was now a hotel. After years of ownership by the Department of the Secretary of State for Scotland, it was finally sold to Miss Kelly, owner of the Flodigarry Hotel. It was opened after some renovations and named the Duntulm Castle Hotel.

Piping lost one of its foremost exponents with the death of John MacDonald of Inverness on 8 June 1953 at the age of eighty-seven. He was buried at Forres and was honoured by having the Queen's Pipers, Brown and Nicol, play at his funeral. Nicol chose *'Lament for the Children'* and Brown played MacDonald's favourite *poibaireachd*, *'Lament for Patrick Og'*. Seton Gordon, in one of the many eulogies, summed up the feelings of the many pipers gathered that day:

> I think he was very like the MacCrimmon in the story. He was the King of Pipers because he combined extreme accuracy and brilliancy of fingering with the most wonderful expression. Like the playing of any musical genius, his gave the impression of being very simple, the sort of thing one could do one's self, and having heard him for two or three hours one went back and played probably 100 per cent better than before hearing him – because the ear had taken in the beauty and the skill and the brilliance of his playing.

Only six weeks after John MacDonald died, Seton Gordon was advised of the sudden death of Bend Or, Duke of Westminster. He died at Lochmore in his seventy-fourth year. It was a blow to Seton, whose worship of the Duke was based not on his wealth, but on his simplicity. Writing a tribute to his friend, he said:

> His was a stimulating yet elusive character, difficult to portray. Indeed to his intimate friends it often seemed that he wished the world should have a

> wrong impression of him. The North-West Highlands have benefited by his afforestation and agricultural schemes, which have not only checked the drift to the towns, but have brought men back to their homelands . . . It is never safe to say that a man was unique, yet in the combination of great wealth and democratic spirit the Duke of Westminster was certainly almost unique. It might be said that it was easy for him to spend large sums in order that one of his employees should benefit by the best surgical skills, yet the continued personal interest in the sufferer came not from wealth but from a kindliness of heart.

(Only two months before he died, with the assistance of his trusted land agent, George Ridley, the Duke purchased Annacis Island, a wooded piece of land of several acres a few miles up the Fraser River from Vancouver, British Columbia. It is now a thriving industrial estate, and still part of the Grosvenor holdings.)

For the first two weeks of July, Seton and Audrey were again in Switzerland. This time they flew from Prestwick to Zurich. From Zurich they left for Zermatt and the village of Riffelalp. While in Switzerland they met writer – naturalist Carl Stemmler and were shown an eyrie where two golden eaglets had been shot the week before. Stemmler, who wrote two books on the golden eagle in Switzerland, told them that the bird is protected in some Swiss cantons, but not all. Those giving official protection as of 1953 were Berne, Wandt, Wallis, Schwyz and Luzern. It was in Wallis that Seton and Audrey saw the eyrie where the young birds had been shot, posing a question as to the effectiveness of the protection. The killers had waited three days, luckily in vain, for the parent birds. Stemmler gave other examples to Seton: in the canton of Tessin during the winter of 1949–50, four eagles were officially poisoned with strychnine. In 1951 a pair nested in a sycamore tree close to a beauty spot, but the profusion of visitors kept the parent birds away for such long intervals that the eaglet starved to death.

Seton's contacts in Italy and Spain informed him that the golden eagle fared badly in these countries, other than a small degree of protection in Spanish national parks. All this lead him to the conclusion that throughout the world, man is the golden eagle's only serious enemy. Despite the fact that in Britain the golden eagle has human enemies, it also has more friends here than anywhere else in the world.

It was surely with tremendous relief that he returned to Trotternish and on 16 July headed across the moor in the certainty that he would find his eagle friends unharmed. He was in fact surprised to see three birds above the rock. At first he was surc that the third one was the 1951 offspring but observing the unsure landing he realised that it was that year's eaglet already airborne. Already its skill in sailing on the breeze was not far behind that of the parents.

An exploration of the 'Prince's Cave' at Loch nan Uamh was talked about with Francis Cameron-Head as early as 1948, but inexplicably they did not actually go to the site until January 1954.

The road from Fort William to Mallaig was little improved and was still a single track width. The distance from Inverailort to Borodale is no more than five miles and both must have passed it dozens of times. There is no question as to the importance that Borrodale had played in Prince Charles Edward Stuart's arrival and departure.

There would have been little more than a hill-track serving Borrodale House in 1746, but it did not lack neighbours. There were several cottages close by. It is now a comfortable country home with two floors, all the rooms having twelve-paned windows, and several dormer windows in the third floor. The original house was destroyed on Cumberland's orders when he learned of its owner's associaton with the '45. The destruction was discovered when the Prince's party returned there after crossing from Uist via Skye. The Prince was taken to the well-disguised cave mentioned in Seton's February 1947 letter to Francis. It is close to the beach and possibly a mile from Borrodale House, across level meadows, overlooked by the larger and more imposing Arisaig House, now a hotel. It is not easy to find the cave entrance among the loose rocks which form the small cliff and when the author visited the site in 1986 with Iain Thornber, it took several minutes of searching even though Thornber was familiar with the area. The chamber is dry and is large enough that an occupant would not be cramped. The cave faces the open loch and one might question why such a spot was chosen as a hide-out. On the Ordnance Survey map another 'Prince Charlie's Cave' is marked, due east, where the Meoble River and Loch Beoraid meet. This cave, which is approximately six miles inland was used on another occasion while the Prince was on the run.

In *Highland Days* Seton wrote: 'So far as I know, no evidence in writing exists of the exact embarkation point of the Prince. For this we must rely on the tradition of the country, and my friend, the late Francis Cameron-Head of Inverailort, and I were grateful to John MacEachan, who lived at the time on the shore of Loch nan Uamh, for showing us the little promontory, covered with heather, bracken, and wind-stunted oaks, where the long-boat from the *L'Heureux* embarked the Prince. There is deep water here to the edge of the tide, and the place is a secluded one. At the time, people lived high above the loch on Mullach Buidhe. John MacEachan remembers no fewer than seventeen families there: not one remains'.

Seton Gordon's diary entry is cryptic:

> 21 January – Prince's Cave Loch nan Uamh – one horned stag – Rhodos in full flower – very attractive strath – sunny and sheltered.

From this 'expedition' came a firm resolve to one day erect a cairn to commemorate the Prince's departure. The spot pointed out by MacEachan is to the south of Borrodale and some distance from the cave itself. As active members of the '45 Association their first thought was the importance of seeking the Association Council's approval. The members lived far and wide, but were very enthusiastic in their cause. The secretary at that time, Marion Cameron, lived in

Largs, and when contacted on the idea she immediately circulated information to the Council.

Although he was an outdoorsman, the health of Francis Cameron-Head was not robust. There were often references to his being 'laid-up' and in April 1955 Seton wrote:

> You must have had a long and grevious illness. I know too well, what influenza does to you and especially when you cannot shake it off. I am sure, now that the good weather has come, it is best to be out in the sunshine; just sitting full in the sun is the best cure. That and Metatone, three times a day after meals. I am sure you will feel quite different after a course of it.
>
> I am much looking forward to Lismore and hope you will soon be fit enough. How many days do you think we should aim at being there? I could I think come on Friday 27 May, to Monday 30 May. I think end of May would show Lismore at its best, dont you?

By 19 May all was confirmed and Seton was able to write:

> . . . the letter has come this morning from Mrs MacGregor, Balygrundle – 'Sir, I will indeed be happy to give the Laird of Inverailort and Mr Seton Gordon lodgings for the weekend 27 May to 30 May. Please let me know the day you will arrive'.
>
> I do hope you are always getting fitter, & the long range weather forecast says warmer weather should set in about 24 May, so it ought to be lovely on Lismore the last weekend of May and I am so much looking forward to it.
>
> Pipe-Major Brown is to play at the Borreraig Cairn on 25 May. He has never been in Skye. The Queen has given him special leave and Flora has invited him to stay.

They stayed at the MacGregor farmhouse at Balygrundle on the east side of the island, and Seton's weather prediction had proved accurate. An expedition across the island to Bernera, a small island off the south-west corner of Lismore was completed in full sunshine and the weekend provided a lift in spirits for his companion. Not long after the weekend on Lismore, Francis Cameron-Head was honoured with a Knighthood in the Order of the Hospital of St John of Jerusalem, which brought speedy congratulations from Seton:

> I was so very glad Francis, as you have worked hard and quietly without ostentation for the order and it is good to feel that you were appreciated – I am addressing this letter to you as SIR Francis Cameron-Head, and I feel I should always thus address you – though for some reason this is not done. As you know, the title Sir, was at one time used to denote those of learning – for example Ministers.
>
> I wish I could do more to help the Order but being so deaf it is not much good my attending meetings . . . Seton.

The Golden Eagle – King of Birds was in the final stages. In a separate section Seton Gordon wrote an account of the eight consecutive years that he watched this one eyrie. He continued watching these, or other birds in the same area for the remainder of his life. He again stressed that the observations were not intended to be a scientific account of the golden eagle's life history, but were meant to give the ordinary reader a picture of the day to day home life of the bird throughout the year:

> Other naturalists have been able to make only occasional observations of this home life. I believe, therefore, that my watching of these birds is unique in having been made all the year round, during eight years on one pair of eagles. I have learnt during this long period that this particular pair – though I cannot say that this applies to all golden eagles everywhere – are mated and remain so throughout the year with every sign of devotion towards each other. I have now known this pair for a total of eleven years – I have seen them grow up and take to family cares and I have admired their excellence as mates and parents. How can I regard them as anything but my friends? I cannot regard them with the cold scientific eye and consider their hormones, their glandular reactions, or their behaviour complexes . . .

During the last few weeks of observation Seton and Audrey lost their collie Dugie, who succumbed to old age. All their dogs were loved, but not so much was written about Dugie as of the earlier collies, Dileas and Dara. No Gordon dog lacked exercise and Seton estimated that in the course of visiting the eyrie, Dugie had walked at least 1500 miles with his master. Many times they were also accompanied by the much smaller, but equally keen walker, Morag, the Cairn terrier.

Seton again crossed the country to Deeside, where he again met Adam Watson. Now twenty-five, Watson had taken up a career in natural history and in 1955 he joined Aberdeen University's Unit of Grouse and Moorland Ecology, operating at Glen Esk. He had also decided to marry, which had brought a postcard from Seton Gordon in March:

> Dear Adam,
>
> Is it true you are marrying a Golden Eagle or is it only a rumour, and you are really engaged to the Snowy Owl of Beinn MacDhui?
>
> Anyhow, warm congratulations to you both.
>
> S. G.
>
> Thanks for note on Eagle castings. Your Derry nature notes most vivid. The Eagle book is down in Collins' June list.

Adam's wife to be, Jenny, was secretary at Aberdeen University's Statistics Department. They were married a few weeks later and by chance Seton met them at Nell McDonald's cottage when they were en route to camp high in the Cairngorms to count ptarmigan. In a follow-up postcard he said:

> Please tell the Snowy Owl that I think she is the perfect mate for a mountain and bird lover. Many congratulations to you both.

As early as 1946 Watson was, in the opinion of Professor Wynne-Edwards of the University of Aberdeen, emerging as the most active and knowledgeable ornithologist in the counties of Banff, Aberdeenshire and Kincardineshire. He took a degree at Aberdeen and chose a study of ptarmigan for his PhD.

Watson became both a climber and a cross-country skier, and in doing so it is possible that he took on a wider perspective of the Cairngorms than Seton Gordon. His postgraduate work and subsequently main area of interest is ptarmigan and grouse ecology. By this time his knowledge of these birds far exceeded that of Seton Gordon, yet he does not diminish the contribution made by his mentor. In 1983, long after election as a Fellow of the prestigious Royal Society of Edinburgh, in a paper on Ecology, Watson wrote:

> Seton Gordon was a link between the old naturalists and the animal ecologists, showing aspects of both in his books on natural history. It was particularly on golden eagles that he brought an ecological approach to questions of numbers, breeding, food supply, and traditional behaviour (1955) . . . he wrote on a wide range of ecological issues, such as weather affecting animal numbers and behaviour, and deer preventing regeneration of the Old Caledonian Forest by over-browsing'.

As Seton had predicted, *The Golden Eagle – King of Birds* was released and put on the shelves by the end of August. The Romeike and Curtice clipping service sent thirty-eight reviews to Upper Duntuilm. It is in many ways a remarkable book and the reviewers were quick to realise this. Few were ornithologists and to read a book by one who had spent fifty years closely observing one bird species was a rare thing for them. There were also reviews from France, the United States and Canada.

A review appeared in the *Natural History Magazine*, published in the United States:

> It is quickly apparent that this book is much more than an account of golden eagle watching in the Scottish Highlands. It is the document of a glorious, harassed, controversial, and often savagely treated creature as seen through the eyes of a perceptive naturalist who for half a century has lived among eagles . . .
>
> Inevitably it must tell the sorry tales of our own South-west, and it is a testament to Mr Gordon that, with all his love for this great bird, he presents an unbiased, unemotional report.
>
> The conservationist and the bird-watcher will find provocative material in this book. There is more to these problems in America than the mere squandering of great riches in golden eagles along the lines of the passenger pigeon and the buffalo. Perhaps this report will help us to see the problem for what it really is and to deal fairly with it; else we will have the familiar

> situation of a succeeding generation leaping to 'save' a great bird when only a fragment of the population remains . . .

Although, as many of the reviewers pointed out, there were few tables in the book, there was information on the status of the golden eagle in the following countries and regions: South-West Asia, South-East Europe, North Africa, North, Central and South America, Norway, Sweden, Finland, Denmark, Russia, Estonia, Germany, Switzerland, Austria, France, Italy, Spain, India and Japan. There is also a worldwide list of animals on which the various eagle populations feed. *The Golden Eagle – King of Birds* sold well in the United States and in the early 1970s was translated into Japanese. A copy was presented to the Oriental Books Department of the Oxford Bodleian Library.

There was firm news about the Loch nan Uamh cairn by May, 1956. Seton suggested that as well as Angus MacPherson, the '45 Association's Honorary Piper, John MacKinnon, the stone-mason chosen to build the cairn and also a piper, should be asked to play. A letter on the cairn's progress was received from the Secretary of the '45 Association.

That summer was an exciting one in the west Highlands. In August the Queen, accompanied by the Duke of Edinburgh and Princess Margaret, came to Skye, as her parents had done in 1933. On the 14th Her Majesty visited Dunvegan Castle, which added to an already important day for Clan MacLeod. Seton wrote to Francis about the forthcoming visit:

> You are a better historian than me. What would you say was the last occasion on which a reigning Monarch visited Portree and Dunvegan?
>
> King Edward VII when on the *Victoria and Albert* landed at Uig incognito but did not go further than the pier, so that hardly counts as a visit.

14 August was the date of the coming of age of Dame Flora's grandsons, John and Patrick. It was also the day when John was accepted as Tanaister and heir nominate by the clan, during a MacLeod Parliament, with representatives from all the major Commonwealth countries and the United States. Only a few days before, it was arranged that the Queen would come to lunch on that day. No reigning monarch had visited the Castle since the sixteenth century, and in a talk to young clan members during the 1968 Parliament, Dame Flora told them of the excitement when the Queen came to Dunvegan:

> Staying at the Castle were two New Zealanders, two Canadians, two Australians and one American. I asked whether we might all have lunch with the Queen and she consented, so we had a wonderful Commonwealth luncheon party on that day and I am terribly happy to think we all shared it.

Seton Gordon had an opportunity for a conversation with the Queen and Princess Margaret when he was presented to them in Portree. The next day he left Skye for the Glenfinnan Gathering. Captain Alwyne Farquharson of Invercauld

A pair of Golden Eagles taken by Seton Gordon (reproduced by kind permission of British Birds*)*

had agreed to be honorary Chief of the Day and arrived with Pipe-Major Robert Brown of Balmoral.

Those invited to be honorary Chief of the Day are chosen for their historical connection, scholarship, or promotion of Scottish affairs at home and overseas. Captain Farquharson represented a clan that supported both the 1715 and 1745 attempts to take the Crown. The Farquharsons were a part of the Confederation of Clan Chattan. A famous forebear, Anne Farquharson, married Angus MacIntosh, twenty-second Chief of the Clan and twenty-third Chief of Clan Chattan. In 1745 he was in service with Loudon's Highlanders who, as this Campbell name suggests, were on the side of the Hanoverians. His wife, aged twenty at the time, set about recruiting his clansmen and led them to join the Prince. She distinguished herself throughout the campaign, on one occasion repulsing 1500 government troops who were about to attack Moy Hall while the Prince was under her roof. Defending the house were five well-placed servants, who did a lot of shouting! It became known as the Rout of Moy. She was taken prisoner after Culloden. With a background so rich in the annals of the Jacobite cause, there were few people better qualified than Captain Farquharson to accept the honour of the Chieftainship of the Day at Glenfinnan.

In the day's piping events Pipe-Major Robert Brown was first in *piobaireachd* for his rendering of *'Patrick Og MacCrimmon'* and Donald MacPherson came second with *'I Got a Kiss of the King's Hand'*.

With Glenfinnan barely behind them the Cameron-Heads began preparations for the cairn unveiling on 4 October. They were helped by Seton, who enthusiastically suggested names of people to invite. When the day of the unveiling dawned the weather could not have been worse. Seton wrote:

> No one who was present will forget the ferocity of that early October day, when the high hills were already deep in snow and the hail lay thick to the tidemark. Opening the ceremony, the Laird of Inverailort spoke strongly of the loyalty and devotion of the Jacobites of today to their sovereign Queen, and their joy that they now have another Prince Charles.

A full account of the ceremony appeared in the *Oban Times*:

> Standing in that hail-raked promontory, this drenched and chilled hundred or so members and friends of the '45 Association had come from many parts of Scotland and England too, to pay homage to the memory of the Young Pretender. They lustily sang 'Sound the Pibroch loud and high from John o' Groats to the Isle of Skye'.
>
> The Countess of Erroll, High Constable of Scotland, one of whose forebears was an active Jacobite, unveiled the cairn and then Mr John MacKinnon, Arisaig, who built the cairn, played two great *piobaireachds 'In Praise of Morag'* and *'My King has Landed at Moidart'*.
>
> The pipes skirled again, this time played by Angus MacPherson, whose forebear, John MacPherson, was present on that fateful day 210 years ago. Angus, who like his ancestor, had been piper to Cluny MacPherson, put his

heart into his rendering of *'The Prince's Salute'* and his grandfather's own setting of *'Lochaber No More'*.

As the plaintive notes were tossed away on the wind the thoughts of those who listened turned to that far-off day when the Prince sailed from Scotland's shores forever.

Under the crest of the '45 Association, the plaque reads:

A REIR BEUL-AITHRIS
IS ANN BHO'N TR'AIGH SO
A SHE ÒL AM PRIONNSA TEARLACH
AIR AIS DO'N FHRAING

THIS CAIRN MARKS
THE TRADITIONAL SPOT FROM WHICH
PRINCE CHARLES EDWARD STUART
EMBARKED FOR FRANCE
20TH SEPTEMBER 1746.

ERECTED BY THE FORTY-FIVE ASSOCIATION 1956

Over Christmas, Audrey developed a bad cold which she could not shake off. By the third week of January, 1957 it had turned to bronchitis and Seton was concerned for her. She was put on M and B tablets (sulphur pyrin) but her temperature would not go down. Seton then heard that Francis Cameron-Head was again unwell and wrote on the 25th:

Dear Francis,

I do hope you feel better? This is one of the Dead Months (*Na Miosan Marbh*) mentioned in *Carmina Gadelica*.

Audrey remains in bed with a bad cough and altho' the bronchitis has cleared on one side, the other side is still affected. The doctor now prescribes penicillin injections.

Today I have a heavy chest cold which adds to the difficulty and am staying in. We have a very nice couple, which makes such a difference . . .

I always look forward to expeditions, for you and I have done so many in friendship – that one from the head of Glen Nevis, past your ancestral home in Glen Dessary, would be particularly interesting . . .

More letters followed in February on historical matters. One of these dwelt on the Cattach, a book of psalms thought to have been written by St Columba. Another note was full of praise for a book by Eona MacNicol, *Columb of Derry*, based on the time of St Columba. In a letter on the 25th he told Francis, 'The day approaches when the long Arctic twilight will be banished by the sun and you will sit in your *grianan* [bower] with the sun's rays renewing your youth. He went on:

Your letter on Columb of Derry is a masterpiece of scholarly thinking (and writing). I felt sure the book would appeal to you as it did to me, and as you say, she makes her heroes LIVE. How thrilling for you to have seen the Cattach*. I have often read of it, but had not realised until I received your letter, that it is no less than Calum Cille's copy of the St Jerome's Psalter. It must have been inspiring to have looked on St Columba's actual handwriting. Audrey is getting about again, but was rather pulled down by her bronchitis. The raven was sitting on Saturday and the golden eagle was building two weeks ago. Give Putchaidh my love. Seton.

*(The Cattach, Cathach, is preserved in the Royal Irish Academy, Dublin)

Seton's interest in the Cattach was all-consuming and he wrote on 5 May: 'The Cattach is indeed enthralling and I am reading the masterly notes and introduction with great care. Thank you, many times, for sending me this valuable paper. What I'd love to do, some time, is to go to Eire with you. Would you come? . . . Audrey is greatly heartened by your encouragement in her attempt to keep the Highland Home Industries alive at Kilmuir. She is writing to you, I think, today'.

The Highland Home Industries was ailing, despite the year by year increase in tourism on the island. It became one of Audrey's crusades to save it and Francis Cameron-Head had generously offered financial help:

5 May, 1957.

Dear Francis,

Thank you very much for all your interest in my plans for the Highland Home Industries depot here.

It is very good of you to say you will invest a few hundreds in my venture. I hope to have a meeting of the interested parties to see the property and hear all details. I find it very difficult to get any satisfactory information from HHI headquarters!

The ten workers, three of whom have worked for HHI twenty-nine years, and none less than ten years and the basket maker about fourty years! – were paid off on 30 April without even a word of thanks for loyal service! I will write a full report of what happens at the meeting. Yours ever, Audrey.

Before his help could be put into action, Francis died suddenly on 14 May. He had suffered an aneurysm while he and Putchaidh were preparing to leave Inverailort for a few days. He never regained consciousness.

What thoughts went through Seton's mind over the next few days he did not record, but in his diary he continued to note the events of the natural world which were so vital to his being, and which he had shared with Francis. He had, many times, expressed eloquently his perception of life and death and what he saw as the fine border between both these experiences. Now suddenly, his friend was dead:

14th May – Took A. to boat : Mowed Lawns : Heard Francis had gone.

15th – Brilliant day : Two terns fishing at low tide off Scarpall and oyster catchers being robbed of sand-eels by common gulls. Thunder & hail 5 p.m.

16th – A bar of grey mist suspended 7 a.m. across Craig Sneosdal – clear light. Tremendous rain at Scourr – almost cloudburst. Saw black-throated diver on Loch Garry. Red rose out at Glenfinnan. Reached Lochailort 8 p.m.

17th – Wild day : Heavy squalls : Played at Francis' grave the second variation of the 'Lament for Donald Ban MacCrimmon' and John MacKinnon played the ground of 'Lament for the Children'. Butterwort in flower.

18th – Left Inverailort 10 a.m. Started up Allt an Utha 10:50 a.m. – 1:25 p.m. reached the ridge at about 2400 ft. *Azalea procumbens* in bloom. Reached home 11:15 p.m.

Allt an Utha lies on the north side of the road, just west of Glenfinnan in the wild reaches of that romantic country. From Sgurr an Utha, Glen Dessary and Glen Pean lie to the north, and to the south-west Loch Shiel and the hills of Moidart give way to the blue islands of Rhum and Eigg. Due west lay Loch nan Uamh and its recently erected cairn. The lonely ridge provided wide views of a land filled with memories of a dear close friend, and the many outings they shared in exploring it.

It was, perhaps, good for Seton's spirits that another visit to Switzerland had been planned for late June and early July. In their previous trips, Seton and Audrey had spent time observing the Alpine swift. The early summer of 1957 was a cool one in Switzerland, so much so that it disturbed the nesting cycle of these birds and some even died of cold and hunger. Before leaving Skye they had arranged to meet with Swiss ornithologist, Hans Arn-Willi at Solothurn, in the northern part of the country. On 25 June they spent an evening in his company to watch a colony of the Alpine swift high up in the round tower of the Jesuit church, a building which dates back to 1689.

The colony was one of the largest in Europe, and that summer it had 169 pairs. The highest number recorded was 229. Arn-Willi had observed them for many years and had kept careful records of their breeding habits and population cycles. He told them that the usual number of eggs in a clutch was three, but that year because of the weather, most nests contained only two. The nests themselves were unusual in that they were made from the bud cases of the beech, blown from the trees and caught in mid-air by the birds. With the added saliva of the nest builders, an adhesive like substance was made which created a strong bonding. The result was a rubber-like structure, so pliable that their host demonstrated how a nest could be flexed without it breaking.

While they waited for the birds to return from their foraging, Arn-Willi told them that the Alpine swift usually makes its appearence at least a month earlier than the common swift. The young leave in September but the parents remain behind for up to two to three weeks longer. The actual stay, for both young and old, was almost twice as long as the common swift, which remained for about three months.

It was a memorable experience to be in the ancient tower to await the return of the swifts as the twilight deepened outside. The first birds appeared at about seven o'clock, coming in through small holes under the eaves. Those that had young to feed brought the food in their pouches. Dusk was well advanced when they left the church, but late-comers were still seen flying towards the small holes in the tower. Other birds seen were a snowfinch, wall creeper, rock bunting, black redstart, ring ouzel and chough. The bird which fascinated them most was the wall creeper, especially its plumage which they described as 'almost tropical in its brilliance'. Above a glacier they saw a golden eagle.

On 19 August, Arthur, Lord Elibank, wrote a letter to Seton in which he voiced his admiration for his friend's accomplishments:

> Dear Seton,
>
> I was thinking today what a tremendous influence for the spreading of good and beauty you have exerted – and are continuing to exert – on the life of the nation through your splendid and inspiring books and articles on animate and inanimate nature.
>
> And none felt this more strongly to be so than your and my dear friend, Edward Grey of Fallodon, himself a knowledgeable lover and master of the same subjects. With all best wishes, yours ever, Arthur Elibank.

Lord Elibank was another keen amateur ornithologist, who between 1910 and 1914 was Parliamentary Private Secretary to Sir Edward Grey, and shared his enthusiasm for bird watching. Lord Elibank's letters show a mischievous sense of humour. He and Seton had an exchange of letters with Encylopaedia Britannica over an erroneous statement on Great Northern Divers. The entry said it nested in the Hebrides. Elibank put Seton up to seeking a retraction by composing letters and sending them to Upper Duntuilm for Seton's signature. The retraction took some time and during the exchange Lord Elibank wrote:

> Recently I had an accident on a bus – and I was lucky to get away with a very badly bruised back instead of a broken spine!
>
> Whilst having an enforced rest I had irritable thoughts about all evil doers(!), and one who stood at the head of the list was he who, most rudely, refused to answer your letters on the breeding habits of our friend the Great Northern Diver, a sleek and handsome bird who, we will hope, is duly grateful for the interest we have displayed in him! Having been most contemptuously ignored, we must now return to the attack . . .

After a delay of several months the Managing Editor of Britannica conceded: 'We have checked with two ornithologists and find that your point is well taken. Our consultants were unable to confirm the statement in question. In view of this we are deleting the reference to the Hebrides in the Britannica article'.

An elated Lord Elibank wrote: 'I think all right-minded persons will agree that we can lift up our voices and chant, 'we have won a famous victory!' And when, in the great Beyond, we meet the spirit of the progenitor of all Great Northern Divers, we can tell him the story of our successful battle to have eliminated from the Encyclopaedia Britannica the false statement that his spouse and their descendants nested in the Hebrides! . . . and we may expect to be greeted by a Guard of Honour of G.N. Divers when we cross the ferryboat on to the further bank of the River Styx!'

The praise given to Seton in Lord Elibank's August 1957 letter can only have been of great encouragement and solace to Seton Gordon, who, with Francis very much on his mind, wrote to Lochiel in early October with the beginning of a plan to honour the memory of his late friend:

> . . . Two or three of Francis' old friends have felt that what we would really like is a cairn to his memory. The feeling is that you should take a leading part in anything which is done in that line. Lady Whyatt, an old friend of Francis thinks we might have a small meeting in November – a preliminary one to discuss the idea . . .

Seton wrote to the *Times* announcing an appeal. In early 1958 a cairn was erected to the memory of the late Laird of Inverailort. It stands on the shore of Loch Eilt near the memorial to his grandfather, Duncan Cameron of Inverailort.

CHAPTER
14

A TIME FOR SADNESS AND A TIME FOR JOY

IN THE MID-1950S, Sir Jamie Stormonth-Darling, Director of the National Trust for Scotland, introduced natural history cruises around the Scottish coast. The earlier ones were led by James Robertson and Alastair Dunnett, editor of the *Scotsman*. The cruises were so successful that within two years the Bergen Line ship *Meteor* was chartered. It accommodated 150 passengers. Each May, two cruises of seven or eight days' duration were arranged. The Earl of Wemyss and March was another cruise leader but in 1959 he was appointed The Queen's Lord High Commissioner to the General Assembly of the Church of Scotland and was available for only the first part of the cruise. The leader that year was the late Lord Polwarth. It helped to have naturalists on board with previous knowledge of the locations visited. Seton and Audrey were ideal candidates to act as nature interpreters and, encouraged by Lord Wemyss, they agreed to accompany the 1959 cruise. (See Appendix 8)

The *Meteor* sailed from Leith on Wednesday, 6 May and the first call was Fair Isle. Here the cruise participants were thrilled to see an American song sparrow, the first ever sighting in the British Isles. After watching Seton and Audrey together on Fair Isle, a fellow passenger later wrote:

> The vision of the Seton Gordons walking together last Thursday made many of us remark on the blissful happiness of a perfect partnership. There was so much unselfish thought for the other, such mutual respect and understanding, so much brightness and good cheer. These conditions inspire and exhilarate others.

On the night of Friday 8 May, the ship sailed for Lerwick. Lady Marjorie Dalrymple had a cabin next to the Gordons and at some unknown hour in the night she was aware of a short 'heavy groan' coming from their cabin. Without his hearing-aid Seton would have been quite unaware of any unusual noise. The Earl of Wemyss was asleep in the pilot's cabin and he recalled:

> Seton came up to the pilot's cabin at about 7:30 a.m. where I was dozing in my bunk. He shook me gently and said twice, 'Audrey's dead'. I arose and did what I could, which was little enough.

> I remember thinking with what marvellous tact and consideration that charming lady had behaved, because Lerwick was the only place between the beginning and the end of the cruise where not only would the ship be tied up to a quayside, but also there were undertakers, coffins, a Registrar and a regular mail steamer to Aberdeen. Not only that, but all the passengers were to go ashore later in the morning and visit the Broch of Clickhimin about a mile away, so the whole process of removing her body could be done quite unobserved.

Seton wrote in his diary, 'When I looked at Audrey in her upper berth at 7:30 a.m., she had gone. Woke David and told him this news'. Arrangements for a seat on the next plane were made for Seton, and Lord Wemyss accompanied him to Edinburgh to be met by Caitriona and Simon.

The writer who had observed them with such perception on their last day together continued:

> The supreme tribute that could be ascribed to Audrey is that she would never have us be sad, but rather that we should each in our small and different ways try to help her beloved partner, the devoted and respected friend of so many of us.
>
> If this succeeds in some measure to express the feelings of such a host of friends, we can have some idea of the shock which her family will have suffered. Many of us cannot be in Skye on Thursday for a memorial service, but there our thoughts and prayers will surely be.

Seton had agreed to write a piece for the *Scotsman* on this cruise and Alastair Dunnett was touched that he provided it despite Audrey's death. At the end of the item, when he described rejoining the ship after Fair Isle, he said:

> I little thought that this was to be the last of many happy expeditons we were to have together. The kindness I received from both the members of the National Trust for Scotland and all the *Meteor*'s crew and passengers made me realise that my wife was well loved, and thanks for a good and useful life that ended that night, swiftly and without suffering were due to be given to the Giver of All Good Things.

Audrey was cremated in Aberdeen and her ashes scattered on the summit of the Braeriach, but a memorial service was held at the Kilmuir Church of Scotland on Thursday 21 May. The list of those attending was long, swelled by many local people, among them Jonathan MacDonald who led the singing of the twenty-third Psalm.

It was Audrey's wish to have her ashes scattered in the Cairngorms where she and Seton had spent many happy days bird-watching. In *Highland Days*, Seton wrote of this journey and its effect on Morag, the Cairn terrier:

> It is a sad day for a dog when the earthly life of his or her mistress ends.

Audrey Gordon, early 1920s

Morag was one of a small and sorrowful party who one summer day climbed to the high Cairngorms to fulfil a wish expressed by my wife, that her ashes might be scattered here, the home of snow bunting, ptarmigan and dotterel where we had spent many days on the Roof of Scotland. The plateau was bright with innumerable flowers of the cushion pink, a plant which had often gladdened my wife's heart and was now to be her memorial. During the

> ceremony Morag lay curled up, tired and miserable. When we had planted a small plant to mark the place and I was kneeling on the ground, Morag came to me and did a thing she had never done before – she began to lick my knees. This action deeply impressed me, for she was reserved by nature and did not show affection when on a walk. This was obviously an occasion of tremendous sadness for her: how I wished that at that moment she might have been gifted with human speech to tell me her thoughts.
>
> That evening, as we were slowly descending the hill to the deep glen beneath, Morag suddenly stopped and showed her sorrow by prolonged and sorrowful barking. The events of the day evidently made a strong impression on her sensitive mind.

In a two year period Seton had lost his closest friend and his wife. It is to his credit and strength of character that his grief was a personal thing. There were several references to his missing both of them, but outwardly he remained the same convivial companion and his interest in events did not diminish. He continued to visit the eagles and noted their progress.

By mid-month he was at Dalness and, with Pamela and Follett Bell, went by train from Bridge of Orchy to the Corrour Forest nursery, and over two days climbed Chno Dearg and Beinn Eibhinn. In the next several days at Dalness, he assisted in one of the first attempts to reintroduce the sea-eagle to the Highlands. Patrick Sandeman was a great friend of Follett Bell's and of Tom Weir, with whom he still enjoys several outings each year into the hills. Patrick modestly refers to his part in this sea-eagle venture as 'minor' but it was born out of a wish to see this bird once again flying over the Highlands.

Knowing that they were still found in Norway he made enquiries about paying to have some young birds brought over to Scotland. Recalling the activities at Dalness during that week, Patrick Sandeman explained:

> I was in correspondence with a Norwegian about paying ransom money for saving young birds that might otherwise be killed by hunters. Thus I paid £10 for each for two young birds and an older one, brought in via Newcastle and Edinburgh. I collected and took them straight to Dalness, where Seton was staying at the time. It was all rather exciting, tethering the birds out, and we let them loose after two weeks. One bird was caught by a farmer in Appin when it raided his chicken house, and was sent to the London Zoo. The second bird was caught in a trap near the Otter Ferry, Loch Fyneside and the third was not seen again.

This attempt was entirely Patrick Sandeman's initiative, aided by Follett Bell and on this occasion Seton Gordon was merely an observer. It was a valiant effort and was not repeated until 1968, when the RSPB released four sea-eagles on Fair Isle. These birds, again from Norway, were taken there by George Waterston and Johan Willoghs. That it also failed was no one's fault, least of all the RSPB staff. Desmond Nethersole-Thompson blamed it on the sea-eagles' inability to catch young fulmars and to stay clear of the 'deadly oil' that they spray at attackers. The birds survived for some months but eventually all succumbed. (See Appendix 9)

In the months following Audrey's death, many people sustained Seton in his sorrowing, and he was frequently away from Upper Duntuilm visiting friends. Looking after himself was not something that he enjoyed or cared to do on a long-term basis. One person who was able to offer sympathy, because of her own recent bereavement, was a friend of both Seton and Audrey, Elizabeth Badger. Her husband Colonel Reginald Badger had died in 1957. He commanded the 12th Lancers, and had long been an invalid as a result of being wounded in the first war. Biddlesden Manor, a 175-acre estate was purchased by the Badgers in 1932. They set about building stables and paddocks, eventually creating a successful horse-breeding business which Betty, as she liked to be called, continued to operate after his death.

Betty was an accomplished rider whose knowledge of horses was equal to that of her late husband. After Reginald died, Betty began staying more frequently in the north, at Shiel Bridge. She had stalked in the Highlands over several years, was keenly interested in bird-watching and began to share this with Seton, as they spent more time together. Betty had two dogs, a spaniel, Rain, and a golden labrador, Honey, who was trained as a guide dog, but was not accepted after training.

By the end of 1959 a decision was made to marry after a suitable time of mourning. Their families and friends were delighted with the news, believing that two such charming people deserved continued happiness for their remaining years. Their engagement was on 2 April, 1960 and only a few people were told at the time. Mrs Putchi Cameron-Head was one of these, and refrained from letting the news out even though people were trying hard to confirm rumours. When it became official there were, inevitably, amusing stories associated with 'gossip'. She said that when people were told that Betty bred mares, the information was misinterpreted and one woman said to her 'Isn't Seton's wife-to-be rather odd – breeding bears for Whipsnade Zoo?'

The wedding was on 2 June in the small church at Glen Shiel with only family members and close friends present. Jonathan MacDonald came from Skye to sing for the occasion. With him was John Graham who, in 1958, had returned to Upper Duntuilm.

Seton's life changed significantly. Between them, he and Betty possessed three homes, Biddlesden Park, Upper Duntuilm and a cottage which Betty built at Shiel Bridge. It was named 'Grianan' (the bower). Duntuilm was kept because Seton did not want to break his ties with Skye or with his many friends there. Several months of the year were spent in the Highlands, divided between Shiel Bridge and Skye, where Betty became a willing watcher of the Trotternish golden eagles.

Adjustments were required for both of them. Seton had new friends to make at Biddlesden and new areas for the exploration of bird habitats in the many reservoirs surrounding Biddlesden. The lakes on the estate contained waterfowl, and the coots soon came to know him. Seton soon endeared himself to the staff. Head groom, Desmond Price, had worked on the estate, except for army

Biddlesden Manor

service, since 1932. Gertrude, his wife had worked in the manor house. To them, Seton was a most wonderful master and Desmond especially enjoyed the time spent walking around the estate with him. They recall that he was most appreciative of any small kindness and always offered a gracious thank you. It impressed them that he was always performing kindnesses and would not let a tramp go by without offering him help, as he and Audrey had done at Upper Duntuilm.

Betty was of course familiar with the west Highlands and had visited Upper Duntuilm. As Seton's wife she was soon accepted by his neighbours. It was universally regarded as a wonderful match, which did not diminish the place Audrey held for almost forty-five years.

Reading Seton Gordon's diary notes after his marriage to Betty, they became fuller as the years passed. There appeared to be no particular pattern to the couple's movement from house to house. He enjoyed staying at Biddlesden and it is strange to read the full nature notes of the surrounding English countryside after years of writing only on the Highlands. Betty made frequent trips to the Newmarket sales each year and Seton sometimes went with her. They seldom drove between Biddlesden and the west Highlands, preferring to use the rail-car/sleeper service from Crewe. Their pattern was based on events and they were just as likely to be found on Skye in winter if there was a reason to be there.

For the first time there was no pressure to write in order to survive, though his pieces were still eagerly accepted. His new wife had a more than adequate personal income, plus a large country home, and their lifestyle reflected this. He continued to enjoy all the pursuits that had absorbed him throughout his life and he was totally in touch with everyday events. All major news items, both national and international, were noted in his diary.

This included reports on the catastrophe that had befallen some bird populations in heavily farmed areas of the British Isles in the early months of 1960. Dead birds were reported in large numbers and many mammals were sharing the same fate. The blame was eventually laid on the treatment of seed with the chemicals dieldrin, aldrin and heptachlor – unknown names that would soon become household words as citizen groups went into action. A special committee of the House of Commons was appointed to examine the situation. It recommended an immediate ban on these toxins.

While field bird populations were suffering such heavy losses, one bird was making a comeback on Speyside. In 1958 ospreys began nesting again at Loch Garten for the first time in many years. The nests were watched over by the RSPB, led by George Waterston, Scottish Representative of the Society. The programme got off to a bad start that first year, and Seton noted: 'Despite a careful watch the eggs were taken on the dark and misty night of 3 June'.

Fortunately a greater vigil was kept in succeeding years and the only failures during the 1960s were '63 and '66, when the nests were lost through gales. Seton went to see the nest in 1960 when the first young were successfully reared. Improbable though it seems, a misunderstanding grew between him and George Waterston. From Seton Gordon's perspective it was perfectly natural that he should want to see first-hand the progress at Loch Garten. From the perspective of the RSPB, they had a tightly controlled nest protection scheme and guests, however knowledgeable or hallowed, could be considered a nuisance if they did not observe all the rules. It is quite certain that Seton was unaware of the impact he was having on the wardens, who were no doubt overawed by this 'grand old man' of nature, as some now called him. For some time George Waterston was given to referring to Seton as 'Old Satan'! The relationship was fortunately healed by the intervention of other RSPB staff, among them Roy Dennis and Michael Everett, both of whom still hold key positions in the Society.

Writing some years later, Seton was quick to give full credit to the dedicated watchers: 'Mr. George Waterston and his team of enthusiastic helpers deserve the thanks and admiration of all bird lovers. I was indebted to the RSPB for the use of their forward hide in making the observations recorded'. That early team included writer Tom Weir, Louis Stewart, Bert Axwell, Bob Dawkin, Valerie Thom and Betty Garden. A rope was put in place at night between the forward hide and the rest tent, so that in the event of robbers appearing help could be immediately summoned.

When a robbery attempt ended with broken eggs left on the ground, George Waterston made a daring proposal to then Scottish Director Philip Brown: invite the public, set up high-powered binoculars and encourage donations. In the early months, several thousand people came – with money! It provided an opportunity for ordinary citizens to show their concern for diminishing wildlife habitat by participating. The money enabled the RSPB to protect areas of habitat for other bird species that might otherwise have been lost to development.

The Loch Garten eyrie was in the crown of an old Scots fir, on a small dry knoll in what Seton described as 'typical greenshank country'. The surrounding ground was acid and spongy and most of the trees were quite stunted. The osprey tree was taller, on its drier rise.

The young ospreys grew visibly during the week Seton spent in the hide. In the last couple of days, one of them began wing exercises, once so vigorously that he rose a couple of feet into the air. 30 July was Seton's last morning at the eyrie. The strongest of the young birds again practised his exercises and as Seton watched he suddenly rose almost vertically and hovered over the eyrie, keeping station perhaps 6 feet above the floor of the nest. To Seton this first hover-flight of a young osprey was a thrilling sight. He had not seen the young of any species rise vertically from the nest and return to it on a first flight. On this last day Seton noted:

> The young ospreys would soon leave their sanctuary and face the dangers which beset all birds of prey from the man with the gun.

He was at Invercauld in September and set out early one morning with Morag specifically to see if, after one of the hottest summers in memory for the Highlands, the snow in Garbh Choire Mor had entirely gone. On the previous occasion there he found a small quantity of snow and some dampness on the spot. In the scree Seton found parsley ferns with newly sprouted leaves, and several varieties of alpine plants were showing flowers for a second time. After a difficult descent into the corrie, he reached its base and examined the ground where the snow would normally be. He wrote:

> The snow had gone, completely and without trace. Gone were the small streams from the snow which usually moisten the ground. Instead of being soft and damp, it was dry and even dusty.

The most remarkable thing about that day was the absence of birdlife. He did not see a ptarmigan or grouse all day. The only bird he saw was a meadow pipit. The sun set behind the Braeriach as Seton and Morag started down towards the Dee. In the late afterglow the path was indistinct as he crossed the shoulder of Carn a' Mhaim. He observed: 'Fourteen hours earlier I had watched the morning light on the hills and glens here. Now a star shone near the zenith and chill air drifted up from the river'.

In the meantime, dinner was proceeding at Invercauld where among the guests was Robert Wolrige Gordon and his wife. Betty did not accompany Seton to Deeside this time, but she was surely aware of her new husband's penchant for arriving late for meals. Writing of that evening, Robert Wolrige Gordon, who was hoping to meet and chat with Seton after not seeing him for several years, said:

> There was a time when I had hoped to see him: it was 1960 and my wife and I were to dine on Upper Deeside. Seton did not appear until about 11 p.m. (we had an hour's drive and were just about to leave). He had been up to the source of the Dee where there was an eternal snowfield. It had melted for the first time since 1756 and he had been to see if there was any snow left. His hostess did not think this was a very good reason for being late for dinner; although indeed he did!

February 1961 found Seton and Betty at Upper Duntuilm. There was severe wind and rain, but outings took place to Glen Conan where they saw an Iceland redwing. Betty went south on the 16th but Seton remained for another ten days and soon followed his old interests, crossing the moor in the company of Morag. He found the 1959 eyrie repaired, but there was no sign of the eagles. Morag was now eleven years old and of the many dogs Seton had owned, she was regarded with special affection. It was all the more devastating to realise, by spring, that she was ailing.

The Holyrood Royal Garden Party was held on 28 June. Caitriona and her daughter Susan accompanied Seton and Betty and although they enjoyed talking to members of the Royal Family, Seton went with the knowledge that Morag was very sick. The next day she died, and Seton wrote, 'A tremendous loss of a loving companion and friend'. He took her body north to bury it on Skye.

Most of August and September was spent in the north to attend the Gatherings before returning to Biddlesden. In October they were joined by Follett and Pamela Bell. When their Highland friends came to stay it gave Seton and Betty an opportunity to show them the variety of birdlife on the estate and in the surrounding country. One of their favourite locations was Wilstone Reservoir, near Tring. On the Biddlesden lakes were mute swans, Canada geese, pochards, mallard, tufted ducks, goosander, and Seton's favourites, the cootes.

Follett Bell remembered that a feature of Biddlesden was Seton playing his pipes as friends arrived or departed. This was not reserved just for Scottish guests, and others were given the same welcome or send-off – whether they liked the pipes or not!

The pipes had played too important a part in Seton's life for him to put them aside when he was in England. In any case there were enough visitors from the piping fraternity to cause surprise to local people in Seton's early days at Biddlesden, as the sound of *piobaireachd* drifted across the English landscape. Both Archibald Campbell and his son, James, came for sessions. Another regular visitor was Iverach McDonald, retired foreign editor for *The Times* of London, and later associate editor. They first met at Glenfinnan, though he lived a short drive from Biddlesden. At his home near Oxford, Iverach McDonald has a large collection of piping records, including some rare ones of John MacDonald of Inverness, and Seton enjoyed listening to them. On an assignment to the United States, McDonald found one recorded at Glenfinnan. The cover was a photograph of John MacLellan playing, while Seton, Angus MacPherson and Colonel Jock were judging.

In the United States, Rachel Carson came into full prominence with her eloquently written book, *Silent Spring*, published in 1962. It presented a clear message that every country should be concerned with the overuse of pesticides and insecticides, and stressed a need for solid data. Data gathering was never Seton's style, and he was sometimes criticised for this by other natural history writers. While Carson and other naturalists came up with the hard evidence of environmental degradation, he continued to enjoy the simple contact with birds, though he did voice alarm when obvious differences in breeding patterns occurred.

This does not mean that Seton's life began to lack significance. Amateur naturalists continued writing to him to share exciting bird-watching experiences, and as a life member and Scientific Fellow of the Zoological Society, he received papers on many different subjects related to natural history, or research on phenomena, such as the Loch Ness monster.

From time to time, dramatic sightings of the Loch Ness monster were reported, though few were taken seriously by the public. A panel of scientists was brought together to look at the evidence presented by the sightings and to draw some conclusions. Their findings were presented in October 1962. The panel was headed by David James, MBE, DSC, MP and its members were: Adrian Head, MA; Dr N. B. Marshall, MA; J. E. Robson, MC, and John Buxton. All were chosen for their expertise in a field of natural history, the latter as a wildlife photographer.

Seton had maintained an interest in the monster after his first contact with Father Dieckhoff of the Fort Augustus Monastery many years before, and was given copies of his very full notes that included a record of sightings. One of the monks, Brother Horan, had a very clear sighting in May 1934, one of the best on record. Dieckhoff told Seton that monsters inhabit Loch Shiel and Loch Morar. The old people named the one in Loch Ness, '*An Niseag*', in Loch Shiel '*An Seileag*' and in Loch Morar '*A Mhorag*' (Gaelic – '*A Vhorag*'). Loch Morar is the second deepest body of water in western Europe at 1080 feet.

Another person with keen interest was Constance Whyte, a medical doctor, whose husband was the canal manager. With Seton Gordon's help she gained access to Father Dieckhoff's papers and in 1957 wrote a book on Highland monster phenomena, *More Than a Legend*. In the opinion of Elizabeth Montgomery-Campbell, who was responsible for organising the 1970 Loch Morar Survey, it was the best one written to that time on the subject. In a note to Seton Gordon following publication of the report, Whyte said, 'It does not really get us much further, but it could help to stop some of the nonsense, don't you think?'

Constance Whyte documented at least seventy sightings of the monster, one of them by the late Charles Farrell in May 1943. Farrell, father of Putchi Cameron-Head, saw the Loch Ness Monster at 5:15 a.m. on 25 May 1943, when on Royal Observer Corps duty. Another observer, in April 1947, was the Inverness-shire County Clerk, J.W. MacKillop, who, in the company of his son and two other men travelling with them had a good view of the monster for several minutes. At the next meeting of the County Council the standing orders were suspended so that MacKillop could give a first-hand account of the sighting.

Whyte had made an earlier contact with Seton in February 1955 when the echo sounding apparatus of a Peterhead trawler produced a graph outline of what could only be perceived as a large and unknown moving shape. In *A Highland Year* Seton Gordon wrote:

> I believe the Loch Ness Monster to be a species of large pinnipide which once inhabited several of the larger Highland lochs.
>
> There is general agreement among witnesses that the neck is long and slender and the body rarely appears above the surface. It is seen more frequently of late because the modern highway has an almost uninterrupted view of the loch. The creature is now, as it were, common property, but formerly those who saw it hesitated to talk of it, for fear of ridicule.

The scientific panel examined transcripts of oral evidence, film, both movie and stills, as well as written evidence from sources such as the Freshwater Biological Association's Laboratory and officials of the Ministry of Agriculture, Fisheries and Food. Their findings showed great empathy with the observers and an acknowledgement that all sightings pointed to the existence of an unexplained animate object in the loch. The Panel concluded:

> We find that there is some unidentified animate object in Loch Ness, which, if it be mammal, amphibian, reptile, fish, or mollusc of any known order, is of such size as to be worthy of careful scientific examination and identification. If it is not of a known order, it represents a challenge which is only capable of being answered by controlled investigation conducted on careful scientific principles.

This was not the last serious 'monster' investigation in which Seton Gordon took an interest.

A recognition of his contribution to nature photography came the following year with the publication of eleven photographs in *British Birds*. The pictures were published in the January 1964 issue and included five of golden eagles, all on the eyrie. In three the young are visible, but the most remarkable is of a male at the moment of dropping a young red grouse into the nest. The flies are swarming and every detail of the birds and the building materials of the eyrie are in sharp focus. The others are of a ptarmigan, dotterel, black-throated diver, whooper swan, puffin and the one of a greenshank pair exchanging on the nest.

Highland Days was published in late 1963. The chapters were mainly previously-published pieces and it was illustrated with black and white line drawings by Keith Shackleton. Several of the seventeen reviews collected by the clipping service regretted that books by Seton Gordon were becoming all too infrequent.

Included in the book were many memories of eagle watching in Trotternish. Though the eyrie was still occupied, the birds no longer laid each year and in 1964 no egg was produced. Seton questioned if pesticides used in sheep dip were having an effect in changing the eagles' breeding pattern. Dieldrin, used in sheep-dip, became suspect and was eventually banned. From then on things improved gradually but it took years to rebuild many of the species affected. Seton Gordon wrote to the Duke of Edinburgh and told him about his hopes and concerns for the Trotternish eagles. His Royal Highness replied with some encouraging news from the Balmoral estate. An eyrie near Pipe-Major Brown's house had been empty for years when, that spring Brown found it occupied by a pair with an eaglet. The Duke was of the opinion that they had moved in after being disturbed at another location. He ended: 'I'm glad you've been converted to the dangers of pesticides, I've been trying to get them controlled for several years'. There were several letter exchanges between them, all on matters relating to the countryside and its problems.

Jonathan MacDonald's father died in June, and Seton Gordon sent a condolence letter which his family still treasures:

3 July, 1964.

Dear Mrs Hector, Mary, and Jonathan,

So Hector is away, and you are left sorrowful. All is well with his soul, for he lived close to goodness, loving kindness and mercy.

It is wonderful for all of you to feel that you have been a loving and united family, tending Hector with affectionate care to the very end. You have been a fine example in these materialistic days, keeping bright and shining the old values.

You will all be weary, especially Mrs Hector, but you will find peace and rest, and I am sure, the nearness of Hector to you all. The inner meaning and beauty of life will come close to you. We both send all three of you our most sincere sympathy.

Yours most sincerely, Seton Gordon.

Jonathan's business was, by this time, flourishing, and his entrepeneurial spirit was becoming more evident. As well as the craft shop, it occurred to him that tourists might like to learn more about crofting and to see how the interior of a blackhouse might have looked. He negotiated with Seton Gordon to take over John Graham's old bothy, as John was now living in a cottage away from Upper Duntuilm. It took several months to make repairs and search for suitable items for interior and exterior displays, but the following year a croft museum was opened. Jonathan was also aware of the need for quality accommodation on the island and was looking for a suitable hotel to buy. The Duntulm Castle Hotel was still in the hands of Miss Kelly and she showed no inclination to dispose of it. However, he was prepared to bide his time until the right opportunity presented itself.

The museum was opened on 27 May 1965, by Seton Gordon. The interior, with its earth floor and simple furnishings, has caught the atmosphere of olden times and a byre was added next to the bothy. The thatched roofs are held down with ropes attached to large rocks. Around the buildings are a number of early farm implements. Colonel Jock, who had created a bothy's interior in a room at Viewfield, also made a speech. Angus Nicolson spoke on some of the old customs. There were displays of weaving, dying and waulking tweed.

A series of lectures were lined up for the last few months of the year. In early November, Seton Gordon was invited to Gordonstoun, where in the audience was His Royal Highness, Prince Charles. The slides were the same ones that had been used for years, black and white pictures mounted in glass. Many people who attended Seton's later talks were impressed at the way he brought these old pictures alive as he described how and where they were taken. The audience soon forgot their age because, like the lecturer, they were timeless. A few days after the lecture, Seton Gordon wrote to the Prince, inviting him to Skye, and he soon received a reply:

Windmill Lodge, Gordonstoun.
9 November, 1965.

Dear Mr. Seton Gordon,

Thank you very much indeed for your letter. It was very kind of you. I did enjoy the talk and the slides. They were simply marvellous. You seldom see such big pictures nowadays. You must have had a very interesting time photographing those eagles. Unfortunately I've never been very close to one. I've seen one or two while out stalking, though I don't remember seeing one while out with Brown. I always love being out with him as he's fascinating to talk to about what happens on the hill.

I would love to come over to Skye next summer and see the eagles, but as you may know, I'm going to Australia in February and wont be back until the beginning of August. But I'd love to come over from Balmoral in August or September if you were going to be there . . .

I believe there's a great deal of wildlife and birdlife in the forests around the school I'm going to, and also some eagles, so I may be able to take some photographs or make a survey. There is also fishing for trout in the streams, which is rather a pleasant thought.

Thank you so much for your letter again and I do hope I can come over to Skye in August or September when I know that I'll be back from Australia.

Yours very sincerely,

Charles.

The Prince was to leave Gordonstoun temporarily, to spend two terms at Timbertop, the country annexe of Geelong Church of England Grammar School, near Melbourne. A letter was written to Seton Gordon on the same day from

Desmond Nethersole-Thompson, who was nearing completion of his book, *The Snow Bunting*, to be published by Oliver and Boyd. He wrote seeking permission to use one of Seton's very early photographs:

> Ivy Cottage, Culrain,
> Ardgay, Rossshire.
>
> Dear Seton Gordon,
> I am now trying to finalise the illustrations for *The Snow Bunting* and wonder whether you would allow me to use your 1909 photograph of the young snow buntings, and possibly one of the habitat prints. I am anxious to show one of these as it was in *Hill Birds of Scotland*, as I have told in the book, that first interested me in our wonderful little bird . . . Yours ever, Desmond Nethersole-Thompson.

Consent was gladly given, and Nethersole-Thompson sent a letter of thanks in which he voiced his concern over the state of the Cairngorms:

> . . . This is indeed a historic print and one I am looking forward to reproducing in the book. I fear that much has changed since those spacious days in 1909. Development – necessary as it probably is for the economy of the Highlands – makes me feel very sad. I also fear that there is worse to come. For these reasons I now spend most of the spring and summer in Sutherland where one can still spend weeks in the field without seeing a single human being . . .

Seton Gordon's eightieth birthday was celebrated on 11 April, 1966, with many expressions of good wishes. He was not able to escape the 'flu that spring, and in a letter exchange with Angus MacPherson shortly after his birthday, eighty-nine year old Angus replied that he too had been laid up with the same 'flu type. He also referred to a prize-winning *piobaireachd* he had composed in response to a challenge issued by the BBC. It was to see if modern pipers were capable of writing a *piobaireachd* to equal the ancient tunes. Sixty-six entries came in from several countries. A distinguished panel of judges unanimously voted Angus the winner. His tune was called, *'Salute to the MacCrimmon Cairn at Borreraig'*. MacPherson was concerned that if the piece was not played at the cairn that year, he might not be alive to hear it subsequently.

Seton Gordon fully recovered and in July did an epic walk with Alwyne Farquharson of Invercauld, who still recalls the day with immense pleasure:

> Our never to be forgotten walk took place 18 July, 1966, when Seton was over eighty! We left at 05:30 hours and reached Bob Scott's cottage at the Derry by about 06:30. It was about a quarter to midnight when we returned, the last hour following the glimmer of the path stretching ahead. It was a fine night and we had taken our shoes and stockings off to ford the head-waters of the Dee at around 9:30 p.m.
>
> It was a walk of perhaps twenty-five miles, and we made only some four

stops of about a quarter of an hour each, during the whole time. It was a glorious day, and one I shall never forget.

Although more than thirty years his junior, I was certainly not as sure footed as Seton. Instinct was in his step, like that which nature gives to wild creatures and he invariably left an impression of physical efficiency with economy of effort. He emerged from this walk down to breakfast before me!

It was a wonderful experience – both a privilege and an education because all along the trail he knew the stories that lay behind the Gaelic placenames, and told them in his own inimitable way and where to look for the plants and the birds, and if his deafness prevented him hearing that song, he could recall it to perfection from his memory. His eyesight, too, was quite remarkable.*

*Seton Gordon's last book, *Highland Summer* takes its name from the first chapter, which is an account of that walk.

There were occasional reminders for Seton of the days when he and Audrey freely roamed the Outer Isles, setting up camp on uninhabited islands. On a 1966 ferry journey from Armadale to Mallaig, Seton fell into conversation with a young man named Michael Robson. In the course of their discussion it was learned that he was a teacher at George Watson's School, Edinburgh, and had been on North Rona, where he had camped and studied birdlife. Seton realised that he was talking to someone with a love of the Hebrides equalling his own. After first visiting them in about 1949, Robson had set foot on many of the smaller islands in both the Inner and Outer Hebrides, familiar to Seton. Robson also possessed several Seton Gordon books and had made a point of going to many of the locations mentioned, following up on the legends and folklore found in them.

In July 1967 he wrote to Seton that he was returning via Uig to camp on Taransay and Pabbay, and offered to bring his slides of North Rona, which was gladly accepted. He later wrote, exciting Seton with visions of old haunts:

> The week on Pabbay was one of uninterrupted pleasure, with mostly fine, calm days. We found a colony of storm petrels and there were fulmars along the north-west shore. Turnstones, whimbrel, ringed plover, and great quantities of snipe were seen.
>
> From here I went on to Taransay where one still morning I sat among old ruins at the north end of the island, the hills of Harris across the calm water, and the wailing of the divers through a grey half-sunlit air.
>
> My return across the Minch was one of the most splendid I have ever had, the light so clear that you could see over the horizon; the Storr a vivid violet in the late evening seen from Portree, and a deep red glow on Beinn na Cailleach.

The letters brought vivid memories of places he had not seen for many years, as the writer explored as he once did. When Robson next wrote in mid-September, it was with news that he had set foot on four islands, helped by the Royal Navy. The islands were Hasgier, Gasker, Mingulay and Soay of the St Kilda group, about which he wrote:

> Being by myself on Soay, I did not feel like taking risks on the cliffs. The weather and the nature of the place added up to a rather frightening atmosphere, and I was quite glad to get off. My last island was Mingulay, where I had four hours. I was there ten years ago, and found little change, except there seemed to be more sand in the village and more people had written their names inside the old manse. And so home by way of Stornoway.

His help from the Royal Navy came about in an unexpected way. On a previous stay on St Kilda, Robson met an officer from a Royal Navy oceanic survey ship who was also exploring the island. He suggested that it might be possible to offer transportation if circumstances allowed. After further follow up, the navy agreed to assist with the 1967 drops, but first a release form had to be signed – and it was made clear that all efforts would made to pick him up, but there would be no absolute guarantee.

Michael Robson's love of the Hebrides has grown stonger with the passage of time, and he still visits them regularly. In 1989 he wrote: 'One thing that Seton Gordon is partly responsible for, and for which I am eternally grateful, is my persistent and, if possible, ever increasing attachment to the Western Islands. This would not have been sustained, however, without the native people themselves and their many kindnesses'.

Although Seton was still very active, his mind still alert and showing a vital interest in everything, he was to some degree beginning to live in the past. With a mind that could conjure up memories of long ago outstanding moments of beauty; dawn, sunset, moonrise and northern lights, it should be expected that those who shared these moments would also retain an affectionate place in his mind. It was with a wealth of memories that he wrote to Putchaidh Cameron-Head in May, 1969:

> Dear Putchaidh,
>
> I hope this reaches you on the 14th, for that is the day, I think, that Francis left us twelve years ago. What a lot he took with him of the real happiness of this world. So often I have said to myself, 'How Francis would have enjoyed that'.
>
> I often think of his humility and his true spirituality, and his wonderful and refreshing gift of never saying an unkind thing of anyone, and always seeing the best in a person's nature.

Another letter said, 'What a number of good visits I have had to Inverailort through the years. Francis, I feel, might have been my [spiritual] brother, and I felt I was able to help and encourage him. It is good that you are carrying on the traditions he started'.

Before the year was out, Seton's longest surviving friend, Sir Malcolm Barclay-Harvey, with whom he had shared many early adventures on Deeside, died on 17 November, aged seventy-nine. Like Francis Cameron-Head, Sir Malcolm was a Knight of the Order of St John of Jerulasem and in later years was Grand Prior of the Order in Scotland. Happily, Seton Gordon's contact with

Dinnet did not end with the death of Sir Malcolm. Violet Barclay-Harvey, Sir Malcolm's daughter, married James Humphrey, a Canadian who had served in both wars. After living several years in Montreal, they bought a house in Aboyne, Rhu na Haven, where Seton and Betty became welcome and frequent guests. Sir Malcolm's grandson, Marcus, after graduating from university and attending agricultural college, took over the management of Dinnet.

Rhu na Haven is on the north bank of the Dee and just downstream on the opposite bank is Seton's old home, Auchintoul, still very much as he remembered it from his boyhood, the garden layout unaltered. From the wide terrace of Rhu na Haven there is a view of Morven, the hill that played such a vital part in his formative years.

Despite the loss of one close friend, for another, 1969 was as he described it, a 'golden' year. Angus MacPherson, in his ninety-second year, was invited to Balmoral, where at a private investiture, Her Majesty bestowed on him the MBE.

Public interest was aroused in 1969 when several sightings of the Loch Morar monster were reported. The late Elizabeth Montgomery-Campbell was an enthusiastic Loch Ness watcher, and a member of the Loch Ness Phenomena Investigation Bureau. Loch Morar had its share of sightings over the years, but five in 1969 of its monster, named '*Mhorag*' (*Vhorag*) by local people, was enough to bring a group together with the common aim of examining this loch more closely. One of the leaders was Montgomery-Campbell.

She wrote to Seton Gordon the following April on letterhead with the banner, 'Loch Morar Survey 1970'. The letter touched upon Seton Gordon's *Afoot in Wild Places* which contained a chapter on the beast of Loch Morar. The chapter began:

> Loch Morar is the deepest of all Scottish Lochs, and its twilight floor is well over 1000 feet, at its deepest point. It is therefore not surprising that it should contain, if the tradition of the district be credited, a strange animal, apparently not unlike the Monster of Loch Ness . . .

In her letter, Montgomery-Campbell wrote:

> . . . In the course of my researches for this Survey I have read *Afoot in Wild Places* and its references to the beast of Loch Morar. These will play a valuable part in the general picture leading up to contemporary accounts.
>
> I am trying to collect as much factual information as I can and would be extremely grateful for any further details you might have on this, or indeed any other eyewitness accounts.
>
> I hope I am not being a nuisance by writing and I would be so grateful if you were able to help us.

Seton Gordon replied that the report he received was from someone now deceased, but that he had talked to some of the older people in Morar before writing the book and some had stories of sightings. From Constance Whyte, Montgomery-Campbell also learned that Francis Cameron-Head had known of several sightings, and also of two sightings on Loch Shiel in 1911, one of them by the headkeeper of the Inverailort Estate. He also told Whyte that in 1946 or 1947, the Loch Morar beast was seen by all of the Commun na h-oigridh camp children while on an outing from Inverailort.

One 1969 sighting made international headlines when two local men out fishing in a substantial boat were bumped by the monster. Unfortunately by the time the press heard of it the men, Duncan MacDonell and William Simpson, both long-distance lorry drivers, were on the road and not available for verification. They had not intended to make their encounter public knowledge, but it was released by a relative. Montgomery-Campbell had to use persuasion to get the event retold for the Loch Morar Survey.

The men estimated that the visible portion of the body was between 25 to 30 feet, with three humps and a skin of rough brown texture. It protruded no more than 18 inches out of the water, including its 'snake-like head'. The body was solid and did not give when pushed by Duncan McDonell's oar.

Other observers were people of high credibility; a retired naval officer, two headmasters, a newspaper executive, and a surgeon. In 1971 the Morar postman and a long-time Loch Morar boatman were added to the list of observers. The latter was an ideal witness, in that he had been sceptical of the existence of the monster for all of the eighteen years he had been the Meoble Estate boatman.

Elizabeth Montgomery-Campbell and co-leader David Solomon published a detailed account of the survey in 1973. It was called *The Search for Morag*. The final paragraph stated:

> If support of the right kind is forthcoming, responsible investigation has a real hope of discovering the truth. If it is not, then another species may be condemned to join those such as the dodo and the trusting Stellar's sea cow which man has succeeded in exterminating. But if the creatures are allowed to become extinct like so many before them, it will not be because they have been slaughtered for profit, nor even because they have died out through neglect. It will be because they have been ridiculed to death.

In June 1970, Jonathan MacDonald purchased the Duntuilm Castle Hotel from Miss Kelly and began extensive renovations. Mrs 'Putchi' Cameron-Head was awarded the OBE in the Queen's Birthday Honours, in recognition for her public work.

Earlier in the year, the Duke and Duchess of Windsor had made a broadcast, to which Seton listened, and afterwards wrote to the Duke. His letter was forwarded to New York where the Duke and Duchess lived for a part of each year, and a reply was sent on 9 June:

> Tne Waldorf-Astoria,
> New York.
>
> Dear Seton,
>
> My apologies for the delay in thanking you for your nice letter of 27 March, however it was forwarded from Paris and has only now reached me.

Your 'few thoughts' after listening to the Duchess' and my broadcast brought back nostalgic memories of Oxford and the Cairngorms when we were young and could follow pursuits we can no longer attempt nor enjoy.

I am afraid my bagpipes have not been with me for thirty years. I last played them in the New Year 1940 in Paris during the last war but have had no time since then to devote to that instrument of music we love so much. However, I still play golf despite an arthritic hip and get lots of relaxation out of that.

It is sad to think how many of our contempories have now passed on. You are fortunate to be living on the Isle of Skye, away from the unpleasantness of this ever changing World. Still I am very happy and in good health (touching wood) as I hope you are. It was nice to hear from you again and with best wishes.

Sincerely yours, Edward.

Seton replied to the Duke from Invercauld Castle on 7 July, and was able to offer the Duke more memories of Deeside:

Dear Edward,

It was splendid to see your handwriting again after many years. As you say there are not many of us left.

Alwyne Farquharson, as you may know, has succeeded to Invercauld and has made it a happy estate – you would find him a man after your own heart. I am on a short visit here and he and I were on Ben A'an yesterday. Large snowfields still and snowbridges over the burns.

You may remember Sandy McDonald of the Derry – I hope to call on his daughter, Nellie, who lives in Braemar, today.

We had Norman Meldrum to pipe last night and he played your very first tune, 'Invercauld's March' round the table, and later, 'MacCrimmon's Sweetheart'.

This evening I hope to go across to hear Robert Brown, perhaps the finest living piper – he is still in the Queen's service but reaches sixty-five, the retiring age, in October. You will remember him, so there are still links with the past.

It is ten years since Audrey left this life and I am now married to Betty Badger, whose husband Reggie, comanded the 12th Lancers.

It is good news that you still play golf and are happy and still on the move, Seton.

Beginning in 1970, Seton Gordon was interviewed several times by the BBC Scottish Home Service. On 6 November, George Waterston interviewed him for the *Countryside* programme, which was broadcast on 3 January, 1971. Waterston was, by this time, a very sick man but his determination and dedication would not let him give in to the acute kidney disease, which eventually led to a transplant. Unfortunately it was not successful, and he hated the restrictions which dialysis then imposed on people. His problems had started during the war when he was taken prisoner on Crete. He was so ill that he heard a fellow soldier wagering that he would not survive the night. With great courage, George was to prove the soldier wrong. He was later operated on by a German doctor and then repatriated under a Red Cross scheme.

Two letters from George Waterston to Seton during the 1971 breeding season, showed that despite all that was being done by the RSPB and the Nature Conservancy, the battles were far from over:

> . . . We certainly have had a most disastrous period recently with the osprey robbery and with oil pollution incidents in Shetland. In addition we have suffered a marked upsurge in egg-collecting in various parts of Scotland as well as England. At least three golden eagle eyries in the Outer Hebrides have gone this past year; and at one eyrie in south-west Scotland the robbers left a knotted nylon rope hanging down the cliff. We know too, of at least two pairs of kites which have been robbed by egg-collectors in Wales. The peregrines have had a very bad year nearly everywhere. There were only three broods out of sixteen normally occupied sites successfully hatched on Speyside . . . The situation is very serious indeed and is most depressing.

A follow-up letter requested help for an eyrie on Skye. A member had reported seeing a notice posted in a hotel lobby which stated that at a nearby location, golden eagles were nesting. He wrote to Seton:

> I remember that we had some trouble with this hotel divulging such information in the past, and I wonder whether you could again do something about it for us? I think you should point out that it is an offence for anyone to disturb a First Schedule Bird, such as a golden eagle, at its nest, and this poster is tantamount to encouraging people to break the law!

This letter also illustrates the restrictions imposed on modern bird watchers, compared to the freedom which Seton Gordon enjoyed for most of his life to observe birds at close quarters without creating an offence under the Protection of Birds Act.

In the meantime *Highland Summer* was published. In its Preface, Seton wrote:

> The Highlands are swiftly changing in character . . . In the old days the family and its neighbours gathered round a peat fire on a winter's evening and held a *ceilidh*, where tales of the past were recited and songs were sung. The company now sit silent beside a television screen, or listen on their wireless sets to the latest bulletin from a materialistic world . . . But there are still Highland areas that have not felt the heavy hand of 'progress', and in this book I have endeavoured to convey to the reader the abiding charm of hill and glen and of the wild creatures which have their home here.

As the final proofs of *Highland Summer* were being approved, Seton sent off an item to the publishers of *Blackwood's Magazine*. It was a fictional piece, as far as is known the only one that he ever wrote. It was called 'Seal Wife', a mythical tale of the fate which befell the children of a Norse king who remarried after his first wife died. Their stepmother was jealous, and cast a spell that turned them into seals, from which they were only allowed back into human form each autumn when the moon was full. A young Hebridean fisherman, Donald Mor, who had made his home on the island of Hasker, by chance saw these 'change-lings' on the night that they became temporarily human. He took one of the seal-skins to see what would happen when the time came for them to return to seal form, and hid it over the lintel of his bothy. It belonged to one of the young princesses, whose name was Fionngala, and he was reluctant to give it back. They met while she was searching for it. She remained with him and they fell deeply in love.

As the autumn progressed she became restless and one day found the skin, which she felt compelled to put on, and reluctantly left her human lover. They were both heartbroken, but she assured him that their love would survive, and she would come to him whenever she could. He was finally persuaded to return to North Uist. Here he met a young University of Glasgow Mathematics Professor, Austin MacConnachie, who had become separated from a group while exploring South Uist. They had come ashore from a yacht sailing through the Hebrides. The Professor learned the story and became fascinated enough to persuade the yacht's owner, Sir Farquhar Matheson, to sail it to Hasker so that he could go ashore there. He saw on the island a group of seals and knew intuitively that one of them was the princess. He told her of his meeting with Donald Mor, her lover.

At the next autumnal full moon, when once again in human form, Fionngala met Donald Mor in a North Uist cave, from where they swam together to Hasker. As they neared the island, in a rising sea and increasing wind, she became aware that they were being followed by a massive bull seal, who had tried unsuccessfully for many seasons to make her his mate. Mad with jealousy the bull, after a fight in the water, drowned Donald Mor. The story ends:

> Dulled by the stupor of grief, Fionngala as in a dream stood, still in human form, alone upon Hasker. Gone was the love of her life; vanished were her dreams of happiness: she could see herself forlorn and weary until the end of time. Cold and trembling she moved slowly to the bothy door, took down her seal's covering from the lintel, where she had placed it earlier that night before swimming the strait to the cave of Uaimh Mhor, wrapped herself in it and slept the sleep of exhaustion.
>
> When she awakened the storm had spent itself, the sky was clear and the eastern horizon flushed with red. Slowly the light strengthened and the hills of Harris, warmed by the sun, rose to the north . . .
>
> As Fionngala looked upon this unfolding beauty, peace entered her heart. She knew then that love had been given her in order to experience the immortality of the human soul, even though it might be held for a time beneath dark spells. She knew, too, in a flood of inner light, that great love is immortal, for it comes from the heart of beauty, which can never die.

In the story was all of Seton's depth of feeling for the Isles, for nature, for legend, and his view of life and death. He incorporated piping when, earlier in the story, his hero piped to the seals. Seton also incorporated many of the island customs he had discovered over the years. Douglas Blackwood replied:

11th March, 1971.

Dear Mr Gordon,

My colleague David Fletcher has passed to me the typescript of your story 'Seal Wife'. We both very much appreciate your having given us the opportunity of considering this story, and it is with very real regret that I cannot see my way to accepting it for publication in my magazine. I do not feel the subject matter quite meets the requirements of *Blackwood's*, but primarily my reason for coming to this decision is that it is too long and is not the sort of story that would divide into two parts.

Believe me, I am very sorry that I have to write in this way and that I must return your manuscript to you. It would give me a deal of pleasure to publish something from your pen in the magazine and I hope that I am not expecting too much in asking you to try again.

Yours sincerely, Douglas Blackwood.

CHAPTER
15

'THE GRAND OLD MAN OF NATURE'

A FEW DAYS before Seton Gordon's eighty-fifth birthday, James Campbell of Kilberry arrived from Cambridge. These visits from so knowledgeable a piper, and the association with the old days, were looked forward to by Seton. They gave him encouragement to keep on with the pipes himself, and he refers to 'much piping' over the next twenty-four hours.

On 11 April, Seton's birthday, there was a complete weather change, from several days of overcast to sunshine all day and a temperature of 60 degrees. There were several telegrams, the one from Caitriona reading 'Curlews in great form!' The first flower appeared on the magnolia, and as though to complement the day, five hot-air balloons passed over Biddlesden.

Each spring and autumn Desmond Price made a huge bonfire. When he began collecting debris and fallen branches around the estate, Seton would say to him, 'Don't light the bonfire without telling me'. Desmond recalls his eagerness to help pile it up and he would stay and warm himself for some time, making frequent visits while the fire was still going. There are several diary entries through the years at Biddlesden of these fires, and one just before his eighty-fifth birthday refers to Desmond lighting the 'Budget Bonfire, which gave out great warmth'. Desmond enjoyed these opportunities to walk around the estate with Seton.

An invitation came for Seton to visit the national headquarters of the RSPB, The Lodge, at Sandy in Bedfordshire. Michael Everett, who came south in 1969, had not met Seton, though they had communicated frequently. Writing of that day Everett said:

> Seton Gordon came here to Sandy as a venerable and much honoured visitor. He was a fund of information and stories, and was treated with great respect. I took him to see the nest of a pair of willow-tits. He was thrilled at this, saying that he hadn't seen such a thing since before the war.

On 19 May, Seton noted: 'Caught overnight train from Crewe to Inverness. Reached osprey hide 10 a.m. Heard about the robbing of the nest at 3 a.m. on 17th, though there was an electric alarm and barbed wire wound all the way up the tree. The police at Boat of Garten arrived in record time and awaited the two men as they returned to their car. The female osprey had returned and brooded the empty eyrie for eight minutes, calling all the time'.

(It is a credit to the RSPB and its volunteers that despite these robbing efforts and two near-disasters by fire, between 1958 and 1988, fifty-four ospreys were fledged. The figure for Scotland is an impressive 600, with 400 of those ringed. Over 300,000 people viewed the Loch Garten eyrie in those thirty years.)

By the third week of January, 1972, Seton and Betty were again at Upper Duntuilm. There were more teatime visits to Viewfield and more piping sessions both there and at Upper Duntuilm, sometimes they held what Seton referred to as a piping *ceilidh*, with as many as six pipers in attendance. One of the regulars was Dugie MacLeod, a joiner by trade and very popular on the island. He was a composer of *piobaireachd* and when Colonel Jock and Evelyn lost their son Johnnie, a career officer in the Cameron Highlanders, to cancer, Dugie composed a *piobaireachd* in his memory. Another composition of his was played when Viewfield went electric – *'A Farewell to the Tilley Lamp'*!

There were sometimes special guests such as the MacFadyen brothers. Colonel Jock in his later years actively encouraged young pipers and clarsach (harp) players, and began a day of competition at the hotel each autumn when their guests were gone. These are still continued by Evelyn MacDonald, and Highland dancing competitions have been added.

A letter in the spring brought news of well deserved recognition from the National Library of Scotland. It asked if Seton Gordon would donate his papers and manuscripts to the National Library archives as part of a plan to assemble a collection from Scottish writers, scientists, artists and men of letters of the present century. Unfortunately this request coincided with an especially sad piece of news:

> 25 April – Very sad to hear from Follett, who rang before breakfast to say the Scottish News announced that Robert Brown had died suddenly. He had returned to Balmoral midday yesterday from a tour of Australia and at 4 p.m. he was away and we shall not hear his piping again. He will be a sad loss to piping and his many, many friends.

After Robert Brown's funeral, Alwyne Farquharson wrote to Seton:

> I never saw the Church at Crathie so full, so packed and masses of flowers at the Altar steps. Bob Nicol played the Ground of *'Donald Ban MacCrimmon'* at the graveside. It must have been a bad moment for him but he played beautifully. The whole piping fraternity was represented. They came from far afield – what a tragic loss indeed!

As well as writing to the Queen when Pipe-Major Brown died, Seton Gordon also wrote to His Royal Highness, the Prince of Wales. Brown had been a part of his life from the time he was old enough to handle a fishing rod. The Prince was at sea, in the frigate HMS *Hermione* when the news came, and it had a profound effect on him, all the more because it was unexpected, after hearing of the Pipe-Major's successful tour. On 5 June, the Prince replied:

> Dear Mr. Gordon,
>
> You were very kind to write about Brown. I was absolutely shattered by his death and burst into floods of helpless tears. I had no idea how much he meant to me and how much of a Highland friend he had been. He taught me so much – he was the first person I used to go fishing with when I was small and he taught me all I know about stalking.
>
> He was what I call a 'nature's gentleman', a man of the forest and mountains and thus one of the greatest pipers Scotland has known. I think your idea of a small memorial to him is splendid. It would carry on a small Victorian tradition and would mean that pipers could pay a tribute to him in the Ballochbuie he knew so well. I will let you know if I can organise something. Thank you so much for suggesting it.
>
> Charles.

The envelope had written on it: 'The Prince of Wales' Tribute to Robert Brown'. Later a pipe-tune was composed by Robert Nicol. It was called *'Bob Brown's Farewell to the Ballochbuie'.*

As a diversion from going to the local reservoirs, Seton and Betty drove to Suffolk to the Minsmere reserve. The warden took them to see the only pair of nesting marsh harriers in Britain at that time:

> We watched both male and female harriers hunting – graceful, airy flight, wings held V-shape. Curlew sandpipers, black-tailed and bar-tailed godwits. In the evening I heard at very close quarters the lovely song of a nightingale in a low tree. The FIRST I've heard since Oxford in 1911.

This was the second time within two weeks that Seton reported hearing birds not heard for some years. The previous occasion was by the Oxford canal, when he heard both a cuckoo and a curlew. He was using an Amplivox hearing-aid, and he reported further hearing improvements as time went on.

Seton and Betty went north in time for Skye Week. 1972 was of special significance, as Colonel Jock made the opening speech and was introduced by Jonathan MacDonald. Jock's speech was to form, but there were disappointments with the piping competitions: 'A very warm sunny afternoon. Ideal for Ceol Mor playing but no one would enter!! Were they afraid of the distinguished judges??'

Two days later, at Borreraig, Angus MacPherson was honoured by having John MacFadyen play his composition *'Salute to the Cairn at Borreraig'.*

While Seton was on Skye, Patrick Cadell of the National Library of Scotland came to Upper Duntuilm. There was a huge accumulation of papers, cuttings, and correspondence to be sorted and readied for transportation to the Library. Cadell left with a large volume of material, and by October, S.M. Simpson, Assistant Keeper of Manuscripts, forwarded the Accession lists for Seton

Pipe-Majors Robert Nicol and Robert Brown (the 'Two Bobs' of Balmoral)

Gordon's approval. They had been sorted into twenty-seven boxes, and included over eighty typescript pieces, representing only a fraction of the total number of articles he wrote, though many others were pasted into scrapbooks. There were manuscripts or galley proofs of at least five of his books, and a large collection of photographs going back to early days on Deeside.

Changes were coming faster in Seton Gordon's life. In February 1973, John Graham decided to leave Upper Duntuilm, this time to retire. He had been unwell for some months, and once or twice Seton had taken him into Portree for massage therapy. On the 15th John went to Portree for X-rays. Fortunately his problem was not life threatening and he enjoyed several years of retirement.

Seton and Betty headed south for Biddlesden and in the following weeks there are several diary comments which serve to show how well he had adapted to life on the estate in the thirteen years since he first came there. March 20th is noted, 'FIRSTS: first Brimstone Butterfly: first Bumble-Bee: first Mowing of Upper Lawn'.

> 26 April – V. clear air and long sunny periods. When I was at the lower lake yesterday afternoon I thought that the pair of cootes there seemed friendly when I called 'Cootie Cootie Cootie!' I wonder if they could perhaps be the pair that had vanished from the bridge, where, until November I had fed them for years.
>
> This evening I went down there and when I called, the cootie came at once – his more timid wife a little later, behaving in the same manner as before. So after many years they have left their territory by the upper bridge and will, I expect, nest this year by the large fallen branch of the horse-chestnut.
>
> Clear, calm evening, almost cloudless.
>
> 27 April – A day of almost continuous sunshine, 60 degrees.
>
> A house-martin (first seen) flew over Biddlesden about 9 a.m.
>
> This evening about 7:30 when I fed the cootie he got the fright of his life. A large pike had been 'warming up' in the shallow water beneath the bridge and just as Cootie was swimming to me, the pike must have seen me on the bridge and shot out, making a big bow-wave and passing right under Cootie & frightened him badly. I am sure he thought I was responsible!

Seton Gordon was invited to open Skye week in 1973. It was early, beginning 5 May. He stayed at Dunvegan in preference to Upper Duntuilm. The official start of the week was 1:45 p.m. and Seton gave his speech in Somerled Square. He remained on the island for the Borreraig ceremony and as there was no running water at Upper Duntuilm he continued to stay as a guest of Flora MacLeod. Seton admitted that John Graham was missed when he lamented, 'No John to sort things out'. Nature was, however, in full swing to his great satisfaction: 'At Upper Duntuilm blackbird singing well on the chimney stack and I heard a thrush. The campanula is not fully in flower, but the lupins are out and the erinus is in full scented bloom'.

Seton gave a talk on Ceol Mor at Portree School. Colonel Jock was in the chair and it was here that the story of 'gulls' of London was told. Seton was assisted by Iain MacFadyen who played *'I Got a Kiss of the King's Hand'*, *'Lament of the Earl of Antrim'* and *'My Dearest on Earth, Give me Your Kiss'*. Seton's introduction of the first tune, his favourite, enthralled the crowd as he described the meeting between the king and the piper. In introducing Iain MacFadyen he mentioned the piper's impressive record that year:

> He comes from a great piping family and his brother John is at the moment teaching in Kenya. Another brother, Duncan, is also a first class piper. I asked Iain today how many successes he's had this summer, and the Games season is not half way through and he has already won eight First Class prizes at the big Gatherings.

The evening ended with Seton remarking how unusual it was for a lay audience to hear a whole programme of *piobaireachd*, and how well they had 'stood up to the strain!' The lecture was recorded by BBC Northern for a later broadcast. This was done by Bill Sinclair, an Inverness businessman and occasional BBC producer. He is an expert in recording birdsong and has worked with both Adam Watson and the late Desmond Nethersole-Thompson on BBC nature programs.

During 1973 and 1974, Desmond Nethersole-Thompson and Adam Watson co-authored a book, *The Cairngorms*. It was published in the summer of 1974 and in mid-June Seton had an unexpected letter and parcel from them:

> My Dear Seton,
>
> Adam and I wish you to have this advance copy of *The Cairngorms* as a little tribute to your wonderful work on the wildlife of the Highlands.
>
> You have meant so much to us both. You inspired Adam and myself when we were schoolboys and gave us the wish to walk the hills and always to try to discover.
>
> We hope that you will like the dedication and will understand why we tried so hard to get hold of that greenshank print. But we wished the dedication to be a little surprise for you and Adam's father. We certainly told no one!
>
> Now, our love to you and may you walk our dear Cairngorms for many a long year. Yours as ever, Desmond and Adam.

The dedication read: 'For Seton Gordon, who lit a spark in us both, and Adam Watson, father of one and friend of both'. In the text there were no less than twelve references to Seton Gordon and seven of his books were listed in the bibliography.

Seton was still a contributing writer for the magazines and newspapers that had printed his articles regularly and was also still in demand as a judge at the *piobaireachd* competitions. On 22 August he was again at Glenfinnan with his usual co-judges, Colonel Jock and Angus MacPherson. Angus had, with great reluctance, given up piping. The honorary Chief that year was Godfrey, Lord MacDonald of Sleat. Seton also judged at the Dunvegan Silver Chanter competition, with James Campbell of Kilberry and Colonel Murray, and at Invergordon with Angus MacPherson and Neil Angus MacDonald.

The Northern meeting was the next event attended by Seton. With fifty-one entries and twelve hours of competition, he thought the numbers were too many. Of these, twelve entered for the Clasp, the most coveted award. Many of the names that had long been associated with the Meeting were missing and a new breed of piper was present. They were younger and more women were entering the competition.

Seton gave cause for concern when he returned to Biddlesden. One Sunday afternoon he was hurrying to the gates to catch the mail and passed the lodge where Desmond and Gertie Price lived. They became aware that he had not returned, and Desmond found him face down in the grass at the side of the driveway. He quickly recovered but appeared dazed. What impressed Gertrude was that Seton did not on this occasion say 'thank you', something he was always so ready to offer. It was as though he had not been aware of what had happened.

He was sufficiently well to pay another visit to Sandy Lodge not long after to give a lecture on the golden eagle to RSPB members. His hearing was further helped by the purchase of a new Willco hearing-aid in January 1975 and it made a noticeable difference in his ability to pick up birdsong from this time on.

A treat on his eighty-ninth birthday was a simultaneous visit from James Campbell and Iverach McDonald. He brought a recording of John MacDonald playing four of Seton's favourite MacCrimmon tunes. Campbell then played *'The Old Man of the Shells'* followed by another record on which the *canntaireachd*, or mouth music of this tune was sung. As a finale, Campbell played *'The Vaunting'*. Ironically it was the setting of this tune which had so upset John MacDonald of Inverness in 1949 when he examined it in Archibald Campbell's book of Ceol Mor.

Almost immediately he and Betty headed north once more and remained in Scotland until 16 July. Visiting Skye for the day, Seton wrote a wry comment, 'Upper Duntuilm still standing! Well very dry and plants are suffering on the wall'. There was a further indication of Seton's remarkable hearing improvement: 'In our plantation, I heard the cuckoo very clearly for quite a long time. Heard a blackbird, also loud and clear. Wonderful to hear them, and also wind in trees!'

Angus Mapherson had celebrated his ninety-eighth birthday on 2 July and Seton went north to see him. Angus told Seton that he was 'feeling his 98 years'. On the same day Seton recorded: 'At 2.15 p.m. beside the Shin, I actually heard the cry of a Curlew – how wonderful to hear them, at last, after MANY years'.

Angus was well enough to attend the Glenfinnan Gathering on 16 August, and with the usual gathering of friends took part in a TV programme produced by the late Russell Harty, who was then with Thames Television. Harty called the progamme 'Finnan Games'!

When Seton arrived at Inverailort he found cameras and lights in the dining room. Next day film crews were out at Glenfinnan where Harty interviewed

Lochiel and Donald, Younger of Lochiel, who made the opening speech. Mrs Putchi Cameron-Head, in her capacity as convenor and organiser was likened in the commentary to a 'head-mistress'. Dinner on the Saturday evening was also filmed, with Seton, Colonel 'Jock' and Angus each saying a few words. Jock played his miniature bagpipes and Angus gave a brief demonstration of mouth music, or *canntaireachd*.

It could not be regarded as an entirely serious 'behind the scenes' look at a Highland Gathering. If it was, it might have been handled less flippantly and with much more sensitivity. The background music was not always appropriate, other than an excerpt from Malcolm Arnold's *'Four Scottish Dances'*. There were excerpts from *'Four Cornish Dances'*, the *'Brandenburg Concerto No. 3'*, and *'Aquarius'*, none of these sounding right for the event. The coverage of the piping competition had no consistency and it is doubtful if anyone watching would have any better idea about *piobaireachd* than before. This is a pity as there was some excellent playing by Jimmy MacGregor of *'Lament for Colin Roy MacKenzie'*. The three judges were not given an opportunity to talk seriously about pipe music. Nevertheless, it was interesting to see them together 'live', as it transpired, for the last time. When Seton departed at 11:30 p.m. on Sunday, he must have known that their chances of judging together again were slim. Their combined ages added to 271 years, with Angus at ninety-eight, Seton at eighty-nine and Jock at eighty-four.

As his ninetieth birthday drew nearer in 1976, Seton's health remained good. There was no reoccurrence of the blackout that he had suffered the previous year. He had published a number of articles on both piping and nature in the previous year and his diaries continued to be a delight to read, still with detailed observations, wherever he happened to be. At Upper Duntuilm in December 1975, he wrote: 'At 10 a.m. It was cloudless over Skye, but dark as night over Harris and magnificent cumulus clouds were towering white at the margin of the inky canopy. In thirty minutes all the dark, stormy area vanished, and at 11 a.m. there was sunshine everywhere. – all was beautiful'.

From the Shiel Bridge cottage was a view of the Five Sisters of Kintail, with Sgurr Fhuaran the most predominant. There were many references to it, and once, after a day of high wind and rain, Seton looked out at sunset and noted:

> The wind, of almost hurricane speed, fell light and a few minutes before sunset the west facing slope of Sgurr Fhuaran, greatest of the Sisters of Kintail, was lit up by pools of glowing red-brown light, rare and unexpected.

Aside from a mind which continued to be sharp, and his ability to walk long distances still, there were the already mentioned signs that his hearing was improved with a better aid. It was, however, his sight which was so remarkable, and was as keen as when he was young. There are two examples which illustrate this. The first occurred when he was driving between Shiel Bridge and Invercauld in his ninetieth year: 'Had sun most of way – it was so clear I saw a man on the Beinn MacDhui plateau, from Aviemore'.

The second example is one that Alwyne Farquharson loves to tell, of a time when Seton was staying at Invercauld. They were dining by candlelight, which was the only light in the room: 'Seton was writing up his daily notes in his finest, smallest handwriting, with no spectacles. I'm ashamed to say that at only half his age, I could not read what he had written with my spectacles on!'

Seton's ninetieth birthday was celebrated with his family. Caitriona and Simon Macdonald-Lockhart had built for themselves a smaller single storey house less than a mile from Newholm. They named it Dunsyre House, after the last hill in the Pentlands, which rises behind it to the north. Their son Hamish was now living at Newholm. The family gathered at Dunsyre House and there were four grandchildren and five great-grandchildren present.

Recognition and congratulations came from many quarters, but especially from other naturalists and publishers. Frank Hamilton, then Deputy Director, Scotland, of the RSPB, wrote:

> Dear Seton,
>
> I send all the good wishes from this office on reaching your ninetieth birthday. You have an advantage over nearly everyone of being able to look back and see the enormous changes that have taken place in bird conservation and the effects of man on birds since the beginning of the century. You can rightly claim to have played a very important part in this by firing many young people with enthusiasm and interest through your writings. Your influence has travelled far and wide and has travelled through every strata of society. It is something of which you can be justly proud . . .
>
> Hoping you are in good health and, once more, all of us send our very warm congratulations.
>
> Yours sincerely, F. D. Hamilton.

A letter came from the editor of *The Field*:

> Dear Mr. Seton Gordon,
>
> Late but not forgotten.
>
> Forgive me for going on leave and failing to realise that I would not return until your milestone was behind you. This little note brings congratulations and good wishes for the future.
>
> You will pass more milestones yet, both actually and metaphorically, so I must be careful not to make a similar dereliction ten years hence. As ever, Wilson Stephens.

Three weeks after Seton's birthday, on 3 May, Angus MacPherson died. He was only two months from his own ninety-nineth birthday. With him went a direct link to the old Highland pipers and a life totally concerned with piping. Seton Gordon wrote an obituary for *The Field* in which he pointed out that Angus MacPherson was not only a Gold Medallist at the Northern Meeting, but he had an unbroken record of attendance at the event. He said of his friend:

> . . . I am sure that no piping expert has continued to judge to the age of

> ninety-eight at the various Highland gatherings. Old men are often tiresome but with Angus the flame of enthusiasm burned brightly until the end.
>
> There is no one who can take his place in the piping world, yet we must be thankful for his long and full life. He was a piping aristocrat, for he was descended from generations of celebrated pipers. His great-great-grandfather was piper to the Chief of Clan MacPherson, at the time of the Jacobite rising of 1745 . . .

Pipe-Major Robert Nicol composed some pipe music in memory of Robert Brown that year and sent it to Seton Gordon for approval. He in turn sent it to the Prince of Wales in June. When the Prince acknowledged it he was sailing in HMS *Bronington*, off Cape Wrath and had sailed past Skye the previous evening. He wrote of seeing a school of porpoises off Loch Eriboll and while sailing up the west coast had watched puffins, guillemots, razorbills and Manx shearwaters 'going about their business'. In October, Nicol's composition was played in a programme of pipe music for the Queen. On the official programme notes it was named *'Pipe-Major Robert Brown's Farewell to the Ballochbuie Forest'*. The Prince wrote to Seton Gordon again expressing delight with the 'splendid' tune, but said 'The Queen felt, as I do, that the title is too long and liked my original suggestion of *'Bob Brown's Farewell to the Ballochbuie'*. I hope you will agree to the shorter version'.

(In 1984 a cairn was erected to the memory of both Brown and Nicol, near the spot at Braemar where they both played and judged *piobaireachd*. The epitaph reads: 'Erected by the Braemar Royal Highland Society and friends, in tribute to the late Pipe-Majors Robert U. Brown, MBE, and Robert B. Nicol of Balmoral. Masters of *Piobaireachd*. August, 1984.')

On Deeside, Seton walked with Alwyne Farquharson and Adam Watson in the Cairngorms. Adam took a picture of Seton wearing his old, patched kilt. A deerstalker hat replaced his bonnet. It was the last picture of Seton taken in the hills. On an earlier occasion Adam and his father met Seton Gordon at Bob Brown's house. Adam's beard was now very long and Seton looked at him and said, 'I'm pleased to meet you for the first time'. Pointing to the clean-shaven Adam senior he continued, 'Your son here has been corresponding with me since he was a schoolboy'. Adam said that the statement might have been mistaken for the confused mind of an old man, until one spotted the mischievous twinkle in Seton's eyes as he said it – a joke against his bearded protégé and a classic example of his sense of humour.

Soon after this, while on the Highland Games tour on Deeside, Seton lectured in Braemar in aid of the Scottish Wildlife Trust. Watson was there and afterwards wrote: 'Some of the slides were ancient and blurred, but his word pictures were as good as any he had ever written. Describing the dawn sunrays as they caught the gold hackles of a brooding eagle's neck, he had us there with him, over fifty years ago'.

In a series of notebooks are recorded the winners and runners-up of piping competitions Seton attended from 1932 onwards. 1976 is no exception. Some people contended that he could not hear them playing, but his written comments show that he listened intently and did not miss a single note that was played. Even for one of the best-known pipers, his comment for *'MacCrimmon's Sweetheart'* said 'Good, one variation too long'. For another, who played his favourite, *'Kiss of the King's Hand'* Seton commented, 'Played ground slow, two mistakes in Siubhal, Crunluath none too good'. One piper earned the comment, 'Well played, but long and heavy tune'.

At Glenfinnan he accorded the comment, 'One variation left out' to a piper who played *'The Glen is Mine'*. For *'MacCrimmon's Sweetheart'* the piper was, Seton thought, guilty of playing the first variation too fast, though he felt that the ground was well played. In 1976, Seton judged at Glenfinnan, Invergordon and Morar, and was present at Blair Castle and Dunvegan Silver Chanter competition.

For a broadcast on 3 October, Seton wrote his notes on an old, slit-open envelope. In his jottings he revealed that the gardener at his parents' house in Aboyne was a piper, and had an early influence on his interest in piping. It was he who first talked about John MacDonald of Inverness, though Seton did not meet MacDonald until the resumption of the Northern Meeting in 1919. He also mentioned Pipe-Major John Burgess, who was recognised as an outstanding piper at a very young age, and at twelve years old was invited to Edinburgh Castle by the GOC, Scottish Command. It was a cold day and the boy's fingers were blue. Seton realised that Pipe-Major 'Wullie' Ross had no idea of the skilled piping he was about to hear, and was amused at his change of expression as the tune progressed. Burgess now enjoys international acclaim.

A month after Seton's broadcast, Dame Flora MacLeod died in her ninety-eighth year. Like Angus MacPherson she was in reasonable health to the end, and was walking with her companion near Ythan Lodge in Aberdeenshire, when taken ill.

Her body was taken to Dunvegan to lie in the Castle Drawing Room, which had been her wish. Seumas MacNeill and John MacFadyen piped together there, playing a selection of MacCrimmon *piobaireachds*. At 9 a.m. on Tuesday, 9 November, Dame Flora left her castle for the last time. Lord MacDonald, as the MacLeods' neighbouring chief, was present. Three other chiefs attended, Tormod Matheson of Matheson, James MacNab of MacNab, and Lochiel, who as as Lord Lieutenant of Inverness-shire, also represented the Queen. In the congregation were Seton Gordon and Colonel Jock MacDonald.

Seton Gordon was asked, among others, to write an appreciation of Dame Flora in the memorial tribute published after her death. He wrote:

> Skye is the poorer for the passing of Dame Flora. All MacLeods, or those connected with the MacLeods, were welcome at the Castle. Walking with her through the castle grounds on MacLeod Day, I was always amazed at the number of people she stopped to talk to. Almost to the end of her long life she was tireless and stopped to welcome strangers as if they were old friends.
>
> As the years passed, her love for Skye grew stronger, as did her love for the

Seton Gordon in his last few months of life. After this picture was taken by Tom Weir he spent a day on the Cairngorms with Adam Watson, walking steadily on the plateau, 'blue eyes sparkling as keenly as ever, and his conversation was full of exciting comments on snow patches, birds, place names and the Cairngorms range itself, which I believe was the most beloved part of Scotland'. He wrote an article in The Field *about it. He died only a fortnight short of 91. (By kind permission of Mr Tom Weir)*

Great Music of the MacCrimmons. As a lifelong piper myself, I was able to introduce her to and keep her in touch with the great pipers of Scotland during the last century. Many of them were present on that day, long ago now, when her father, Sir Reginald MacLeod of MacLeod dedicated the Borreraig Cairn.

Seton Gordon making notes while judging the piobeareachd *at Glenfinnan, 1976 (at 90) (with kind permission of Diana Head Parkin)*

I recall the blue sea, the Castle rising five miles away on the far shore, the clear grace notes of a great piper, the distant seagull voices – all this formed a picture of beauty and inspired my old friend Charles Cammell to write for the *Scotsman* one of his best poems, *'Pibroch Voices'*. Dame Flora attended regularly the *piobaireachd* competition at the Skye Gathering. She inaugurated a unique competition, open only to winners of the Gold Medal at Inverness, Oban, or the Dunvegan Medal at Portree. The prize is a silver chanter, to recognise the tradition that their hereditary pipers, the MacCrimmons, owed their piping gift to a magic silver chanter given by a fairy. The Silver Chanter Competition has become one of the premier piping competitions in the world . . .

In the church I thought of that day forty-one years before, when Pipe-Major Robert Reid had played *'Lament for the Children'* at her father's grave, and I had played *'MacCrimmon will not Return'* at the Castle. Now his talented daughter was to make her last journey to the same burial ground.

Following the burial the pipers payed their respects to a great lady with *'Lament for the Children'*. She had brought fame to Skye and encouragement and understanding to *piobaireachd*, Ceol Mor, the great music of the bagpipe.

Of Seton's friends who had kept alive the old Highland traditions and had lived into old age, now only Colonel Jock was left. It is said that he, with his laconic humour, thought it was hardly worth leaving the graveyard after Dame Flora's funeral! He survived Seton by four years and died on 1 June, 1981 at the age of ninety.

Seton and Betty did not go north at all during the early part of 1976. There were plans to go later, once spring was underway. Seton continued writing articles. Alastair Dunnett, then editor of the *Scotsman*, ran a small nature column for which Seton wrote. It was a format which had run its course by the mid-1970s, but Dunnett kept it going because he thought there was still a valuable contribution to be made by observant people of Seton's calibre, though towards the end his pieces became perfunctory and, in the opinion of the editorial staff, repetitious. Dunnett felt they did nothing to add to his renown and regretfully sent a few back, with a note explaining how sorry he was. Once, on a visit to the editor's office, at about this time, Seton remarked sadly, that he had never before had anything refused by the *Scotsman*. Alastair Dunnett said, 'It made no difference to our friendship'.

In an interview with Tom Weir, Seton reflected on his long and mainly happy life. He said how sorry he felt for modern ornithologists compared to the freedom he had enjoyed in watching golden eagles, 'Nowadays you have to apply for a permit to watch, let alone take photographs. I would not want to do it now'.

Memories now made up 75 per cent of his enjoyment of the Highlands. He thought of all the wonderful people he had known and the kindness and hospitality he had received. When asked about his feelings on outliving his contemporaries and his views on death, Seton Gordon was forthright:

I feel it is something to look forward to, for the people you have known and want to meet again. One believes in a future life because of one's own experience. I am impressed with the goodness of people, and I believe in telepathy.

> I have often felt it very strongly . . . There is less to do here at Upper Duntuilm when you lose the strength to go on long cross-country walks . . . but I like to spend the summer here and take a walk every day. It is a wonderful place for sunsets.

Seton's diaries for 1976 and 1977 are missing, but it is certain that they were filled with the same joyous notes as the previous ones. Winter was nearly over, and by 18 March, 1977, the early spring flowers were blooming. It was usual for Betty to retire for the night before Seton as he liked to stay and finish off his diary notes and any other piece of work which was to hand. What particular event had pleased him during that day will probably never be known. Seton finished his notes, turned off his study lights and made for the stairs.

Early on the morning of the 19th the Prices received a call from Betty. On getting up she had discovered that Seton had got no further than the foot of the stairs. She told Gertude Price, very calmly, that Mr Gordon was dead.

Arrangements were made, as with Audrey, that Seton be cremated and his ashes scattered in the Cairngorms, his first love of all Scottish mountains. From here the whole range of the Highlands can be seen. Far to the west, his equally beloved Cuillin Hills lie beyond the Five Sisters of Kintail.

Condolence letters expressed disbelief that Seton had gone, and all referred to his gentle ways and kindliness. Sir Peter Scott wrote, 'Seton had become a legend when I was a young man and we have very happy memories of his visits to Slimbridge. But the most marvellous thing was the liveliness and youthfulness of his mind right into old age . . .'

The Hon. Pamela Bell recalled their long association:

> . . . He was such a wonderful person and will be so terribly missed, not only by yourself, Dear Betty, and all the rest of his family, but by his many, many friends everywhere. I don't think there ever was a more lovable character. Always so gentle and kind and so entertaining and full of fun!
>
> We have so many happy memories of him throughout the years. Some in Skye, lots at Dalness and latterly some at Biddlesden . . .
>
> All sweet memories that can never be forgotten and Scotland has lost one of the greatest, and most lovable personalities ever, in the passing of your beloved Seton . . .

There were letters from RSPB staff members. George Waterston particularly, paid tribute to Seton for starting his own early interest in birds.

Michael Everett wrote from Sandy Lodge, '. . . We will miss Seton for his wisdom and kindly advice – and also for his courtesy. As a Highland gentleman of the 'old school' he was surely without equal. For my part I shall always regard it as a great privilege to have known him'.

Jonathan MacDonald was particularly affected by Seton's death:

> Sunday night.
>
> Dear Mrs Gordon,
>
> It is with a very real sense of sorrow that I begin to write to you. I have

just finished (at 11:30 p.m.) writing a paragraph on my good friend for tomorrow morning's radio and as I think over it I can hardly believe that he is gone forever from this scene. What a sad occasion for us all and I cannot find words to express how my feelings go out to you in this hour of sorrow. Gone from us now is one that people felt should never change. He was such a part of the Highlands and in every way was a landmark.

Tonight all the memories rush back to my mind and I recall all the interesting conversations we had over the years and all the fine letters he wrote me. He had a wonderful life and you made his last years very happy . . .

Seton was one of nature's gentleman and I shall always count myself fortunate to have known him for so long. My life will be so much more empty now that he is gone but we shall live with our very happy and pleasant memories of him. I would like to express the sympathy of all my family to yourself, to Caitriona, Alasdair and Bridie. We think of you all and give thanks for a life that has been devoted to Skye and to the Highlands.

Yours sincerely, Jonathan.

Seton's other protégé, Adam Watson, wrote an obituary for *Scottish Birds*:

. . . With his passing ends the period of wholly exploratory naturalists in Scotland and their extraordinary breadth of interests. He was long the last practitioner, overlapping for decades with the modern period when scientific method dominated ornithology. Astride two centuries, Seton had a timeless attitude, exemplified by the patched, decades-old kilt he wore on every occasion, sun or snow, mansion or bothy . . .

Only days before his death, *The Field* published a letter of his about Whooper Swans, simple and evocative as usual. It was a good farewell from the grand old man.

A final and fitting tribute came from Donald Berwick of Burnage, Manchester, who wrote to Seton on 12 April, without the knowledge that he had died. It summed up the immense pleasure that Seton had given to his readers over the years:

Dear Seton Gordon,

For over fifty years my wife and I have been visiting the Highlands and Islands of Scotland. When planning our holidays, reference to your books has been a great help and inspiration to us.

The *Cairngorm Hills of Scotland*, so splendidly illustrated with your photographs, was our first introduction to your nature writings.

Your description of Sandwood Bay and Cape Wrath area [*Highways and Byways in the West Highlands*] so impressed us that we made a number of visits to that remote district.

The first occasion we saw a golden eagle was when we were eating our sandwiches on the summit of Cul Mhor. It flew from behind a group of boulders about fifty yards away . . .

Our travels have taken us on many of the islands of the Hebrides, Orkney, Shetland and Fair Isle as well as many parts of the coast from the Mull of Galloway Cape Wrath.

We would be pleased if you would accept the enclosed photograph as a token of thanks for the pleasure your books have given us.

Yours sincerely, Donald Berwick.

Many years ago the Wiltshire naturalist Richard Jefferies wrote:

> The exceeding beauty of the earth, in her splendour of life, yields a new thought with every petal. The hours when the mind is absorbed by beauty are the only hours we live. All else is illusion, or mere endurance.

There can be few better words to describe Seton Gordon's life. By this standard his long, full span was lived to the fullest and there is little doubt that his last diary note was another testimony to the constant wonder that filled his hours.

BIBLIOGRAPHY

OXFORD

Vera Brittain: *The Women at Oxford* (Harmondsworth 1987)
Willie Elmhirst: *A Freshman's Diary, 1911–1912* (Blackwell 1969)
Jan Morris: *The Oxford Book of Oxford* (Oxford University Press 1978)
The private diaries of Irene Martin, a contemporary of Audrey Gordon's at Lady Margaret Hall.

FIRST WORLD WAR

Douglas Botting: *The U-Boats* (Time Life Books Inc. 1979)
E. K. Chatterton: *Q Ships and their Story* (Conway Press 1972)
Robert Grant: *U-Boat Intelligence 1914–1918* (Archon Books 1969)
Lord Hankey: *Supreme Command 1914–1918* (Allen & Unwin 1961)
Liddell Hart: *The Real War* (Pan Books 1970)
Ernst Hashagen: *The Log of a U-Boat Commander* (Putnam 1931)
Gilbert Murray: *The Foreign Policy of Sir Edward Grey* (Clarendon Press 1915)
James Pope-Hennessy: *Queen Mary* (Allen & Unwin 1959)
F. J. Reynolds: *The Story of the Great War* (Collier 1919)
Lowell Thomas: *Raiders of the Deep* (Doubleday 1929)
Admiral Sir Reginald Tupper: *Reminiscences* (Jarrolds 1928)
The Duke of Windsor: *A King's Story* (Thomas Allen 1947)

EDWARD GREY

Seton Gordon: *Earl Grey of Fallodon and his Birds* (Cassell 1937)
Edward Grey: *The Charm of Birds* (Hodder & Stoughton 1927)
Edward Grey: *The Fallodon Papers* (Constable & Co. 1926)
R. M. Trevelyan: *Grey of Fallodon* (Longmans, Green & Co. 1937)

YOUSSOUPOFF

R. K. Massie: *Nicholas and Alexander* (Athenium 1967)
Prince Felix Youssoupoff: *Lost Splendour* (Jonathan Cape 1953)

THE DUKE OF WINDSOR

Eric Acland: *The House of Windsor* (Dominion Books of Canada 1939)
Reprint from the Times: *King and People* (Times Publishing Company Ltd. 1935)
The Duke of Windsor: *A King's Story* (Thomas Allen Ltd. 1947)

RAMSAY MACDONALD

Lord Elton: *The Life of James Ramsay MacDonald* (Collins 1939)
David Marquand: *Ramsay MacDonald* (Jonathan Cape 1977)
Hubert Hessel Tiltman: *J. Ramsay MacDonald* (Stokes & Co. 1929)
L.MacNeill Weir: *The Tragedy of Ramsay MacDonald* (Secker 1938)

SECOND WORLD WAR

Winston Churchill: *Blood, Sweat and Tears* (Putnams 1941)
Winston Churchill: *The Gathering Storm* (Houghton Mifflin 1948)
Winston Churchill: *Their Finest Hour* (Houghton Mifflin 1949)
Winston Churchill: *Triumph and Tragedy* (Houghton Mifflin 1953)
Francis de Guigand: *Operation Victory* (Hodder & Stoughton 1952)
Dwight Eisenhower: *Crusade in Europe* (Da Capo Press 1948)
Chester Wilmott: *The Struggle for Europe* (Collins 1952)

HIGHLANDS
T. Ratcliffe Barnett: *Autumns in Skye, Ross and Sutherland* (John Grant 1930)
Evan MacLeod Barron: *Prince Charlie's Pilot* (R. Carruthers 1913)
James Boswell: *The Journal of a Tour to the Hebrides* (Oxford University Press 1926)
Robert Chambers: *A History of the Rebellion of 1745–6* (W & R Chambers 1827)
David Daiches: *Charles Edward Stuart* (Pan Books 1973)
Ian Grimble: *Clans and Chiefs* (Blond and Briggs 1980)
Samuel Johnson: *A Journey to the Western Isles of Scotland* (Oxford University Press 1926)
Charles MacDonald: *Moidart; Or Among the Clanranalds* (1889 reprinted by Mercat Press/Iain Thornber 1989)
Alasdair A. MacGregor: *Over the Sea to Skye* (W & R Chambers 1927)
H.V. Morton: *In Search of Scotland* (Methuen 1933)
John Prebble: *Culloden* (Penguin Books 1967)
Alexander Smith: *Summer in Skye* (Sampson Low, Marston & Co. 1865)
Otta Swire: *Skye and its Legends* (Oxford University Press 1952)
Constance Whyte: *More than a Legend* (Hamish Hamilton 1957)
The papers and articles of Donald B. MacCulloch

APPENDICES

APPENDIX 1:
A HISTORY OF THE 1923 AND 1924 'MARLOCH' EMIGRANTS.

The Red Deer and District Archives Committee has much material on the 1923 and 1924 embarkations from the Hebrides on the *Marloch*. The most thorough description is by the man who was responsible for the scheme, the Rev. Father R.A. MacDonell. The original paper is in the Glenbow Museum, Calgary, Alberta. Copies are also in the archives of St Benedict's Abbey, Fort Augustus, Scotland.

It was only his determination which made the scheme work, and the 1923 emigration almost fell apart when fifty families arrived, more than was originally planned for; especially as many of them had little money. Father MacDonnel had arranged the appraisal of thirty-five farms, already worked by Russian farmers who wished to return to their native land in the hope of finding a new paradise!

In the autumn of 1922 a delegation of four men went out from various Hebridean islands to meet Father MacDonell and inspect several areas in Western Canada. The Red Deer district of Alberta was chosen as offering the best opportunities. The original agreement was for the settlement of eighteen families, and a farm of 1100 acres was made available to house and teach the men some basic farming. Each family should have at least $750 to purchase a farm and buy some equipment.

Eventually fifty families started on their way, many of them almost penniless. Independently of the delegation, thirty men had left Barra earlier in 1922, some with families, and had settled in Ontario. They later moved on to Red Deer and joined the 1923 contingent in the search for farms.

The majority of the settlers were successful, and few went back to Scotland, though three bachelors out of a total of fourteen, returned to seafaring and eventually found their way back. There were only two single women in the 1923 emigration. One of them, Morag MacKinnon, now lives with her daughter in Invermere, a town in the beautiful Windermere valley of British Columbia in the shadow of the Rocky Mountains. She had already left Barra for work in Glasgow before joining her family for the journey to Canada. She married another Hebridean with the same surname, and they lived in Calgary, Alberta for many years.

Donald MacDonald of Sidney, Vancouver Island, BC, sailed on the *Marloch*. He was only four years old, but nevertheless has vivid memories. His family were not immediately placed. While they stayed at the Immigration Hall in Edmonton, his eighteen-month-old sister, Jessie, died of scarlet fever. Eventually they went to a farm to the west of Edmonton. In the last war Donald went back to the Hebrides as a soldier and met his future wife on South Uist. She recalled in 1923 standing by the shore on Eriskay, to watch the *Marloch* sail past, having no idea that a very young boy on it would one day return and take her back to Canada as his bride.

Mr Michael Maclean of Sylvan Lake, Alberta, went to Red Deer in 1923 at the age of twelve with the Barra group who had left the island in early 1922, and had stopped in Chatham, Ontario. His father was a sea captain and knew nothing about farming, but in Chatham he learned the rudiments of it and was determined to have his own farm, which was the reason for the eventual move to Alberta. Their knowledge was sufficient that when the 1923 immigrants arrived, the Barra men were able to teach them harnessing and ploughing. Young Micheal became more adept than his father and eventually managed a team of five horses.

An amusing recollection of Michael Maclean's was the ignorance of Ontarians about the west, and his father was implored not to go because of the danger of Indians. In fact they saw none for some weeks after arriving in Alberta. Maclean senior was also persuaded to purchase a stove for $64 and ship it out as they would not be available in Red

Deer. He was not very pleased to discover that he could have purchased one there for $22.

Rachel Munden, who lives in the Fraser Valley, east of Vancouver, sailed on the *Marloch* with her family. While the *Marloch* was steaming from Glasgow, John Morrison, her father, wrote on behalf of himself and sixteen other men who were sailing, a letter to Donald Ferguson, Esq., JP, of Boisdale House, Lochboisdale. His use of language is a credit to the education system in place at that time in the Islands:

> Dear Sir,
>
> We, the undersigned, on the eve of our departure to seek our fortunes in the Dominion of Canada, beg to record our great respect for you and to express our appreciation of your manifold services on our behalf. We always found in you one who was keenly sensitive to the needs and welfare of the common people, and who at all times endeavoured to do his utmost to promote their happiness.
>
> In this zeal for the amelioration of the lot of your fellow islanders, you have followed in the steps of your late respected father, whose memory is still cherished by us with feelings of the deepest affection. We rejoice that you have continued to show the same spirit of kindness towards us, and testified in many ways that our interests be very close to your heart.
>
> We especially desire to thank you for your great assistance to us in our preparation to emigrate, for your wise and practical guidance in the disposal of our stock, lands, and homesteads.
>
> That you may be long spared to show the same self-sacrifice for your fellow men and that the blessing of Almighty God, may rest with you and your family is our fond hope and unanimous desire; and we assure you, that your good name will ever remain fresh in our memories. We are, Sir, with profound respect and gratitude, Your obedient servants . . .

Maclean and MacDonald have returned to the Hebrides several times, and both have been told that their Gaelic is better than is heard at the present time.

APPENDIX 2:
NIALL RANKIN.

When Niall Rankin crossed to the Flannan Isles during the time of the Cain and Abel observations he was beginning a career as a wildlife photographer. Then in his early twenties, Rankin was a free spirit, who thought himself to be a fortunate and privileged man. He travelled widely and in 1924 was, like Seton three years earlier, the official photographer on the Oxford Universtiy Arctic Expedition, which also visited Spitsbergen. He shared with Seton Gordon an enduring love for the Highlands. He died in Bechuanaland in 1965, at the age of sixty-one, and many of his photographs appeared in Seton Gordon's books. His obituary in *British Birds* said: 'In the Highlands he was all things – laird, farmer, stalker, shooter, climber, conservationist, yachtsman, ornithologist'. The writer, G. K. Yeates, also said, 'The pity is that he was always so busy with his next expedition that he rarely had time to write up the records of his last – or even to print his negatives. . . . If he loved to chase the emperor goose to the Yukon or the albatross to Antarctica, at heart he would not have exchanged them for the black-throated diver or the great skua of his beloved Highlands and Islands. He was a very great bird-photographer. Unfortunately much of his work was known only to a few, for he published little and exhibited even less . . . all we have are *Haunts of British Divers* (1947) and *Antarctic Isle* (1951)'.

From 1929 to 1931 Rankin was a staff photographer for *The Field* and in 1931 married Lady Jean Dalrymple, daughter of the twelfth Earl of Stair. During the second world war Niall Rankin rose to the rank of colonel in the Scots Guards and later became a member of the Royal Company of Archers, the Queen's Bodyguard. In 1947, Lady Jean was asked by Queen Elizabeth (the Queen Mother) to be a Woman of the Bedchamber and in 1957 was made a Lady-in-Waiting.

APPENDIX 3:
SIR DAVID YOUNG CAMERON.

David Young Cameron was then at the pinnacle of his career and it was an honour for Seton Gordon that he was selected to illustrate the new book. Born in 1865, his mother, Margaret Cameron, was a gifted watercolour artist. After a frustrating period in jobs which he hated, at the age of twenty he entered the Mound School of Art in Edinburgh. While still a student there he was invited, in 1886, to exhibit in the Royal Scottish Academy.

In 1889, D.Y. was elected an Associate of the Royal Society of Painter-Etchers. In 1906 he became a member of the Royal Society of Painters in Water Colours, having attained an associate membership of the Royal Scottish Academy. In 1918 he became a full member.

In 1917 D.Y. was asked by the Canadian Government to visit France and he spent several months with the Canadian army there. From this came his paintings, 'The Battlefield of Ypres' and 'Garment of War', showing the utter desolation he saw. It influenced D.Y'.s abhorrence of war and violence, and almost every letter he wrote emphasised this, particularly when he found someone who shared his views.

Knighted in 1924, the following year Sir D.Y. was invited by the Speaker of the House of Commons to take charge of the redecoration of St. Stephen's Hall. In the same year he became Chairman of the Faculty of the British School at Rome. Other honours came in the 1930s when he was appointed King's Painter and Limner in Scotland.

APPENDIX 4:
CHARLES CAMMELL'S POEM *'PIBROCH VOICES'*.

This was composed on the occasion of the unveiling by MacLeod of Macleod of the monument to the MacCrimmons at Borreraig, Skye on 2 August, 1933.

Thou art stealing, stealing the heart of me, Pibroch;
Wounding, wounding me with the wild voice of thee:
Voice of the mountian, voice of moorland and sea-waste,
Voice of the Isles, captured and chained by MacCrimmon.

Nature's voice heard by them, chiefs among pipers:
Caught and held fast by them, set here forever,
The sea-voice and hill-voice and moor-voice of Scotland,
In the pibrochs of Skye on the pipes of MacCrimmon.

Wound! Wound! How bitter are the stabs of thee,
Deep, deep, to the heart of me, sword of the Pibroch.
Gathered are the tears in thee; all the sad years in thee:
All the wounds and the woes in the voice of MacCrimmon.

There's a new note in thee; is it man or fay?
Is it God's voice in thee, crying to me, Pibroch?
Past all the pain of thee, through the refrain of thee,
Hope! the last strain on the pipes of MacCrimmon!

Charles Cammell was a part of the Edinburgh literati during the 1930s and was an unsuccessful contender for both the Chair of Fine Art and the Chair of Rhetoric and English Literature at Edinburgh University, despite a list of imposing supporters, including Seton Gordon; Pittendrigh MacGillivray, Sculptor Royal for Scotland and Francis J. Grant, Lord Lyon King of Arms.

Cammell met Seton Gordon in 1932 at the the home of the Countess of Tankerville, another of his supporters for the Fine Arts post. A champion fencer who acquired the skill while living in Geneva after the First World War, Cammell was, above all, a prolific and sensitive poet who published several collections. John MacDonald of Inverness considered 'Pibroch Voices' to be the poem that best reproduced the spirit of the Highland bagpipe. The poem also appeared in 'Songs of Skye', published in 1934, an Anthology of verse. In the opinion of Cammell, Seton Gordon was the most romantic and picturesque Scottish personality of his time.

In January 1934, Seton Gordon became godfather to Cammell's son, Donald Seton Cammell, who was born in the Outlook Tower, which stands near St Giles Cathedral. Charles Cammell and his wife, Iona, had rooms in the tower. Donald became a talented painter.

APPENDIX 5:
THE IONA COMMUNITY.

The Iona Community is an ecumenical community of men and women seeking new ways of living the Gospel in the world. Its roots were in the docks area of Clydeside. George MacLeod was minister of Govan Parish Church.

Despite his tenure during the depression, with a full church, and a willingness to participate in the problems of the area, he felt that something more was required. His dream was a ministry whose clergy were totally in touch with working people. His vision included the rebuilding of Iona as a 'visible, tangible sign of the unity of worship and work, church and industry, spiritual and material'. In that first small group there were craftsmen and young ministers. After a period on the island, each group returned to the cities, to the industrial areas and the new housing schemes built after the war.

There are now 200 full members, most of them in Britain. Their belief is that the Community is an integral part of the Christian faith. Members are expected to lead a disciplined life which includes prayer, Bible study, and a tithe of 10 per cent of their income. A part of this supports other charitable groups who promote peace, world development, justice and healing.

There are 800 Associates and 3000 Friends, who contribute money and work, but are not bound by the strict rules imposed upon the members.

APPENDIX 6:
THE VENERABLE ORDER OF THE HOSPITAL OF ST. JOHN OF JERUSALEM.

The Order was founded in Britain in 1831, and St John's Gate, Clerkenwell became its Headquarters. The St John Ambulance was established by the Order in 1877 and the St John Ophthalmic Hospital, Jerusalem, in 1882. Queen Victoria granted a Royal Charter in 1888, which made it a British Royal Order of Chivalry, with the Sovereign as its head. Prince Henry, Duke of Gloucester became the Grand Prior, as is the present Duke. Francis Cameron-Head and Seton were members of the Scottish Priory, and Sir Malcolm Barclay-Harvey later became its Prior.

APPENDIX 7:
THE AUTHOR'S FIRST MEETING WITH SETON GORDON.

Sunday, 17 July 1949, was memorable for the author, because it was after Seton Gordon returned to Upper Duntuilm from the eyrie that their first meeting took place, following a walk around the tip of Trotternish from Staffin. After an invitation to join him on the garden seat at the side of the house, overlooking the Minch, a pleasant hour was spent talking on many things; giving Seton Gordon an account of a night spent on Beinn na Caillich, so recently climbed, a look at the Upper Duntuilm weather station, during which Seton pointed to Clisham, the highest hill on Harris and said that it represented maximium visibility for weather reporting purposes. He also told of the recent visit to Switzerland and how overawed they were by the size of the mountains. Talking of birdlife on Skye, he recounted the loss of species due to the severe winters prior to 1949 and said that it would take many years to bring the numbers up again. Asked about the chances of seeing a great skua he said that none bred on Skye but were occasionally seen. The hour passed all too quickly and the author rejoined his walking companions for the return to Staffin. It was an hour which in 1983 he had an opportunity to share with Adam Watson when they compared notes on the thrill of their first meeting with Seton Gordon.

In a subsequent visit to Upper Duntuilm the following January, one evening Seton Gordon sat me at his desk in his study and played the pipes for two hours while a peat fire glowed in the grate. A plan to spend a summer helping with the meteorological station did not take place because National Service and a posting to Hong Kong intervened.

APPENDIX 8: LORD CHARTERIS OF AMISFIELD AND THE EARL OF WEMYSS AND MARCH.

Lord Charteris first met Seton Gordon in the 1920s at Grogary Lodge on South Uist. It was rented by Guy Benson, stepfather to Martin Charteris and David Charteris, now twelfthth Earl of Wemyss and March. The Gordons occasionally stayed there when they visited the Outer Hebrides. When the Royal Family took their holiday on Deeside each year, it provided Seton with further opportunities to meet and walk with Martin Charteris, who before joining the Royal staff had served in the King's Royal Rifle Corp, rising to the rank of Lieutenant Colonel. His pedigree was Highland, though he was very modest about it. The second son of Hugo Francis, Lord Elcho, who was killed in the first war, he was a direct descendant of an earlier Lord Elcho, who kept a diary of the part he played in the '45.

APPENDIX 9: THE RETURN OF THE SEA EAGLE.

On 31 August, 1975 at Shiel Bridge, Seton passively noted: 'Listened 4:30 p.m. to broadcast on the Isle of Rhum and the young sea-eagles from Norway to be released there'.

This third attempt to reintroduce the sea-eagle into Scotland was at the initiative of the Nature Conservancy Council. The birds came from Bodo, on the coast of Norway, midway between Trondheim and Tromso. The Council had the assistance of Harald Misand of Bodo, an ornithologist who had studied the sea eagle with as much keenness as Seton Gordon had studied the golden eagle. The population density of these birds was such that Misand had no problem in providing fledglings from different parents, thus reducing the possibility of inbreeding.

There is a NATO airbase at Bodo and the RAF were asked to assist by transporting the birds to Kinloss. Permission was given by the Air Ministry and the routine Nimrod flight was used between Bodo and Kinloss, cutting down the total delivery time to less than eight hours.

The fledglings were kept in cages on the island, and were fed on fish, offal, venison and goat meat. Before release, as a halfway measure, they were tethered out. They were banded with a metal ring with a number and a return address, as well as colour tags for immediate identification. The birds were discouraged from becoming tame, and after release it did not take them long to become independent in their search for food. (Rhum sea-eagles have been seen in Shetland and Northern Ireland. Regrettably, there have been two known cases of poisoning and five others have suffered an unknown fate.)

The results have been encouraging. In the eleven years to 1986 eighty-two young sea-eagles were released with a survival rate of more than 75 per cent. There have been several attempts at nesting and disappointments when eggs broke or were abandoned. In 1985 two chicks were hatched, but died in a freak snowstorm at the end of April. Fortunately another pair were luckier and successfully raised a single chick which flew in July of that year, the first sea-eagle raised in Scotland for seventy years.

It is ironic that after never having had an opportunity to report, or record sea-eagle activity directly, in Seton Gordon's eighty-ninth year a large-scale attempt was now being made to bring the bird back, though its success or failure could not be judged for at least two or three years.

INDEX